Impact of Open Innovation on the World Economy

Orlando Lima Rua
Polytechnic of Porto, Portugal

A volume in the Advances in Finance, Accounting, and Economics (AFAE) Book Series

IGI Global
PUBLISHER of TIMELY KNOWLEDGE

Published in the United States of America by
IGI Global
Business Science Reference (an imprint of IGI Global)
701 E. Chocolate Avenue
Hershey PA, USA 17033
Tel: 717-533-8845
Fax: 717-533-8661
E-mail: cust@igi-global.com
Web site: http://www.igi-global.com

Library of Congress Cataloging-in-Publication Data

Names: Rua, Orlando Lima, 1974- editor.
Title: Impact of open innovation on the world economy / Orlando Rua, editor.
Description: Hershey, PA : Business Science Reference, [2022] | Includes bibliographical references and index. | Summary: "This publication presents chapters to build on the available literature in the field of open innovation and its linkage to entrepreneurship, strategy and marketing in the context of organizations and countries, as a reference resources for entrepreneurs, managers, technology developers and policy makers to adopt and implement new business and social solutions"-- Provided by publisher.
Identifiers: LCCN 2021031857 (print) | LCCN 2021031858 (ebook) | ISBN 9781799886655 (hardcover) | ISBN 9781799886662 (paperback) | ISBN 9781799886679 (ebook)
Subjects: LCSH: Entrepreneurship. | New business enterprises. | Marketing. | Technological innovations.
Classification: LCC HB615 .I485 2022 (print) | LCC HB615 (ebook) | DDC 658.4/21--dc23
LC record available at https://lccn.loc.gov/2021031857
LC ebook record available at https://lccn.loc.gov/2021031858

This book is published in the IGI Global book series Advances in Finance, Accounting, and Economics (AFAE) (ISSN: 2327-5677; eISSN: 2327-5685)

British Cataloguing in Publication Data
A Cataloguing in Publication record for this book is available from the British Library.

For electronic access to this publication, please contact: eresources@igi-global.com.

Advances in Finance, Accounting, and Economics (AFAE) Book Series

ISSN:2327-5677
EISSN:2327-5685

Editor-in-Chief: Ahmed Driouchi, Al Akhawayn University, Morocco

MISSION

In our changing economic and business environment, it is important to consider the financial changes occurring internationally as well as within individual organizations and business environments. Understanding these changes as well as the factors that influence them is crucial in preparing for our financial future and ensuring economic sustainability and growth.

The **Advances in Finance, Accounting, and Economics (AFAE)** book series aims to publish comprehensive and informative titles in all areas of economics and economic theory, finance, and accounting to assist in advancing the available knowledge and providing for further research development in these dynamic fields.

COVERAGE

- Behavioral Economics
- Economic Downturn
- Finance
- Economics of Intellectual Property Rights
- Interest Rates and Annuities
- E-Accounting
- Finance and Accounting in SMEs
- Economics of Risks, Uncertainty, Ambiguity, and Insurance
- Macroeconomics
- Economics of Natural and Environmental Resources

The Advances in Finance, Accounting, and Economics (AFAE) Book Series (ISSN 2327-5677) is published by IGI Global, 701 E. Chocolate Avenue, Hershey, PA 17033-1240, USA, www.igi-global.com. This series is composed of titles available for purchase individually; each title is edited to be contextually exclusive from any other title within the series. For pricing and ordering information please visit http://www.igi-global.com/book-series/advances-finance-accounting-economics/73685. Postmaster: Send all address changes to above address.

Editorial Advisory Board

Table of Contents

Detailed Table of Contents

This research is based on the premise that the open innovation model enhances the firms' competitive advantage. Therefore, this study aims to analyze the relationship between open innovation and competitive advantage. A quantitative methodology was adopted with a survey of 251 small and medium-sized enterprise (SMEs) top managers in the hospitality sector. The primary data collected were subjected to descriptive and inferential statistical analysis treatments, highlighting the application of the structural equations model. The findings show that open innovation enhances hotel competitive advantage. In practical terms, this study will guide, on the one hand, the firms' top managers of the hospitality sector in the definition of open innovation strategies to develop the relevant resources and capacities for achieving competitive advantage. On the other hand, it can contribute to the meaning of effective government programs to support firms in this sector.

COVID-19 has contributed to global public health and economic crises. While most developed countries have successfully adopted mass vaccination programs, in developing countries, the vaccination rates have remained extremely low. The vaccine divide has further aggravated the economic impacts of the pandemic. This chapter argues that since COVID is a global problem, vaccines should be equally accessible to all countries. A wider availability of vaccines is not achievable unless poor countries develop their capability to produce vaccines locally. The production of generic vaccines requires low level of R&D capability, which is achievable by firms in poor countries if they receive technological support. The chapter discusses the relevance of the open innovation model that focuses on firm- and institution-level collaboration in improving the capability of firms in the developing world. The flexibilities in the TRIPS Agreement could also be used to address the existing vaccine divide.

Open innovation practices are recurrent in the business environment due to resource and technology limitations in most companies. The search for complementary resources, especially among SMEs, begins to be a current practice due to the possibility of resorting to partnerships and collaborative processes. Thus, through a case study analysis of a Portuguese SME based in Aveiro, Portugal, it was possible to analyze the innovation process and the adoption of open innovation practices in this SME. Through a qualitative study, it was possible to understand the importance of SMEs in the Portuguese business fabric, as they increasingly seek to apply innovative processes in their processes. However, the case analyzed reveals that open innovation may involve an inter-organizational partnership where the company analyzed uses an intermediate model of open innovation, since it does not sell surplus technology, internalizing only external resources. This case study serves as a teaching case as well as a pedagogic tool.

The growing complexity of innovation has led to transition to an open innovation approach. Achieving sustainable economic growth based on knowledge and innovation depends on the efficiency and intensity of interactions between the government, business sector, and academia. Searching for ways to improve the innovation performance of small and medium-sized enterprises is high on the agendas of policy makers in developed and even more in developing countries. Through innovation policy, a favorable environment and stimulating system is created in which innovation activities are realized, information and knowledge are flowed, and cooperation between different actors is established. Academia plays a key role in the open innovation approach and is perhaps the most important partner for small and medium-sized enterprises. The subject of the research is the effects of innovation policy support on science to business collaboration in Serbia, with additional emphasis on the national innovation system and innovation performance of Serbia.

The study aims to analyze the related publications on open innovation and entrepreneurship on the Web of Science in the period from 2011 to 2020. The study methodology was bibliometrics and researched on the themes open innovation and entrepreneurship analyzing the following aspects: main authors, analysis by year, main institutions, funding agencies, keywords, main newspapers, main countries and languages, areas of knowledge, and the relationship between authors with the most publications and the most cited. In addition, the authors sought to analyze the co-citation of the aspects listed above. The results of the study, through CiteSpace, encompass multiplicity and diversity as to the authors who most published on the topic, and they found the institution that stood out the most in terms of publications.

This chapter describes the interplay between marketing and innovation, between the "emergent marketing paradigm" and open innovation, and at a further level, between "sustainable marketing paradigm" and post open innovation, not to mention how these two disciplines provide ground for each other in increasing market share, boosting firm performance and producing value-added results for society. Over the last decade, both marketing and innovation have been navigating into a new phase. The third wave of open innovation, together with the "sustainable marketing paradigm," heralds a profound change concerning how sustainable value is created through open value networks (OVNs) in a post-innovation era.

This study aims to present the evolution mechanism of the aerospace industry cluster in terms of new quadruple helix and open innovation. This study analyzed aerospace clusters located in Gyeongnam province in the Republic of Korea. It emphasizes the importance of active cooperation among industry, government, and university participating in innovation cluster. In addition, this study points out that the cooperation of clusters in other regions is also important. It also emphasizes that a common open innovation culture among participating actors strengthens these collaborative ecosystems. In the past, Korea has been dependent on imports for most of the civilian and military sectors from US as a latecomer in the aerospace industry. At present, however, it produces its own advanced trainer called the T-50. This has a unique development path as a latecomer, and the aerospace innovation cluster played a major role in this development.

Innovation policies of the United States of America (USA) seem to be more effective and efficient than the innovation policies of the European Union (EU). In this work, a brief review about the innovation policies of the two regions is carried out, followed by their comparison and critical discussion. Unequivocally, the innovation policies

Preface

Alexy et al. (2016) argue that one of the leading academic discussions about management innovation lies in explaining differences within organizations' performance with similar characteristics and operating under identical market conditions. In the relationship between open innovation (management model) and organizational performance, the company's management competence depends on the ability of top managers to mobilize and distribute available resources, including knowledge about the development of business ecosystems (suppliers, customers, and others stakeholders).

Although researchers have a growing interest in exploring open innovation, the conceptual and potential applications of using open innovation in the various sectors of activity are still rarely explored (Vrgovic et al., 2012). Due to the opening of organizations to new market perspectives, the concept of open innovation quickly gained prominence, both as a contemporary management approach within the business community and a theoretical concept intensively studied by researchers (Teplov et al., 2019).

The impact of the open innovation model is one of the primary management topics of discussion at the beginning of this century (Huizingh, 2011). This statement reflects positively on the results achieved by companies in leveraging the organization's value chain, with strategic business objectives aligned through management innovation (West et al., 2014). This issue also promotes the intentional use of knowledge to accelerate internal innovation and expand markets (Chesbrough, 2006).

The open innovation model highlights the need for companies to acquire valuable resources from third parties and share internal resources to develop new products and services; however, this model does not clarify when and how a company obtains external knowledge and shares internal knowledge (Kuo-Nan & Tidd, 2012).

Therefore, open innovation confronts managers with complex analysis and interpretation of the specificities of each organization and the market in which this one is inserted, despite the individual character (each organization) and the management model being specific. For Chesbrough (2003), open innovation is generally structured on a tripod, strategy, structure/processes, and culture. Still, according to this author, mobility makes it impossible to keep all the best talents in the same R&D, as these are expensive for the organization. And in the gradual and progressive transformation of ideas, organizations need to look for alternative content (ideas and concepts) to generate innovation, sharing costs and benefits. Chesbrough (2003) realized that these transformations could quickly be exchanged in rapidly changing environments, which organizations had capitalized for now.

Based on the set of independent parts of the organization's ecosystem, the decisions of top managers become strategic, as it involves innovation between organizations (internal and external sources of innovation), placing open innovation significant attention among researchers who study innovation in management. However, companies continually seek new ways to improve performance and gain a competitive advantage (Zhang et al., 2012).

This book discusses and addresses the trends and challenges of innovation to the business and countries' economic and social development.

The editor will seek chapters addressing different aspects of this research area and related topics.

OBJECTIVE OF THE BOOK

This comprehensive and timely publication aims to be an essential reference source, building on the available literature in the field of open innovation and its linkage to entrepreneurship, strategy and marketing. Thus, the book aims to reflect on such an essential issue as open innovation in organizations and countries, providing relevant academic work, empirical research findings, and an overview of this relevant field of study.

It is hoped that this text will provide the resources necessary for policymakers, technology developers and managers to adopt and implement solutions to measure the *Impact of Open Innovation on the World Economy.*

TARGET AUDIENCE

Organizations, academicians, researchers, advanced-level students, technology developers, policymakers, and the government will find this text helpful in furthering their research exposure to pertinent topics in Innovation, Entrepreneurship, Strategy and Marketing, promoting, therefore, their research efforts in this field.

ORGANIZATION OF THE BOOK

The book is organized into 10 chapters. A brief description of each of the chapters follows:

Chapter 1 establishes the relationship between open innovation and competitive advantage. A quantitative methodology was adopted with a survey of 251 small and medium-sized enterprises (SMEs) top managers in the hospitality sector. The results show that open innovation enhances hotels' competitive advantage.

Chapter 2 considers that COVID-19 has contributed to global public health and economic crises. This paper argues that since COVID is a global problem, vaccines should be equally accessible to all countries. The chapter discusses the relevance of the open innovation model that focuses on firm- and institution-level collaboration in improving the capability of firms in the developing world. The flexibilities in the TRIPS Agreement could also be used to address the existing vaccine divide.

Chapter 3 argues that, through a qualitative study, it was possible to understand the importance of SMEs in the Portuguese business fabric, as they increasingly seek to apply innovative processes in their processes. However, the case analysis reveals that open innovation may involve an inter-organizational partnership. The company analyzed uses an intermediate open innovation model since it does not sell surplus technology, internalizing only external resources.

Chapter 4 searches for ways to improve the innovation performance of small and medium-sized enterprises is high on policymakers' agendas in developed and even more in developing countries. Through innovation policy, a favourable environment and stimulating system is created in which innovation activities are realized, information and knowledge are flowed, and cooperation between different actors is established. Academia plays a key role in the open innovation approach and is perhaps the most important partner for small and medium-sized enterprises.

Chapter 5 aims to analyze the related publications on Open Innovation and Entrepreneurship on the Web of Science from 2011 to 2020. The study methodology was bibliometrics and researched on the themes open innovation and entrepreneurship. The study results encompass a multiplicity and diversity as to the authors who most published on the topic, and it was found the institution that stood out the most in terms of publications.

Chapter 6 describes the interplay between marketing and innovation, between the "emergent marketing paradigm" and open innovation, and at a further level, between "sustainable marketing paradigm" and post open innovation, not to mention how these two disciplines provide ground for each other in increasing market share, boosting firm performance and producing value-added results for society. Over the last decade, both marketing and innovation have been navigating into a new phase. The third wave of open innovation, together with the "sustainable marketing paradigm," heralds a profound change concerning how sustainable value is created through Open Value Networks (OVNs) in a post-innovation era.

Chapter 7 points out the evolution mechanism of the aerospace industry cluster in terms of new quadruple helix and open innovation. This study analyzed aerospace clusters located in Gyeongnam province in Republic of Korea. It emphasizes the importance of active cooperation among industry, government and university participating in innovation cluster. In addition, this study points out that the cooperation of clusters in other regions is also important. It also emphasizes that a common open innovation culture among participating actors strengthens these collaborative ecosystems.

Chapter 8 compares innovation policies of the United States of America (USA) and European Union (EU). In this work, a brief review of the innovation policies of the two regions is carried out, followed by their comparison and critical discussion. Both USA and EU recognize the importance of innovation in the current pandemic crisis. In comparison to EU, USA provides a higher investment in research and development (R&D), a more flexible regulation in some areas (e.g., copyright) and more coordinated agencies for the transposition of the laboratory inventions to the market ("Lab-to-Market"). This seems to contribute to a less fragmented market and more effective promotion and marketing of new inventions in USA.

Chapter 9 aims to analyze the linkage between open innovation and firm performance. A quantitative methodology was adopted with a survey of 251 small and medium-sized enterprises (SMEs) top managers in the hospitality sector, particularly in hotels. The findings show that open innovation enhances hotels' performance.

Chapter 10 establishes the different implementation modes of Open Innovation (OI) companies adopt when engaging with startups. A comprehensive and systemized literature review was performed to identify and describe the most critical issues to be considered when companies engage with startups. The authors have identified the main barriers to corporate-startup collaboration and, in doing so, to provide a comprehensive framework able to shed new light on the proposed issue and to provide guidance to future research directions.

REFERENCES

Alexy, O., Bascavusoglu-Moreau, E., & Salter, A. J. (2016). Toward an Aspiration-Level Theory of Open Innovation. *Industrial and Corporate Change*, *25*(2), 289–306. doi:10.1093/icc/dtw003

Chesbrough, H. W. (2003). The era of open innovation. *MIT Sloan Management Review*, *44*(3), 35–41.

Chesbrough, H. W., & Crowther, A. K. (2006). Beyond high tech: Early adopters of open innovation in other industries. *R & D Management*, *36*(3), 229–236. doi:10.1111/j.1467-9310.2006.00428.x

Huizingh, E. K. (2011). Open innovation: State of the art and future perspectives. *Technovation*, *31*(1), 2–9. doi:10.1016/j.technovation.2010.10.002

Kuo-Nan, H., & Tidd, J. (2012). Open versus closed new service development: The influences of project novelty. *Technovation*, *32*(11), 600–608. doi:10.1016/j.technovation.2012.07.002

Teplov, R., Albats, E., & Podmetina, D. (2019). What Does Open Innovation Mean? Business Versus Academic Perceptions. *International Journal of Innovation Management*, *23*(1), 805–811. doi:10.1142/S1363919619500026

Vrgovic, P., Vidicki, P., Glassman, B., & Walton, A. (2012). Open innovation for sme's in developing countries-an intermediated communication network model for collaboration beyond obstacles. *Innovation (North Sydney, N.S.W.)*, *14*(3), 290–302. doi:10.5172/impp.2012.14.3.290

West, J., Salter, A., Vanheverbeke, W., & Chesbrough, H. (2014). Open innovation: The next decade. *Research Policy*, *43*(5), 805–811. doi:10.1016/j.respol.2014.03.001

Zhang, D., Linderman, K., & Schroeder, R. G. (2012). The moderating role of contextual factors on quality management practices. *Journal of Operations Management*, *30*(1-2), 12–23. doi:10.1016/j.jom.2011.05.001

Chapter 1
Impact of Open Innovation on the Competitive Advantage of Hospitality Sector SMEs

Orlando Lima Rua
Center for Organisational and Social Studies, Porto School of Accounting and Business, Polytechnic of Porto, Portugal & Research Center of Business Sciences, University of Beira Interior, Portugal

Francisco Eugenio Musiello-Neto
University of Rovira i Virgili, Brazil

Mario Arias-Oliva
Complutense University of Madrid, Spain

ABSTRACT

This research is based on the premise that the open innovation model enhances the firms' competitive advantage. Therefore, this study aims to analyze the relationship between open innovation and competitive advantage. A quantitative methodology was adopted with a survey of 251 small and medium-sized enterprise (SMEs) top managers in the hospitality sector. The primary data collected were subjected to descriptive and inferential statistical analysis treatments, highlighting the application of the structural equations model. The findings show that open innovation enhances hotel competitive advantage. In practical terms, this study will guide, on the one hand, the firms' top managers of the hospitality sector in the definition of open innovation strategies to develop the relevant resources and capacities for achieving competitive advantage. On the other hand, it can contribute to the meaning of effective government programs to support firms in this sector.

DOI: 10.4018/978-1-7998-8665-5.ch001

INTRODUCTION

Open innovation became an increasingly established topic in the management literature at the beginning of this century (Lee et al., 2010). Alexy et al. (2016) argue that one of the leading academic discussions about this topic is the explanation of the differences in competitiveness in organizations with similar characteristics and operating under equivalent market conditions. For Aranha et al. (2017), the considerable increase in the number of academic studies on open innovation in recent years does not reflect robustness in the concept, which still needs understanding and deepening of the principles of open innovation aimed at SMEs.

Regarding the relationship between open innovation and competitive advantage, firms' management competence depends on the ability of top managers to mobilize and distribute the available resources, which includes knowledge about the development of business ecosystems (Alavi & Leidner, 2001). The impact of the open innovation management model has currently been one of the topics of significant discussion within the management (Huizingh, 2011). Positively, this allows the leverage of firms' value chains, with strategic business objectives aligned through management innovation (West et al., 2014). It intentionally uses knowledge input and output flow to accelerate internal innovation and expand markets for retention of external knowledge, taking on the contours of the paradigm of closed innovation (Chesbrough & Crowther, 2006).

In contrast to the traditional view of closed innovation, open innovation is based on a solid prior knowledge developed in the innovation management literature, including approaches related to R&D outsourcing, i.e., outsourcing, inter-firm collaboration, and organization-environment interaction (Ferreira & Teixeira, 2018). Open innovation thus emerges as an emerging paradigm to replace the previous paradigma of closed innovation (Chesbrough, 2003a).

The nature of open innovation suggests that a greater openness facilitates the generation of innovative products to external sources of knowledge in organizations, which encourages the flow of knowledge and information between firms (Chesbrough & Crowther, 2006; Crescenzi et al., 2016; Shearmur & Doloreux, 2016). Huizingh (2011) recognizes the evolution of the concept in its various perspectives, concluding that further discussions are needed for its understanding and implementation due to the scarcity of academic studies, particularly related to SMEs. In this context, SMEs' top managers practices are particularly vital to ascertain (1) whether there is an effective relationship between management innovation activities and its environment and (2) whether they are driven by technological developments, which correspond to the growing trend towards the interconnectedness of people, solutions and organizations (Martins & Lino, 2014).

Firms expect responses in business environments marked by uncertainty and vulnerability, where top managers are required to have the flexible and diversified capacity to overcome market instability to adapt to highly competitive market dynamics in a globalized environment (Lião et al., 2015). Simultaneously, these organizations use integrated business strategies as a compass to orient themselves in the face of business competition. Fayoumi and Loucopoulos (2016) argue that organizations have several business languages proposing to meet some business aspects (e.g., rules, decisions, goals, processes, organizational structure, etc.). More profitable returns on their investment are derived from these, regardless of their nature, thus maximizing the increase in the firm's value chain to the extent of the qualifications and skills that human resources can effectively put into practice.

This market dynamics accelerates the competition intensification and creates new products, processes shorter product and service life cycles, flexibility for market service, new inputs and changes in production organization patterns (Wendra et al., 2019). These are some of the elements that configure the so-called new competition, which is opposed to the widespread offer of standardized products. In this sense, the market dynamics (vulnerability and uncertainty) concerns the open innovation business model, recreating collaboration and partnership environments with research and development (R&D) institutions to develop and commercialize intellectual property and create economic value to the organization (Chesbrough, 2003a; Weiblen, 2014). Therefore, for Weiblen (2014), the term "open" in business models is grounded in the logic of the firm's collaboration with its ecosystem, which is oriented towards the model's design. Strategic decisions focus on creating value for the organization.

This research sought to evaluate the relationship between open innovation and competitive advantage. The following research question emerged: What is the relationship between open innovation and competitive advantage?

THEORETICAL BACKGROUND

Open Innovation

Concept and Evolution

The phenomenon of innovation continues to attract the interest of management scholars. "Ubiquitous" product and technological innovation and its various subdomains have emerged concerned with aspects such as business model innovation and process innovation (Birkinshaw & Mol, 2009).

When analyzing the historical behavior of American corporations throughout the 20th century realized that the management innovation model was closed, concerning new ideas and their discrimination in the market. From this observation, this researcher identified two pressing issues for maintaining this management model for most of the 20th century: (1) do these companies have the best talent and, therefore, are their ideas the best? and (2) are we the creators, are we the best marketers of our ideas? Chesbrough, 2003b).

Although one can attribute the origin of the innovation concept to the studies of economist Joseph Schumpeter (1883-1950), this researcher describes that to innovate is to produce other things, or the same things in another way, to combine materials and forces differently to make new combinations. In his studies, the author developed the concept of innovation further. In his 1911 work "Theory of Economic Development", Schumpeter this the role of the innovative entrepreneur (manager) in the development process. The same author, in 1934 defines innovation as a broader set of typologies of this process, namely five typologies: (a) product innovation, (b) process innovation, (c) organizational innovation, (d) management innovation, and (e) marketing innovation (Croitoru, 2012). Moreover, for these authors, over the years, this thinking began to fall with momentum as social transformations took place, the expansion of markets became a reality, the dissemination and qualification of knowledge and, finally, the globalization of research, technology and innovation itself, which were replicated to companies (competition).

For Chesbrough (2003b), the mobility of knowledge makes it impossible to keep the best talents in R&D processes, because they have a high cost for the organization. Regarding the gradual and progressive transformation of ideas, organizations need to look outside in search of alternative content to generate innovation to share costs and benefits. These transformations could quickly be exchanged in rapidly changing environments, which for the moment had been capitalized by firms. A new paradigm emerged - open innovation, in which the external environment can and should be considered for the management innovation strategies, R&D departments are no longer the only source of innovation for organizations, because they need to innovate with increasing speed. Thus, innovation becomes part of a continuous flow in a collaborative process, from the internal to the external environment and vice-versa (Chesbrough, 2003b).

In this context, scholars sought an extensive review of the academic literature on business models between 1997 to 2018 to identify varied concepts (Vils et al., 2017). The main areas with conceptual highlights are e-business and information technology for organizations; strategy focused on value creation and competitive advantage, innovation and technology management, creation and acquisition of value based on internal and external relationships with customers and suppliers (Zott et al., 2011).

Inclusively, organization openness has increasingly become a trend for management; it aims to analyze how a new management model can influence the firm's innovation. In addition, the open innovation model identifies the main variables that can affect the relationship between innovation and competitive advantage (Lopes & De Carvalho, 2018). The open innovation model highlights the need for firms to acquire valuable resources from third parties and share internal resources to develop new products and services (Teplov et al., 2019).

Open Innovation Classification

Empirical research has pointed to ambiguity in open innovation, which can cause embarrassment in managers' understanding of the nature of open innovation. It can combine different types of open innovation, and the main factors that can influence the combination of various open innovations (Yuan & Li, 2019). For these authors, there is a gap in researching the structuring of open innovation activities in understanding how firms associate the degree of involvement with their level of adoption.

Gassmann and Enkel (2004) classified open innovation as the outside-in, inside-out, and coupled processes. This classification was later applied in the studies of Dahlander and Gann (2010), Enkel et al. (2009), Van de Vrande et al. (2009), and Rohrbeck et al. (2009), among others. Gassmann et al. (2010) pointed out the mechanisms that help firms understand and manage intentional knowledge flows for each dimension of open innovation. Similarly, academic research devotes its energies to inbound rather than outbound or coupled open innovation (Chesbrough & Bogers, 2014).

The dimensions of open innovation are addressed as firms extract external knowledge intensively from different research channels or sources of innovative ideas. The following are the dimensions of open innovation (Chesbrough, 2003a):

1. *Outside-in process*: to enrich the firm's knowledge base through the generation of ideas, the integration of suppliers, clients, and external knowledge sources can configure the increase of an organisation's innovation capacity. This process is also referred to as inbound. In this context, the organizational modes for open innovation outside-in stand out (e.g., licenses, patents, investments in minority stakes, acquisitions, joint-ventures, R&D contracts and research funding, purchase of technical and scientific services and non-equity alliances);
2. *Inside-out process*: making profit through internal ideas-driven to market, selling or partnering to acquire intellectual property and multiply technology, transferring ideas to the external environment (open innovation) inside-out (e.g., licensing, based on new ventures, selling innovation projects, joint-venture for

commercialization of technology, providing technical and scientific services, corporate venture investments and non-equity alliances); and

3. *Coupled process* or *value co-creation*: consists of connecting the outside in and inside-out processes through alliances with complementary partners in which exchange (give and take) is crucial for success because this open innovation approach combines the outside-in process with the inside-out process (whose goal is to bring ideas to market) (Gassmann et al., 2010).

Firms cooperate with other stakeholders, such as partner firms (e.g., strategic alliances, joint-ventures), suppliers and customers, and universities and research institutes to co-create value approaches. Coupled process combines internal (inside-out) and external (outside-in) R&D strategic processes. Chesbrough and Crowther (2006) adopt only outside-in and inside-out processes in their works. Moreover, Van de Vrande et al. (2009) adopt technology exploration and exploitation to define inbound and outbound open innovations.

Despite the approaches in which the open innovation model was structured, Chesbrough (2012) clarifies the following elements of obstruction for conducting management innovation; (a) high mobility of skilled and experienced people: when changing jobs, they take with them part of their internal knowledge sharing it with other firms, (b) the growth of private venture capital: these capitals started to create new ways to commercialize ideas and (c) the speed of commercialization of products and services: a factor that reduces the life of the product technology.

Competitive Advantage

Concept and Evolution

For Porter (1985), competitive advantage is gained when a firm can add value to a product or process. This statement goes beyond its production cost and cannot be concurrently implemented by current or potential competitors. It indicates a firm's position relative to its competitors or market leadership. Anning-Dorson (2018) states that it is possible to explain how firms create competitive advantage through innovation. Innovation acts as a mediator of organizational leadership in the relationship with a competitive advantage, where leadership, too, mediates between innovation and competitive advantage. The implication is that the impact of leadership may differentiate the relationship between performance measures, innovation to assess innovation and competitive advantage in the context of emerging markets, which has not received the necessary attention (Anning-Dorson, 2018).

Porter (1990) argues that firms can use their capabilities and competencies to promote business growth and gain competitive advantages. This author refers to the example of developed countries and, consequently, more competitive than others (developing countries) by using internal productive capacities and structures capable of transforming them into competitive advantages, something that companies from these (developing) countries cannot. He also identifies two sources of competitive advantage for the organization. The first refers to the lower production cost achieved by the company, which provides greater productivity by marketing its product more effectively and choosing more competitive prices. The second refers to the differentiation of products and services, the ability to offer the customer a superior final value product or service in terms of product quality, specific features, and/or support services. These sources are embedded in the competitive process, directly implying the creation of competitive advantages and their long-term sustainability.

However, Barney (2001) mentions that the firm must consider the available resources that can be the differential for the construction and consolidation of the market. Thus, a competitive advantage is gained when the organization effectively implements a strategy or an innovation capable of creating value for the market and the customer. Therefore, the most significant value creation opportunities are being seized by retail chains that will provide real value and maintain a competitive advantage but require constant improvements to service quality and innovative business models related to sustainable elements (Bilińska-Reformat et al., 2019). Simão and Franco (2018) state that firm's product or service, when compared with competitors, must be durably grounded in the market. Analyzing the impact of different sources of knowledge (internal and external) for organizational innovation adoption and decision making can stimulate the introduction of new management practices since many of the ideas and skills of organizational innovation originate from external sources (Barney, 2001).

The relationship between innovation and competitive advantage lies in the fact that the firm uses, in a more effective way, its resources (internal and external) to manage them for the generation of innovations, and these are likely to gain competitive advantage. However, Nuryakin (2018) argues that market orientation for product and service innovation is empirical evidence on the importance of competitive advantage to enhance superior performance in SMEs by top managers. Competitive advantage fundamentally arises from the value that a firm can create for its buyers that exceeds the cost of manufacture by the firm (Porter, 1985). An organization has a competitive advantage when it implements a value creation strategy that cannot be simultaneously implemented by any competitor or potential competitor (Barney, 1991).

SME activities are constrained by the uncertainty of critical resources such as finance, expertise, time, market access, and logistics are more limited and uncertain than those of large companies (Wosche et al., 2017). Developing products with high levels of advantage and new product development is advantageous given the specific resource constraints that challenge new product development for SMEs, i.e., financial expertise, experience, access to networks. These firms invest in innovations that will build customer loyalty, which thus increases sales and drives SME growth (Love & Roper, 2015). Therefore, as competition increases, product life cycles decrease, and consequently, there is product change; a key quest for SMEs refers to building observable product advantages in their new products to increase adoption in market dynamics, as firms seek competitive advantages and survival through the use of different sources and resources, which is essential for firm survival and superior performance (Anwar, 2018).

Björkdahl et al. (2018), state that firms move to renew their product offerings, incorporate technologies into their products to profit from the value they create for customers; this will enhanced control since firms can create a constant demand for their products/services if they constantly readjust their strategies. In this way, firms can reshape the market through their innovations, to which they can contribute some external sources or agents. Economic performance is enhanced by the ability of firms to offer solutions to changing needs and structures (OECD, 2007). More firms recognize that change is essential and mandatory because these ones are constantly facing a rapidly changing market (Björkdahl et al., 2018).

This contribution to internal R&D can give firms access to complementary resources needed to turn an idea into a successful product/service (Pihlajamaa et al., 2017). Suddenly, many of theme seek external partners and expertise to compete in this dynamic and rapidly changing context.

Competitive Advantage in Hospitality Tourism

The dynamics of tourism as an activity and an industry, combined with growing environmental concerns, require continuous efforts to search for new approaches, tools, and perspectives to acquire environmental knowledge by organizations in the hospitality sector (Martínez-Martínez et al., 2019). As a result of this triangulation (environmental knowledge, organizational learning, and business performance), Razumova et al. (2015) investigate the factors that influence environmental innovations, and innovation in the hospitality sector based on business learning processes.

Factors that influence innovation are varied, such as developing innovative projects, other to the company, or even related to the environment. These factors can be grouped into: innovation inputs, factors that directly influence innovative activities/projects, and institutional factors, such as market and firm characteristics that affect the propensity to undertake innovation activities (Divisekera & Nguyen, 2018). However, it is an increasingly uncertain and competitive market for the hospitality sector, as tourism SMEs are often pressured to innovate across a wide range of innovation types (Martie-Louise et al., 2019). The diversity of innovation creates synergies in which capabilities developed for a specific demand can improve innovation outcomes.

The competitive advantage to be reflected as a research strategy conducted for the tourism industry has gained increasing relevance in recent years. Several aspects related to this area (hospitality) are referenced in specialized literature. For Martie-Louise et al. (2019), most research on innovation in tourism is based on cross-sectional data. Moreover, for this author, innovation diversity creates synergies in which capabilities developed for one type can improve the outcomes of other types of innovation since it (1) defines and examines innovation diversity and its relationship with SME performance and (2) considers the role of uncertainty and dependence on tourism markets in this relationship.

Despite growing empirical research in recent decades on innovation, it has not yet been possible to build an integrated model focused on the innovative behavior of SMEs in the tourism industry, particularly for the hospitality sector. In addition to these factors, the relationship between competitiveness and strategy in the hospitality industry substantially affects how hospitality companies operate, either by structure or demand (Ioncica et al., 2008). Also, according to these authors, to attract and make loyal customers, it is necessary to offer an unforgettable experience and accommodation. Going beyond this experience as hotel chains innovate to create a unique environment is required. Thus, technology is an important strategic asset that allows hotel chains to improve their performance and competitiveness with innovation. On a global scale, the role of technology in strengthening the competitive advantage of a hotel is recognized, hence its contribution to hotel success (Nyheim et al., 2005). Moreover, human resources in the hospitality sector can represent a competitive advantage for hotel companies that aim to make tourism a sustainable activity (Chung & Annunzio, 2018).

In this context, tourism becomes an industry in which the supply structure is highly volatile, and the solid and consistent part is the demand. Thus, the decision to travel precedes the acts of consumption (Ioncica et al., 2008). The activities of the hospitality sector are related to hotel and restaurant services or market segments and activities related to entertainment, culture and sports.

Research Hypothesis

In achieving competitive advantage as an organizational strategy, the foundation in the organization's core competencies is the combination and application of uniquely used internal elements at levels beyond what competitors perform (Drechsler & Weißschädel, 2018). Astuti et al. (2018) argue that many companies share the corporate identity and competitive advantage to established market strategies in internal processes and financial performance, and non-financial performance of the company. It is essential to comprehensively understand the relationship between organizational strategy and competitive advantage. Managers design policies and strategies in alignment with organizational strategy and organizational performance (Park et al., 2019).

For Prahalad and Hamel (1995), although it is essential to focus on the market and the final product/service, the competitive advantage primarily comes from the competence of the management (top manager), serves as an intermediary between the product/service and the market. In this sense, Akbar and Tracogna (2018) stress that the main resources made available by firms should be shared, focusing on the nature of transactions and specifically on three variables: (1) the frequency of hotel destination (platform) transactions, (2) the uncertainty of platform transactions, and (3) the specificity of shared assets.

Akbar and Tracogna (2018) report that booking platforms such as Airbnb could be considered evidence that transactions have relatively low levels of frequency, uncertainty. However, based on more detailed analysis of the transactions that occur on Airbnb, one can make the following conclusions: (a) sharing private houses or apartments seems to be characterized by level of uncertainty such as lack of knowledge about the identity of the parties involved, the quality of the accommodation offered, and the safety of the area around the accommodation; (b) these transactions may suffer from a lack of specificity, houses are generally not purpose-built for short-term rental. Thus, essential components of the housing value package (services) are missing. While uncertainty can be managed by the platform owner providing guarantees, this requires a platform in the archetypal form (person to person) and intensifying platform integration mechanisms, such as reputation building procedures which implies an increase in investment costs for the owner's platform, and (c) frequency, too, can be an issue, particularly for the supply of private homes that are not permanently available to be rented. These assets are shared intermittently, and the relative transactions have low frequency, so their economic value to the hosts is limited.

These organizations have launched many initiatives to obtain adequate and timely decision support as an important factor in achieving and sustaining competitive advantage (Knabke & Olbrich, 2018). Furthermore, it aims to analyze how open innovation can affect firm and innovation performance as a variable that affects the organizational strategy and competitive advantage relationship. Hong et al. (2019) set out to assess how open innovation can positively influence the superior performance of organizations, since available organizational resources are essential for better performance in the organization. As organizational boundaries become increasingly porous and knowledge flows more freely, open innovation receives great attention in management studies. However, the relationships between human resource management practices and open innovation have not yet been examined.

Auh and Menguc (2005) identified that competitive advantage (intensity) increases from the resources, limitations, lack of opportunities, and survival of competitors for the firm's future growth. Competitive advantage features superior competition among the activities of competitors (competitors), survival of the strongest competitors, imitation, promotion and price competition. Hughes and Morgan (2007) discussed the different levels of the intensity of competitive advantage as an influencer on open innovation in services for obtain compatitive advantage.

Firstly, differentiation can decrease threats and involve competition with high innovative ability. Competitive advantage probably undermines competitors' actions and creates differentiation benefits. Auh and Menguc (2005) argue that by continuously introducing unique services, innovative firms can stay one step ahead of competitive imitation; consequently, these highly innovative firms are more successful in winning promotion wars. Second, from an information processing standpoint, highly innovative firms are in a better position when they are open to new external knowledge because they can quickly obtain and interpret a wide variety of information from competitors; they can use it to expand creative responses to problems that allow them to be superior in competitive advantage to competitors. Third, firm requirements increase the likelihood of successful innovation attempts. Highly innovative firms are more willing to clarify their goals and resolve internal conflicts; they innovate successfully.

Innovative firms can convert competitive threats into valuable opportunities through product and/or service differentiation; this will lead to creative responses to competitors' actions and superior determination to innovate successfully, all who can help (e.g., stakeholders) these innovative firms are increasingly globalized and segmented market oriented than in minimally competitive markets (Tsai & Yang, 2013).

Thus, it is intended to test the following hypothesis:

H1: Open innovation has a positive effect on competitive advantage.

RESEARCH METHODS

Sample Design and Data Collection

The sample was drawn from Portuguese hospitality sector firms. A questionnaire was used as the primary data source and was carried out from 28 October 2018 to 27 April 2019. The identification of firms was made through Portugal's Hotel,

Restaurant and Similar Association (Associação da Hoteleira, Restauração e Similares de Portugal-AHRESP) database, which features 1727 hotels, of which 717 were disregarded for not having active e-mail. Thus, in this study, we have used non-probabilistic and convenient sampling.

Hotel executive directors were the elements of research, and the unit of analysis is individual. 348 responses were received, of which 97 were eliminated because (1) the survey was not fully covered, (2) the hotel had no employee designated for this purpose, and/or (3) the manager did not have time to respond to the survey. Thus, 251 complete and validated questionnaires were obtained, and the sample size was considered appropriate according to Krejcie et al. (1970). This score corresponds to a response rate of 24.85%, which is regarded as good as the average response rate of the top management survey is in the range of 15-20% (Menon et al., 1999). According to Hair et al. (2016), this sample size is considered suitable for data analysis using structural equation modelling of partial square composition (PLS-SEM). It allows analysis even with small sample sizes.

Measures

We measured the constructs of this study with scales from previous research. The two dimensions of open innovation, inbound and outbound, were assessed using six items from Sisodiya et al. (2013) and five items from Cheng and Huizingh (2014). The three dimensions of competitive advantage, cost, service, and product were analyzed according to the ten items recommended by Kaleka et al. (2002).

RESULTS

Descriptive Analysis

Table 1 shows the descriptive statistics of the sample's demographics.

Table 1. Descriptive analysis

Item	%
Gender:	
Male	62.5
Female	37.5
Age (years old):	
1-258	19.3
26-35	26.9
36-45	42.6
46-55	8.4
> 55	2.8
Academic qualifications:	
vocational qualification	55.6
bachelor degree	28.9
master degree	12.6
PhD	2.9
Professional experience (years):	
1	7.3
2-5	48.7
6-10	30.8
>10	13.2

Source: Own elaboration.

Partial Least Square Structural Equations Modeling (PLS-SEM)

Results of the Measurement Model

The reliability of the variables was studied by analyzing the internal stability and consistency of Cronbach's alpha, which must be greater than 0.7 (Chin, 2010). The Cronbach's alpha for both constructs is excellent (Table 2) (Pestana & Gageiro, 2010). Results show that the measurement model meets all general requirements. First, all reflective items have a load higher than 0.707, which means that the reliability of individual indicators (loading) is higher than 0.5. Second, all-composite reliability values and Cronbach's alpha values are higher than 0.70, suggesting acceptable model reliability. Third, the average variance extracted (AVE) values of all constructs are higher than 0.50, indicating an adequate convergent validity and implying that our set of indicators represent the same underlying construct (Hair et al., 2016).

Table 2. Standardised factor analysis loadings, CR, AVE, Mean and SD

First-order constructs	Item	Loadings	CR	AVE	Mean	SD
Open innovation			.962	.698		
(α = .957)	OI_9	.903			4.74	1.482
	OI_10	.897			4.71	1.523
	OI_3	.892			4.84	1.653
	OI_2	.888			4.67	1.666
	OI_5	.884			4.68	1.653
	OI_8	.862			4.84	1.497
	OI_4	.716			5.03	1.535
	OI_7	.698			4.53	1.622
	OI_6	.690			4.65	1.671
	OI_11	.686			4.53	1.621
	OI_1	.635			5.12	1.605
Competitive advantage			.959	.678		
(α = .952)	CA_3	.967			4.92	1.171
	CA_10	.958			4.98	1.156
	CA_4	.954			4.94	1.158
	CA_7	.941			4.81	1.214
	CA_2	.928			4.93	1.165
	CA_9	.927			5.06	1.177
	CA_8	.924			4.87	1.172
	CA_6	.911			4.74	1.209
	CA_1	.904			4.93	1.170
	CA_11	.888			4.92	1.199
	CA_5	.872			4.88	1.216

Source: Own elaboration.

The composite reliability coefficient was also used to test the convergent validity (Chin, 1998). As can be seen from Table 2, using the parameters of Gefen and Straub (2005) that advocate a minimum level of 0.6, the variables exponentially exceed the required value. In this study, the method proposed by Fornell and Larcker (1981) was used, which suggests using the AVE with a minimum value of 0.5 to prove convergent validity. All variables also did reach the required value.

Discriminant validity is determined by construct and is related to the level at which it differs and stands out from the other constructs of the model, thus making it necessary to have no correlations with other latent variables, and it can be gauged from the principle that all cross loads cannot be higher than the loading of each indicator (Hair et al., 2016). Henseler et al. (2015) propose Heterotrait-Monotrait Ratio (HTMT) to assess the discriminant validity, which is a new and advanced criterion and is one of the effective methods to evaluate it. Therefore, HTMT was used to assess the discriminant validity of the constructs, and its values are given in Table 3. All the values were less than 0.90; hence, discriminant validity had also been established for all constructs.

Table 3. HTMT

HTMT	1.	2.
1. Competitive advantage		
2. Open innovation	.339	

Source: Own elaboration.

Results of the Structural Model

For this purpose, the significance of the model was assessed based on path coefficients, t-values, and standard errors. The hypotheses tested the direct and indirect effects through the bootstrapping procedure using Smart PLS 3 (Henseler et al., 2015). The PLS algorithm followed by bootstrapping techniques was used to calculate each exogenous construct's relative strength.

According to Chin (1998), the hypothesis is significant, who advocates a minimum structural coefficient of 0.2. As displayed in Table 4, open innovation had a significant and positive relationship with competitive advantage ($\beta = 0.291$, $t = 3.930$; LL = 0.149, UL = 0.437); thus, H1 is supported.

Table 4. Path analysis: direct effects

Hypothesis	Original Sample (O)	Sample Mean (M)	Standard Error (STERR)	T-Statistics (O / STERR)	L.L.	U.L.	Result
H1. OI -> CA	0.291	0.295	0.074	3.930*	0.149	0.437	Supported

Note: *p<0.001.
Source: Own elaboration.

DISCUSSION AND CONCLUSION

The results support the relationship between open innovation and competitive advantage. In this sense, open innovation requires the organization to identify and understand emerging technologies and expand its technological knowledge base to maintain cutting-edge technologies, which creates competitive advantage (Distanont & Khongmalai, 2018). The acquisition of external technologies is particularly crucial for a company in a highly turbulent market environment because it can suppress organizational inertia and capture the value of entrepreneurial capability (Lichtenthaler, 2010). On the other hand, in a stable market environment, a firm depends on existing market knowledge (external) and technological knowledge (internal) to fulfill organizational goals and objectives. Therefore, management innovation allows the firm to present new or improved products before its competitors and thus thrive and create competitive advantages (Goksoy et al., 2013).

Competitive advantage may result from goods and services that exhibit notable differences from typical products in the respective domain or lower cost than competitors (Porter, 1985). This author states that the components of competitive advantage originate in a firm's ability to maximize the efficiency of its production process, develop goods and services of superior quality, and develop services to which customers respond with high rates of satisfaction. Open innovation is a strategy that firms use to create a competitive advantage by introducing superior, cheaper and faster services (Chesbrough, 2003b).

For Ilmudeen (2021) innovation in products and services creates value for organizations and consumers. In turn, this connection can lead to a long-lasting relationship between stakeholders. This theoretical contribution meets Distanont and Khongmalai (2018), who show that innovation increases competitive advantages in organizations in the external factors (partnerships) that influence and amplify innovation in SMEs. This relationship between stakeholders and positive outcomes for the organization promote the growth of the entire regional and national economy (Lichtenthaler, 2010). This linkage capacity points to the organization maintaining its market position, requiring it to possess financial capacity, organizational capacity, and relationship capacity (stakeholders) as a significant and positive contribution to gaining competitive advantage (Lichtenthaler, 2010).

For Goksoy et al. (2013), the business environment is highly dynamic; organizations need to develop new competitive advantages to keep up with the speed of technological changes, customer demands, and global competition. They also mention that innovation can be a key driver of competitiveness, but it can also be risky and create uncertainty. The practical approach to strategy development and implementation best describes performance in service and industrial firms. Porter

(1990) states that the components of competitive advantage originate in a firm's ability to maximize the efficiency of its production process.

We developed this research based on the conceptual model Chesbrough (2003b) proposed to better mature the relationship between open innovation and competitive advantage, thus pointing to a set of contributions to the theory. The model used different measurement scales to validate the model with more robust measurement instruments for analysis. This study thoroughly analyzes the psychometric properties of all the latent variables in the structural model (PLS-SEM) and represents the paths between the constructs. Subsequently, the role of the open innovation construct was emphasized, in the proportion that it can enhance or influence the attraction of resources necessary for the development of the activity of the hospitality sector, namely organizational and technological resources. The observed results clearly show open innovation as an essential construct that allows attracting resources, but, by itself, is not relevant for organizational performance. Open innovation as an innovation in the top management of the organizations studied only shows relevance when there is a relationship with a direct and positive effect. Open innovation is an antecedent of resources and technology, an important contribution of this research.

The results of this study contribute to the development of new instruments and programs to support SMEs of the hospitality sector. By identifying the resources, technologies and dynamic capabilities that influence the firms' performance, directly or indirectly, through the available and necessary resources, this study is beneficial for top managers because it stimulates entrepreneurial behaviors.

The practical contributions of this research proved to be important for companies in the hospitality industry to achieve a competitive advantage. Therefore, top managers should develop the firm's capabilities as they allow them to use organizational resources to obtain competitive advantage. This study showed that open innovation is an indispensable factor for getting organizational and technological resources and the dynamic capability of top managers. In turn, these present themselves as causal links with an inductive effect on top managers to develop their management capability.

Some limitations stand out in the course of this study. The first one refers to the sending of the survey. We should also mention that given the number of firms studied (251), we chose to apply the survey to firms whose e-mail address was registered at AHRESP. Although the number of respondents is significant, a larger sample would allow a more refined analysis of the results. In addition, this is a non-probabilistic convenience sample. The second limitation concerns the metrics that assess innovation management and its superior performance. We chose for respondents only top managers/leaders. However, because it is an electronic survey, this does not characterize whether the top manager responded to the survey. We also understand that evaluating the different constructs of this study based on a single person's opinion (top manager/leader) may not accurately reflect the reality of firms, since decisions are made by a team that may have different views about the activity studied.

This research suggests some lines of future investigations, namely:

(1) to analyze the mediating/moderating effect of environmental factors on the relationship between open innovation and competitive advantage in large firms and insufficiently structured sectors of the economy, to identify whether top managers have developed entrepreneurial skills when they perceive that in an external environment with a high level of hostility they can lead firms to achieve competitive advantage; and

(2) replicate the research in other sectors of the economy, whether technology-intensive or not, or in quite structured sectors (automotive, pharmaceutical, agribusiness, etc.) to identify the existence of innovation ecosystems that support sectors where late technologies characterize innovations.

REFERENCES

Akbar, Y. A., & Tracogna, A. (2018). The Sharing Economy and the Future of the Hotel Industry: Transaction cost theory and platform economics. *International Journal of Hospitality Management*, *71*, 91–101. doi:10.1016/j.ijhm.2017.12.004

Alavi, M., & Leidner, D. E. (2001). Review: Knowledge management and knowledge management systems: Conceptual foundations and research issues. *Management Information Systems Quarterly*, *25*(1), 107–133. doi:10.2307/3250961

Alexy, O., Bascavusoglu-Moreau, E., & Salter, A. J. (2016). Toward an Aspiration-Level Theory of Open Innovation. *Industrial and Corporate Change*, *25*(2), 289–306. doi:10.1093/icc/dtw003

Anning-Dorson, T. (2018). Innovation and competitive advantage creation. *International Marketing Review*, *35*(4), 580–600. doi:10.1108/IMR-11-2015-0262

Anwar, M. (2018). Business Model Innovation and SME performance - Does Competitive Advantage mediate? *International Journal of Innovation Management*, *22*(7), 1–31. doi:10.1142/S1363919618500573

Aranha, E. A., Garcia, N. A. P., Silva, G. N. R., & Santos, P. (2017). Open Innovation and Business Model in Brazilian Small Business. *International Journal of Business Management and Economic Research*, *8*(5), 1008–1015.

Astuti, E., Suhadak, Rahayu, S. M., & Wilopo. (2018). The influence of information technology strategy and management support to the internal business process, competitive advantage, financial and non-financial performance of the company. *International Journal of Web Information Systems, 14*(3), 317–333. doi:10.1108/IJWIS-11-2017-0079

Auh, S., & Menguc, B. (2005). Balancing exploration and exploitation: The moderating role of competitive intensity. *Journal of Business Research, 58*(12), 1652–1661. doi:10.1016/j.jbusres.2004.11.007

Barney, J. (1991). Firm Resources and Sustained Competitive Advantage. *Journal of Management, 17*(1), 99–120. doi:10.1177/014920639101700108

Barney, J. B. (2001). Resource-based theories of competitive advantage: A ten-year retrospective on the resource-based view. *Journal of Management, 27*(6), 643–650. doi:10.1177/014920630102700602

Bilińska-Reformat, K., Kucharska, B., Twardzik, M., & Dolega, L. (2019). Sustainable development concept and creation of innovative business models by retail chains. *International Journal of Retail & Distribution Management, 47*(1), 2-18.

Birkinshaw, J., & Mol, M. J. (2009). The sources of management innovation: When firms introduce new management practices. *Journal of Business Research, 62*(12), 1269–1280. doi:10.1016/j.jbusres.2009.01.001

Björkdahl, J., Fallahi, S., & Holmén, M. (2018). Organizing for parallel business models in established firms. In Academy of Management Proceedings (Vol. 2018, No. 1, p. 14950). Academy of Management. doi:10.5465/AMBPP.2018.14950abstract

Cheng, C. C. J., & Huizingh, E. K. R. E. (2014). When Is Open Innovation Beneficial? The Role of Strategic Orientation. *Journal of Product Innovation Management, 31*(6), 1235–1253. doi:10.1111/jpim.12148

Chesbrough, H. W. (2003a). The era of open innovation. *MIT Sloan Management Review, 44*(3), 35–41.

Chesbrough, H. W. (2003b). Xerox PARC-1. The Achievements and Limits of Closed Innovation. In H. W. Chesbrough (Ed.), *Open Innovation: the new imperative for creating and profiting from technology* (pp. 1–10). Harvard Business School Press.

Chesbrough, H. W. (2012). Open innovation: Where we've been and where we're going. *Research Technology Management, 55*(4), 20–27. doi:10.5437/08956308X5504085

Chesbrough, H. W., & Bogers, M. (2014). Explicating open innovation: clarifying an emerging paradigm for understanding innovation. In H. W. Chesbrough, W. Vanhaverbeke & J. West (Eds.), New frontiers in open innovation (pp. 3-28). Oxford University Press.

Chesbrough, H. W., & Crowther, A. K. (2006). Beyond high tech: Early adopters of open innovation in other industries. *R & D Management*, *36*(3), 229–236. doi:10.1111/j.1467-9310.2006.00428.x

Chin, W. W. (1998). The Partial Least Squares approach to structural equation modelling. In G. A. Marcoulides (Ed.), *Modern methods for business research* (pp. 295–336). Lawrence Erlbaum Associates Publisher.

Chin, W. W. (2010). How to write up and report PLS analyses. In V. E. Vinzi, W. W. Chin, J. Henseler, & H. Wang (Eds.), *Handbook of Partial Least Squares: Concepts, Methods and Applications in Marketing and Related Fields* (pp. 655–690). Springer. doi:10.1007/978-3-540-32827-8_29

Chung, K. L., & D'Annunzio, N. (2018). Talent Management Practices of Small Mediumsized in the hospitality sector: na entrepreneurial owner-manager perspective. *WorldWide Hospitaity and Tourisn Themes, 10*(1), 101-116.

Crescenzi, R., Nathan, M., & Rodríguez-Pose, A. (2016). Do inventors talk to strangers? On proximity and collaborative knowledge creation. *Research Policy*, *45*(1), 177–194. doi:10.1016/j.respol.2015.07.003

Dahlander, L., & Gann, D. M. (2010). How Open Is Innovation? *Research Policy*, *39*(6), 699–709. doi:10.1016/j.respol.2010.01.013

Distamont, A., Khongmalai, O., Rassameethes, R., & Distanont, S. (2018). Collaborative triangle for effective community water resource management in Thailand. *Kasetsart Journal of Social Sciences*, *39*(3), 374–380. doi:10.1016/j.kjss.2017.07.015

Distanont, A., & Khongmalai, O. (2018). The Role of Innovation in Creating Competitive Advantage. *Kasetsart Journal of Social Sciences*, *41*(1), 15–21. doi:10.1016/j.kjss.2018.07.009

Divisekera, S., & Nguyen, V. K. (2018). Determinants of innovation in tourism evidence from Australia. *Tourism Management*, *67*, 157–167. doi:10.1016/j.tourman.2018.01.010

Drechsler, A., & Weißschädel, S. (2018). An IT strategy development framework for small and medium enterprises. *Information Systems and e-Business Management, 16*(1), 93–124. doi:10.100710257-017-0342-2

Enkel, E., Gassmann, O., & Chesbrough, H. (2009). Open R&D and open innovation: Exploring the phenomenon. *Journal compilation. R & D Management, 39*(4), 311–316. doi:10.1111/j.1467-9310.2009.00570.x

Fayoumi, A., & Loucopoulos, P. (2016). Conceptual modeling for the design of intelligent and emergent information systems. *Expert Systems with Applications, 59*(15), 174–194. doi:10.1016/j.eswa.2016.04.019

Ferreira, J. L. M., & Teixeira, A. A. C. (2018). Open innovation and knowledge for fostering business ecosystems. *Journal of Innovation & Knowledge, 4*(4), 253–255. doi:10.1016/j.jik.2018.10.002

Fornell, C., & Larcker, D. (1981). Evaluating structural equation models with unobserved variables and measurement error. *JMR, Journal of Marketing Research, 18*(1), 39–50. doi:10.1177/002224378101800104

Gassmann, O., & Enkel, E. (2004). Towards a Theory of Open Innovation: Three Core Process Archetypes. *R&D Management Conference*, 1-18.

Gassmann, O., Enkel, E., & Chesbrough, H. (2010). The future of open innovation. *R & D Management, 40*(3), 213–221. doi:10.1111/j.1467-9310.2010.00605.x

Gefen, D., & Straub, D. (2005). A practical guide to factorial validity using PLS-graph: Tutorial and annotated example. *Communications of the Association for Information Systems, 16*(1), 91–109. doi:10.17705/1CAIS.01605

Goksoy, A., Vayvay, O., & Ergeneli, N. (2013). Gaining competitive advantage through innovation strategies: An application in warehouse management processes. *American Journal of Business and Management, 2*(4), 304–321.

Hair, J., Hult, G. T. M., Ringle, C., & Sarstedt, M. (2016). *A Primer on Partial Least Squares Structural Equation Modeling (PLS-SEM)*. Sage.

Henseler, J., Ringle, C. M., & Sarstedt, M. (2015). A new criterion for assessing discriminant validity in variance-based structural equation modeling. *Journal of the Academy of Marketing Science, 43*(1), 115–135. doi:10.100711747-014-0403-8

Hong, J. F. L., Zhao, X., & Stanley, S. R. (2019). Collaborative-based HRM practices and open innovation: A conceptual review. *International Journal of Human Resource Management, 30*(1), 31–62. doi:10.1080/09585192.2018.1511616

Hughes, M., & Morgan, R. E. (2007). Deconstructing the relationship between entrepreneurial orientation and business performance at the embr.,ic stage of firm growth. *Industrial Marketing Management*, *36*(5), 651–661. doi:10.1016/j.indmarman.2006.04.003

Huizingh, E. K. (2011). Open innovation: State of the art and future perspectives. *Technovation*, *31*(1), 2–9. doi:10.1016/j.technovation.2010.10.002

Ilmudeen, A., Bao, Y., Alharbi, I. M., & Zubair, N. (2021). Revisiting dynamic capability for organizations' innovation types: Does it matter for organizational performance in China? *European Journal of Innovation Management*, *24*(2), 507–532. doi:10.1108/EJIM-06-2019-0144

Ioncica, M., Madalina, T., Catalina, B., & Incica, D. (2008). The factors of competitiveness in the hospitality industry and the competitive strategy of firms. *Academia de Studii Economice, Buscuresti. Piata Romana*, *17*(2), 213–218.

Kaleka, A. (2002). Resources and capabilities driving competitive advantage in export markets: Guidelines for industrial exports. *Industrial Marketing Management*, *31*(3), 273–283. doi:10.1016/S0019-8501(00)00148-6

Knabke, T., & Olbrich, S. (2018). Building novel capabilities to enable business intelligence agility: Results from a quantitative study. *Information Systems and e-Business Management*, *16*(3), 493–546. doi:10.100710257-017-0361-z

Koplin, J., Seuring, S., & Mesterharm, M. (2007). Incorporating sustainability into supply management in the automotive industry – the case of the Volkswagen AG. *Journal of Cleaner Production*, *15*(11-12), 1053–1062. doi:10.1016/j.jclepro.2006.05.024

Krejcie, R. V., & Morgan, D. W. (1970). Determining Sample Size for Research Activities. *Educational and Psychological Measurement*, *30*(3), 607–610. doi:10.1177/001316447003000308

Lee, S., Miyoung, J., & Haemoon, O. (2018). Enhancing customers' positive responses: Applying sensory marketing to the hotel website. *Journal of Global Scholars of Marketing Science*, *28*(1), 68–85. doi:10.1080/21639159.2017.1410772

Lião, Y.-W., Wang, Y.-M., & Tu, Y.-M. (2015). Understanding the dynamics between organizational IT investment strategy and market performance: A system dynamics approach. *Computers in Industry*, *71*, 46–57. doi:10.1016/j.compind.2015.02.006

Lichtenthaler, U. (2010). Intellectual property and open innovation: An emperical analysi. *International Journal of Technology Management*, *52*(3/4), 372–391. doi:10.1504/IJTM.2010.035981

Lopes, A. V. B. V., & De Carvalho, M. M. (2018). Evolution of the open innovation paradigm: Towards a contingent conceptual model. *Technological Forecasting and Social Change*, *132*, 284–298. doi:10.1016/j.techfore.2018.02.014

Love, J. H., & Roper, S. (2015). SME innovation, exporting and growth: A review of existing evidence. *International Small Business Journal*, *33*(1), 28–48. doi:10.1177/0266242614550190

Martie-Louise, V., Williams, A. M., Ritchie, B. W., Gronum, S., & Betts, K. S. (2019). Innovation Diversity and Uncertainty in Small and Medium Sized Tourism Firms. *Tourism Management*, *72*, 257–269. doi:10.1016/j.tourman.2018.11.019

Martínez-Martínez, A., Cegarra, J. G. C. N., García-Pérez, A., & Moreno-Ponce, A. (2019). Environmental knowledge strategy: Driving success of the hospitality industry. *Management Research Review*, *42*(6), 662–680. doi:10.1108/MRR-02-2018-0091

Martins, S. O., & Lino, J. A. (2014). Influência das Práticas de Inovação Aberta na Prospecção de Conhecimentos para a Criação de Valor em Ambientes de Alta Complexidade sob Condições de Incerteza e Imprevisibilidade. *Revista de Administração e Inovação*, *11*(1), 295–318. doi:10.5773/rai.v11i1.1320

Menon, A., Bharadwaj, S. G., Adidam, P. T., & Edison, S. W. (1999). Antecedents and consequences of marketing strategy making: A model and a test. *Journal of Marketing*, *63*(2), 18–40. doi:10.1177/002224299906300202

Nuryakin, M. (2018). Competitive advantage. and product innovation key sucesso of batik sme's marketing performance in Indonesia. *Academy of Strategic Management*, *17*(2), 1–17.

Nyheim, McFadden, & Connolly. (2005). Technology strategies for the hospitality industry. Upper Saddle River, NJ: Pearson Prentice Hall.

Organisation for Economic Co-Operation and Development (OECD). (2007, Setembro 28). *Teachers Matter. Attracting, Developing and Retaining Effective Teachers. Country Note Korea*. Retieved from www.oecd.org/edu/teacherpolicy

Park, J., Song, H., & Qiu, R. T. R. A. (2019). Review of research on turism demand forecasting: Lauching the annals of tourism research curated collection on tourism demand forecasting. *Annals of Tourism Research*, *75*, 338–362. doi:10.1016/j.annals.2018.12.001

Pestana, M. H., & Gageiro, J. N. (2010). Análise de Dados para Ciências Socais: A Complementaridade do SPSS (5th ed.). Edições Sílabo.

Pihlajamaa, M., Kaipia, R., Säilä, J., & Tanskanen, K. (2017). Can supplier innovations substitute for internal R&D? A multiple case study from an absorptive capacity perspective. *Journal of Purchasing and Supply Management, 23*(4), 242–255. doi:10.1016/j.pursup.2017.08.002

Porter, M. E. (1985). *Competitive Advantage*. Free Press.

Porter, M. E. (1990). *Competitive Advantage of Nations*. Free Press. doi:10.1007/978-1-349-11336-1

Prahalad, C., & Hamel, G. (1995). *Competindo pelo Futuro*. Campus.

Razumova, M., Ibáñez, J. L., & Rey-Maquieira, J. P. (2015). Drivers of environmental innovation in majorcan hotels. *Journal of Sustainable Tourism, 23*(10), 1529–1549. doi:10.1080/09669582.2015.1062016

Rohrbeck, R., Hölzle, K., & Gemunenden, H. (2009). Gemünden opening up for competitive advantage How Deutsche Telekom creates an open innovation ecosystem. *R & D Management, 39*(4), 420–430. doi:10.1111/j.1467-9310.2009.00568.x

Shearmur, R., & Doloreux, D. (2016). How open innovation processes vary between urban and remote environments: Slow innovators, market-sourced information and frequency of interaction. *Entrepreneurship and Regional Development, 28*(5/6), 337–357. doi:10.1080/08985626.2016.1154984

Simão, L., & Franco, M. (2018). External knowledge sources as antecedents of organizational innovation in firm workplaces: A knowledge-based perspective. *Journal of Knowledge Management, 22*(2), 237–256. doi:10.1108/JKM-01-2017-0002

Sisodiya, S. R., Johnson, J. L., & Grégoire, Y. (2013). Inbound open innovation for enhanced performance: Enablers and opportunities. *Industrial Marketing Management, 42*(5), 836–849. doi:10.1016/j.indmarman.2013.02.018

Teplov, R., Albats, E., & Podmetina, D. (2019). What Does Open Innovation Mean? Business Versus Academic Perceptions. *International Journal of Innovation Management, 23*(1), 805–811. doi:10.1142/S1363919619500026

Tsai, K.-H., & Yang, S.-Y. (2013). Firm innovativeness and business performance: The joint moderating effects of market turbulence and competition. *Industrial Marketing Management, 43*(8), 1279–1294. doi:10.1016/j.indmarman.2013.06.001

Van De Vrande, V., De Jong, J. P. J., Vanhaverbeke, W., & De Rochemont, M. (2009). Open innovation in sme's: Trends, motives and management challenges. *Technovation*, *29*(6-7), 423–437. doi:10.1016/j.technovation.2008.10.001

Vils, L., Mazzieri, M., Rodrigues, G., Da Silva, A., & Queiroz, M. J. (2017). Business model innovation: A bibliometric Review. *International Journal of Innovation*, *5*(3), 311–324. doi:10.5585/iji.v5i3.243

Weiblen, T. (2014). The open business model: Understanding an emergent concept. *Journal of Multi Business Model Innovation and Technology*, *2*(1), 35–66. doi:10.13052/jmbmit2245-456X.212

Wendra, W., Sule, E. T., Joeliaty, J., & Azis, Y. (2019). Exploring dynamic capabilities, intellectual capital and innovation performance relationship: Evidence from the garment manufacturing. *Business: Theory and Practice*, *20*, 123–136. doi:10.3846/btp.2019.12

West, J., Salter, A., Vanheverbeke, W., & Chesbrough, H. (2014). Open innovation: The next decade. *Research Policy*, *43*(5), 805–811. doi:10.1016/j.respol.2014.03.001

Wosche, T., Haase, H., & Kratzer, J. (2017). Resource scarcity in sme's: Effects on incremental and radical innovations. *Management Research Review*, *40*(2), 195–217. doi:10.1108/MRR-10-2015-0239

Yuan, X., & Li, X. (2019). The combination of different open innovations: A longitudinal case study. *Chinese Management Studies*, *13*(2), 342–362. doi:10.1108/CMS-02-2018-0410

Zott, C., Amit, R., & Massa, L. (2011). The business model: Recent development and future research. *Journal of Management*, *37*(4), 1019–1042. doi:10.1177/0149206311406265

ADDITIONAL READING

Lichtenthaler, U. (2011). Open innovation: Past research, current debates, and future directions. *The Academy of Management Perspectives*, *25*(1), 75–93.

Musiello-Neto, F., Rua, O. L., Arias-Oliva, M., & Silva, A. F. (2021). Open innovation and competitive advantage on the hospitality sector: The role of organizational strategy. *Sustainability*, *13*(24), 13650. doi:10.3390u132413650

Peteraf, M. (1993). The cornerstones of competitive advantage: A resource-based view. *Strategic Management Journal*, *14*(3), 179–191. doi:10.1002mj.4250140303

Van Lieshout, J.W.F.C., van der Velden, J.M., Blomme, R.J., & Peters, P. (2021). The interrelatedness of organizational ambidexterity, dynamic capabilities and open innovation: a conceptual model towards a competitive advantage. *European Journal of Management Studies*. doi:10.1108/EJMS-01-2021-0007

KEY TERMS AND DEFINITIONS

Competitive Advantage: Considered strategic resources, including six dimensions: reputational resources; access to financial resources; human resources; cultural resources; relational resources; and informational resources.

Hospitality Sector: Sector of the tourism industry that comprises a growing competitive activity that sustains a representative position in the tourism production chain and requires the ability to constantly adapt to the changes, needs and desires of the customer, as the satisfaction, safety and pleasure of the tourist have a vital role in generating wealth and employment in any country, with implications for the economy, the environment and the population.

Open Innovation: The open innovation concept is an emergent paradigm based on the assumption "that firms can and should use external ideas as well as internal ideas, and internal and external paths to market" (Chesbrough, 2003a, p. 59).

SME: Small and medium-sized enterprises.

Chapter 2
The Relevance of Open Innovation for the Generic Pharmaceutical Industry in Developing Countries:
Open Innovation to Address Vaccine Divide

Mamun Ala
Australian Institute of Business, Australia

Kuldeep Kaur
Australian Institute of Business, Australia

Dilraj Wadhwa
Australian Institute of Business, Australia

ABSTRACT

COVID-19 has contributed to global public health and economic crises. While most developed countries have successfully adopted mass vaccination programs, in developing countries, the vaccination rates have remained extremely low. The vaccine divide has further aggravated the economic impacts of the pandemic. This chapter argues that since COVID is a global problem, vaccines should be equally accessible to all countries. A wider availability of vaccines is not achievable unless poor countries develop their capability to produce vaccines locally. The production of generic vaccines requires low level of R&D capability, which is achievable by

DOI: 10.4018/978-1-7998-8665-5.ch002

firms in poor countries if they receive technological support. The chapter discusses the relevance of the open innovation model that focuses on firm- and institution-level collaboration in improving the capability of firms in the developing world. The flexibilities in the TRIPS Agreement could also be used to address the existing vaccine divide.

INTRODUCTION

COVID-19 has had serious and multi-dimensional impacts on all countries irrespective of their socioeconomic status. It is not only a worldwide public health crisis; it has also contributed to an unprecedented global economic crisis. Long-term lockdowns and disrupted international supply chains have affected both manufacturing and service sectors and resulted in job loss and/or significant reductions in income (Pak et al., 2020).

The literature on the economic evaluation of COVID-19 and the optimal strategy to escape the pandemic is still emerging; however, it is argued that mass vaccination has both health and economic benefits (MacIntyre, 2021). In 2021, many developed countries have adopted mass COVID vaccination programs in mitigating the outbreaks of the virus as well as the main strategy towards economic recovery (MacIntyre, 2021; Moghadas, 2021). Accordingly, these countries have been able to reduce uncertainty and panic, thereby open their economies. Unfortunately, only a few selected developing countries have been able to successfully combine lockdowns with mass vaccination. In many developing and least developed countries (LDCs), the vaccination rates have remained extremely low; as a result, the economic impacts of the pandemic have been felt more badly by them.

Attaining self-sufficiency in original vaccines requires a country to have an advanced pharmaceutical and biotechnology sector (consisting of research-intensive firms), which is non-existent in most developing and least developed countries. These countries also do not afford buying a vaccine for every citizen. The statement by the United Nations "No one is safe, until everyone is safe" indicates that since COVID-19 is a global problem, current gaps in the vaccination rates between countries are unacceptable and that to help stop the spread of the disease, vaccines should be equally accessible to people in poor countries. Unless the global community undertakes a wholistic approach in addressing the vaccine divide, the pre-existing economic divide is likely to become further worse (Muro & Austin, 2021).

This paper discusses the relevance of the open innovation model in improving the capability of pharmaceutical and biotechnology firms in the developing world in producing generic versions of vaccines for COVID-19 and other diseases. Chesbrough et al. (2006, p.1) define open innovation as 'the use of purposive inflows and outflows of knowledge to accelerate internal innovation, and expand the markets for external use of innovation, respectively'. At the center of open innovation is the facilitation of research and development (R&D) spillovers, which can be understood as the voluntary and involuntary exchange of commercially viable technological information (Steurs, 1994; Chesbrough & Bogers, 2014). The authors emphasize that a wider availability of vaccines for COVID and other diseases is not achievable unless poor countries develop their capability to produce vaccines locally. The production of generic vaccines needs lesser degree of innovation capability, which is achievable by firms in poor countries given that they receive technological support from multinational companies (MNCs) and international organizations. Essentially, the issue of transfer of technology by MNCs to firms in developing countries is typically a contentious issue as technology development involves huge costs. Nevertheless, the pandemic has also served as an eye opener for all to realize the importance of collective approaches in dealing with global problems.

The rest of the paper is organized as follows. Section 2 discusses current COVID situation and vaccine divide. Section 3 looks at the importance of multi-actor partnership and collaboration in open innovation framework. Section 4 presents a discussion on commonly used models of open innovation in the pharmaceutical sector. Section 5 discusses how open innovation can be used to take advantage of the flexibilities embedded in the TRIPS Agreement of the WTO for fair access to COVID vaccines. Section 6 concludes this paper.

CURRENT COVID SITUATION AND VACCINE DIVIDE

The scientific community is still fully clear about the COVID virus and the most effective therapy however many studies show that vaccines protect people from getting severely ill or dying from the disease (Heinz & Stiasny, 2021; Saeed et al., 2021). As mentioned already, COVID-19 vaccines have not yet reached to many people in low-income countries. Table 1 and Table 2 below indicate that in comparison with high income countries, only few developing countries (e.g., India, Sri Lanka, Vietnam, Morocco) have achieved mentionable success in vaccinating their population.

Table 1. The list of countries with the COVID vaccination rates more than 50% (as of 22nd of November 2021) and some key demographic and macroeconomic indicators

	Name of the country	Vaccination rate (%)	Population in millions (in 2019)	Life expectancy in years (in 2019)	Per capita GDP in 2019 (in USD)	Unemployment rates (%)		
						2019	2020	Change
1	UAE	98.10	9.8	77.97	43103	2.28	5.00	2.72
2	Singapore	92.99	5.70	83.50	65641	3.10	5.19	2.09
3	Cuba	89.47	11.33	78.80	9100	1.67	3.87	2.20
4	Portugal	89.04	10.29	80.68	23285	6.46	7.20	0.74
5	Chile	87.38	18.95	80.18	14742	7.29	11.51	4.22
6	China	84.82	1398	76.91	10217	3.62	4.24	0.62
7	Cambodia	83.19	16.49	69.82	1643	0.13	0.13	0
8	Iceland	82.87	0.34	82.56	68883	3.93	6.43	2.5
9	South Korea	82.33	51.71	83.23	31846	3.78	3.94	0.16
10	Spain	81.74	47.13	83.49	29565	14.10	15.67	1.57
11	Qatar	80.54	2.83	80.23	62088	0.12	3.45	3.33
12	Argentina	79.22	44.94	76.67	9912	9.84	11.67	1.83
13	Canada	79.21	37.59	82.05	46327	5.73	9.60	3.87
14	Japan	78.97	126.3	84.36	40113	2.40	2.97	0.57
15	Malaysia	78.19	31.95	76.16	11414	3.31	4.55	1.24
16	Denmark	78.13	5.81	81.20	60213	5.02	5.66	0.64
17	Italy	77.83	59.73	83.20	33567	9.95	9.20	-0.75
18	Norway	77.30	5.35	82.91	75826	3.69	4.62	0.93
19	Ireland	77.19	4.93	82.30	80779	4.95	5.92	0.97
20	Finland	76.96	5.52	81.79	48712	6.80	7.9	1.10
21	Australia	76.73	25.37	82.90	55057	5.16	6.49	1.33
22	Netherlands	76.70	17.34	82.01	52295	3.38	4.09	0.71
23	France	76.44	67.25	82.58	40380	8.44	8.62	0.18
24	Brazil	75.91	211	75.88	8897	11.93	13.67	1.74
25	New Zealand	75.00	4.98	81.71	41999	4.07	4.55	0.48
26	United Kingdom	74.42	66.84	81.20	42354	3.90	4.34	0.44
27	Ecuador	74.25	17.37	77.01	6223	3.84	5.34	1.50
28	Sri Lanka	74.01	21.8	76.98	3852	4.27	4.84	0.57
29	Sweden	71.75	10.28	82.96	51687	6.83	8.45	1.62
30	Turkmenistan	71.51	5.94	68.19	7612	3.74	4.38	0.64
31	Germany	69.89	83.09	80.94	46467	5.00	5.90	0.90

Continued on following page

Table 1. Continued

	Name of the country	Vaccination rate (%)	Population in millions (in 2019)	Life expectancy in years (in 2019)	Per capita GDP in 2019 (in USD)	Unemployment rates (%)		
						2019	2020	Change
32	Saudi Arabia	69.34	34.27	75.13	23140	6.13	8.22	2.09
33	Austria	68.90	8.88	81.79	50122	4.49	5.77	1.28
34	Lithuania	68.86	2.794	76.13	19555	6.26	8.43	2.17
35	United States	68.48	328.3	78.79	65279	3.50	8.31	4.81
36	Vietnam	67.95	96.46	75.40	2715	2.04	2.27	0.23
37	Colombia	67.66	50.34	77.29	6425	9.96	15.44	5.48
38	Mongolia	67.85	3.23	69.87	4340	5.31	4.33	-0.98
39	Israel	67.44	9.054	82.80	43589	3.80	4.33	0.53
40	Latvia	67.1	1.914	75.24	17795	6.31	8.19	1.88
41	Switzerland	66.71	8.58	83.70	85300	4.39	4.94	0.55
42	Greece	66.59	10.72	81.94	19151	17.31	16.85	-0.46
43	Iran	66.63	82.91	76.68	3115	11.14	10.96	-0.18
44	Thailand	66.44	69.63	77.15	7817	0.72	1.02	0.30
45	Turkey	65.89	83.43	77.69	9127	13.67	13.92	0.25
46	Morocco	65.54	36.47	76.68	3230	9.10	10.15	1.05
47	Peru	64.93	32.51	76.74	7028	3.03	6.24	3.21
48	Hungary	62.53	9.77	76.02	16733	3.42	4.35	0.93
49	Estonia	62.04	1.33	78.50	23718	4.45	6.46	2.01
50	Oman	59.15	4.98	77.86	15343	1.84	4.97	3.13
51	Poland	54.57	37.97	77.86	15695	3.28	3.55	0.27
52	Mexico	58.24	127.6	75.05	9946	3.48	4.71	1.23
53	India	55.04	1366	69.66	2101	5.27	7.11	1.84
	AVERAGE	**73.11**	**92.76** (Total 4823.3m); Unvaccinated - 349.42 m	**78.85**	**29460**	**5.49**	**6.83**	**1.34**

Sources: Alas and Matthews (2021) and Macro trends (2020).

Table 2. The list of countries with the COVID vaccination rates less than 50% (as of 22nd of November 2021) and some key demographic and macroeconomic indicators

	Name of the country	Vaccination rate (%)	Population in millions (in 2019)	Life expectancy in years (in 2019)	Per capita GDP in 2019 (in USD)	Unemployment rates (%)		
						2019	2020	Change
1	Tunisia	49.44	11.82	77.97	3352	15.13	16.69	1. 56
2	Azerbaijan	49.40	10.11	73.00	4806	4.84	6.27	1. 43
3	Indonesia	48.64	270.6	71.72	4135	3.62	4.11	0.49
4	Slovakia	47.25	5.45	77.47	19273	5.75	6.79	1.04
5	Serbia	47.07	6.95	75.69	7412	10.40	9.08	-1.32
6	Kazakhstan	45.44	18.51	73.18	9813	4.80	6.05	1.25
7	Russia	43.52	144.4	73.08	11498	4.60	5.73	1.13
8	Bolivia	39.62	11.51	71.51	3552	3.46	5.61	2.15
9	Jordan	39.74	10.10	74.53	4405	16.85	18.5	1.65
10	Romania	39.25	19.37	75.46	12890	3.91	4.84	0.93
11	Pakistan	35.01	216.6	67.27	1285	3.98	4.65	0.67
12	Botswana	34.91	2.30	69.59	7971	17.21	17.7	0.49
13	Belarus	34.52	9.42	74.23	6839	4.71	5.28	0.57
14	Bangladesh	31.87	163	72.59	1856	4.22	5.30	1.08
15	Guatemala	31.27	16.6	74.30	4639	2.36	4.65	2.29
16	Nepal	30.03	28.61	70.78	1195	2.85	4.44	1.59
17	Philippines	29.68	108.1	71.23	3485	2.24	6.90	4.66
18	Ukraine	29.53	44.39	71.83	3663	8.19	9.48	1.29
19	Tajikistan	28.60	9.32	71.10	891	6.66	7.50	0.84
20	Georgia	28.07	10.62	73.66	4698	11.57	12.05	0.48
21	Lebanon	27.59	6.86	78.93	7584	6.04	6.61	0.57
22	Myanmar	26.81	54.05	67.13	1477	1.79	0.50	-1.29
23	Zimbabwe	24.33	14.65	61.49	1156	5.02	5.73	0.71
24	Libya	23.3	6.78	72.91	7686	18.34	19.39	1.05
25	Bulgaria	22.23	6.98	74.91	9828	4.23	5.71	1.48
26	Moldova	21.98	2.67	71.90	4494	5.10	4.71	-0.39
27	Mauritania	21.91	4.65	64.92	1673	10.13	10.66	0.53
28	Egypt	20.86	100.4	71.99	3019	9.73	10.45	0.72
29	Mozambique	18.45	30.37	60.85	504	3.19	3.39	0.29

Continued on following page

Table 2. Continued

	Name of the country	Vaccination rate (%)	Population in millions (in 2019)	Life expectancy in years (in 2019)	Per capita GDP in 2019 (in USD)	Unemployment rates (%)		
						2019	2020	Change
30	Nicaragua	18.64	6.46	71.60	1374	5.14	5.82	0.68
31	Angola	17.53	31.83	61.15	2810	6.93	7.70	0.77
32	Kyrgyzstan	16.24	6.46	71.6	1374	6.72	7.89	1.77
33	Iraq	16.35	39.31	70.6	5659	12.76	13.74	0.98
34	Algeria	14.45	43.05	76.88	3976	11.81	12.83	1.02
35	Namibia	13.39	2.5	63.71	5037	19.75	20.35	0.60
36	Liberia	9.54	5.06	64.10	622	2.89	3.30	0.41
37	Afghanistan	8.86	38.04	64.83	502	11.98	11.73	-0.25
38	Senegal	7.45	16.74	67.94	1430	6.47	7.10	0.63
40	Kenya	7.25	52.57	66.7	1817	2.60	2.98	0.38
40	Gabon	6.53	2.17	66.47	7767	19.60	20.50	0.90
41	Syria	4.50	17.07	72.7	1079	8.16	9.03	0.87
42	Zambia	4.26	17.86	63.89	1305	11.91	12.17	0.26
43	Ethiopia	3.44	112.1	66.6	856	2.04	2.79	0.75
44	Nigeria	2.81	19.66	59.31	879	8.53	9.01	0.48
45	Papua New Guinea	2.79	19.66	59.31	879	2.37	2.74	0.37
46	Sudan	2.57	19.66	59.31	879	16.76	17.71	0.95
47	Niger	2.01	19.66	59.31	879	0.46	0.69	0.23
48	Madagascar	1.60	26.67	67.04	526	1.67	1.92	0.25
49	Mali	1.56	19.66	59.31	879	7.24	7.50	0.26
50	Tanzania	1.44	58.01	65.46	1086	1.96	2.16	0.20
51	Yemen	1.75	29.16	66.12	632	12.90	13.42	0.52
52	South Sudan	0.75	11.06	57.58	343	12.01	12.66	0.65
53	DRC	0.13	86.79	60.68	581	4.10	4.60	0.5
	AVERAGE	**20.90**	**39.13** (Total 2034.58m); Unvaccinated - 1609.35m	**68.64**	**3748**	**7.36**	**8.12**	**0.77**

Sources: Alas and Matthews (2021) and Macro trends (2020).

Table 1 reveals that the group of countries with the COVID vaccination rates more than 50% (as of 22nd of November 2021) had achieved an overall vaccination rate of 73.11%, which indicates only 26.89% (349.42 million out of 4823.29 million people) remained unvaccinated (Alas & Matthews, 2021). The average life expectancy in these countries in 2019 was 78.85 years, while the average per capita GDP (in 2019) was USD 29,460. Only six of the 53 countries are lower middle-income economies - those with a Gross National Income (GNI) per capita between $1,036 and $4,045 (World Bank, 2020), namely Sri Lanka ($4010), Mongolia ($3790), Iran ($3640), Vietnam ($2590), Morocco ($3200), India ($2120) and Cambodia ($1530) (Macro Trends, 2020). In contrast, Table 2 reveals that the group of countries with the COVID vaccination rates less than 50% (as of 22nd of November 2021) had achieved an overall vaccination rate of only 20.90%, which indicates 79.10% (1609.35 million out of 2034.58 million people) remained unvaccinated (Alas & Matthews, 2021). The average life expectancy in these countries in 2019 was 68.64 years (10 years lower than the first group). The average per capita GDP (in 2019) was only USD 3748. Out of the 53 countries, ten countries (almost one-fifth) are very low-income economies - those with a Gross National Income (GNI) per capita less than $1,036 (Macro Trends, 2020; World Bank, 2020). Importantly also, the average unemployment rates in the countries in Table 2 were also considerably higher than their counterparts in Table 1 (7.36 versus 5.49 in 2019 and 8.12 versus 6.83 in 2020).

Overall, Table 1 and 2 depict unacceptable gaps in the vaccination rates between rich and poor countries as well as the disproportionate economic outcomes of the pandemic. The data strongly indicates the need for the local production of affordable vaccines in low-income countries with the support from the global community. As the authors believe that open innovation model can be useful in improving the capability of pharmaceutical and biotechnology firms in the developing world in producing generic vaccines, the next section presents a discussion on open innovation, and the importance of multi-actor partnership and collaboration in open innovation.

OPEN INNOVATION – THE IMPORTANCE OF MULTI-ACTOR PARTNERSHIP AND COLLABORATION

In the face of rapidly changing scientific, technological and sociological conditions, businesses rely on innovation to grow and stay competitive. The industry's traditional strategy has been to foster innovation within specialized research and development units. However, this strategy has limitations as these internal R&D efforts do not always transform into commercial products or services that benefit the company; there are always a lot of potentially useful innovation generated outside of firms (Yeong et al, 2021). Calantone and Stanko (2007) argue that due to the high cost of establishing specialized structures, a firms' innovation efforts are not frequent and therefore, they need outside expertise.

In recent decades, the concept of open innovation has provided a new language for many practitioners and business leaders to logically change the prevailing R&D concept and move away from internal focus to outward interaction (Chesbrough, Lettl & Ritter, 2018). The literature suggests a paradigm shift towards open innovation, a model that does not exclude traditional internal creativity but also allows internalizing the externally generated innovation (Houdson, 2016). According to Chesbrough (2003, p. 43), "open Innovation is a paradigm that assumes that firms can and should use external ideas as well as internal ideas, and internal and external paths to market, as the firms look to advance their technology. Open Innovation combines internal and external ideas into architectures and systems whose requirements are defined by a business model." This indicates open innovation is predicated on the notion that a business can leverage knowledge, ideas, technology, and R&D knowledge from a variety of external sources to boost innovation and thereby bring value to its consumers. In other words, when a business follows an open innovation approach, it does not seek to produce the greatest ideas completely on its own, rather it tries to maximize the use of internal and external ideas, to improve cost and risk management, and to speed technology development. Suppliers, research institutes, universities, consumers, competitors, and businesses with complementary offers are frequently cited as sources of information (Von Hippel, 1988).

The early players in open innovation include the 'high-technology' industries such as information technology, computers, and pharmaceuticals. Beyond these early adopters, industries in the fields of medical devices, chemicals, and bioscience tools and services were among the first to embrace the open innovation approach (Chesbrough & Crowther, 2006). Taking Chesbrough's concept of open innovation as a starting point and emphasizing its expansive character, scholars have attempted to develop the open innovation paradigm by defining openness in a variety of ways (West & Bogers, 2017; Bogers et al., 2017). Three distinct forms of open innovation processes have been recognized based on the route in which new information is spread (Gassmann & Enkel, 2004). Specifically:

- the *inbound process* entails integrating an organization's internal knowledge with knowledge derived from external sources;
- the *outbound process* entails generating profits for the organization through the transfer of internally generated knowledge or intellectual property to external entities; and
- the *coupled* process entails combining both inbound and outbound processes through the formation of alliances with complementary external entities (Gassmann & Enkel, 2004; Santoro et al., 2019).

The literature suggests that in the context of healthcare, inbound open innovation (integrating internal knowledge with external knowledge) is the most widely used strategy (Wass & Vimarlund, 2016). Internal openness confers that companies can utilize new knowledge from internal networks that are within the boundary of an organization. Internal knowledge (e.g., information, ideas, and solutions) can come from other employees of the same organization who have in-depth understanding of the organization's goals, available resources, and work processes. Essentially, when knowledge is explicit to the problem or challenge, its use, incorporation and application is easier. Open innovation does not necessarily mean that the idea must come from outside the organization; to increase the dynamic capability of innovation, organizations need to have its own knowledge pool (Chesbrough, Lettl & Ritter, 2018; Yun et al., 2020). The ability to access, absorb, and assimilate innovation-relevant knowledge, information, and creativity from employees outside the formal innovation unit may also be considered as an important a source of innovation. (Vaiman, 2010). This notion is consistent with the argument by Bogers, Foss and Lyngsie (2018) that employees' knowledge diversity promotes firms' ability to benefit from open innovation. Thus, more opportunities to communication with the internal sources contributes towards employee's ability to combine their own knowledge with new information.

In contrast, external search by a firm or employees involves seeking information from diverse outside knowledge sources to address innovation challenges. In effect, R&D workers who also invest time and energy in external search efforts will be more likely to recognize new market or technological opportunities compared to colleagues who focus exclusively on internal research (Salter et al., 2015). Individual employees need organizational consent and support from direct managers to interact with external knowledge, however, external engagement by R&D professionals is often overlooked by the organization Laursen & Salter, 2020). The literature suggests that when the employees are externally engaged, they are in a better position to combine internal and external knowledge rudiments into innovative ideas that may lead to new developments for their organization (Rubin & Abramson, 2018). The deployment of outside ideas opens prospects to ingress ideas from external players, and disables the propensity common to many large, established organizations, to stick with "tried and tested" approaches and solutions (Hargadon & Sutton, 1997).

Some scholars have used evolutionary economics to understand the role of collaboration in open innovation that underpins the importance of a systems perspective and focuses on an industry-specific system of innovation (Christensen et al., 2005 cited in Bianchi et al, 2011). Lundvall et al. (2009, p. 214) suggest that a firm's learning or capability is influenced by its attitude as well as 'the meso and macroeconomic contexts' specific to it. Therefore, the local environment (such as R&D infrastructure and domestic competitiveness) and institutions (academic, research-oriented and political) and external institutions and firms (e.g., MNCs) influence the innovativeness of firms (Metcalfe, 1994). Accordingly, establishing effective networks of relationships between industries, academia, national and international institutions and the government to foster innovation is at the heart of the evolutionary approach (Iammarino & McCann, 2006; Frenken, 2007). Specifically, the principal aim of supporting a system of innovation would include creating an environment to mitigate firms' uncertainties about regulatory and technological changes, encouraging collaborative R&D and innovation through reducing the risks from R&D-related uncertainties and promoting cooperation between various industry-related players in the private and public sector (Lundvall & Borrás, 2005; Nelson, 2008).

To sum up, while all forms of open innovation involve higher involvement in collaborative research and innovation, scholars argue that open innovation is more than collaborative inventing. It involves independent actors relying on each other's ability to create and capture vale (Chesbrough, Lettl & Ritter, 2018). Therefore, collaborating partners need both value creation and value capturing capabilities for and capture. This indicates, to be able to collaborate with MNCs and international organizations in producing vaccines locally, firms in poor countries need proactive efforts to improve their value creation and value capturing capabilities both at organizational and employee levels.

COMMONLY USED MODELS OF OPEN INNOVATION IN THE PHARMACEUTICAL SECTOR

In the pharmaceutical sector, greater operational complexity, new technology, the lack of availability of highly skilled professionals outside of big pharmaceutical corporations, and increased time and financial constraints may have accelerated the emergence of open innovation. In recent decades, many multinational pharmaceutical firms have utilized the full potential of open innovation by using external sources of innovation through access to ideas, technologies, and R&D initiatives (Hunter & Stephens, 2010). For instance, many firms have addressed the gaps in their own project portfolios by licensing or through mergers and acquisitions. Pharmaceutical firms also outsource their know-how to decrease new drug development costs or time as well as to get access to external information and know-how that they do not want to own for strategic reasons (Schuhmacher et al., 2013). This section has explored some commonly used models of open innovation that pharmaceutical firms adopt in developing mutually beneficial collaborative relationship with other actors including firms, research companies and government agencies. Schuhmacher et al. (2013) suggest four types of open innovation models as below:

- Knowledge creator – Organizations that use the 'knowledge creator' model have 'an inward preference for innovation management coupled with a lower proportion of externally acquired R&D projects than the industry standard' (Schuhmacher et al., 2013, p. 1135). These organizations rely heavily on internal innovation management, and even when innovation is obtained outside, it is generated primarily through internal resources and know-how. Garvin (1993) asserts that the organization who believe in knowledge creation place a premium on encouraging inventive knowledge by stressing regular experience confronting and overcoming challenges, trying new approaches, profiting from experience, and conveying information. Schuhmacher et al. (2013) identified Boehringer Ingelheim (BI) and Novartis as 'knowledge creators' that continue to adhere to this more traditional R&D model, which is based on internal R&D projects, skills, and know-how and supplemented by targeted licensing, university collaborations, and academic partnerships.
- Knowledge translator – A 'knowledge translator' is characterized as a predisposition for utilizing external resources and expertise to advance domestically created innovation. Knowledge translators focus on analysing new information, interpreting it in terms of the requirements and interests of their organization, and changing it into forms better suited to the application (Holden & von Kortzfleisch, 2004). Organizations (such as GSK) are considered as 'Knowledge translators' as the main project portfolio of these organizations are predominantly driven by internal research, while they manage their R&D projects effectively through outsourcing, collaborations, and partnerships.
- Knowledge integrator – Knowledge integrators take benefit from the expertise of outsiders by acquiring, assimilating, modifying knowledge and use it for internal innovation or to solve ill-structured problems posed by the organization (Sun, et al., 2020; Zahra & George, 2002). These organizations have a propensity for incorporating externally produced innovation into a model that is mostly based on internal resources and know-how. They derive value from their in-house experience in R&D management, while obtaining most of their R&D pipeline from licensing or acquisition. Sanofi appears to successfully use this model (Schuhmacher et al., 2013)., and knowledge leverage.
- Knowledge leverage – These organizations emphasize externally produced innovation in conjunction with an extroverted approach to innovation management (Schuhmacher et al., 2013). Outside sources provide most of the ideas, know-how, technologies and resources necessary to identify and develop novel medications. These organization gathers technology and

expertise from external sources and understands how to maximize the value of internal and external resources.

Choosing an open innovation model that best fits to a firm's interests, needs and capabilities warrants a careful judgment. As pharmaceutical R&D has become increasingly complex, large research-based pharmaceutical companies such as Novartis, Sanofi, and AstraZeneca make use of traditional collaboration and partnership models as well as other open innovation models such as crowdsourcing, innovation centers, open-source innovation to virtual R&D are also becoming more popular (Schuhmacher, Gassmann & Hinder, 2016). An increased use of vaccines worldwide to curb infectious diseases has also resulted in many joint ventures; these research collaborations are mainly aimed towards gaining access to the broader set of skills and technologies required for vaccine development. (World Health Organization Report, 2011). Furthermore, many technology-intensive firms transfer their proprietary technology to external academic and institutional laboratories to benefit from generous research grants from the government. For example, AstraZeneca has used academics from Oxford University and collaborated with Vaccitech to develop COVID vaccine; the company has signed exclusive agreements including further development and large-scale manufacturing and distribution of COVID vaccine around the globe (University of Oxford, 2020). AstraZeneca has established 25 different manufacturing sites in 15 countries to manufacture COVID Vaccines. On the other hand, Pfizer collaborated with BioNTech's founders to create the vaccine, while US based Moderna collaborated with National Institute of Allergies and Infectious Diseases (NIAID) to produce another vaccination for COVID-19 (GAVI, 2022).

The above-mentioned collaboration trends indicate that the models of open innovation adopted in the pharmaceutical sector is largely determined by individual firms' objectives (Bianchi et al., 2011). Typically, an MNC would develop mutually beneficial collaborative relationship with other MNCs, research companies and government agencies. They are least likely to collaborate with pharmaceutical/biotechnology firms in poor countries unless they have the required in-house capabilities and sustainable absorptive capacity (West & Gallagher, 2006: Martinez-Grau & Alvim-Gaston, 2019). The reason behind the innovative MNCs' reluctance in technology transfer and the unavailability of sophisticated technologies to firms in poor countries can also be explained by the economics of innovation. As suggested by Chesbrough et al. (2006), in recent years, new drug or vaccine development is increasingly becoming unsustainable, mainly due to the rising cost of R&D and shortened product life cycles. It is argued that since the early 2000s, the growth in R&D expenditure in pharmaceutical has exceeded the growth of their annual sales. Since the market for generic drugs is also becoming competitive as many MNCs are also interested in ensuring that a large part of their revenue comes from the sale of generic drugs (Chesbrough et al., 2006). The production of many generic drugs or vaccines also requires companies to perform R&D and innovative activities, which are often beyond the capability of firms in poor countries.

USING OPEN INNOVATION TO TAKE ADVANTAGE OF THE FLEXIBILITIES EMBEDDED IN THE TRIPS AGREEMENT OF THE WTO FOR FAIR ACCESS TO COVID VACCINES

It is impossible to overestimate the importance of worldwide cooperation in identifying and developing solutions to combat the pandemic. Massive efforts were made by researchers, doctors, scientists, approval boards, regulatory bodies, governments and manufacturers to get vaccines on the market as rapidly as possible, while keeping the same high standards and quality that are required for any new drug. According to the World Health Organization (2022), there are 23 approved COVID-19 vaccines in public and there are around 139 clinical trials underway for with the support from academia, research organizations and government bodies. The World Bank is collaborating with the WHO, UNICEF, GAVI (Global Alliance for Vaccines and Immunization), and other international organizations to help LDCs gain access to vaccinations through programs like Access to COVID-19 Tools–Accelerator (ACT-A), which includes the COVAX vaccine. Additionally, the World Bank has pledged US$12 billion in financing for poor countries in order to procure and deploy COVID-19 vaccines as well as build national health and immunization systems (GAVI, 2022; Pate, Bali & Kulaksiz, 2021). However, there are still numerous obstacles to overcome in ensuring that everyone has access to COVID vaccines. Many poor nations are concerned that most supplies have been reserved by developed countries and relatively little is available for them (Cheng, 2020). Many LDCs also face challenges related to vaccination transportation, storage, and distribution (Pate, Bali & Kulaksiz, 2021). Taken together, the local production of affordable vaccines in low-income countries using open innovation is the key to address the current vaccine divide.

As mentioned in the preceding section, MNCs are unlikely to collaborate with these low-technology pharmaceutical/biotechnology firms in less developed countries that are also deprived of infrastructure and institutional support from their governments. Therefore, they need support and intervention from the supranational organizations (such United Nations, World Health Organization and World Trade Organization) and global leaders. Pharmaceutical firms from both developed and developing countries can also explore the flexibilities embedded in the TRIPS (Trade-Related Aspects of Intellectual Property Rights) Agreement of the World

Trade Organization (WTO). The Agreement requires all WTO members to protect intellectual property (IP) such as patents, trademarks and copyrights. While the TRIPS Agreement was negotiated in 1994, it was implemented in developed countries in 1995 and in developing countries in 2005. However, TRIPS initially provided the least developed countries (LDCs) with an extension period of 10 years (2005–15) to allow them to undertake preparation for TRIPS. On 29 June 2021, at a formal meeting of the TRIPS Council, the WTO members agreed to extend the transition period for LDCs for another 13 years (until 1 July 2034) (United Nations 2021). As stated in the TRIPS Preamble[1] of the Agreement, 49 LDCs were granted an extended transition period beginning from 2005, to enable them 'to create a sound and viable technological base'. Although they were allowed to infringe patent rights during the transition period until 1 July 2034, the WTO envisages that LDCs will be able to operate within a strict regulatory regime and shift their strategic focus from imitation to innovation.

While the WTO has encouraged the governments in the least developed countries to developing a supportive technological regime for their domestic industries, the organization encourages cooperative relations between developed countries and LDCs to promote innovation in the pharmaceutical industry in LDCs and so it has appealed to developed countries to facilitate technology transfer to LDCs. Specifically, it expects the developed country members to promote and encourage the transfer of technology to LDCs. This is clearly stated in the Article 66.2[2] and 67[3] and was reiterated in a WTO press release on 29 November 2005[4] (World Tarde Organization, 2006). The WTO's expectation from developed countries in regard to providing technical assistance to LDCs is in line with the three key objectives of the TRIPS Agreement (as stated in Article 7 of the TRIPS): promoting technological innovation; promoting the diffusion of technical knowledge in a manner that ensures mutual benefits for technology creators and users, and that promotes social as well as economic welfare; and ensuring a balance between rights and obligations (of technology creators and users) (World Tarde Organization, 2006). Unfortunately, TRIPS Agreement has neither enhanced the flow of international technology transfer nor it has enhanced domestic innovation in poor countries, rather firms have been increasingly facing difficulties in accessing superior technology (Ala, 2013) which can be seen in the current race of vaccine development and manufacturing by the primary and private pharmaceutical giants.

Although TRIPS attempts to compel the WTO members to provide patent protection, there are some flexibilities (such as compulsory licensing[5] and parallel imports[6] embedded in the Agreement which enables countries to deal with public health emergencies. For example, the government can grant temporary compulsory licenses to domestic companies to produce patented drugs, or some pharmaceutical products can be sourced through parallel imports at cheaper prices. However, the literature suggests that even an effective use of the provision of compulsory licensing will not be possible unless the pharmaceutical sector in a WTO member has sufficient manufacturing capacities. Nevertheless, for developing countries with low technology base that were required to implement TRIPS in 2005 (unlike LDCs who are granted with an extension period) can still benefit from the flexibilities (such as compulsory licensing and parallel imports) embedded in the Agreement to deal with public health emergencies such as COVID-19 if they receive technological support from external actors.

However, only the TRIPS agreement will not solve the issue and as recommended by Dr. Ozlem Tureci, co-founder of BioNTech (cited in Pate, Bali & Kulaksiz, 2021), the teamwork and partnership across disciplines, fields, industries, and nations are vital to confront the current pandemic. Cross-sector collaboration also extends to the production and distribution of vaccines, leading to new ways to overcome supply, demand, and delivery constraints. For example, vaccines in LDCs lack access to ultra-cold chains to store vaccines as well as other hurdles such as lack of training, incorrect or incomplete information, and vaccine apprehension. Thus, more efforts and collaboration are required to develop vaccines suitable to such climate conditions. An equal distribution of vaccinations between countries and within countries is essential to stop this pandemic (Organisation for Economic Co-operation and Development, 2021; United Nations, 2020).

FUTURE RESEARCH DIRECTIONS

This paper examined the role of open innovation and the collaboration between MNCs and low-technology pharmaceutical/biotechnology firms in poor countries in addressing the current vaccine divide and emphasized the support and intervention from the supranational organizations (such United Nations, World Health Organization and World Trade Organization) and global leaders. Nonetheless, MNCs may not be willing to transfer their patented technology to firms in less developed economies that have inadequate patent protection laws, infrastructure and institutional support. Future studies should explore the specific role of the governments in developing and least developed countries in patent and regulatory reform, technology infrastructure development and implementing well-defined incentive mechanisms for the local and foreign firms that are collaborating in vaccine/drug development.

CONCLUSION

While many scholars suggest that open innovation is more relevant in the context of high-tech industries, there are also proponents of open innovation for low-tech industries such as generic pharmaceuticals or bio-tech sectors (Bianchi et al., 2011; Gassmann, Enkel & Chesbrough, 2010). The key argument for open innovation is the existing inefficiencies in markets for technology, especially in the pharmaceutical and biotechnology sectors. Often MNCs deal with transactions related to their IP assets secretly, which results in information asymmetry and therefore, higher prices of imported technology (Chesbrough et al., 2006); in most cases firms in developing and least developed countries are unable to afford technology. As already discussed in the paper, when MNCs adopt an open innovation model, it enables them to achieve more economies of scale than that from the traditional closed model (Gassmann, 2006; Michelino et al., 2015). However, given that pharmaceutical/biotechnology firms in poor countries generally lack in-house competencies to produce high quality vaccines, to improve their dynamic capability they should also proactively engage in collaborative R&D with research-intensive foreign firms and/or MNCs and seek to be part of an innovation network or system of innovation. Being part of an innovation network is likely to make it easier to access complementary technological resources to develop the generic vaccines. Finally, the authors believe that in line with the TRIPS Agreement's promises in relation to transfer of technology, the WTO should be more proactive in promoting firm- and institution level collaboration between developed, developing and least-developed countries. Importantly also, the mass production of generic vaccines in collaboration with firms from developing countries may bring both economic and non-economic benefits for knowledge-intensive MNCs in terms of royalty through licensing, access to new markets, improved competitive advantage, branding, learning from partner firms, and giving back to the global community.

REFERENCES

Ala, M. U. (2013). A firm-level analysis of the vulnerability of the Bangladeshi pharmaceutical industry to the TRIPS agreement: Implications for R&D capability and technology transfer. *Procedia Economics and Finance*, *5*, 30–39. doi:10.1016/S2212-5671(13)00006-3

Alas, H., & Matthews, A. L. (2021). *Vaccination rates by country*. https://www.usnews.com/news/best-countries/articles/covid-19

Bianchi, M., Cavaliere, A., Chiaroni, D., Frattini, F., & Chiesa, V. (2011). Organisational modes for Open Innovation in the bio-pharmaceutical industry: An exploratory analysis. *Technovation*, *31*(1), 22–33. doi:10.1016/j.technovation.2010.03.002

Bogers, M., Zobel, A. K., Afuah, A., Almirall, E., Brunswicker, S., Dahlander, L., Gawer, A., Gruber, M., Haefliger, S., & Hagedoorn, J. (2017). The open innovation research landscape: Established perspectives and emerging themes across different levels of analysis. *Industry and Innovation*, *24*(1), 8–40. doi:10.1080/13662716.2016.1240068

Calantone, R. J., & Stanko, M. A. (2007). Drivers of outsourced innovation: An exploratory study. *Journal of Product Innovation Management*, *24*(3), 230–241. doi:10.1111/j.1540-5885.2007.00247.x

Cheng, M., & Larson, C. (2020). Race for virus vaccine could leave some countries behind. *ABC News*. Retrieved from https://abcnews.go.com/Health/wireStory/race-virus-vaccine-leave-countries-71313932

Chesbrough, H. (2003). *Open innovation: The new imperative for creating and profiting from technology*. Harvard Business Press.

Chesbrough, H. (2006). *Open business models: How to thrive in the new innovation landscape*. Harvard Business Press.

Chesbrough, H., & Crowther, A. K. (2006). Beyond high tech: Early adopters of open innovation in other industries. *R & D Management*, *36*(3), 229–236. doi:10.1111/j.1467-9310.2006.00428.x

Chesbrough, H., Lettl, C., & Ritter, T. (2018). Value creation and value capture in open innovation. *Journal of Product Innovation Management*, *35*(6), 930–938. doi:10.1111/jpim.12471

Christensen, J. F., Olesen, M. H., & Kjær, J. S. (2005). The industrial dynamics of Open Innovation—Evidence from the transformation of consumer electronics. *Research Policy*, *34*(10), 1533–1549. doi:10.1016/j.respol.2005.07.002

Frenken, K. (Ed.). (2007). *Applied evolutionary economics and economic geography*. Edward Elgar Publishing. doi:10.4337/9781847205391

Garvin, D. A. (1993). Building a learning organization. *Harvard Business Review*, *71*(4), 78–91. PMID:10127041

Gassmann, O. (2006). Opening up the innovation process: Towards an agenda. *R & D Management*, *36*(3), 223–228. doi:10.1111/j.1467-9310.2006.00437.x

Gassmann, O., & Enkel, E. (2004). Towards a theory of open innovation: three core process archetypes. *Proceedings of the R&D Management Conference,* 6–9.

GAVI. (2022). *The COVID-19 vaccine race.* Retrieved from https://www.gavi.org/vaccineswork/covid-19-vaccine-race

Heinz, F. X., & Stiasny, K. (2021). Profiles of current COVID-19 vaccines. *Wiener Klinische Wochenschrift, 133*(7), 271–283. doi:10.100700508-021-01835-w PMID:33725201

Hippel, E. V. (1988). Cooperation between Rivals: The Informal Trading of Technical Know-how. *The Sources of Innovation*, 76-92.

Hodson, R. (2016). Open innovation. *Nature, 533*(7602), S53–S53. doi:10.1038/533S53a PMID:27167389

Holden, N. J., & Von Kortzfleisch, H. F. (2004). Why cross-cultural knowledge transfer is a form of translation in more ways than you think. *Knowledge and Process Management, 11*(2), 127–136. doi:10.1002/kpm.198

Howell, J. M., & Sheab, C. M. (2001). Individual differences, environmental scanning, innovation framing, and champion behavior: Key predictors of project performance. *Journal of Product Innovation Management, 18*(1), 15–27. doi:10.1111/1540-5885.1810015

Hu, Y., McNamara, P., & McLoughlin, D. (2015). Outbound open innovation in bio-pharmaceutical out-licensing. *Technovation, 35*, 46–58. doi:10.1016/j.technovation.2014.07.004

Hunter, J., & Stephens, S. (2010). Is open innovation the way forward for big pharma? *Nature Reviews. Drug Discovery, 9*(2), 87–88. doi:10.1038/nrd3099

Iammarino, S., & McCann, P. (2006). The structure and evolution of industrial clusters: Transactions, technology and knowledge spillovers. *Research Policy, 35*(7), 1018–1036. doi:10.1016/j.respol.2006.05.004

Laursen, K., & Salter, A. (2020). Who captures value from open innovation—The firm or its employees? *Strategic Management Review, 1*(2), 255–276. doi:10.1561/111.00000009

Lundvall, B. Å., & Borrás, S. (2005). Science, technology and innovation policy. The Oxford handbook of innovation, 599-631.

Macro Trends. (2020). *GNI Per Capita by Country.* Retrieved from https://www.macrotrends.net/countries/ranking/gni-per-capita

Martinez-Grau, M. A., & Alvim-Gaston, M. (2019). Powered by open innovation: Opportunities and challenges in the pharma sector. *Pharmaceutical Medicine*, *33*(3), 193–198. doi:10.100740290-019-00280-5 PMID:31933287

Metcalfe, J. S. (1994). Evolutionary economics and technology policy. *Economic Journal (London)*, *104*(425), 931–944. doi:10.2307/2234988

Michelino, F., Lamberti, E., Cammarano, A., & Caputo, M. (2015). Measuring open innovation in the Bio-Pharmaceutical industry. *Creativity and Innovation Management*, *24*(1), 4–28. doi:10.1111/caim.12072

Muro, M., & Austin, J. (2021). The vaccine divide will drive even worse economic divides. *The Avenue*. Retrieved from https://www.brookings.edu/blog/the-avenue/2021/09/13/the-vaccine-divide-will-drive-even-worse-economic-divides/

Nelson, R. R. (2008). Economic development from the perspective of evolutionary economic theory. *Oxford Development Studies*, *36*(1), 9–21. doi:10.1080/13600810701848037

Organisation for Economic Co-operation and Development. (2021). *Race to vaccinate - Understanding the policy challenges around COVID-19 vaccines*. Retrieved from https://www.oecd.org/coronavirus/en/vaccines

Pak, A., Adegboye, O. A., Adekunle, A. I., Rahman, K. M., McBryde, E. S., & Eisen, D. P. (2020). Economic consequences of the COVID-19 outbreak: The need for epidemic preparedness. *Frontiers in Public Health*, *8*, 241. doi:10.3389/fpubh.2020.00241 PMID:32574307

Pate, M. A., Bali, S., & Kulaksiz, S. (2021). *Safer Together—Unlocking the Power of Partnerships against COVID-19*. Retrieved from https://blogs.worldbank.org/health/safer-together-unlocking-power-partnerships-against-covid-19

Regalado, A. (2012). Money seeks idea. *Technology Review*, *115*(6), 75–76.

Rubin, G. D., & Abramson, R. G. (2018). Creating value through incremental innovation: Managing culture, structure, and process. *Radiology*, *288*(2), 330–340. doi:10.1148/radiol.2018171239 PMID:29969069

Saeed, H., Osama, H., Madney, Y. M., Harb, H. S., Abdelrahman, M. A., Ehrhardt, C., & Abdelrahim, M. E. (2021). COVID-19; current situation and recommended interventions. *International Journal of Clinical Practice*, *75*(5), e13886. doi:10.1111/ijcp.13886 PMID:33278855

Salter, A., Ter Wal, A. L., Criscuolo, P., & Alexy, O. (2015). Open for ideation: Individual-level openness and idea generation in R&D. *Journal of Product Innovation Management*, *32*(4), 488–504. doi:10.1111/jpim.12214

Schuhmacher, A., Gassmann, O., & Hinder, M. (2016). Changing R&D models in research-based pharmaceutical companies. *Journal of Translational Medicine*, *14*(1), 1–11. doi:10.118612967-016-0838-4 PMID:27118048

Schuhmacher, A., Germann, P. G., Trill, H., & Gassmann, O. (2013). Models for open innovation in the pharmaceutical industry. *Drug Discovery Today*, *18*(23-24), 1133–1137. doi:10.1016/j.drudis.2013.07.013 PMID:23892183

Steurs, G. (1994). *Spillovers and Cooperation in Research and Development* [Unpublished doctoral dissertation]. KU Leuven.

Sun, Y., Tüertscher, P., Majchrzak, A., & Malhotra, A. (2020). Pro-socially motivated interaction for knowledge integration in crowd-based open innovation. *Journal of Knowledge Management*, *24*(9), 2127–2147. doi:10.1108/JKM-04-2020-0303

United Nations. (2020). *Recover better - Economic and Social Challenges and Opportunities*. Retrieved from https://www.un.org/development/desa/en/wp-content/uploads/2020/07/RECOVER_BETTER_0722-1.pdf

United Nations. (2021). *WTO members agree to extend TRIPS transition period for LDCs until 1 July 2034*. Retrieved from https://www.un.org/ldcportal/wto-members-agree-to-extend-trips-transition-period-for-ldcs-until-1-july-2034/

University of Oxford. (2020). *Oxford University announces landmark partnership with AstraZeneca for the development and potential large-scale distribution of COVID-19 vaccine candidate*. Retrieved from https://www.ox.ac.uk/news/2020-04-30-oxford-university-announces-landmark-partnership-astrazeneca-development-and

Vaiman, V. (2010). Managing talent of non-traditional knowledge workers: Opportunities, challenges, and trends. In *Talent Management of Knowledge Workers* (pp. 1–22). Palgrave Macmillan. doi:10.1057/9780230277526_1

Wass, S., & Vimarlund, V. (2016). Healthcare in the age of open innovation–A literature review. *The HIM Journal*, *45*(3), 121–133. doi:10.1177/1833358316639458 PMID:27105481

West, J., & Bogers, M. (2017). Open innovation: Current status and research opportunities. *Innovation*, *19*(1), 43–50. doi:10.1080/14479338.2016.1258995

West, J., & Gallagher, S. (2006). Challenges of open innovation: The paradox of firm investment in open-source software. *R & D Management*, *36*(3), 319–331. doi:10.1111/j.1467-9310.2006.00436.x

World Bank. (2020). *The World Bank in Middle Income Countries*. Retrieved from https://www.worldbank.org/en/country/mic/overview#1

World Health Organization. (2011). *Increasing access to diagnostics through technology transfer and local production*. Retrieved from https://www.who.int/phi/publications/Increasing_Access_to_Vaccines_Through_Technology_Transfer.pdf?ua=1

World Health Organization. (2022). *The COVID-19 vaccine tracker and landscape*. Retrieved from https://www.who.int/publications/m/item/draft-landscape-of-covid-19-candidate-vaccines

World Trade Organization. (2006). *Agreement on Trade-Related Aspects of Intellectual Property Rights as Amended by the 2005 Protocol Amending the TRIPS Agreement*. Retrieved from https://www.wto.org/english/docs_e/legal_e/trips_e.htm#part1

World Trade Organization. (2021). *Compulsory licensing of pharmaceuticals and TRIPS*. Retrieved from https://www.wto.org/english/tratop_e/trips_e/public_health_faq_e.htm

Yeong, S. P., King, L. M., & Dol, S. S. (2015). A review on marine search and rescue operations using unmanned aerial vehicles. *International Journal of Marine and Environmental Sciences*, *9*(2), 396–399.

Yun, J. J., Zhao, X., Jung, K., & Yigitcanlar, T. (2020). The culture for open innovation dynamics. *Sustainability*, *12*(12), 5076. doi:10.3390u12125076

Zahra, S. A., & George, G. (2002). The net-enabled business innovation cycle and the evolution of dynamic capabilities. *Information Systems Research*, *13*(2), 147–150. doi:10.1287/isre.13.2.147.90

ADDITIONAL READING

Chiaroni, D., Chiesa, V., & Frattini, F. (2009). Investigating the adoption of open innovation in the bio-pharmaceutical industry: A framework and an empirical analysis. *European Journal of Innovation Management*, *12*(3), 285–305. doi:10.1108/14601060910974192

Getz, K. A., & Kaitin, K. I. (2012). Open innovation: The new face of pharmaceutical research and development. *Expert Review of Clinical Pharmacology*, *5*(5), 481–483. doi:10.1586/ecp.12.44 PMID:23121265

Michelino, F., Lamberti, E., Cammarano, A., & Caputo, M. (2015). Measuring open innovation in the Bio-Pharmaceutical industry. *Creativity and Innovation Management*, *24*(1), 4–28. doi:10.1111/caim.12072

Mortara, L., & Minshall, T. (2011). How do large multinational companies implement open innovation? *Technovation*, *31*(10-11), 586–597. doi:10.1016/j.technovation.2011.05.002

Musiello-Neto, F., Rua, O. L., Arias-Oliva, M., & Silva, A. F. (2021). Open innovation and competitive advantage on the hospitality sector: The role of organizational strategy. *Sustainability*, *13*(24), 13650. doi:10.3390u132413650

KEY TERMS AND DEFINITIONS

Absorptive Capacity: An organization's ability to identify, value, integrate, renovate, and use new knowledge from external sources.

Developing Country: A country with lower levels national income and industrialization where people have inadequate access to health care and education.

Generic Vaccine: A vaccine that is chemically identical to the patented one and includes the same active ingredients.

Intellectual Property: It is a type of property that is the creation of mind such as a new product or service, design, symbol, process, idea, and image.

Least Developed Countries (LDCs): A country with low levels of social, economic, and technological development where a large proportion of people live in extreme poverty.

Open Innovation: An organizational practice involving the readiness to share knowledge and information with people outside and inside the firm for suggestions and solutions.

System of Innovation: A network of people, business, research organizations and institutions who have direct interaction in regard to the creation, distribution, and use of scientific knowledge or technology.

TRIPS Agreement: The Trade-Related Aspects of Intellectual Property Rights is an international agreement between the members of the World Trade Organization to protect intellectual property rights using regulatory mechanisms.

Vaccine Divide: The gap between people in developed and less developed countries in terms of their access to vaccines.

ENDNOTES

1 TRIPS Preamble: 'Members ... Recognizing also the special needs of the least-developed country Members in respect of maximum flexibility in the domestic implementation of laws and regulations in order to enable them to create a sound and viable technological base' (WTO 2006).

2 Article 66.2 of the TRIPS Agreement: 'Developed country Members shall provide incentives to enterprises and institutions in their territories for the purpose of promoting and encouraging technology transfer to least-developed country Members in order to enable them to create a sound and viable technological base'(World Trade Organization, 2006).

3 Article 67 of the TRIPS Agreement states: 'In order to facilitate the implementation of this Agreement, developed country Members shall provide, on request and on mutually agreed terms and conditions, technical and financial cooperation in favour of developing and least-developed country Members. Such cooperation shall include assistance in the preparation of laws and regulations on the protection and enforcement of intellectual property rights as well as on the prevention of their abuse, and shall include support regarding the establishment or reinforcement of domestic offices and agencies relevant to these matters, including the training of personnel' (World Trade Organization, 2006).

4 WTO press release no. 424/2005: 'The decision by the WTO's Council for Trade-Related Aspects of Intellectual Property Rights (TRIPS) extends the transition period for least-developed countries (for pharmaceutical products until 2016), and includes commitments on technical assistance to help them prepare to apply the agreement ... The decision also reiterates developed countries' commitment to provide technical and financial cooperation to help the least-developed countries implement the TRIPS Agreement and respond to needs that the least-developed countries have promised to identify, preferably over the next two years ... The decision was agreed by consensus among all members, as is standard practice in the WTO' (World Trade Organization, 2006).

5 Compulsory licensing: 'When the authorities license companies or individuals other than the patent owner to use the rights of the patent — to make, use, sell or import a product under patent (i.e. a patented product or a product made by a patented process) — without the permission of the patent owner. Allowed under the WTO's TRIPS (intellectual property) Agreement provided certain procedures and conditions are fulfilled' (World Trade Organization, 2006).

6 Parallel import: 'When a product made legally (i.e. not pirated) abroad is imported without the permission of the intellectual property right-holder (e.g. the trademark or patent owner). Some countries allow this, others do not' (World Trade Organization, 2006).

Chapter 3
Open Innovation:
A Successful Case Study of a Portuguese Company Seeking Complementary Resources

Ana Inês
University of Aveiro, Portugal

Maria Hespanha
University of Aveiro, Portugal

Mariana Leite
University of Aveiro, Portugal

Patrícia Pires
University of Aveiro, Portugal

António Carrizo Moreira
https://orcid.org/0000-0002-6613-8796
University of Aveiro, Portugal

ABSTRACT

Open innovation practices are recurrent in the business environment due to resource and technology limitations in most companies. The search for complementary resources, especially among SMEs, begins to be a current practice due to the possibility of resorting to partnerships and collaborative processes. Thus, through a case study analysis of a Portuguese SME based in Aveiro, Portugal, it was possible to analyze the innovation process and the adoption of open innovation practices in this SME. Through a qualitative study, it was possible to understand the importance of SMEs in the Portuguese business fabric, as they increasingly seek to apply innovative processes in their processes. However, the case analyzed reveals that open innovation may involve an inter-organizational partnership where the company analyzed uses an intermediate model of open innovation, since it does not sell surplus technology, internalizing only external resources. This case study serves as a teaching case as well as a pedagogic tool.

DOI: 10.4018/978-1-7998-8665-5.ch003

INTRODUCTION

Innovation is one of the most commonly used business strategies (Dantas & Moreira, 2011) to: (i) generate new products/processes and processes, (ii) adapt and developed new technologies, (iii) deploy changes within organizations in order to improve business competitiveness.

Innovation is one of the main drivers of business performance (Ribau et al., 2019; Zimmermann et al., 2020). It is normally related to the successful commercialization of the result of the generation and development of new ideas, transformed into products, services or processes (Dantas & Moreira, 2011; Hungund & Mani, 2019). The organizational climate is important for successfully promoting innovation within the firm. For that an innovation culture supporting free expression of ideas, divergent thinking practice, and risk aversion is mandatory (Popa et al., 2017).

If historically, most of the organizational knowledge and innovation was generated internally (Chesbrough, 2003), with the globalization of the technology and the business world, there are only a limited number of firms that would be able to compete by using exclusively their internal resources. Moreover, in an increasingly competitive world, where competitive advantages are ephemeral and hardly sustainable in the long term due to technological change (Bianchi et al., 2010; Lööf & Heshmati, 2006; Parida et al., 2012), innovation and technology have become key elements in the development of the knowledge economy. If innovation is important, inter-organizational relationships based on open innovation (OI) and technological alignment are important for the business success (Carvalho & Moreira, 2015; Silva & Moreira, 2021).

Open innovation, as defined by Chesbrough (2003), consists of using internal and external sources of knowledge and technology. Although the resource-based view of the firm has been extensively used to defend the importance of the internal source of knowledge and innovation as a competitive advantage, external sources of knowledge seek to accelerate internal innovation processes, to increase the potential for entering into new markets and to obtain better business performance (Bernal-Torres & Frost-González, 2015; Chesbrough, 2003, 2006; Hungund & Mani, 2019; Lööf & Heshmati, 2006).

Unlike the traditional model of innovation, where all the knowledge, technology and innovation is coordinated and internalized and controlled by the company, OI is characterized by a porous organization in which firms interact with their partner organizations to internalize and externalize knowledge and technology (Torres et al., 2015). The concept of OI assumes that organizations use both external and internal ideas and knowledge to enhance their innovations (Boger et al., 2018). As firms are applying business models to enhance their R&D capabilities, and taking into account the characteristics normally associated with small and medium-sized firms

(SMEs), OI is very important to leverage the development and competitiveness of SMEs. In fact, resource constraints and the small size of SMEs force them to interact with the outside world in order to gain access to the resources and knowledge they need, but do not have. Consequently, OI plays a very important role in its growth and competitiveness.

Open innovation has been widely studied, especially in large companies. Although it is still a relatively unexplored area in the scope of SMEs, the apparent relationship between OI and SMEs has aroused growing interest on the part of the scientific community, which has been studying it in an attempt to understand what are the factors that lead SMEs to adopt this type of innovation, namely the conditions and benefits of OI in SMEs. Thus, as there are few studies on OI in countries that are at an intermediate level of technological development, as is the case of Portugal, which has the characteristics from a peripheral country (Milici et al., 2021; Silva et al., 2021; Teixeira & Lopes, 2012), and taking into account the composition of the Portuguese business fabric, in which the majority of companies are SMEs, representing around 99.9% of the total business fabric, it was decided to assess a Portuguese firm that values OI as an engine for growth and differentiation (Silva et al., 2021; Teixeira & Lopes, 2012).

To this end, a company was chosen – for confidentiality reasons is going to be named VERTICAL – which due to its history of partnerships with the University of Aveiro and its interaction with external agents, follows an OI strategy and seeks to leverage its technology, knowledge and competitiveness on external resources, having a predominant role in the development of the company, through an innovative and entrepreneurial capacity. As such the main objective of this chapter is to explore how this SME uses OI strategy as part of its innovation strategy. Taking into account that OI serves as a management business model that uses internal and external sources of knowledge and technology with people and organizations outside the company to tap into externals sources of knowledge and technologies, analyzing the characteristics of a small firms is of added values to present how small companies muddle through the implementation of OI business model as the compete in the market. As a result, this case study seeks to cover two different situations: to serve as an example of OI strategy and to prepare this case study for class discussion, serving academic as well as practitioners perspectives. The chapter constitutes an important tool for SMEs managers as well as for graduate students to discuss the importance of the implementation of OI approaches to generate competitive advantages.

This chapter is divided into six sections. After the introduction, the Section 2 presents the literature review, which aims to frame the work with regard to OI in SMEs and their impact on the Portuguese business fabric. In Section 3, the methodology used for the preparation of this case study is reported. In Section 4, the company is presented, followed by the presentation of the case study, where the company will be presented and a systematic description of the results of the interview conducted with the CEO of the chosen company will be made. Section 5 presents the results. Section 6 presents the discussion of the results. Finally, the conclusion is presented in Section 7.

LITERATURE REVIEW

Impact of SMEs in the Portuguese Economy

The importance of SMEs is transversal to most industrialized economies, especially in the European Union, constituting their economic base (Moreira, 2009). In fact, SMEs are usually referred to as the backbone of the European economy (Schmiemann, 2009), since they represent 99% of all European companies (Coelho & Matias, 2010). In other words, the importance of SMEs is not exclusive to the Portuguese reality.

According to the criteria defined in European legislation, the main factors that determine whether a company is an SME are related to the number of employees and turnover (European Commission, 2020). A medium-sized enterprise employs fewer than 250 employees and its annual turnover does not exceed 50 million euros. A small company has fewer than 50 employees and a microenterprise fewer than 10 employees (Carvalheira & Moreira, 2015; European Commission, 2020).

The weight of SMEs in the Portuguese economic fabric is quite significant, as they represent 99.9% of the total number of firms. Of these, 95.4% are micro; 4% are small companies and only 0.6% are medium-sized (Carvalheira & Moreira, 2015). According to 2017 data, there are 1259234 SMEs in Portugal, of which 1212059 are micro enterprises (PORDATA, 2017). Overall, SMEs still account for 79% of total employment, playing an important role in the development of the Portuguese economy (Carvalheira & Moreira, 2015), generating employment, and being a source of entrepreneurial skills and innovation. SMEs are also crucial to the Portuguese economy, especially for the support they provide to large companies, serving as a complement to their activities throughout the value chain. Indeed, multinationals tend to turn to SMEs for subcontracting activities due to their technological expertise and mastery of certain technologies (Moreira, 2009).

However, despite the fact that 99.9% of companies are SMEs, the truth is that large companies are responsible, despite representing only 0.1% of the total number of companies, for 20% of employment and more than 20% of sales volume (Moreira, 2009).

Advantages, Limitations and Strategies of SMEs

SMEs have major limitations, such as lack of both R&D resources and structured innovation processes. In terms of advantages, SMEs stand out for being less bureaucratic, more flexible and having a greater propensity to take risks. Given their limitations they are also forced to interact more with customers, suppliers, research centers and other firms (Carvalho & Moreira, 2015). The globalization process has also motivated companies to establish these outward-based proactive behaviors (Coelho & Matias, 2010; Ribau et al., 2017).

In the current economic context, marked by stiff competitiveness, competing internationally is essential for economic survival. Thus, due to their more flexible organizational structure, SMEs have competitive advantages that large companies generally do not have, since SMEs are nimble and more resilient to crises and can more easily reconvert their business. However, one of the major obstacles SMEs face is the fact that they cannot take advantage of economies of scale (Carvalheira & Moreira, 2015; Moreira, 2009), despite their specific know-how (Coelho & Matias, 2010; Silva et al., 2021).

Another problem of SMEs is related to their organizational structure, characterized by the lack of financial resources and the scarcity of human resources (Coelho & Matias, 2010; Hungund & Mani, 2019; Moreira, 2009).

Given the limitations of SMEs, OI is an excellent opportunity for them to collaborate with external entities, especially at regional level, in order to increase their probability of success and to create opportunities for improvement and growth. These outward-oriented interactions allow for mutual knowledge sharing between entities involved (Odriozola-Fernández et al., 2019; Radwizon & Bogers, 2019).

Open Innovation and SMEs

Due to their small size and consequent resource limitation, SMEs are likely to adopt OI processes, since they do not have all the necessary resources, knowledge and technologies (Santoro et al., 2019; Van de Vrande et al., 2009). Therefore, OI is a means to obtain external resources and competences quickly and efficiently, facilitating the development and commercialization of new ideas. Open innovation is opposed to the traditional model of closed innovation, and has two dimensions that must exist simultaneously: on one hand, the absorption of knowledge and technology and, on the other hand, the transfer of knowledge and technology to other organizations. Those two dimensions encompass what is referred to as inbound and outbound OI.

All practices entail the establishment of inter-organizational relationships with external organizations that leverage the other organizations discoveries, technologies and knowledge, which encompass the inbound dimension of OI (Chesbrough, 2006;

Chiaroni et al., 2011). Huizingh (2011) poses that inbound OI refers to the internal use of external knowledge.

Inbound innovation is characterized by outside-in processes that involve the opening up of the innovation processes of the firm to integrate external knowledge and technologies from suppliers, customers or other firms to enrich the firm's own knowledge base (Enkel et al., 2009), increase the firm's innovativeness (Gassmann et al., 2010; Inês et al., 2021; Laursen & Salter, 2006). Within this process, innovation networks (Dittrich & Duysters, 2007; Enkel, 2010) and the use of innovation intermediaries are notoriously important (Gassmann et al., 2010; Lee et al., 2009).

The outbound dimension reflects the possibility of the firm to explore the market, or other external organizations, to complement the internal paths of the firm to reach the market. As such, this outbound dimension represents an opportunity to seek external organizations with business models that are more appropriate to market a particular technology that the firms is not willing to utilize (Chesbrough, 2006; Chiaroni et al., 2011; Inês et al., 2021). This dimension refers to the external exploitation of internal knowledge (Huizingh, 2011). Inside-out OI refers to the sale of intellectual property and multiplying technology by transferring ideas from the external environment (Enkel et al., 2009). Companies establishing inside-out OI processes as the main key of their business are focused in sourcing their knowledge and innovation, with the purpose of quickly bringing ideas to the market. The decision of changing the focus of exploitation outside company borders seeks the creation of profits via intellectual property licensing and/or multiplying technologies and transferring ideas to other companies, thereby generating revenues from licensing, joint-ventures and spin-offs (Enkel et al., 2009).

These dimensions are related to three knowledge processes: research, knowledge retention and exploitation, and the former can be undertaken both inbound and outbound (Lichtenthaler and Lichtenthaler, 2009). According to existing studies, there are several OI modes; however Abulrub and Lee (2012) have developed a classification of 13 OI types: (1) purchasing external technology; (2) licensing-in; (3) joint-ventures; (4) joint development; (5) R&D outsourcing; (6) venture capital; (7) mergers and acquisitions; (8) customer involvement and (9) external networking; (10) selling internal technologies; (11) licensing-out; (12) spin-offs; and (13) Open source.

There are several reasons explaining why SMEs can benefit more from OI adoption than large firms, namely the fact that they are less bureaucratic, more flexible and more responsive to market needs (Silva et al., 2021; Carvalho & Moreira, 2015). Indeed, several studies address the benefits of OI adoption in SMEs (Carvalho & Moreira, 2015; Chiaroni et al., 2011). However, in relation to the Portuguese context, it should be noted that many companies are still in an intermediate state of technological development. Thus, in comparison with firms located in countries with higher rates of technological development (such as the USA, Sweden, Finland or the Netherlands), Portuguese companies, in general, tend to adopt a closed innovation model (Teixeira & Lopes, 2012). However, there are still few studies regarding the adoption of OI in Portugal, especially in SMEs, so it is in our interest to assess the extent to which Portuguese companies value innovation as an engine for growth and differentiation (Milici et al., 2021; Silva et al., 2021).

Although the Portuguese innovation model is generically closed, Portuguese firms consider acquiring external technologies and knowledge as vital for their business. In other words, usually the most widespread aspect of OI in Portuguese firms is the absorption of external knowledge (Teixeira & Lopes, 2012).

Although the innovation model most frequently used in Portugal could be considered as 'closed innovation', Portuguese firms consider the use and acquisition of external technology as vital to their businesses. That is, usually the most widespread aspect of OI in the Portuguese business environment is the absorption of external knowledge (Teixeira & Lopes, 2012).

Silva et al. (2021) consider that the propensity of SMEs to adopt OI depends on five dimensions: (1) human, technological, financial resource allocation; (2) leadership; (3) planning and processes; (4) general context; and (5) transactional context. Of these, the importance of leadership should be emphasized. Indeed, the attitude of the owner or head of SMEs is a key determinant of the firm's performance and adoption of innovation models (Chiaroni et al., 2011; Van de Vrande et al., 2009). It is the leader who is also responsible for designing and conveying the organizational culture, affecting how innovation is perceived within the firm. Through an organizational culture that supports creativity and knowledge dissemination among the various employees of the company it becomes easier for the company to solve problems and create synergies (Raposo et al., 2014). Felício et al. (2019) consider that the SME's ambidextrous capacity, i.e. the ability to respond simultaneously to disruptive or incremental innovation processes, allows a better adaptation to new routines, based on the ability to assimilate knowledge.

Vis-à-vis large firms, the innovation process of SMEs is different, since SMEs are particularly focused on creating networks with other firms, research centers, customers and suppliers (Carvalho & Moreira, 2015). Portuguese SMEs are positively influenced in their performance and innovation levels through cooperation. Collaborative activities with other firms and institutions allow them to access technological knowledge and resources useful for the rapid development of organizations, access to new markets, economies of scale, and risk and cost sharing (Teixeira & Lopes, 2012; Carvalho & Moreira, 2015). Sources of collaboration include educational entities, research centers, suppliers, customers, and companies from other sectors. Typically, competing entities are avoided and government institutions appear only as a funding source. These collaborative activities with partners are most evident in the experimentation or prototyping, design, and engineering phases. The relationships established are long-term oriented, typified by partnerships, alliances, and organizational networks (Carvalho & Moreira, 2015). Typically, in Portuguese SMEs, cooperation between companies results in the creation of radical innovation processes rather than incremental innovation (Raposo et al., 2014). Social networks also appear as facilitating agents for the formation of strategic partnerships and increased contact with suppliers and customers (Franco et al., 2016).

RESEARCH METHOD

Based on the objectives defined in the introduction section, a case study-based qualitative methodology was adopted, where it is possible to interpret and explain the observable phenomena within certain specific contexts (Wahyuni, 2012).

The qualitative approach followed allows a greater understanding of the phenomena analyzed. It follows an interpretive and descriptive approach of the reality, using a single case study, whose objective is complemented by the desire to be analyzed and discussed in the classroom. This conjecture is supported by Yin (2009), who defends the use of case studies for the analysis of complex social phenomena, given the dynamism and complexity that they involve.

One of the main advantages of the case study is the fact that information may originate from several sources. The most used source of information, however, is interviews (Rowley, 2002). In fact, it is the interview that allows interviewees to express themselves, allowing interviewers to collect information about a certain topic (Alshenqeeti, 2014).

Based on the objective initially outlined, the choice of the company to be analyzed was based on the following criteria: being a Portuguese SME; being at an early stage of its development and internationalization process; having limited resources in order to seek to complement these resources with external partners; and actively using OI.

The Portuguese SME chosen, which for confidentiality reasons is called VERTICAL, was selected for fulfilling the criteria defined above, enhancing the possible discussion of the case study in the classroom, which we consider of added interest.

In order to guarantee reliability, all the processes and analyses used during the research were described and the main instruments used in data collection were identified, such as the interview guide.

The previously prepared script was structured taking into account the theme to be developed – OI in Portuguese SMEs – and was inspired by the survey conducted by Teixeira and Lopes (2012) and Abulrub and Lee (2012). The script addressed 12 key aspects: (1) presentation of the company, referring to its history, mission, objectives, human resources, sector of activity, awards, etc.; (2) CEO's opinion about the importance of SMEs; (3) organizational culture; (4) new product development process; (5) R&D activities; (6) use of external technology; (7) partnerships and collaborations; (8) relationship with the public policy and funds; (9) innovation processes in the company; (10) open innovation; (11) importance of the CEO in the innovation processes; and (12) the role of social networks.

The main method used for data collection was the semi-structured interview, using open-ended questions, in order to deepen the above-mentioned themes (Fisher, 2007). The open structure allows exploring data obtained during the interviews, with the objective of gaining a more in-depth understanding of the topic (Fisher, 2007). The interviews allowed the collection of primary data, which provided relevant information and concrete answers to the objectives defined above.

The interviews took place at VERTICAL's facilities, in Gafanha da Nazaré, Portugal and took about 50 minutes. It was audio-recorded in order to collect all the information more efficiently. It should be noted that the CEO authorized both the recording and the disclosure of the content of the interview. During the course of the interview, the script was adapted, according to the answers given during the interview.

As VERTICAL's CEO had been part of the company's staff since its inception, he was contacted to provide the most reliable information about the company. We had the opportunity to schedule two semi-structured interviews to address the evolutionary perspective of the company regarding strategy, main innovation activities, financial indicators as well as partnerships. As we had previous knowledge about the company, the two interviews lasted approximately 30 minutes each. The two interviews were audio recorded so that subsequent content analysis could be carried out. Subsequently, the interviews were transcribed to ensure the conformity of the results and facilitate further analysis of the data. With the second interview it was possible to complement the previous one. This second interview helped with the triangulation of some content, and supported further elaboration on key points that were not analyzed during the first interview. Both interviews took place at VERTICAL's facilities, so the interviewers could observe events in their natural setting, rather than relying on pre-arranged single interviews.

The interviews and the complementary visit to the company's facilities allowed the researchers to analyze managerial actions regarding innovation activities. The interviewers sought to maintain a passive and unobtrusive presence, in order not to interfere with on-going events and activities. Data from all sources were collected and transcribed into a single case story, helping to identify missing information.

After conducting the interview a transcript was made and the CEO's responses were analyzed and interpreted critically. In order to reduce subjectivity, we also applied a triangulation, crossing the information obtained through the interview, with secondary sources, namely information available online, both on the company's website, as well as in newspaper and magazine articles (Fusch et al., 2018). This method of collecting data from various sources helped triangulate data and aided the researchers not only to collect more comprehensive relevant information, but also to verify its consistency, in order to increase the robustness of the results.

Finally, authenticity was achieved by crossing information from various sources and validating the information in a second interview. In order to portray the reality faithfully and fairly, the interview was conducted in the presence of at least two interviewers, which reduces the bias in understanding the reality and the possible bias during the interview.

CASE STUDY PRESENTATION

Company History

VERTICAL started its business with a single patented product – PLTS, acronym for People Lifting and Translation System – and six employees. It was created in 2011 by Mr. Manoel. The current CEO joined in as partner with marketing responsibilities, trying to reach foreign markets in the construction industry, where the PLTS could be employed. Mr. Manoel had previous experience working at height, as the owner of a specialized Brazilian company, created in 2002 and focusing mainly on the construction industry. In 2010, As a result of safety problem in the construction industry, this Brazilian company came up with the innovative idea, but did not have the resources to develop it. As such, VERTICAL was created with the objective of developing high-tech equipment and new solutions for working at height. This led to the creation of an innovative PLTS system, which was patented afterwards. Mr. Manoel stepped out as a result of a company turnaround and VERTICAL was taken over by its current CEO with the support of external investment.

Between 2011 and 2013 VERTICAL had no sales activities: the focus was on product development, patenting and bureaucratic work. Only in 2013, VERTICAL was formally registered as a company. A young, dynamic and flexible factory was set up in Aveiro as a result of the turnaround process. Nowadays, VERTICAL is a company with a strong customer focus, concerned with the development of solutions that meet the needs of its customers.

The company's activity began in January 2014, when the current CEO joined VERTICAL on a full time basis. Between 2013 and 2014, VERTICAL managed to certify product quality, produce catalogs, design a website and establish several partnerships. By 2016, the company, to compensate for its limited resources, typical of micro-companies, actively participated in several competitions, having earned some awards for its innovative activities. Currently, VERTICAL is dedicated to the development of new products/services, having launched three new products in 2019.

Mission, Vision, Values and Objectives

VERTICAL's mission is to develop simple yet effective equipment that is both safe and productive for working at height. The three main pillars of this company are safety, productivity and innovation. Innovation is undoubtedly one of VERTICAL's competitive advantages, given that it was created to develop new equipment. Safety is also critical, as the main downstream business sector is construction, an industry with high occupational accident rates. Sustainability and social responsibility are also important values that govern the company's operations. The CEO claims he is concerned about using environmentally friendly materials in the manufacture of PLTS.

The company focuses on the development of new projects with innovative technologies that can solve problems that are emerging in working at height. The main need the company wishes to address is the risk and low productivity associated with working at height. According to the CEO, about 40% of a worker's day is lost to the resettlement of their life-lines and other safety issues. Therefore, VERTICAL's value proposition is (a) a 40% reduction in cleaning and maintenance costs, and (b) social inclusion, as PLTS enables the employment of handicapped individuals.

Organizational Structure

VERTICAL is a micro-company with only three employees. It is currently looking for a fourth employee to join the sales team. Being a micro-company, it relies heavily on technical partners who collaborate temporarily with the company in certain areas. Partnerships with universities mean that an intern is currently part of the team, but this cannot solve structural problems. The CEO is responsible for both the financial and marketing functions of the company. VERTICAL also has a technical department.

Product and Service Portfolio

PLTS is innovative equipment that allows work to be performed at heights of up to 120m with both horizontal and vertical movement. A worker can reach any part of a structure/building using a single harness and a remote control. Its innovative design also allows anyone, including the physically disabled or paraplegic individuals to carry out vertical work safely and efficiently. PLTS is versatile as it fits any structure, whether a building, bridge, oil rig or wind tower. This patented technology enables safer, faster work, as it takes only six seconds to reach a height of 120m. It also makes work cheaper, as it increases the productivity of work at height. PLTS is still considered the safest lifting system in the world, consisting of seven mechanisms. Of these, the lifting system is based on the first winch in the world that lifts people using a single harness, i.e. without the need for safety baskets. This replaces the use of more conventional methods such as scaffolding, lifting platforms and ropes.

PLTS is VERTICAL's core product. However, it has several models, which have a total of 13 different applications, of which the following stand out: *PLTS no limits*, which allows horizontal and vertical movements, using a simple harness, initially designed for the construction industry, but can be used in maintenance services, such as cleaning exterior or interior glass; *PLTS freedom*, which is most suitable for elevators; *PLTS4two*, which combines *PLTS no limits* with a basket (which allows the transportation of heavy loads such as stones, windows or glass) and a distance limiting bar; *PLTS wind* for the repair of wind power towers; *PLTS home*, designed to be installed in homes or hospitals, to allow quick access to multiple rooms without the use of a wheelchair; and *PLTS deep*, suitable for accessing mines. However, the interview with the representative of the company's technical department revealed that only *PLTS no limits* is currently for sale, and that it meets European standards and has European certification. In addition to PLTS, the company also sells accessories, which are developed by its R&D team. These are mainly equipment to make the work more practical and safer.

In terms of services, VERTICAL has created the PLTS Academy, a program, integrated into its strategy, to train and certify individuals, including the disabled and amputees, and other companies to install and use the PLTS technology and products. When the PLTS system is sold, at least one VERTICAL representative, accompanied by a team that is subcontracted in Portugal or in the destination market, must supervise the installation of the product on site. A representative of VERTICAL must be physically present wherever the PLTS service is being provided.

Market and Competitors

VERTICAL was created to meet the needs of markets in different industries: construction, renewable energy, services and maintenance for vertical structures, and tourism. The company's target is mainly maintenance companies in those sectors. VERTICAL is a company that works in the B2B segment. The company was established to develop the necessary parts and equipment for which there was not yet an offer in those markets. The two main industries that the company is dealing with are the construction and renewable energy sectors, as the company also develops internal elevators for wind energy turbines.

The main competitors are predominantly international companies. There is no manufacturer of similar equipment at national level. For example, one competitor,

TRACTEL, a multinational company, provides lift and maintenance equipment, suspended work platforms, and fall arrest systems in more than 120 countries, featuring similar products to those sold by VERTICAL, or that can replace them.

Awards and Partnerships

PLTS was recognized as an internationally innovative technology, having being awarded several distinctions. In 2013, VERTICAL won the award "Best Idea of the Year" in a competition sponsored by the Business Incubator of the University of Aveiro, Portugal. This was an important step as it allowed the VERTICAL staff to participate in an immersion program in Silicon Valley, California, USA. VERTICAL also received an Honorable Mention in the EDP Innovation Prize, in the same year, which was the first honorable mention given by EDP since the beginning of these awards. Then, VERTICAL was invited to join the EDP Starter program, an accelerator program for companies and technologies related to the energy sector, which underpinned VERTICAL staff to establish important networking relationships.

Also as a start-up, VERTICAL participated in The Lisbon Transatlantic Challenge. Apart from a 5,000€ prize, VERTICAL was part of the 10 winners from a pool of 500+ participants. As a result, VERTICAL could present the PLTS to investors and public policy decision makers from Brazil, USA, and UK, which allowed the company to expand its network of contacts and increase its business opportunities. In 2014, the company is invited by EDP to create a partnership to develop a pilot project for wind towers. The partnership later materialized in the entry of EDP into VERTICAL's capital as an investor (Isento, 2015). In 2015, VERTICAL received investment from Rising Ventures, a business angel, and EDP Ventures, which joined as VERTICAL's shareholders.

RESULTS

After briefly introducing VERTICAL, its CEO highlighted the importance SMEs have in the Portuguese business fabric and in the development of the national economy. He believes that there is an increasing concern with innovation; however, he also stated that compared to large companies, the lack of financial, technological, or human resources of SMEs are indisputable. Thus, the CEO considers that this forces SMEs to establishing partnerships and collaborations with other entities, which underpins OI initiatives. He also mentioned that due to the lack of financial resources to hire technicians, the collaboration with the University is crucial, as it allows the absorption of knowledge in a more accessible way, for example through protocols for internships.

The CEO recognizes that organizational culture is one of the organizational pillars supporting competitive advantages and it is open to explore both outbound and inbound OI. However, as a microenterprise, it does not have many technologies to license out.

VERTICAL's new product development process always starts with the identification of a market problem/need. There are two possible processes: (1) internally the company recognizes that a product could be improved in order to create more added value for the customer; and (2) the company receives feedback from customers, or even requests, regarding possible product improvements or new product developments. Therefore, contact with customers is fundamental. In the energy sector, the main input to VERTICAL's innovation processes comes mostly from the outside, namely from partners with whom VERTICAL works, such as EDP. It is the technical operatives in the field who, given the difficulties encountered, provide ideas for new developments processes and products. After recognizing the market needs, especially through the difficulties experienced by customers, the company creates a product concept. Only after the validation of this concept, VERTICAL moves on to its technical development. In terms of innovation, the CEO claims that the company does both incremental and radical innovation. The former through the adaptation of existing products to customer needs and projects the company faces. The latter, working all the way into the market, but normally facing more resistance from the market.

VERTICAL's core R&D activity is carried out internally, and is focused on the development of mechanical parts that give the firm a competitive edge. VERTICAL invests heavily in R&D, having R&D expenses reached 15% of sales volume. In the case of electronic developments, or those related to robotics, VERTICAL subcontracts specialized companies. That is, due to the company's limited resources, all activities that do not belong to the company's core know-how are subcontracted. For the company it does not make sense to invest in in-house production, since it does not have sufficient production scale that could amortize this investment. Its priority is to focus on its core activities, using OI to complement its resources.

VERTICAL has only one patented technology, the first PLTS system – the *no limits*. However, the company does not generate surplus technologies, nor does it buy patents or licenses. VERTICAL only uses technology already available on the market to apply in their products.

Besides EDP in the energy sector, VERTICAL has partnerships with other external entities, among which the University of Aveiro stands out, through internships and dissemination of job offers. VERTICAL also works with a professional school, in order to allow students to have a first contact with the labor market. There are other partnerships at the R&D level, namely with suppliers. There is no kind of collaboration with competitors, due to the fact that they are mainly international.

The objective of the partnerships is mainly the absorption of knowledge from the partners, integrating their inputs. Suppliers end up helping more in the innovation process, to the extent that they have more technical knowledge. VERTICAL resorts to their suppliers when it wants to solve the problems it encounters along the way. These long-term relationships are based on a mutual exchange, as VERTICAL also shares knowledge with suppliers. Usually, partnerships for the development of new products are made at the prototyping stage. There are no partnerships with the government. It should be noted that EDP, the largest Portuguese energy company in Portugal, is one of three investment funds that currently co-sponsors the company; these funds are key to access strategic partnerships.

VERTICAL has already participated in a European project, but the impact on the company turned out to be negative. However, the CEO recognizes that EU funds are essential to leverage any investment, also helping in the company's internationalization process. In addition to this financial advantage, the funds bring with them some disadvantages, namely the fact that they condition the company in terms of the adoption of long-term strategies, since they commit the company to the short-term project that was developed for the contribution of the funds.

Financial issues are one of the major constraints for VERTICAL, as the company may sacrifice innovation activities to comply with large orders it may receive. However, VERTICAL's CEO assumes that he has a propensity for risk-taking and recognizes that the company is sought after for its innovation culture and its risk-taking perspective.

Currently VERTICAL has no social media strategy, as it prefers to participate in international fairs to gather contacts for future business.

In summary, VERTICAL claims to be an SME that adopts an OI approach, collaborating with various external entities, with which they share some knowledge and from which they receive inputs. Its product development processes are not solely in-house, thus using external sources of technology to accelerate its innovation processes.

DISCUSSION

Obstacles of the Innovation Process

Innovation consists of the creation of ideas, which are then transformed into products, services, or processes, subsequently successfully commercialized (Hungund & Mani, 2019). Moreover, technological innovation emerges as a differentiating driver in creating value for customers. Thus, VERTICAL can be considered an innovative company as it brings new products to the market, solutions that do not yet exist, and there is recognition and appreciation of this newness by customers.

As explained by VERTICAL's CEO, contact with the environment is seen as crucial and mandatory: the innovation process starts mainly from internal initiative, i.e., it starts from observing reality, from contact with customers and/or partners, from whom they collect feedback and inputs that are integrated into innovation processes. In fact, as it happens with SMEs, limited resources, or even the underdevelopment of internal capabilities, led VERTICAL to take risks and adopt OI processes through the exploitation of knowledge created outside the company. Building networks with customers or suppliers can improve the product development process, because it is the customers who, by using the product, can give feedback on aspects they would like to see improved or give ideas for new products that would help their work. In turn, suppliers, having the technical knowledge, often help VERTICAL in the development of new solutions.

During the interview it was possible to perceive that VERTICAL faces external and internal obstacles to innovation. The external ones are related to the degree of innovation of the product, i.e., when the product represents a radical innovation it is necessary to take measures – namely training and evangelization of the market – in order to speed up the acceptance of the product. On the other hand, internal obstacles are related to limited financial resources, resistance to change, and technical resources. Although the CEO states that there is no resistance to change within VERTICAL – explained by its small size – there are challenges that derive from such limited financial and technical resources.

In fact, as already mentioned in the literature review, SMEs have more difficulties due to their limited production, distribution, marketing and funding for R&D resources and capabilities that are essential for the innovation process. In addition, VERTICAL, as most of SMEs, have financial limitations, lack of qualified personnel or specific knowledge in certain areas that cover activities from the development to the commercialization stages (Marcolin et al., 2017). Another obstacle is the fact that SMEs are not able to take advantage of economies of scale, which is also seen in VERTICAL.

Limited financial resources are seen as the main barrier to innovation, causing the company to focus on providing services rather than developing more technologically advanced products. The CEO states that the lack of an R&D department forces this choice, which does not happen in large companies that have enough resources to focus on both activities.

Finally, limitations in terms of technical resources, i.e. know-how and knowledge, are also seen as a barrier to innovation. Because of VERTICAL's small size it does not have specialized staff in different areas, it is forced to focus on its core competencies (in this case, mechanics), and when it needs specific expertise, it resorts to outsourcing or collaboration. External agents are seen as a faster and more efficient way to obtain resources and necessary skills (Silva et al., 2019), which is in agreement with the case study analyzed in this chapter. Thus, VERTICAL's core competencies are complemented with external technologies, namely in the area of robotics and electronics, which are outsourced. Such behavior is explained by the literature, in that SMEs need to invest in mastering certain technologies so that they excel in serving specialized niche markets (Moreira, 2009). To respond to these difficulties, the CEO states that VERTICAL resorts to partnerships to circumvent the obstacles common to SMEs.

Research and Development

The R&D activity is done internally, although there is no functional department concentrating this activity. Mechanical technology is the core activity and VERTICAL's main know-how. That is, for the design of other components, VERTICAL resorts to collaboration with external entities, usually for developments in robotics and electronics. We conclude that the company exploits its core competencies and uses the context environment to obtain resources.

VERTICAL is involved in incremental and radical innovation, which demonstrates some organizational ambidexterity. That is, VERTICAL either improves its existing products by adding features, adapting to new projects or to emerging customer needs or it identifies opportunities and develops completely the new solutions. As such, it is possible to claim that VERTICAL flows the principles of ambidexterity, as according to Felício et al. (2019), ambidexterity involves the organization's ability to develop disruptive innovation, which requires a creative and dynamic environment with flexible rules, something we can find at VERTICAL, and which, at the same time, ensures incremental innovation in its current activities.

From the R&D efforts resulted, so far, only one patented technology, the PLTS system, in its first model, the *no limits*. However, special attention is being paid to this aspect and, at the time of the interview, other technologies were being analyzed for patenting purposes. However, no surplus technologies are generated in the company, nor does the company buy patents or licenses. As highlighted by the interviewee, VERTICAL only uses technology available in the market for application in the products.

It should also be noted that, according to the CEO, there is a high investment in R&D activities. This does not seem to be in accordance with the existing literature, which states that most SMEs do not invest significantly in R&D as a result of lack of resources. However, this may mean that VERTICAL, due to its need and active search for international markets, has behaviors typical of a Born Global, in that this type of company differs from other SMEs by the high investment in R&D, which allows SMEs to generate radical innovations (Franco & Hasse, 2016).

Open Innovation

Because VERTICAL relies on collaboration with various external entities to complement their internal development processes, resulting in knowledge sharing and integration of inputs into the innovation processes.

Additionally, and taking into account VERTICAL's innovation activities, it was found that external technologies are integrated into the company's products – as much as possible using open source technologies – i.e., there is no acquisition of patents or licenses. However, when analyzing the flow of technologies from R&D in an outbound perspective, VERTICAL shows an apparent divergence with the definition of open innovation, i.e., the technologies developed are not sold to other entities, not generating surplus technologies (all technologies developed are incorporated only in its product portfolio), nor does it make acquisitions, mergers or spinoffs. As such, based on the definition of OI, we recall that it has two dimensions that must exist: the absorption of knowledge and technology, but also its transfer to other organizations (Teixeira & Lopes, 2012). The latter is done mainly through the licensing of intellectual property, the launch of spin-off companies, mergers and acquisitions, and cooperation with the academic world.

Given the above, we conclude that VERTICAL adopts an outside-in OI model, in which companies absorb only outside technology, and there is no technology transfer to other entities. In other words, this proves what was concluded by Teixeira and Lopes (2012) that, although companies believe they practice OI, this does not always correspond to reality. In short, VERTICAL corroborates the studies done in Portugal, which state that the OI model is more widespread in terms of absorption of knowledge than in term of its transfer.

Factors Influencing Open Innovation Adoption: Culture

Culture is seen as a crucial factor to the adoption of open innovation, being creativity mandatory to foster an innovation-based culture. Thus, the work environment created by leaders in the organization should foster divergent thinking, leading employees to share their ideas, which is essential for any organization to practice OI processes (Hungund & Mani, 2019).

In line with the existing theory, it is possible to conclude VERTICAL fosters the adoption of an OI culture. According to the CEO, the company has implemented a very strong culture of innovation, conducive to exchanges and learning with the outside world. In fact, he states that there is a constant care in understanding failure and that, through error, they manage to draw knowledge and know how.

The CEO's recurring connection between leadership and culture is notorious, stating on several occasions that in addition to culture being a pillar of the organization, it is defined and deployed by top managers.

Factors Influencing Open Innovation Adoption: Cooperation and Partnerships

Cooperation and partnerships are central topics in OI since it is through them that most SMEs have access to the external resources and technologies they need. As such, this OI model is about collaboration with external actors (Marcolin et al., 2017). In this context, the use of external entities allows SMEs to overcome their technical and/or financial limitations, as occurs with VERTICAL, which use its partners in order to obtain technical know-how. In fact, OI is a very effective way for SMEs to obtain resources and skills that they do not possess. As such, SMEs seek strategic alliances, acquiring knowledge from other companies, combining technology and internal resources with external resources, to increase their competitive advantage. Furthermore, through external resources, organizations shorten the innovation time, reducing costs and risks and increasing the flexibility of their operations (Xiaobao et al., 2013).

There are several actors that play an essential role in the firms' innovation process of. Thus, the Triple Helix Model emerges, in which the university, the industry and the government are the main institutional actors in this process (Simões et al., 2020; Torkkeli et al., 2007). According to this, the innovation spiral involves research activities, government institutions, and business/enterprises in various reciprocal relationships in order to create a flexible innovation system (Marcolin et al., 2017). Innovation thus results from numerous institutional combinations produced by networks of relationships, which entail mutual exchange (Torkkeli et al., 2007).

Such conclusions are corroborated by this case study. VERTICAL considers its partnerships and collaborations as a pillar of its business. Indeed, the company recognizes external entities as a source of resources and knowledge, thus focusing on mutual exchange and knowledge sharing. Moreover, according to the CEO, the relationships established with suppliers tend to have a long-term orientation. This is tuned to the literature that states that most SMEs seek to establish long-term relationships with their partners (Carvalho & Moreira, 2015). Most of the time, the outward connection is made by internal initiative, since the firm considers contacts with external partners as crucial for the development of useful equipment for the target audience.

In the specific case of VERTICAL, there is only cooperation with suppliers, customers, educational institutions. The reason for not connecting with either government or competitors is related to: the size of the company; the inability to benefit from institutional support; and the size of its competitors, especially the international ones. The non-collaboration with competitors also corroborates the literature, which states that this type of collaborations is avoided (Carvalho & Moreira, 2015).

The partnerships with suppliers and other entities (namely EDP and technical partners) are those that stand out the most, since they allow VERTICAL to better absorb knowledge, integrating their inputs into innovation processes. In the specific case of suppliers, they end up contributing to the innovation process, insofar as they have technical knowledge. However, it is only about integration of inputs from suppliers, as VERTICAL shares some feedback with them. Suppliers are involved mainly at the R&D level, at the prototyping stage, and in conducting technical studies. EDP has a slightly different input in the development of new products, since it is also a client, entering more at the stage of product ideation and testing. Another aspect of the partnership with EDP is access to funds and network of partners since EDP participates in VERTICAL through an investment fund. In conclusion, collaborative activities with partners are more evident in the prototyping stages.

Although not as prominent, partnerships with customers and educational institutions are also important to VETICAL, as they support the development of new products, helping to overcome limitations in technical and human resources. Contact with customers is often sought, as it allows their feedback to be integrated into VERTICAL's innovation processes and to better adapt products to their needs. In terms of partnerships with educational institutions, we highlight the partnerships with the University of Aveiro and with professional schools. Through the partnership with the University, VERTICAL allows students to do internships, participates in events, and supports masters' students by providing information for research and statistical studies. Through the partnership with professional schools, VERTICAL aims to integrate students into the business world, with the purpose of obtaining human resources that accompany and strengthen the team.

Factors Influencing Open Innovation Adoption: Leadership

Due to SME's simplified organizational structure, the decision-making process is usually centralized and important decisions, such as the adoption of OI, are highly influenced by the characteristics of CEOs. Strong leadership from the CEO is necessary to mitigate the various challenges that arise when establishing a culture conducive to open innovation (Ahn et al., 2017). As the CEO argues, "innovation always depends on leadership," leaving it up to top management to build an innovative vision and culture. Thus, in agreement with Ahn et al. (2017), we can conclude that the role of CEOs is really determinant in establishing an atmosphere favorable to the adoption of OI in SMEs, since the strong support of top management encourages the adoption of OI, helping to address possible internal resistance.

Regarding the propensity to take risks, we can conclude that, in VERTICAL's case, there was a change of perspective regarding risk-taking, much due to the CEO's own characteristics, who likes to embrace risks. This propensity, combined with the speed and quality in product development, is recognized and valued by customers, who seek the company for cooperative efforts. Thus, this behavior fosters innovation activities and contact with the outside world, also increasing the value perceived by the customer.

Factors Influencing Open Innovation Adoption: Organizational Structure

Although the literature is not unanimous about the influence of age and size or the organization in the adoption of OI, the recurrent mention of the interviewee to the company's size raised the analysis of this factor.

We can conclude from the case study that the size of the company has influence in two specific factors: culture, and the establishment of cooperative partnerships. Due to the fact that VERTICAL is a small-sized company, with limited technical and human resources, and with specific know how, we conclude that:

- The organizational culture is strongly influenced by the leader as VERTICAL has a very small number of employees, with a similar background and know-how, which facilitates the diffusion of the leader's dynamism.
- Cooperation is justified by the lack of financial, technological and/or human resources, as a result of VERTICAL's small size. Consequently, to overcome these limitations, VERTICAL embraces outside-in OI practices with external entities.

Factors Influencing Open Innovation Adoption: Social Networks

With social networks it is possible to tap customers generated knowledge/ by. In fact, customers can contribute with ideas for new products, also helping to identify possible problems (Candi et al., 2018). Considering the size of SMEs, social networks emerge as an attractive low-cost tool to access knowledge from their customers, which will allow them to develop new products, improve existing ones or even anticipate market trends (Franco et al., 2016). However, VERTICAL's CEO mentions that it is necessary to have a long-term social strategy to get this kind of results.

Although VERTICAL's CEO refers the firm gets feedback from their customers, they do not use social media. This is a consequence of the lack of resources and the type of market Vertical addresses.

CONCLUSION

Taking all of the results into account, it is possible to assert that VERTICAL is an interesting case study that contributes to the theory of OI and it is an interesting case study for classroom discussion on the need of SMEs, especially microenterprises with huge resource limitations that can affect their business horizons taking OI into account. The main conclusions, based on data collected, gathered and analyzed, are shown in Table 1. Table 2 also shows the main types of OI used by VERTICAL.

Table 1. Open innovation VERTICAL's approach

	OI in SMEs	VERTICAL
Mode of OI	● Extensive adoption of inbound OI; ● Exploitation/Absorption of external knowledge and technology to accelerate the innovation processes; ● In-house developed technology is seldom transferred to third parties; ● Main external contributors: customers, suppliers and universities.	● Absorbs external technology and knowledge; ● Involvement of external actors play an important role to advance innovation processes and in the creation of new products; ● Leverages partnerships with clients, suppliers and universities; ● In-house developed technology is not transferred to other entities. ● Adopts inbound OI ● Does not exhibit any inside-out processes of OI.
Resources and capacities	● Limited resources (financial, human and know-how) forces SMEs to interact with the external environment to access to knowledge and resources in need;	● Reduced dimension: microenterprise actively seeking growth. ● Constraint financial and human resources pressures the company into involving external actors; ● Interacts with customers, suppliers and universities, so to advance innovation processes and to access new markets; ● Focus on the core activities (R&D), leveraging a specialized know-how, and outsources production activities.

Continued on following page

Table 1. Continued

	OI in SMEs	VERTICAL
Organizational culture	● Higher flexibility and less bureaucracy than larger companies: SMEs are more willing to take risks; ● More reactive and proactive to external stimuli to overcome limitations; ● Propensity to foster OI: employees can freely express themselves, sharing ideas.	● Innovative culture, which promotes exchanges with the external environment; ● "Learn by doing" approach; ● Encourages employees to share their ideas; ● Low resistance to change.
Networks	● Networks are the preferred sources of external knowledge and a way to overcome their constraints; ● External actors are seen as essential in the innovation process; ● Networks are mainly established at a local level; ● Usage of strategic alliances, or mergers and acquisitions; ● SMEs tend to avoid partnering up with direct competitors; ● Universities, suppliers, customers and governments are often involved in the innovation process;	● Development of strategic long-term alliances and partnerships with suppliers; ● Supplier's input is used to develop specific equipment and to access technical knowledge; ● The universities are used as a source of specialized human capital and knowledge; ● Customers' feedback is essential to improve and to develop new products; ● Partnerships with main competitors or the government are not sought; ● The established networks grant access to external knowledge, bridging internal resources' constraints.
Leadership and Top management	● The CEO's orientation towards innovation is crucial for reducing internal resistance to and implementing OI; ● The role of the top management is essential due to reduced size; ● Entrepreneurial leaders are more prone to adopt OI and to use social networks to gain extra resources.	● An innovative culture was implemented and fomented by the top management; ● Critical thinking and idea sharing is encouraged; ● The CEO is comfortable with taking risks;
Social Media	● Useful and low-cost tool; ● Allows quick access external knowledge and information; ● Leveraged for idea creation, problem-solving in existing products and for predicting market tendencies.	● Residual social media presence; ● VERTICAL's target market does not have a significant social presence; ● Digital tools are used to interact with customers and suppliers, to participate in fairs and to send product catalogues.

Through the information collected and the literature covered and after analyzing the case study, it is possible to claim that there are various characteristics that define VERTICAL's innovation model. As such, the results suggest that VERTICAL adopts an intermediate model of OI, with VERTICAL sharing knowledge with external entities and acquiring technology. However, there is no concern in exploiting it outwardly. As highlighted by the CEO, the company only uses technology available in the market for application in its products. However, VERTICAL has a strong component of sharing and acquiring knowledge and technology from external entities. Through the information analyzed in the literature review it is possible to suggest that VERTICAL, like most Portuguese companies, seeks partnerships to internalize external knowledge and technology due the lack of internal resources.

Both VERTICAL's organizational culture and the entrepreneurial orientation of the CEO seem to enable the adoption of OI strategies, highlighting the crucial role of leaders in SMEs with major impact on the organization innovative culture.

Through partnerships and cooperation with other external entities, SMEs in general, and VERTICAL in particular, have access to external resources needed to carry out their activities and create value. Thus, VERTICAL creates partnerships with its suppliers and other technical entities. Through them, the company seems to have the ability to overcome its difficulties and obstacles, such as scarcity of resources, by absorbing knowledge and integrating resources.

Although the social strategy (the active presence in social networks) has been considered as a source of advantage for SMEs, enabling the adoption of OI activities, VERTICAL is not actively present in social networks. As the firm operates in the B2B segment, where 80% of its target market is not strongly influenced by social networks, VERTICAL's presence on social networks was not an effective channel for communication between the company and its customers.

In a future research, it would be interesting to analyze a larger sample of innovative SMEs, in order to observe the different cases and how their processes may differ given these determinants.

Table 2. Types of OI and VERTICAL's approach

Types of Open Innovation	Processes	VERTICAL's OI Approach
Outside-in (The absorption of external knowledge and technology)	Purchasing external technologies	X
	Licensing-in	
	Joint ventures	
	Joint development	X
	Outsourcing R&D	X
	Venture Capital	
	Mergers and Acquisitions	
	Customer Involvement	X
	External Networking	X
Inside-out (The transfer of knowledge and technology to other organizations)	Selling Internal technologies	
	Licensing-out	
	Spin-Off	
	Open Source	

REFERENCES

Abulrub, A.-H., & Lee, J. (2012). Open innovation management: Challenges and prospects. *Procedia: Social and Behavioral Sciences*, *41*, 130–138. doi:10.1016/j.sbspro.2012.04.017

Ahn, J. M., Minshall, T., & Mortara, L. (2017). Understanding the human side of openness: The fit between open innovation modes and CEO characteristics. *R & D Management*, *47*(5), 727–740. doi:10.1111/radm.12264

Alshenqeeti, H. (2014). Interviewing as a data collection method: A critical review. *Sciedu Press*, *3*(1), 39–45. doi:10.5430/elr.v3n1p39

Bernal-Torres, C. A., & Frost-González, S. (2015). Innovación abierta en empresas colombianas: Reto a superar. *Revista Venezolana de Gerencia*, *20*(70), 262–267. doi:10.31876/revista.v20i70.19996

Bianchi, M., Campodall'Orto, S., Frattini, F., & Vercesi, P. (2010). Enabling open innovation in small- and medium-sized enterprises: How to find alternative applications for your technologies. *R & D Management*, *40*(4), 414–430. doi:10.1111/j.1467-9310.2010.00613.x

Bogers, M., Chesbrough, H., & Moedas, C. (2018). Open innovation: Research, practices, and policies. *California Management Review*, *60*(2), 5–16. doi:10.1177/0008125617745086

Candi, M., Roberts, D. L., Marion, T., & Barczak, G. (2018). Social strategy to gain knowledge for innovation. *British Journal of Management*, *29*(4), 731–749. doi:10.1111/1467-8551.12280

Carvalheira, A. M., & Moreira, A. (2015). Searching for opportunities and trust in international markets. In L. C. Carvalho (Ed.), *Handbook of Research on Entrepreneurial Success and Its Impact on Regional Development* (pp. 675–701). IGI Global. doi:10.4018/978-1-4666-9567-2.ch028

Carvalho, A. S., & Moreira, A. C. (2015). Open innovation profile in small and medium-sized firms. The perspective of technology centres and business associations. *International Journal of Innovation and Learning*, *18*(1), 4–22. doi:10.1504/IJIL.2015.070242

Chesbrough, H. (2003). *Open innovation: The new imperative for creating and profiting from technology*. Harvard Business School Press.

Chesbrough, H. (2006). Open innovation: A new paradigm for understanding industrial innovation. In H. Chesbrough, W. Vanhaverbeke, & J. West (Eds.), Open innovation: Researching a new paradigm (pp. 1–12). Oxford University Press.

Chiaroni, D., Chiesa, V., & Frattini, F. (2011). The open innovation journey: How firms dynamically implement the emerging innovation management paradigm. *Technovation*, *31*(1), 34–43. doi:10.1016/j.technovation.2009.08.007

Coelho, D. A., & Matias, J. C. (2010). Innovation in the organisation of management systems in Portuguese SMEs. *International Journal of Entrepreneurship and Innovation Management*, *11*(3), 324–329. doi:10.1504/IJEIM.2010.031905

Dantas, J. G., & Moreira, A. C. (2011). *O Processo de Inovação*. LIDEL.

Dittrich, K., & Duysters, G. (2007). Networking as a means to strategy change: The case of open innovation in mobile telephony. *Journal of Product Innovation Management*, *24*(6), 510–521. doi:10.1111/j.1540-5885.2007.00268.x

European Commission. (2020). *User guide to the SME Definition*. European Commission.

Felício, J. A., Caldeirinha, V., & Dutra, A. (2019). Ambidextrous capacity in small and medium-sized enterprises. *Journal of Business Research*, *101*, 607–614. doi:10.1016/j.jbusres.2019.02.061

Fisher, M. (2007). Strengthening the empirical base of operations management. *Manufacturing & Service Operations Management*, *9*(4), 368–382. doi:10.1287/msom.1070.0168

Franco, M., & Haase, H. (2016). Internationalisation of born globals: The role of strategic alliances. *European Journal of International Management*, *10*(2), 181–201. doi:10.1504/EJIM.2016.074471

Franco, M., Haase, H., & Pereira, A. (2016). Empirical study about the role of social networks in SME performance. *Journal of Systems and Information Technology*, *18*(4), 383–403. doi:10.1108/JSIT-06-2016-0036

Fusch, P., Fusch, G. E., & Ness, L. R. (2018). Denzin's paradigm shift: Revisiting triangulation in qualitative research. *Journal of Social Change*, *10*(1), 19–32. doi:10.5590/JOSC.2018.10.1.02

Gassmann, O., Enkel, E., & Chesbrough, H. (2010). The future of open innovation. *R & D Management*, *40*(3), 213–221. doi:10.1111/j.1467-9310.2010.00605.x

Huizingh, E. (2011). Open innovation: State of the art and future perspectives. *Technovation*, *31*(1), 2–9. doi:10.1016/j.technovation.2010.10.002

Hungund, S., & Mani, V. (2019). Benchmarking of factors influencing adoption of innovation in software product SMEs: An empirical evidence from India. *Benchmarking*, *26*(5), 1451–1468. doi:10.1108/BIJ-05-2018-0127

Inês, A. I., Pires, P. M., Leite, M. P., & Moreira, A. C. (2021). As pequenas e médias empresas e o desafio da inovação aberta. *Gestao e Desenvolvimento*, *29*, 199–221. doi:0.34632/gestaoedesenvolvimento.2021.10030

Isento, G. (2015). *S.T.E.P. eleva-te para trabalhares em altura*. https://www.publico.pt/2015/11/12/p3/noticia/step-elevate-para-trabalhares-em-altura-1824869

Laursen, K., & Salter, A. (2006). Open for innovation: The role of openness in explaining innovation performance among U.K. manufacturing firms. *Strategic Management Journal*, *27*(2), 131–150. doi:10.1002mj.507

Lichtenthaler, U., & Lichtenthaler, E. (2009). A capability-based framework for open innovation: Complementing absorptive capacity. *Journal of Management Studies*, *46*(8), 1315–1338. doi:10.1111/j.1467-6486.2009.00854.x

Lööf, H., & Heshmati, A. (2006). On the relationship between innovation and performance: A sensitivity analysis. *Economics of Innovation and New Technology*, *15*(4-5), 317–344. doi:10.1080/10438590500512810

Marcolin, F., Vezzetti, E., & Montagna, F. (2017). How to practice open innovation today: What, where, how and why. *Creative Industries Journal*, *10*(3), 258–291. doi:10.1080/17510694.2017.1393178

Milici, A., Ferreira, F., Pereira, L., Carayannis, E., & Ferreira, J. J. (2021). Dynamics of open innovation in small- and medium-sized enterprises: A metacognitive approach. *IEEE Transactions on Engineering Management*, 1–14. Advance online publication. doi:10.1109/TEM.2020.3042458

Moreira, A. C. (2009). Desafios das PME num contexto de globalização. *Revista Percursos & Ideias*, *1*, 43–58.

Odriozola-Fernández, I., Berbegal-Mirabent, J., & Merigó-Lindahl, J. M. (2019). Open innovation in small and medium enterprises: A bibliometric analysis. *Journal of Organizational Change Management*, *32*(5), 533–557. doi:10.1108/JOCM-12-2017-0491

Parida, V., Westerberg, M., & Frishammar, J. (2012). Inbound open innovation activities in high-tech SMEs: The impact on innovation performance. *Journal of Small Business Management, 50*(2), 283–309. doi:10.1111/j.1540-627X.2012.00354.x

Popa, S., Soto-Acosta, P., & Martinez-Conesa, I. (2017). Antecedents, moderators, and outcomes of innovation climate and open innovation: An empirical study in SMEs. *Technological Forecasting and Social Change, 118*, 134–142. doi:10.1016/j.techfore.2017.02.014

PORDATA. (2017). *Pequenas e Médias Empresas (PME).* Obtido de Empresas e Pessoal: https://www.pordata.pt/Subtema/Portugal/Pequenas+e+M%C3%A9dias+Empresas+(PME)-378

Radziwon, A., & Bogers, M. (2019). Open innovation in SMEs: Exploring inter-organizational relationships in an ecosystem. *Technological Forecasting and Social Change, 146*, 573–587. doi:10.1016/j.techfore.2018.04.021

Raposo, M. L., Ferreira, J. J., & Fernandes, C. I. (2014). Local and cross-border SME cooperation: Effects on innovation and performance. *Revista Europea de Dirección y Economía de la Empresa, 23*(4), 157–165. doi:10.1016/j.redee.2014.08.001

Ribau, C. P., Moreira, A. C., & Raposo, M. (2017). SMEs innovation capabilities and export performance: An entrepreneurial orientation view. *Journal of Business Economics and Management, 18*(5), 920–934. doi:10.3846/16111699.2017.1352534

Ribau, C. P., Moreira, A. C., & Raposo, M. (2019). The role of exploitative and exploratory innovation in export performance: An analysis of plastics industry SMEs. *European Journal of International Management, 13*(2), 224–246. doi:10.1504/EJIM.2019.098149

Rowley, J. (2002). Using case studies in research. *Management Research Review, 25*(1), 16–27.

Santoro, G., Ferraris, A., & Winteler, D. J. (2019). Open innovation practices and related internal dynamics: Case studies of Italian ICT SMEs. *EuroMed Journal of Business, 14*(1), 47–61. doi:10.1108/EMJB-05-2018-0031

Schmiemann, M. (2009). *SMEs were the main drivers of economic growth between 2004 and 2006.* Obtido de https://ec.europa.eu/eurostat/documents/3433488/5284033/KS-SF-09-071-EN.PDF/7e1c1766-90e8-453d-aa57-352a1842dc2b

Silva, A. D., Ferreira, F. A., Carayannis, E. G., & Ferreira, J. J. (2021). Measuring SMEs' propensity for open innovation using cognitive mapping and MCDA. *IEEE Transactions on Engineering Management*, *68*(2), 396–407. doi:10.1109/TEM.2019.2895276

Silva, L. F., & Moreira, A. C. (2021). Alignment in collaborative new product development. Comparing small and large firms. *International Journal of Business Innovation and Research*, *24*(2), 167–196. doi:10.1504/IJBIR.2021.112813

Simões, P. C., Moreira, A. C., & Mendes Dias, C. (2020). Portugal's changing defense industry: Is the triple helix model of knowledge society replacing state leadership model? *Journal of Open Innovation*, *6*(4), 183. doi:10.3390/joitmc6040183

Teixeira, A. C., & Lopes, M. (2012). Open innovation in Portugal. *Acta Oeconomica*, *62*(4), 435–458. doi:10.1556/aoecon.62.2012.4.2

The Next Big Idea. (n.d.). *Startups - Vertequip*. Obtido em maio de 2019, de The Next Big Idea: https://thenextbigidea.pt/startups/vertiquip

Torkkeli, M., Kotonen, T., & Ahonen, P. (2007). Regional open innovation system as a platform for SMEs: A survey. *International Journal of Foresight and Innovation Policy*, *3*(5), 336–350. doi:10.1504/IJFIP.2007.016456

Torres, L., Ibarra, E., & Arenas, A. (2015). Open innovation practices: A literature review of case studies. *Journal of Advanced Management Science*, *3*(4), 362–367. doi:10.12720/joams.3.4.362-367

Van de Vrande, V., De Jong, J., Vanhaverbeke, W., & De Rochemont, M. (2009). Open innovation in SMEs: Trends, motives and management challenges. *Technovation*, *29*(6-7), 423–437. doi:10.1016/j.technovation.2008.10.001

Wahyuni, D. (2012). The research design maze: Understanding paradigms, cases, methods and methodologies. *Journal of Applied Management Accounting Research*, *10*(1), 69–80.

Xiaobao, P., Wei, S., & Yuzhen, D. (2013). Framework of open innovation in SMEs in an emerging economy: Firm characteristics, network openness, and network information. *International Journal of Technology Management*, *62*(2/3/4), 223–250. doi:10.1504/IJTM.2013.055142

Zimmermann, R., Ferreira, L., & Moreira, A. C. (2020). How supply chain strategies moderate the relationship between innovation capabilities and business performance. *Journal of Purchasing and Supply Management*, *26*(5), 100658. doi:10.1016/j.pursup.2020.100658

ADDITIONAL READING

Fréchet, M., & Goy, H. (2017). Does strategy formalization foster innovation? Evidence from a French sample of small to medium-sized enterprises. *M@n@gement, 20*(3), 266–286. doi:10.3917/mana.203.0266

Henttonen, K., & Lehtimäki, H. (2017). Open innovation in SMEs: Collaboration modes and strategies for commercialization in technology-intensive companies in forestry industry. *European Journal of Innovation Management*, *20*(2), 329–347. doi:10.1108/EJIM-06-2015-0047

Marangos, S., & Warren, L. (2017). A mapping for managers: Open innovation for R&D intensive SMEs in the life sciences sector. *European Journal of Innovation Management*, *20*(2), 210–229. doi:10.1108/EJIM-12-2015-0133

Moreira, A. C. (2021). Introduction to the Special Section: Innovation. *Management Letters. Cuadernos de Gestión*, *21*(2), 79–82. doi:10.5295/cdg.211470ac

Patrício, R., Moreira, A. C., & Zurlo, F. (2021). Enhancing design thinking approaches to innovation through gamification. *European Journal of Innovation Management*, *24*(5), 1569–1594. doi:10.1108/EJIM-06-2020-0239

Presenza, A., Abbate, T., Meleddu, M., & Cesaroni, F. (2017). Small- and medium-scale Italian winemaking companies facing the open innovation challenge. *International Small Business Journal*, *35*(3), 327–348. doi:10.1177/0266242616664798

Ramirez-Portilla, A., Cagno, E., & Brown, T. E. (2017). Open innovation in specialized SMEs: The case of supercars. *Business Process Management Journal*, *23*(6), 1167–1195. doi:10.1108/BPMJ-10-2016-0211

Teirlinck, P., & Spithoven, A. (2013). Research collaboration and R&D outsourcing: Different R&D personnel requirements in SMEs. *Technovation*, *33*(4-5), 142–153. doi:10.1016/j.technovation.2012.11.005

KEY TERMS AND DEFINITIONS

Inside-Out Open Innovation: It is the part of the open innovation business that requires companies to allow unused and/or underutilized ideas or technologies to be released / commercialized outside the company in order to be incorporated in other companies and their business models.

Open Innovation: It consists of a business management model that uses internal and external sources of knowledge and technology with people and organizations outside the company. It involves the use of purposive inflows and outflows of knowledge to accelerate internal innovation and expand the markets for its external use. This open innovation model is important for companies that acknowledge that there are many professionals, technologies and knowledge outside the company that may underpin the competitive strategy of the organization.

Outside-In Open Innovation: It is part of the open innovation business model that involves opening up a company's innovation processes of external inputs and contributions from individuals and companies in order the complement the internal competitive base of the company.

Chapter 4
The Effects of Innovation Policy on Science-to-Business Collaboration:
The Case of Serbia

Isidora Avram Beraha
Institute of Economic Sciences, Serbia

Sonja Obrad Đuričin
Institute of Economic Sciences, Serbia

ABSTRACT

The growing complexity of innovation has led to transition to an open innovation approach. Achieving sustainable economic growth based on knowledge and innovation depends on the efficiency and intensity of interactions between the government, business sector, and academia. Searching for ways to improve the innovation performance of small and medium-sized enterprises is high on the agendas of policy makers in developed and even more in developing countries. Through innovation policy, a favorable environment and stimulating system is created in which innovation activities are realized, information and knowledge are flowed, and cooperation between different actors is established. Academia plays a key role in the open innovation approach and is perhaps the most important partner for small and medium-sized enterprises. The subject of the research is the effects of innovation policy support on science to business collaboration in Serbia, with additional emphasis on the national innovation system and innovation performance of Serbia.

DOI: 10.4018/978-1-7998-8665-5.ch004

INTRODUCTION

Along with the unambiguity about the contribution of innovation to economic growth, the concept of open innovation is gaining in importance. The increasing adoption of more open approaches to innovation emerged because of the firms' aspirations to take advantage of collective creativity through open innovation (Chesbrough & Appleyard, 2007). The growing interest in finding new ways of knowledge generation has emerged given that it is the main source of innovation. The search for new sources of knowledge for innovation has removed the barriers to collaboration which is an alternative to the traditional closed perspective of research and development (R&D) (Avalos-Quispe &Hernandez-Simon, 2019). The open innovation concept is based on the use of both internal and external resources to implement innovation activities. According to Chesbrough (2003), open innovation refers to the combination of internal and external knowledge for the creation and commercialization of new products and services. The focus is on the collaboration between various actors in the innovation system. Open innovation allows firms to improve their innovation success by using internal and external ideas, internal and external paths to market, and inflows and outflows of knowledge (Bogers et al., 2018), and enables academia to apply and commercialize the results of conducted R&D activities more efficiently. Achieving sustainable economic growth based on knowledge and innovation depends on the efficiency and intensity of interactions between the three main groups of actors i.e., government, business sector, and academia which is also at the core of the triple helix model of innovation.

In an increasingly competitive market, the success and growth of enterprises are affected by the ability to use both internal and external ideas through collaboration (Suh & Kim, 2012). Establishing a collaborative relationship between the actors in the triple helix model aims at the free flow of knowledge and information. This assumes abandoning the traditional practice in which companies were closed in their innovation processes. Innovation requires much more than the capacity to turn new ideas into commercial products. For innovation activity, it is necessary to provide material resources, appropriate business skills, an adequate intellectual property protection system, and a culture of entrepreneurship. Alexander et al. (2015) emphasize that universities and public research organizations are possible partners for organizations that tend to either partially or entirely replace their traditional roles of in-house R&D functions. Focusing only on internal R&D and the development of internal capabilities and routines is no longer sufficient to cope with increasing costs, shorter product life cycles, and greater technological complexities (Berchicci, 2013). Gaining a competitive advantage in a globalized business environment requires the use of external sources of knowledge. The main role of open innovation is the use of external resources through collaboration. As stated by Suh & Kim (2012), it can be achieved through technology acquisition and transfer, R&D collaboration, joint venture activity, and networking. Open innovation in small and medium-sized enterprises (SMEs) is of particular interest as they often lack the resources to implement the innovation process internally. Despite limited capacities, SMEs continue to use the closed model of innovation i.e., rely on internal sources of knowledge to develop new products and services (Santoro, et al., 2018) which is partly due to a lack of capacity to leverage key networks (Ortega-Argilés, et al., 2009).

The idea that SMEs are more prone to innovation activities and risk undertaking is certainly not new. Owning to their flexible organizational structure and the overlap between the ownership and management functions, SMEs respond more efficiently to increasing competitive pressure. Compared to large enterprises, the advantages of SMEs are reflected in less bureaucracy and stronger ability to adapt to market and technological changes (Đuričin & Beraha, 2016). However, the innovation activity of SMEs is constrained by the lack of resources and capabilities. Because of the limited resources, they carry out significantly fewer R&D activities than large companies (Đuričin & Beraha, 2021). Innovations in SMEs occur in everyday operation, rather than as the result of R&D activities. Large companies are more capable to acquire funds for innovation. Collaboration with external sources of knowledge within the concept of open innovation becomes an effective way for SMEs to overcome these barriers. Given that SMEs are the most important segment of every country's economy, creating an environment that encourages innovation success is of great importance.

While there is extensive academic literature confirming the positive relationship between economic growth and innovation (e.g., Ulku, 2004; Pece at al., 2015; Maradana et al., 2017), the relationship between openness and innovation/performance in SMEs remains insufficiently explored (Barge-Gil, 2013). Furthermore, there is evidence confirming the positive effects of university-industry collaboration on scientific productivity (Garcia et al, 2019), but there is a gap in investigating and evaluating the effectiveness of this collaboration for SMEs. Limited capacities hamper the innovative activity of SMEs which emphasizes the role of policymakers in creating a collaborative environment. Research results on the effects of the open innovation approach on SME performance should have important implications on policy measures to support innovation among SMEs. Also, understanding how collaboration with academia affects innovation performance could have important implications on SME management. Being aware of the mentioned gaps in the literature, the subject of this research is the innovation policy support to collaboration between academia and the business sector in Serbia. The paper aims to analyse the effects of the Collaborative Grant Scheme Program that is implemented by the Innovation Fund of the Republic of Serbia on SME beneficiaries. Additionally, it provides a review of the national innovation system and innovation performance of Serbia.

BACKGROUND

Considering innovation as the introduction of new solutions in response to problems, challenges, or opportunities that arise in the social and/or economic environment (Edler & Fagerberg, 2017), it is the backbone of economic growth and development of national economies in a highly globalized world economy. Globalization has caused fundamental changes in all spheres of work and life, and above all, it has led to the interconnection of all countries and economies in the world through the flow of goods and services, people, capital, and information. National economies can no longer build their competitive advantage on traditional factors of production, but rather on innovative and knowledge-intensive economic activities (Đuričin & Beraha, 2021). Dynamic changes in the global market have imposed the need for companies to continuously find new and better ways to meet the needs of consumers, apply new knowledge, and develop modern technologies.

Side by side with globalization, an increasingly competitive environment, and growing consumer demands, a major change in the sources of innovation has occurred. As distinguished by Philipson (2019), those changes were caused by the following key forces: shorter life cycles, lower variable production costs, intellectual property, network economics, and knowledge production and transfer. In an uncertain market environment, knowledge becomes a basic source of innovation. The growing complexity of innovation has necessitated the abandonment of traditional closed, in-house research and development (R&D) activities and the transition to an open innovation approach. Discovering new sources of knowledge for innovation has removed the barriers to collaboration, thus giving an alternative to the traditional closed perspective of R&D (Avalos-Quispe & Hernandez-Simon, 2019). The use of external technology allows companies to mitigate some of the challenges related to a shorter product life cycle, faster production renewal, and increasing R&D costs (Rigby & Zook, 2002).

The idea of "open innovation" was first introduced into theory and practice by Chesbrough (2003, a, b). This approach has gained in importance in a short time and even though there is no consensus on whether companies that rely on external R&D activities achieve better innovative performance, it is quite certain that "closed innovation" is no longer sustainable. As pointed out by Chesbrough (2004, p. 23), a shift has occurred from "closed innovation where companies must generate their own ideas and then develop, build, market, distribute, service, finance, and support them on their own, to open innovation paradigm that assumes that firms can and should use external as well as internal ideas, and internal and external paths to market, as they look to advance their technology". Elmquist et al. (2009) argue that the most important characteristic of open innovation is that the innovation process does not necessarily take place within the company but involves a larger number of actors. Instead of relying solely on internal capacities and capabilities, cooperation with other participants in the innovation system enables companies to overcome the limitations arising from limited resources and capabilities for innovation and take advantage of collective creativity.

While it was previously believed that innovation processes had to be controlled by the company (Elmquist et al., 2009), it is now seen as an open process in which the benefits are realized from the sharing of knowledge, ideas, and information between different stakeholders. The need for more open innovation systems arose because of increasing competitive pressure on the one hand, and of the increasing complexity of the processes themselves which required greater resources on the other hand. West & Bogers (2013) argue that external sourcing is usually initiated by improved efficiency through scale economies and access to innovations (or innovation-producing capabilities) not held by the focal firm. The process of open innovation most often begins with outsourcing to contract service organizations and proceeds with more strategic modes (Gassman et al., 2010).

The growing importance of the open innovation approach has further highlighted the triple helix system perspective. At the core of the triple helix system are the university-industry-government interactions that form an innovation system format defined according to systems theory as a set of components, relationships, and functions (Ranga & Etzkowitz, 2013). The triple helix concept emphasizes the dynamism of relationships and interactions between the three most important types of actors, as well as the role of academia as a generator of knowledge that finds its full application in the business sector. The role of the government is to create a system that defines and regulates the innovation process of enterprises (Vaivode, 2015).

Although much of the innovation has come from large companies, the role of SMEs in the innovation process is significant and cannot be questioned. SMEs make up the largest part of all national economies. Also, they are the largest generator of new jobs and contribute to the generation of more than half of the GDP of national economies, and as such are the engines of economic growth. Due to their size, SMEs are more flexible and more prone to risky and innovative business ventures. However, despite being the most vibrant part of any economy, SMEs also face the most barriers to innovation. Compared to large enterprises, SMEs have significantly fewer resources and fewer capabilities for R&D activities. Limited in-house innovation capacities of SMEs need to be compensated by sourcing external knowledge for internal use (Rajalo & Vadi, 2021).

Developing relationships between participants in the triple helix model is particularly relevant for SMEs that find it most difficult to gain external knowledge. An important source of SMEs' innovation capacity refers to their ability to collaborate with both public and private partners (Pierre & Fernandez, 2018 according to Gronum et al., 2012; Keizer et al., 2001; Lasagni, 2012).

Given the contribution of innovation to sustainable economic growth, governments play an active role in fostering innovation and creating an enabling environment for innovation activities. Government innovation policy measures are important in countries experiencing dynamic economic growth because they need to enable further sustainable progress, and even more in developing countries that are still struggling with low innovation performance. Much of the policy attention has been on the three helixes of universities, industries, and governments. For countries seeking to stimulate knowledge-based economic development, an innovation strategy based on the triple helix systems might be an attractive, novel perspective for policymakers (Ranga & Etzkowitz, 2013). Policy measures and programs are to be directed at building and developing the linkages and networking between different actors in the national innovation system including governmental support institutions, business enterprises, academia, incubators, innovation clusters, and other business associations. The performance of national innovation systems is significantly determined by the intensity and quality of collaboration between the three main groups of actors.

Growing investment in policy measures to stimulate innovation has imposed the need to evaluate the effects achieved. This is particularly relevant in developing countries which usually have limited resources. There are studies confirming the positive effects of innovation policies on the performance of SMEs (e.g., Foreman-Peck, 2013; Diaz-Puente et al., 2009; Radicic et al., 2014; Motohashi, 2001; Veugelers, 2008). However, such surveys for developing countries are scarcer. The creation of support measures in developing countries is insufficiently based on data, which is why full effects are often lacking. Any attempt to assess the effects of innovation policy is important because it provides an opportunity for more rational use of available funds and justifies the continued implementation or redesign of support measures.

RESEARCH METHODOLOGY AND OBJECTIVES

Because of the complexity of innovation and the dynamism of the environment in which they occur, measuring the effects of policy measures is a difficult and challenging task. Edler & Fagerberg (2017) pointed out that the immediate effects are more possible to assess compared to the wider effects such as on innovation, productivity, and jobs which are of particular interest to policymakers. In addition to the complexity of innovation, an additional aggravating circumstance is the long period of time in which the wider effects occur. Also, when evaluating policy measures, it is necessary to consider the innovation system as a set of relationships and interactions between different actors because it has an indirect impact on the effects of the measure.

To assess the effects of the innovation policy on science-to-business collaboration in Serbia, the research was conducted by a combination of desk and field methods. Field research was conducted by a survey that included the beneficiaries of the Collaborative Grant Scheme Program implemented through the Innovation Fund of the Republic of Serbia. Desk research included collection and analysis of data on the relevant national regulation, data on measures and programs of innovation policy and the size of funds for financing innovation activities, and data on actors in the innovation system of the Republic of Serbia.

The survey was conducted on a sample of SMEs funded through the Collaborative Grant Scheme Program in the period 2012-2018. Out of a total of 96 received applications, 74 submitted projects met the eligibility requirements, and 14 projects were approved and funded. The projects were implemented by a consortium of SMEs and academia i.e., universities and research institutions. 30% of funded projects were in the food and agriculture sector, 14% in the electrical engineering sector, 14% in natural sciences, while the rest of the projects were in the ICT sector, environmental protection, medical and therapeutic devices, energy and energy efficiency, software and application development and mechanical engineering. The average duration of funded projects is 24 months, and the average value is 300,000 euros. 43% of SMEs that are project consortium holders are based in Belgrade, the capital of Serbia. The realization of the research sample is 50%.

The survey questionnaire was delivered to the E-mail addresses of all project consortium holders. According to the propositions of the Program, the holders of the consortium are micro enterprises and SMEs. The questionnaire contains 5 sections: general information about Program beneficiaries; objectives, expectations, and barriers related to participation in the Program; direct and indirect effects of projects on business performance of beneficiaries; effects of projects on other companies and organizations; the importance of the Program for the realization of innovation projects. Primary data obtained during the research were processed using the methods of descriptive statistical analysis.

Considering that there is no generally accepted evaluation method, as well as that the success of support measures is determined by the national innovation system, the main objectives of this paper are:

1. To review the Serbian innovation system in terms of the legislative framework and identification of the most important groups of actors.
2. To analyze the innovation performance of Serbia.
3. To analyze the effects of the innovation policy support to science to business collaboration on the performance of SMEs that were beneficiaries of the Collaborative Grant Scheme Program of the Serbian Innovation Fund in the period 2016-2018.

In line with the role of SMEs in innovation and the growing importance of the open innovation approach for SME innovation performance, the focus of research in this paper is on the effects of policy support to science and business collaboration on SMEs. Also, a review of the innovation system in which this cooperation takes place is provided, as well as the analysis of the innovation performance based on the European Innovation Scoreboard and the Global Innovation Index for 2020 in order to identify areas where improvements are needed.

MAIN FOCUS OF THE CHAPTER

Review of the National Innovation System of Serbia

The effectiveness of the national innovation system together with the way in which innovations are realized significantly determines the growth of innovation in an economy (Marjanovic et al., 2019). National innovation systems are more than frameworks for interaction; however, they are also repositories of various resources that firms depend on in their innovation activities and home to various institutions influencing these (Edler & Fagerberg, 2017, p.8). At the core of the concept of a national innovation system is the assumption that innovation is the result of interactions between actors engaged in the process of knowledge creation, distribution, and application. These actors primarily include private enterprises, academia (universities and research institutes), and governmental institutions.

Innovation policy can be defined as a public intervention to support the generation and diffusion of innovation (Edler et al., 2016). Through innovation policy, the government creates conditions for the development and application of innovation which becomes key to promoting the innovation system and improving the innovation performance of national economies (Beraha, 2019). Successful innovation policy governance, in addition to creating adequate programs and measures, implies their implementation in a way that provides effective collaboration between all actors in the innovation system and builds an interactive system of connections that serves to solve general social problems.

The review of the national innovation system of Serbia starts from the analysis of the regulatory framework. The relevant national legal regulation is the Law on Innovation Activity ("Official Gazette of RS", No. 110/05, 18/10 and 55/13). The Law regulates the basic principles, goals, and organization of the application of scientific knowledge, technical and technological knowledge, inventiveness and invention, in the function of creation and realization of new and improved products, processes, and services. Innovation activity includes activities undertaken to create new products, technologies, processes, and services or significant changes to existing ones, in accordance with the needs of the market. An invention is a concept, idea, and method for obtaining a new product or process, including the discovery of new technology (product or process) for the exploitation of natural resources. Innovation is the successful market application of an invention, i.e., the application of a new or significantly improved product, process, or service (includes significant improvements in technical characteristics, components, and materials, firmware, user orientation, or other functional characteristics), marketing methods, or new organizational methods in business, organization work or relations of the legal entity with the environment and can be:

- Product innovation - as the application of a new or significantly improved product, which is new for the legal entity (does not have to be new to the market) and is not a change of aesthetic nature or exclusively the sale of innovated products produced and developed by another legal entity.
- Process innovation - as the application of a new or significantly improved method of production or delivery (including significant changes in technique, equipment, or software, but not exclusively organizational and managerial changes) that is new or improved for the observed legal entity, regardless of who developed it.
- Organizational innovation - as the application of new or significant changes in the structure or methods of management, with the intention to improve the use of knowledge, quality of products or services in the legal entity, or increase the efficiency of business flows.
- Marketing innovation - as the application of a new marketing method, including significant changes in design, packaging, marketing, promotion, and billing of products.

In accordance with the Law, the Republic of Serbia, the Autonomous Province, and local self-government units may provide financing for innovation activities in order to achieve the goals of innovation policy. Economic instruments that provide and encourage innovation are the funds of the budget of the Republic of Serbia, the funds of the autonomous province, the budget of the local self-government unit, the funds of international financial organizations, the Innovation Fund, other funds, economic incentives, and other measures in accordance with the Law.

The budget funds can be used in the form of grants if they do not exceed 50% of the necessary funds for the implementation of certain innovation activities and projects. These funds may be allocated on the basis of a public invitation to submit a request for the allocation of funds. The Law governing the state aid of small value (de minimis), as well as by-laws and other general acts, apply to the financing of innovation activities from the budget of the Republic of Serbia.

Innovation policy sets goals and provides systemic conditions for the creation, development, and implementation of innovations. It is realized through innovation and development projects. Innovation projects last up to one year, and development projects up to two years. Beneficiaries of government incentive measures and budget funds for the development of innovation activity can only be entities registered in the Register of Innovation Activity. The Ministry in charge of scientific research and technological development keeps the Register. The Register is publicly available on the Ministry's website, and it provides an updated list of registered legal entities and individuals, especially registered companies and innovation projects. Also, the Innovation Fund is a beneficiary of budget funds, i.e., it uses funds to finance the preparation, implementation, and development of programs, projects, and other activities in the field of innovation policy implementation.

In accordance with the Law on Innovation Activity, the national innovation system consists of a set of organizations, institutions, and their connections that are in the function of generating, diffusing, and applying scientific and technological knowledge in the Republic of Serbia. Based on the insight into the Register of innovation activities, the following actors have been identified:

1. Registered legal entities - innovation organizations (development and production centers, research and development centers, and innovation centers) and innovation infrastructure (business-technological incubators, science-technology parks, organizations for stimulating innovation activities in the priority area of science and technology and technology transfer centers).
2. Registered individuals.
3. Specially registered companies: high-tech companies and medium-tech companies.

Registered individuals, high-tech and medium-tech companies are excluded from the discussion on key actors in Serbia's national innovation system. High-tech and medium-tech companies are exempted due to their low share in the total number of registered companies. Also, individuals are excluded due to their instability, i.e., the fact that a large number is deleted from the Register. Accordingly, the most important actors in the national innovation system are large enterprises, SMEs, science, and academia, innovation infrastructure, organizations performing innovation activities, start-up companies, actors for promotion and advancement of innovation, governments departments, and ICT companies.

Innovation Performance of Serbia

There is a positive trend in the number of companies in the field of innovation, scientific and technical activities. However, their performance in terms of employment, turnover, export, and added value is still below the average of developed countries. Based on data on R&D expenditure as a percent of GDP for 2018, Serbia with an average value of 0.92 percent is ranked 34th out of 72 countries. There are differences in the structure of sources of R&D funding in Serbia in relation to the tendencies in developed economies. With the government being the leading source of funding for R&D, Serbia is not close to achieving the goal set by the Lisbon Strategy where it was said that appropriate funding of R&D is one-third from public funds and two-thirds from private funds. However, the structure of R&D funding sources slightly shifts in favor of the business sector, thus emphasizing the need to analyze the effects of existing innovation policy and suggest future directions for development.

An assessment of the innovative performance of the Republic of Serbia is performed based on the indicators from the European Innovation Scoreboard Report and the Global Innovation Index Report for 2020.

European Innovation Scoreboard conducts a comparative assessment of research and innovation performance of EU member states and a group of selected countries, including the Republic Serbia. Innovation performance is measured based on the Summary Innovation Index consisting of four groups of indicators and 10 dimensions, respectively a total of 27 indicators. The four basic groups of indicators include the following: Systemic conditions, Investments, Innovation activities, and Impacts. Systemic conditions are related to the basic drivers of innovative performance that are tracked through the three dimensions - human resources, attractive research system, and environment that encourages innovation. Investments in the public and private sectors are monitored through two dimensions - finance and support to innovation and research activities and investments of business entities. Innovation activities include various aspects of innovation in the private sector and are monitored through the dimensions of innovators, connections, and intellectual property. Impact indicator monitors the effects of innovation activity of business entities on employment and sales.

Based on the value of the Summary Innovation Index, Serbia is a moderate innovator. The 2020 Report indicates some progress in the level of performance, but Serbia still lags significantly behind average values at the EU level. The best performance is achieved in the following dimensions: Innovators, Firm investments, and an Innovation-friendly environment. The weakest dimensions include Intellectual assets, Attractive research system, and Finance and support.

Despite some progress, the enterprises' investment in R&D remains insufficient. Because of the underdeveloped financial system and financial market, financing innovative business ventures continues to be difficult in Serbia. Also, the level of collaboration between different actors in the innovation system is modest which is a consequence of the lack of awareness of the importance of the flow of information and knowledge.

In addition to the assessment of innovation performance in relation to the average performance of EU member states, the Global Innovation Index evaluates the innovation performance of Serbia in relation to 126 countries of the world. The Global Innovation Index covers 84 indicators and is calculated based on the average scores of the two sub-indices – Innovative Abilities and Innovative Outcome. Innovative Abilities Sub-Index measures the innovative potential of the economy and consists of five pillars – institutions, human capital and research, infrastructure, market sophistication, and business sophistication. Sub-index Innovative result measures the innovativeness of the product output and consists of two pillars – knowledge and technological ability and creative ability.

According to the Global Innovation Index, Serbia is ranked 53rd which is an improvement by four positions relative to 2019. Compared to the surrounding countries, Serbia is better ranked only than North Macedonia, Bosnia and Herzegovina, and Albania. The most favorable position is achieved in the fields of Knowledge and technology outputs and Infrastructure, while the least favorable position is achieved in terms of Market sophistication which refers to access to credit, investors protection, tariff rates, and local competition.

Based on the values of the observed indicators, the innovation performance of Serbia is assessed as relatively unsatisfactory in all dimensions. This is particularly relevant considering Serbia's position relative to countries with similar income levels. Such an assessment indicates that it is necessary to approach designing innovation policy with much more understanding and attention. Effective innovation policy must first respect the national innovation system as a context in which innovations are realized (Edler & Fagerberg, 2017). Also, an evaluation is necessary to identify policy measures with the most effects, as well as to identify areas, sectors, and/or technologies with the most potential, thus providing directions for future policy interventions (Beraha, 2019).

Analysis of the Effects of Innovation Policy on Science to Business Collaboration

The issue of innovation policy evaluation has been attracting the attention of both academics and policymakers over the past decades. Edler et al. (2012) emphasize the increasing importance of evaluation as a policy and management supporting tool and a tool to assess policies to justify or re-direct funding. Despite hundreds of surveys and evaluations of government interventions, the question of the effects of innovation policy remains uncertain. This is mainly due to the dynamic and systematic character of innovation activity and the complexity of the cause-effect relations in this field (Arnold, 2004).

A comprehensive evaluation of the innovation policy in Serbia has not been conducted so far and there is no evidence of whether and how successful innovation support measures are. A lack of data on the effects of previous measures reduces the possibility of more rational and efficient use of limited budget funds and achieving better innovation performance. The motivation for this paper is rooted in the need to provide insight into the effects of innovation policy and information on which to base future intervention.

The main objective of this paper is to analyze the effects of the Collaborative Grant Scheme Program implemented by the Innovation Fund in the period 2016-2018. The Program aims to initiate the collaboration of private sector companies and public R&D institutions in joint innovation projects to create new products and services and innovative technologies with market potential.

The program is intended for consortia that develop new commercially applicable technologies, services and products from all fields of science and technology. The objectives of the Program are to create a strategic framework to support R&D and innovation, enhance cooperation between public research organizations and the private sector to improve research capacity, strengthen the ability of SMEs to innovate and increase business investment in R&D. The period of project realization is between 12 and 24 months, and projects can be from all areas of science and technology and any industrial sector. Applicants must be a consortium composed of at least one privately owned Serbian company and one registered scientific research institution and may have a maximum of 5 members. The maximum amount of co-financing is EUR 300,000 per individual innovation project with mandatory co-financing by the consortium in the amount of at least 30% of the total project budget.

The basic characteristics of the 2016-2018 project cycle of the Program are systematized below showing the total value of approved funds, the average value of funded projects, the total number of received and approved project proposals, the average duration of projects, and the distribution of approved projects by sectors.

- The total value of projects financed in the observed period within the Program is EUR 4,376,267, with the Fund's participation amounting to EUR 3,000,000.
- The average value of the project is 312,591 EUR, and the average participation of the Fund is 214,286 EUR.
- Out of a total of 96 received applications, 74 submitted projects met the eligibility requirements, and 14 projects were approved and funded.
- The average duration of funded projects is 24 months.

- Out of a total of 14 funded projects, 30% are from the food and agriculture sector, 14% from the electrical engineering sector, 14% from the natural sciences sector, and the rest from the ICT sector, environmental protection, medical and therapeutic devices, energy and energy efficiency, software and application development and mechanical engineering.

The general information about the Program beneficiaries indicates that micro and SMEs (MSME) are the initiators and holders of the consortia that implemented the projects, as well as that more than a third of these companies are from the ICT sector. This information is systematically presented below.

- 50%, 12.5%, and 37.5% of consortia holders are micro, small and medium-sized enterprises respectively, while members of the consortia are scientific research institutions, i.e., faculties and scientific research institutes (36.4% and 27.2% respectively) and privately-owned enterprises (36.4%).
- All MSMEs operate in the form of a limited liability company.
- Approximately 38% of MSMEs operate in the ICT sector, while the remaining are evenly distributed in the sectors of medicine, mechanical engineering, optoelectronics, new materials, and nanotechnology.
- The main initiators of the implemented projects are the MSME holders of the consortia.

The effects of science to business collaboration projects were analyzed from the perspective of cooperation between consortium partners, goals and expectations of MSMEs from participation in the Program, as well as the effects on business performance indicators and MSME products/processes/activities.

The survey results have shown that the level of cooperation within the consortia was evaluated as high and significantly high by per half of the surveyed MSME holders, respectively. The collaboration is achieved primarily through the implementation of project activities and co-financing, as well as through the exchange of technical and R&D skills. Project implementation is very important for innovation/R&D activities of 57% and extremely important for 43% of MSMEs. Also, it is extremely, very, and moderately significant for the growth of 14%, 43%, and 29% of MSMEs, respectively.

Most MSMEs participated in the Program with the aim of developing a new product. Other identified objectives include improvement of existing technology, development of a new process, improvement of an existing product/service, and development of new technology. Regarding the expectations from the participation in the Program, 86% of MSMEs expect revenue growth, entry into new markets/increase in market share, and profit growth 71% expect an increase in exports/start of export activities, 57% expect an increase in company value, while 43% expect growth in the number of employees.

Direct effects of the Program on business performance indicators of MSMEs include an increase in the number of employees, sales revenues, net profit, exports, efficiency, and productivity. Approximately 86% of the surveyed MSMEs pointed to an increase in the number of employees, while per slightly less than third increased exports and sales revenues. MSMEs have optimistic expectations for the duration of the positive effects of implemented projects and the initiated cooperation with the academia. Namely, one-third believe that they will last less than 3 years, one-third that they will last 6 and more years, 16.7% that they will last 4 to 5 years and 16.7% stated that they could not assess. The effects of innovation projects on business performance indicators of MSMEs are presented in Figure 1.

Figure 1. Project effects on business performance indicators of MSMEs
Source: Authors' survey

The implementation of innovation projects has resulted in the development of R&D activity and new products/services in per 86% of MSMEs. Also, as much as 70% of surveyed MSMEs realized technological innovation, and 43% developed innovation activity. The effects of innovation projects on products/processes/activities of MSMEs beneficiaries are presented in Figure 2.

Figure 2. Project effects on product/process/activity of MSMEs
Source: Authors' survey

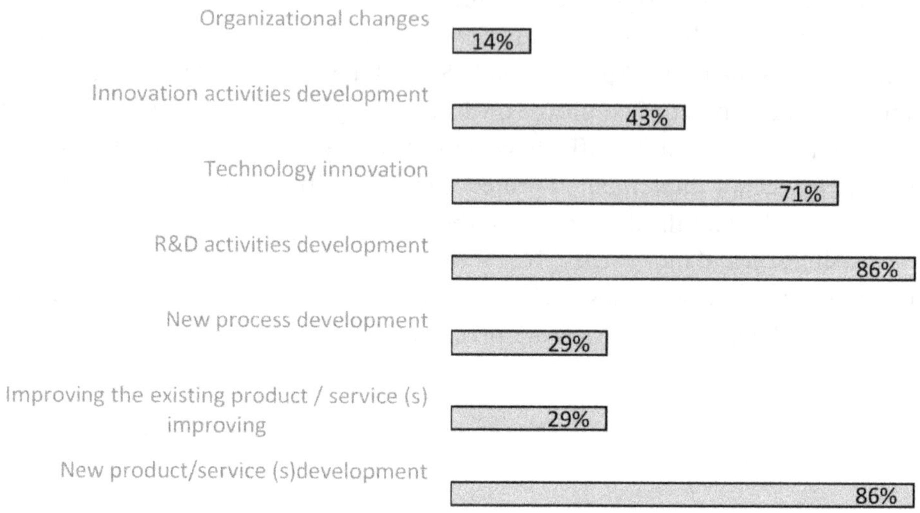

The analysis reveals that the effects of innovation projects implemented under the Program are positive. Firstly, the level of established cooperation between MSMEs and academic institutions was assessed as high and significantly high. Also, the goals and expectations of MSMEs from participating in the Program have been largely achieved. The realization of innovation projects had direct positive effects on the business performance of MSMEs, and above all on the number of employees, sales revenue, and exports. The expected duration of the positive effects unequivocally confirms the importance of initiated cooperation for MSMEs. As a result of the cooperation within this Program, MSMEs have developed R&D activities and new products/services, enhanced their innovation activities, and developed technological innovation.

The positive effects of innovation policy measures on enterprises have been confirmed by other research results. Herrera & Sanchez-Gonzalez (2013) found that government funding stimulates investment in the field of applied research and technological development of enterprises of all sizes and that it significantly increases private R&D effort in small enterprises. Antonioli et al., (2012) revealed that funded companies are found to be more likely to upgrade their competencies, compared with similar non-subsidized companies, while innovation cooperation with other business partners is not significantly affected by the policy. Foreman-Peck (2013) studied the effects of SME innovation policy and determined that SMEs receiving UK government support for innovation were more likely to innovate than unsupported comparable enterprises and that they grew significantly faster over the observed period. Raposo, et al. (2014) analyzed the effects of local and cross-border cooperation between SMEs on company innovation and performance and concluded that it positively impacts the company performance and innovation levels. Czarnitzki & Licht (2006) examined the input and output additionality of public R&D subsidies in Western and Eastern Germany and found a large degree of additionality in public R&D grants regarding innovation input measured as R&D expenditures and innovation expenditures, as well as regarding innovation output measured by patent applications. Research conducted by Đuričin & Beraha (2021) indicates that potentials for the development of innovation activities of medium-sized agricultural enterprises in Serbia can be improved through cooperation with food processing companies, primarily through strengthening the cooperation between science and business and more intensive transfer of technological solutions to the business sector. Chen, et al. (2013) highlight the importance of enhancing cooperation within the triple helix model by introducing facilitators of national innovation policy, such as non-governmental research institutes closely tied to the industry, to foster knowledge absorption and dissemination and enable SMEs to overcome human and technological constraints to innovation activity.

SOLUTIONS AND RECOMMENDATIONS

Given that innovation policy interventions directly or indirectly impact the innovation activity and performance of the national innovation system and spill-over to the entire economy and society, measuring their effects provides a key information input for more rational use of limited budget funds, creating programs and measures tailored to the needs of the users and finally improving the innovation performance of the entire economy. Many governments have long recognized the importance of monitoring and evaluating the effects of policy measures. However, because of the nature and characteristics of the phenomenon of innovation, this issue continues to be quite challenging.

In circumstances where a small number of enterprises, particularly SMEs, have the resources and capabilities to independently perform R&D activities, cooperation has gained in importance. R&D activities of scientific research institutions and organizations that perform innovation activities create knowledge that needs to be transformed into the business sector through various mechanisms of collaboration and communication.

The policy approach to innovation that is based on the triple helix system can be an attractive and novel perspective for policymakers, particularly in countries that intend to promote knowledge-intensive development (Ranga & Etzkowitz, 2013).

National innovation system development is a precondition for the establishment of close relations of cooperation between the government, business, and academia in which the free flow of information and knowledge takes place. Governments have an important role to play in creating stimulating conditions for innovation and achieving synergetic effects through the cooperation of the science and business sector.

The Government of the Republic of Serbia implements innovation policy to support innovation, encourage the creation of new and development of existing innovation companies, improve R&D capacity, foster technology development, transform innovation into new products and services, and promote cooperation and knowledge transfer between business and academia. However, the analysis has shown that Serbia is progressing but still not achieving satisfactory innovation performance.

The starting point for creating an efficient and effective innovation policy in Serbia and further encouraging cooperation between science and business is the establishment of a model for the evaluation of previous interventions. The availability of data on the success and effects of implemented programs and measures provides an opportunity not only to assess the situation but also to plan future investments and improve policy interventions.

The results of the research presented in this paper support previous findings in this field. Singh et al. (2019), suggest that open innovation benefits SMEs in terms of organizational performance enhancement. The results of the research conducted by Suh & Kim (2012) showed that technology acquisition is the most efficient type of collaboration for R&D of service SMEs. The study by Avalos-Quispe & Hernandez-Simon (2019) analyzed the collaboration between SMEs and academia over an open innovation setting in Mexico. The results showed that the knowledge created by the group of SMEs can be observed as an indirect way of learning, where the main output observed from the collaboration was found in internal improvements. The results obtained by Carrasco-Carvajal & Garcia-Perez-De-Lema (2021) show that innovation capability has a significant and positive influence on inbound and outbound practices and that inbound practices have a positive influence on the performance of SMEs. Based on data gathered from 135 SMEs, Santoro et al. (2019) found a positive relationship between knowledge sourcing strategy and internationalization.

The results of this research are the first attempt in Serbia to analyze and measure the effects of an innovation policy program. As such, they provide valuable insights for policymakers in the direction of increasing support for science to business collaboration. Evidence of the positive effects of the Program that promotes science-to-business collaboration is a clear signal that it needs to be further improved and expanded.

The basic recommendation that emerges from this research refers to the introduction of monitoring and qualitative and quantitative evaluation of policy effects through a set of indicators that would provide information on program users; goals, expectations, and barriers related to the implementation of innovation projects, direct and indirect effects of programs on business performance of beneficiaries; effects on other participants in the national innovation system and importance of programs for the realization of innovation projects. Introducing a model for the analysis and assessment of effects of the government investments in innovation activities on direct beneficiaries, and the economy and society requires the collection of accurate data. A system that collects information on all innovation policy measures, results, and effects has not been introduced yet. Another recommendation is related to further strengthening of cooperation between science and business through a larger volume of funds, a larger number of programs, and regular monitoring of achieved results.

FUTURE RESEARCH DIRECTIONS

The practice of monitoring and evaluating the effects of policies has not yet been developed in Serbia. Also, the number of research and scientific papers dealing with this issue is scarce. Being aware of this gap, the research presented in this paper is the first attempt to analyze the effects of a single innovation policy program. The value of this research is in the pioneering attempt to show and analyze the effects of innovation policy. The selection of the science to business collaboration program aims to raise attention to the importance of this issue, as well as to provide policymakers with insights and relevant data for further interventions.

Serbia's innovation performance compared to countries with similar income levels points to the need to improve innovation policy and further develop the national innovation system. Continuous progress measured by the European Innovation Scoreboard and the Global Innovation Index confirms that there is potential for innovation in Serbia. Accordingly, this issue deserves much more attention from both the academic and professional community and policymakers.

The research results are a solid starting point for future research, which would include an analysis of the effects of the Collaborative Grant Scheme Program in other project cycles, as well as of other programs implemented through the Innovation Fund and the Ministry of Education, Science, and Technological Development. However, the analysis conducted in this paper does not apply quantitative methods, which is the main disadvantage of this research. Future research should include the application of more complex evaluation methods so that more accurate conclusions can be drawn.

CONCLUSION

It is widely accepted that innovation is a basic precondition for the dynamic growth and development of national economies. It is the most important source of new value creation, new products and services, new ways of producing and delivering existing products and services, new jobs, increasing productivity and competitiveness, and new and improved ways to solve social problems. Along with raising awareness of the importance of innovation, the open innovation approach is gaining in importance. This is because of circumstances in which individual enterprises, especially SMEs, which make up the bulk of all economies, lack the resources and capabilities to innovate independently. The use of external knowledge significantly enhances innovation performance. The synergetic effects achieved through collaboration between government, business sector, and academia are at the core of the triple helix model of innovation.

The role of SMEs in national economies puts them at the center of attention in all discussions of sustainable economic growth and development. Since innovation is the driver of such growth and development, finding ways to improve the innovation performance of SMEs is high on the agendas of policymakers in developed, and even more in developing countries. Government innovation policies reflect the desire to design support measures that will enable SMEs to exploit their potential and overcome their constraints. Through innovation policy, a favorable environment and stimulating innovation system are created in which innovation activities are realized, information and knowledge flow, and cooperation between different actors is established. Academia plays a key role in the open innovation approach and is perhaps the most important partner for SMEs. Academia is the source of knowledge generation that further finds its application in the business sector. The business sector, academia, and government are the most important actors in the national innovation system that shapes the conditions in which innovation ventures take place.

The implementation of an efficient and effective innovation policy implies information on how successful the intervention is. However, innovation policies evaluation is still challenging, despite an extensive discussion that has been going on for the last two decades. Numerous studies have been conducted but consensus has not been reached on the evaluation methodology. This is due to the complexity and dynamism of the phenomenon of innovation and the difficulty of monitoring and measuring the effects of policy measures.

The motivation for the research presented in this paper arose because of the lack of evidence on the effects of the innovation policy in Serbia. The choice to analyze the effects of science to business collaboration program is a result of the need to affirm and systematically support the open innovation concept in Serbia. Also, the research results contribute to the existing body of literature in the field of open innovation in SMEs.

The results of a survey conducted on a sample of the Collaborative Grant Scheme Program beneficiaries in the period 2016-2018 indicated the positive effects of cooperation on MSMEs. The positive effects were observed in terms of the level of cooperation between MSMEs and academia, new product/service/process development, R&D activity development, innovation activity enhancement and technological innovation development, and business performance of MSMEs. Regarding business performance indicators, the effects of the increase in the number of employees, sales revenues, and exports are especially emphasized. The analysis of the effects of the Program was preceded by a review of the national innovation system, within which the legislative framework was analyzed, and key actors were identified. Also, an analysis of Serbia's innovation performance according to the European Innovation Scoreboard and the Global Innovation Index for 2020 is provided with an aim to point out the fields where improvements are needed.

Based on the results of the analysis, recommendations are given to policymakers regarding the introduction of a model for continuous monitoring and measuring of the effects of innovation policy and further increasing and expanding support for science to business collaboration.

Being aware of the methodological shortcomings, future research directions are proposed. They refer to the application of a quantitative methodology for the evaluation of innovation policy measures and programs in Serbia.

Despite the methodological shortcomings, the value of this paper lies in the fact that this is the first attempt to analyze the effects of innovation policy in Serbia. As such, these results are a significant input for guiding further innovation policy.

ACKNOWLEDGMENT

This research was supported by the Ministry of Education, Science and Technological Development of the Republic of Serbia.

REFERENCES

Alexander, A. T., Miller, K., & Fielding, S. (2015). Open for business: Universities, entrepreneurial academics and open innovation. *International Journal of Innovation Management*, *19*(06), 1540013. doi:10.1142/S1363919615400137

Antonioli, D., Marzucchi, A., & Montresor, S. (2012). Regional Innovation Policy and Innovative Behaviour: Looking for Additional Effects. *European Planning Studies*, *22*(1), 64–83. doi:10.1080/09654313.2012.722977

Arnold, E. (2004). Evaluating research and innovation policy: A systems world needs systems evaluation. *Research Evaluation*, *13*(1), 3–17. doi:10.3152/147154404781776509

Avalos-Quispe, G. A., & Hernández-Simón, L. M. (2019). Open Innovation in SMEs: Potential and Realized Absorptive Capacity for Interorganizational Learning in Dyad Collaborations with Academia. *Journal of Open Innovation: Technology, Market, and Complexity*, *5*(3), 1–14.

Avalos-Quispe, G., & Hernandez-Simon, L. (2019). Open Innovation in SMEs: Potential and Realized Absorptive Capacity for Interorganizational Learning in Dyad Collaborations with Academia. *Journal of Open Innovation*, *5*(3), 72. doi:10.3390/joitmc5030072

Barge-Gil, A. (2013). Open Strategies and Innovation Performance. *Industry and Innovation*, *20*(7), 585–610. doi:10.1080/13662716.2013.849455

Beraha, I. (2019). Ocena inovativnih performansi Republike Srbije. *Ekonomski vidici, 25*(3-4), 137-151.

Berchicci, L. (2013). Towards an open R&D system: Internal R&D investment, external knowledge acquisition and innovative performance. *Research Policy*, *42*(1), 11–127. doi:10.1016/j.respol.2012.04.017

Bogers, M., Chesbrough, H., & Moedas, C. (2018). Open Innovation: Research, Practices, and Policies. *California Management Review*, *60*(2), 5–16. doi:10.1177/0008125617745086

Carrasco-Carvajal, O., & García-Pérez-De-Lema, D. (2021). Innovation Capability and Open Innovation and its Impact on Performance in SMEs: An Empirical Study in Chile. *International Journal of Innovation Management*, *25*(04), 2150039. doi:10.1142/S1363919621500390

Chen, C.-Y., Lin, Y.-L., & Chu, P.-Y. (2013). Facilitators of national innovation policy in a SME-dominated country: A case study of Taiwan. *Innovation*, *15*(4), 405–415. doi:10.5172/impp.2013.15.4.405

Chesbrough, H. (2004). Managing Open Innovation. *Research Technology Management*, *47*(1), 23–26. doi:10.1080/08956308.2004.11671604

Chesbrough, H. (2006). Open innovation: A new paradigm for understanding industrial innovation. In Open innovation: Researching a new paradigm. Oxford University Press.

Chesbrough, H. W., & Appleyard, M. M. (2007). Open Innovation and Strategy. *California Management Review*, *50*(1), 57–76. doi:10.2307/41166416

Chesbrough, H. W. (2003). *Open Innovation* (1st ed.). Harvard Business School Publishing.

Chesbrough, H. W. (2003a). The era of open innovation. *MIT Sloan Management Review*, *44*(3), 35–41.

Chesbrough, H. W. (2003b). *Open Innovation: The New Imperative for Creating and Profiting from Technology*. Harvard Business School Press.

Cornell University. INSEAD, & The World Intellectual Property Organization. (2020). *Global Innovation Index 2020: Who Will Finance Innovation?* Available at: https://www.wipo.int/edocs/pubdocs/en/wipo_pub_gii_2020.pdf

Czarnitzki, D., & Licht, G. (2006). Additionality of public R&D grants in a transition economy. The case of Eastern Germany. *Economics of Transition*, *14*(1), 101–131. doi:10.1111/j.1468-0351.2006.00236.x

Díaz-Puente, J. M., Cazorla, A., & Ríos, I. (2009). Policy Support for the Diffusion of Innovation among SMEs: An Evaluation Study in the Spanish Region of Madrid. *European Planning Studies*, *17*(3), 365–387. doi:10.1080/09654310802618028

Đuričin, S., & Beraha, I. (2016). SME clustering in Serbia: finding the right business partners and improving the business environment for SMEs. In S. M. E. Clustering (Ed.), *Finding the right business partners and improving the business environment for SMEs* (pp. 213–236). Konrad Adenauer Stiftung.

Đuričin, S., & Beraha, I. (2021). Assessment of the Innovation Capacity of Business Entities in the Republic of Serbia. In *Finance, Innovation and Technology: new models and structures* (pp. 179–198). Institute of Economics - Ss. Cyril & Methodius University.

Đuričin, S., & Beraha, I. (2021). Identifying medium-sized agricultural enterprises with the greatest potential for innovation development. *Ekonomika Poljoprivrede*, *68*(1), 213–227. doi:10.5937/ekoPolj2101213D

Edler, J., & Fagerberg, J. (2017). Innovation policy: What, why, and how. *Oxford Review of Economic Policy*, *33*(1), 2–23. doi:10.1093/oxrep/grx001

Edler, J., Berger, M., Dinges, M., & Gok, A. (2012). The practice of evaluation in innovation policy in Europe. *Research Evaluation*, *21*(3), 167–182. doi:10.1093/reseval/rvs014

Edler, J., Cunningham, P., Gök, A., & Shapira, P. (2016). *Handbook of Innovation Policy Impact*. Edward Elgar Publishing. doi:10.4337/9781784711856

Elmquist, M., Fredberg, T., & Ollila, S. (2009). Exploring the field of open innovation. *European Journal of Innovation Management*, *12*(3), 326–345. doi:10.1108/14601060910974219

European Commission (2020). *European Innovation Score board 2020*. Luxembourg: Publications Office of the European Union. Available at: file:///C:/Users/Isidora/Downloads/ET-AY-20-002-EN-N%20Online%20(1).pdf

Foreman-Peck, J. (2013). Effectiveness and efficiency of SME innovation policy. *Small Business Economics*, *41*(1), 55–70. doi:10.100711187-012-9426-z

Garcia, R., Araújo, V., Mascarini, S., Santos, E. G., & Costa, A. R. (2019). How long-term university-industry collaboration shapes the academic productivity of research groups. *Innovation*, 1–15.

Gassmann, O., Enkel, E., & Chesbrough, H. (2010). The future of open innovation. *R & D Management*, *40*(3), 213–221. doi:10.1111/j.1467-9310.2010.00605.x

Gronum, S., Verreynne, M. L., & Kastelle, T. (2012). The Role of Networks in Small and Medium-Sized Enterprise Innovation and Firm Performance. *Journal of Small Business Management*, *50*(2), 257–282. doi:10.1111/j.1540-627X.2012.00353.x

Herrera, L., & Sánchez-González, G. (2013). Firm size and innovation policy. *International Small Business Journal*, *31*(2), 137–155. doi:10.1177/0266242611405553

Keizer, J. A., Dijkstra, L., & Halman, J. I. M. (2001). Explaining Innovative Efforts of SMEs: An exploratory Survey among SMEs in the Mechanical and Electrical Engineering Sector in The Netherlands. *Technovation*, *22*(1), 1–13. doi:10.1016/S0166-4972(00)00091-2

Lasagni, A. (2012). How Can External Relationships Enhance Innovation in SMEs? New Evidence for Europe. *Journal of Small Business Management*, *50*(2), 310–339. doi:10.1111/j.1540-627X.2012.00355.x

Malik, K., Glynn, S., Butler, J., & Miles, I. (2003). Developing innovation policies for the knowledge economy in Europe. *Innovation*, *5*(2-3), 225–233. doi:10.5172/impp.2003.5.2-3.225

Maradana, R. P., Pradhan, R. P., Dash, S., Gaurav, K., Jayakumar, M., & Chatterjee, D. (2017). Does innovation promote economic growth? Evidence from European countries. *Journal of Innovation and Entrepreneurship*, *6*(1), 1. doi:10.118613731-016-0061-9

Motohashi, K. (2001). *RIETI Discussion Paper Series 01-E-006 Use of plant level micro-data for SME innovation policy evaluation in Japan*. Academic Press.

Ortega-Argilés, R., Vivarelli, M., & Voigt, P. (2009). R&D in SMEs: A paradox? *Small Business Economics*, *33*(1), 3–11. doi:10.100711187-009-9187-5

Pece, A. M., Simona, O. E. O., & Salisteanu, F. (2015). Innovation and Economic Growth: An Empirical Analysis for CEE Countries. *Procedia Economics and Finance*, *26*, 461–467. doi:10.1016/S2212-5671(15)00874-6

Philipson, S. (2019). Sources of innovation: Consequences for knowledge production and transfer. *Journal of Innovation & Knowledge.*

Pierre, A., & Fernandez, A. S. (2018). Going deeper into SMEs' innovation capacity: An empirical exploration of innovation capacity factors. *Journal of Innovation Economics & Management*, *25*(1), 139–181. doi:10.3917/jie.pr1.0019

Radicic, D., Pugh, G. T., Hollanders, H., & Wintjes, R. (2014). *The Impact of Innovation Support Programmes on SME Innovation in Traditional Manufacturing Industries: An Evaluation for Seven EU Regions*. UNU-MERIT Working Paper No. 2014-033.

Rajalo, S., & Vadi, M. (2021). Collaboration potential between low-capacity SMEs and academic researchers determined by symmetry of motivation. *Technovation*, *107*(C), 102304. doi:10.1016/j.technovation.2021.102304

Ranga, M., & Etzkowitz, H. (2013). Triple Helix Systems: An Analytical Framework for Innovation Policy and Practice in the Knowledge Society. *Industry and Higher Education*, *27*(4), 237–262. doi:10.5367/ihe.2013.0165

Raposo, M. L., Ferreira, J. J. M., & Fernandes, C. I. (2014). Local and cross-border SME cooperation: Effects on innovation and performance. *Revista Europea de Dirección y Economía de La Empresa*, *23*(4), 157–165. doi:10.1016/j.redee.2014.08.001

Rigby, D., & Zook, C. (2002). Open market innovation. *Harvard Business Review*, *80*(10), 80–89. PMID:12389463

Santoro, G., Mazzoleni, A., Quaglia, R., & Solima, L. (2021). Does age matter? The impact of SMEs age on the relationship between knowledge sourcing strategy and internationalization. *Journal of Business Research*, *128*(C), 779–787. doi:10.1016/j.jbusres.2019.05.021

Santoro, G., Ferraris, A., Giacosa, E., & Giovando, G. (2018). How SMEs Engage in Open Innovation: A Survey. *Journal of the Knowledge Economy*, *9*(2), 561–574. doi:10.100713132-015-0350-8

Singh, S. K., Gupta, S., Busso, D., & Kamboj, S. (2021). Top management knowledge value, knowledge sharing practices, open innovation and organizational performance. *Journal of Business Research*, *128*(C), 788–798. doi:10.1016/j.jbusres.2019.04.040

Spithoven, A., Vanhaverbeke, W., & Roijakkers, N. (2012). Open innovation practices in SMEs and large enterprises. *Small Business Economics*, *41*(3), 537–562. doi:10.100711187-012-9453-9

Suh, Y., & Kim, M. S. (2012). Effects of SME collaboration on R&D in the service sector in open innovation. *Innovation (North Sydney, N.S.W.)*, *14*(3), 349–362. doi:10.5172/impp.2012.14.3.349

Ulku, H. (2004). *R&D, Innovation, and Economic Growth: An Empirical Analysis*. IMF Working Paper No. 04/185.

Vaivode, I. (2015). Triple Helix Model of University–Industry–Government Cooperation in the Context of Uncertainties. *Procedia: Social and Behavioral Sciences*, *213*, 1063–1067. doi:10.1016/j.sbspro.2015.11.526

Veugelers, R. (2008). The Role of SMEs in Innovation in the EU. A Case for Policy Intervention? *Review of Business and Economic Literature*, *0*(3), 239–262.

West, J., & Bogers, M. (2013). Leveraging External Sources of Innovation: A Review of Research on Open Innovation. *Journal of Product Innovation Management*, *31*(4), 814–831. doi:10.1111/jpim.12125

ADDITIONAL READING

Bogers, M., Chesbrough, H., & Moedas, C. (2018). Open innovation: Research, practices, and policies. *California Management Review*, *60*(2), 5–16. doi:10.1177/0008125617745086

Carayannis, E. G., & Rakhmatullin, R. (2014). The quadruple/quintuple innovation helixes and smart specialisation strategies for sustainable and inclusive growth in Europe and beyond. *Journal of the Knowledge Economy*, *5*(2), 212–239. doi:10.100713132-014-0185-8

Chesbrough, H. W., & Appleyard, M. M. (2007). Open Innovation and Strategy. *California Management Review*, *50*(1), 57–76. doi:10.2307/41166416

Chiaromonte, F. (2006). Open innovation through alliances and partnership: Theory and practice. *International Journal of Technology Management*, *33*(2-3), 111–114.

Flanagan, K., & Uyarra, E. (2016). Four dangers in innovation policy studies – and how to avoid them. *Industry and Innovation*, *23*(2), 177–188. doi:10.1080/13662716.2016.1146126

Hung, K. P., & Chou, C. (2013). The impact of open innovation on firm performance: The moderating effects of internal R&D and environmental turbulence. *Technovation*, *33*(10/11), 368–380. doi:10.1016/j.technovation.2013.06.006

Magro, E., & Wilson, J. R. (2013). Complex innovation policy systems: Towards an evaluation mix. *Research Policy*, *42*(9), 1647–1656. doi:10.1016/j.respol.2013.06.005

Perkmann, M., & Schildt, H. (2015). Open data partnerships between firms and universities: The role of boundary organisations. *Research Policy*, *44*(5), 1133–1143. doi:10.1016/j.respol.2014.12.006

KEY TERMS AND DEFINITIONS

Evaluation of Innovation Policy: An analysis and assessment of efficiency, effectiveness and impact achieved by a particular policy measure.

Innovation: A new or significantly improved product, process or service (includes significant improvements in technical characteristics, components and materials, firmware, user orientation or other functional characteristics), marketing methods or new organizational methods in business.

Innovation Performance of a Country: A series of indicators in areas that are relevant to innovation, such as the national system, investments in R&D, cooperation between participants in the innovation system, human resources, etc.

Innovation Policy: A government intervention including measures, programs, incentives, and other instruments aimed at supporting the creation and diffusion of innovations.

National Innovation System: A framework in which innovation activities are realized within an economy. It includes legislation, interactions and relations between various actors, innovation policy measures and all other factors that directly or indirectly affect the circumstances in which the innovation is realized.

Open Innovation Concept: The use of external resources to implement innovation activities.

Triple Helix Model of Innovation: A set of interactions between government, academia, and business sector to promote economic and social development.

Chapter 5
Open Innovation and Entrepreneurship:
Reflections of the State of the Art in the Period 2011–2021

Luciana Aparecida Barbieri da Rosa
https://orcid.org/0000-0001-9240-0236
Universidade Federal de Santa Maria, Brazil

Maria Carolina Martins Rodrigues
https://orcid.org/0000-0003-2575-8611
Independent Researcher, Portugal

Luana Inês Damke
https://orcid.org/0000-0003-0379-6262
Universidade Federal de Santa Maria, Brazil

Tais Pentiado Godoy
https://orcid.org/0000-0001-5021-5315
Universidade Federal de Santa Maria, Brazil

Waleska Yone Yamakawa Zavatti Campos
https://orcid.org/0000-0001-5050-1557
Pontifical Catholic University of Rio de Janeiro, Brazil

Larissa Cristina Barbieri
Federal Institute of Education, Science, and Technology of Rondônia, Brazil

ABSTRACT

The study aims to analyze the related publications on open innovation and entrepreneurship on the Web of Science in the period from 2011 to 2020. The study methodology was bibliometrics and researched on the themes open innovation and entrepreneurship analyzing the following aspects: main authors, analysis by year, main institutions, funding agencies, keywords, main newspapers, main countries and languages, areas of knowledge, and the relationship between authors with the

DOI: 10.4018/978-1-7998-8665-5.ch005

most publications and the most cited. In addition, the authors sought to analyze the co-citation of the aspects listed above. The results of the study, through CiteSpace, encompass multiplicity and diversity as to the authors who most published on the topic, and they found the institution that stood out the most in terms of publications.

INTRODUCTION

Eighteen years after the publication of Chesbrough's book (2003) and studies on open innovation have been studied in academia, which indicates its importance each year. Open innovation has been attracting the attention of national and international researchers about new business models aimed at competitiveness and innovation aspects (Li & Huang, 2019). Chesbrough (2003) already emphasized a facilitator in using comprehensive sources of conceptions, encouraging companies to search for the improvement of their technological capacities and principles. West and Borgers (2014) add that this sharing allows for the acquisition of innovations by sharing resources between

This perspective enhances the importance of open innovation for small and medium-sized enterprises (SMEs) due to the lack of resources and capacities to effectively increase their creations. In this sense, external collaboration is essential to promote access to the lacking inputs (Van de Vrande et al., 2009; Pan-Fagerlin & Wang, 2021).

In the last decade, there have been some changes in research regarding open innovation considering size, where the focus was previously on multinational companies that have become SMEs (Borges et al., 2017). Among such perspectives, we can gain innovation practices (Vanhaverbeke, 2017), modes of collaboration (Henttonen & Lehtimäki, 2017), elaboration of strategic SMEs (Freel & Robson, 2017).

Lee *et al.* (2018) embrace that the 4th Industrial Revolution is being lived; with this, the performance of open innovation is linked to the primordial understanding of the effects of culture in this area. In this scenario, it is evident that open innovation has a fundamental premise to use the available internal resources more efficiently and subsidise with accessible external resources (Bogers et al., 2018). Chesbrough (2017) points out that there are different perspectives in exploring these new opportunities focused on entrepreneurship. Knowing the relevance of open innovation to a business environment, the study question emerges: What are the contributions on Open Innovation and Entrepreneurship in the Web of Science in the period from 2011 to 2020?". This study aims to analyse the related publications on Open Innovation and Entrepreneurship on the Web of Science from 2011 to 2020.

The following will be the theoretical framework of the study.

THEORETICAL FRAMEWORK

Entrepreneurship on Different Vertices

Much is said about entrepreneurship these days, but the term began to be popularized more than half a century ago. In the 1940s, economist Joseph Schumpeter used the word as the centrepiece of his theory of creative destruction. Although entrepreneurship has been a topic discussed for centuries, it was in the 1980s that it became an object of study in almost all areas of knowledge in most nations. Since then, it has assumed a prominent place in the economic policies of developed countries and the development process (Baggio & Baggio, 2015).

According to Schumpeter, entrepreneurship would only happen through versatile people with technical skills to produce, organize financial resources, internal operations and make sales (Schumpeter, 1982). For Hisrich & Peter (2004, p. 33) "The role of entrepreneurship in economic development involves more than just increasing production and per capita income and involves initiating and constituting changes in the structure of business and society".

In this way, economists describe entrepreneurship as an essential process in economic development, and their models consider the principles of society (Baggio & Baggio, 2015). Entrepreneurship is a set of practices capable of guaranteeing the generation of wealth and better performance for the societies that support and practice it; still, it is also known that there is no fundamental theory in this regard. Entrepreneurship is the joint involvement of processes and people, which leads to the transformation of ideas into opportunities. Correctly implementing these opportunities leads to successful businesses (Santos et al., 2016; Dornelas, 2018).

Therefore, entrepreneurship emerged to present differentials to existing organizations, with the purpose that transactions were not lost, but rather to develop innovation in them to face competitiveness and reduce costs (Dornelas, 2018). For Hisrich and Peter (2004), entrepreneurship is a process of creating something different and with value, dedicating the necessary time and effort, assuming the corresponding financial, psychological and social risks and receiving the consequent rewards of economic and personal satisfaction.

It is observed that entrepreneurship comprises entrepreneurs who start a new business and the organization's employees (Ribeiro et al., 2019). Entrepreneurship is conceptualized as a cultural manifestation, which employs attitudes and behavioural forms that change from one region to another according to the way of life of each location (Braga et al., 2018).

The essence of entrepreneurship lies in the perception and use of new opportunities within the business scope. It is always about creating a new way of using national resources, in which they are displaced from their traditional use and subjected to new combinations (Baggio & Baggio, 2015). For entrepreneurship to fulfil its purpose, a detailed study of the context in which the entrepreneur is inserted is essential, analyzing the internal and external variables that can contribute to the organization (Castro et al., 2021). Thus, entrepreneurship can be defined as the art of knowing how to do it with creativity, motivation, determination, and innovation, aiming to produce transformation.

In addition to these, it is known that there are still different notions about entrepreneurship. Eckhardt & Shane (2003) and Shane and Venkataraman (2000) understand that it refers to generating new goods, services, raw materials, markets, and production methods and Organisations using new means, ends, or half-end relationships. Other authors see entrepreneurship in a more revolutionary and transformative way in the social and institutional spheres (Rindova et al., 2009). These examples demonstrate that fundamentally different understandings permeate research in the field and create difficulties for research and field developments due to a lack of consensus on, after all, what entrepreneurship is (Lopes *et al.,* 2019).

There are multiple concepts of "entrepreneur" and "entrepreneurship" arising from various ways of thinking. Entrepreneurship is defined as the search for opportunities beyond the resources you currently control (Stevenson, 2004; Carlsson, 2013). Thus, the dialogue and the relaxation of the convictions of each one, represent the phenomenon necessary, like exchange and combination of knowledge to know the whole. An advance to build such a dialogue is explaining at least part of the varied understandings present in the field, which need to be considered as a whole (Lopes et al., 2019).

Despite the wide variation of understandings and concepts, Davidsson (2016) believes that the multiple ways of understanding entrepreneurship tend to accommodate two definitions: (1) entrepreneurship is the creation (or attempt to create) a new activity economical; and (2) entrepreneurship is anything that concerns those who create and run their own businesses/companies/organisations. However, he recommends using the first of the two understandings, as it is the understanding that imposes itself as a trend in the field. In other words, for the author, more and more researchers are focused on understanding entrepreneurship as an effort to create a new economic activity (Davidsson, 2016; Wiklund et al., 2011).

To undertake is to identify opportunities and turn them into a profitable business. When an entrepreneur perceives a consumer need, he can create a way to solve the problem, offering a product or service that gives a better-quality experience to the customer. This solution can be turned into a business. Entrepreneurship is essential in societies; through it, companies seek innovation, transforming knowledge and ideas into new products placed on the market.

The Relationship between Open Innovation and its Importance in Entrepreneurship

The organizations expand their business, and with the increase in applied technology, organizations are looking for different ways to maintain business competitiveness and not lose their customers. Thus, the private and public sectors must innovate to meet market demand, as innovative activities become fundamental for business competitiveness.

Innovation itself is a necessary and fundamental means for sustainable economic development, creating new technologies and transforming the standard of living (Pinto, 2016; Turchi & Moraes, 2017). Innovation, when implemented, aims to increase the effectiveness and operational efficiency of organizations, that is, in the various business operations, marketing, human resources policies and organizational structure, whether in the way of management or how the administration is performed (Rauta, 2020).

In this way, innovation emerges as a decisive element in business action. For economists, innovation is like the engine of development; that is, it is perceived as a continuous process that seeks to add value, a new opportunity to differentiate and have creative thinking in the face of changes, employing dynamic knowledge in the way of thinking (Lu et al., 2019). The concept of innovation is seen as one that adds, increases or develops improvements in products, processes or services, acquiring a gain in productivity or quality that results in greater competitiveness in the market (ANPEI, 2017; Aquino, 2018).

The application of innovation takes place fundamentally in the combination of information and knowledge elements; it is in the interaction and sharing of these elements which leads to new knowledge for the development of new products, services and innovative processes (Lu et al., 2019). However, developing a culture of innovation is necessary, seeking to expand the interaction between all innovation systems, focusing on behaviour patterns (Azevedo, 2017, 2018).

Organizations do not innovate alone; they depend on internal and external information and knowledge, thus the reference to the open innovation model (Open Innovation) emerges. Thus, collaborative activities have moved from a closed to an open innovation strategy (Park & Kwon, 2018). The open innovation model considers the collaboration between different social actors, aiming to channel innovative ideas and research knowledge outside organization s. as part of its innovation process (Zien & Buckler, 1997; Chesbrough, 2006; Dodgson et al., 2006; Lu et al., 2019).

However, open innovation means the generation and use of ideas internally and externally in organizations (Chesbrough, 2006; Dodgson et al., 2006; Zien & Buckler, 1997). Open innovation can be defined as the use of purposive inflows and outflows of knowledge in the organization, to accelerate internal innovation, and expand the markets for external use of innovation, respectively (Chesbrough, 2006; Chesbrough et al., 2006). It can also be defined as an interpellation in which the innovation process involves exploration, knowledge and internal and external continuity of the organization (Lichtenthaler, 2011).

The open innovation model involves strategic networks, alliances and partnerships that collaborate both in the innovation process and in the conception of knowledge and reduction of invested risks (Haubert et al., 2019). Open innovation becomes an essential form of competitiveness for some business sectors, such as information technology (Chesbrough, 2006; Dodgson et al., 2006; Zien & Buckler, 1997).

Open innovation is a paradigm where organizations can and need to use external experiences; it is necessary to combine internal and external knowledge to develop innovative processes and products (Chesbrough et al., 2006). Second, Jackson & Richter (2017), open innovation is an innovative structure that suggests that organizations search for new technologies, new ideas, markets, and business models.

Therefore, the meaning of open innovation is to be observing the interaction of the market, and the best opportunities can be acquired outside the company (Chesbrough, 2012). In this way, open innovation reveals a new mental model, and the sharing of intellectual property among cooperating organizations is one of the purposes and a challenge (Haubert et al., 2019).

Thus, how technological complexity grows and organizations seek to reduce risks, costs, and the time for the development of innovations, there is soon an increase in business interest regarding the use of open innovation (Lazzarotti et al., 2017). The open innovation model is intended for the organization to create partnerships with research institutes, universities, students, and small specialized companies (Freitas et al., 2017). The variety of ideas and the exchange between organizations and universities, governments and research centres allow the management of pre-existing external sources so that organizations can renew themselves in a more dynamic and accessible way, revealing a new perspective and new trends for organizations (Chesbrough, 2012).

The use of open innovation in companies in the United States and Europe is considered more than a fad, as they believe its use necessary, and 78% of the companies studied intensively adopt open innovation practices in processes than in 3 years. Before research (Chesbrough & Brunswicker, 2015). The literature also evolves concerning the external relations of organizations on the concept of open innovation and the measurement of the efficiency of the open innovation process (Thomas, 2018).

According to Fleming & Waguespack (2007) and Wasserman & Faust (1994), open innovation involves not fully structured activities that have not been tested empirically. Still, the relationships within and between organizations need to be aligned with the technological environment, objectives, skills, and social capital, which is very important for these interactions' success. For Chesbrough (2003), open innovation needs to be studied in organizations outside the USA. The initial definitions were based on North American culture and may differ from the existing companies in developing countries.

Therefore, open innovation is an essential strategy that organizations use to create competitive advantage, combining with internal and external resources, thus requiring collaboration to identify new paths and generate new technologies to continue competing in the market (Yun & Liu, 2019).

METHODOLOGY

Literature Survey: The Methodologic Approach

The present study is a bibliometric analysis. According to Liang and Liu (2018), it has been widely applied in library and information science studies and uses statistical tools to analyse studies published in academic. Bibliometrics is a research methodology characterised by descriptive statistics of citation data and network analysis of authors, years, journals, institutions, countries, and keywords. This article aims to expand the knowledge concerning related publications to Open Innovation and Entrepreneurship, based on the articles researched on the topic, in the last decade, in the Web of Science.

Rousseau (2001) and Camps et al. (2006) define Bibliometrics as a subject that allows a quantitative study of scientific production by analysing its nature and transfer of science in a specific period. Also, bibliometrics aims to evaluate the technical or scientific activity of a particular area of knowledge through a quantitative study of publications Silva (2004). According Modak et al. (2019) bibliometrics is a branch of science that aims to analyse bibliographic information in a quantitative way The growing number of articles and their research complexity has led to the creation of visualisation tools that can produce maps, graphs and diagrams to illuminate patterns, trends and processes, the CiteSpace. According to Chen et al. (2010), the CiteSpace is the most popular bibliometric visualization tool used in the current study, allowing the researcher to take time-series snapshots of the knowledge domain and merge these into a visual map. Additionally, different types of bibliometric networks can be constructed with CiteSpace: (1) cocitation networks of authors, documents and journals; (2) co-occurring author keywords and keywords plus; (3) co-authorship networks of authors; (4) co-authors' institutions and (5) co-authors' country.

Bibliometrics is according to Booksten (1979), can adopt various methods of analysis and is based on the laws of bibliometrics, Zipf (ranking of word frequency), Lotka (authors publishing in a specific discipline or author productivity) and the best-known Bradford (scattering of articles or journal productivity). In this way, based on the importance of knowing the most frequent keywords, the most productive authors, areas and journals, we seek to structure bibliometrics considering its contribution to the field of management (Zupic & Čater, 2015).

Sample Definition

The study basis consists in the Scientifics articles of bibliography data from one of the most renowned academic databases - ISI Web of Science (WoS), between the years 2011 and 2020,

To collect pertinent bibliography data, we perform a keyword search, Open innovation and Entrepreneurship, in the WoS database, one of the largest multidisciplinary databases comprising aspects of national and international abstracts and longitudinal studies were described in mars, 2021. The research was refined so that only scientific articles and books in the database are included with the keyword Open Innovation and Entrepreneurship. Excel spreadsheets were created to analyze data, to compare.

Data Collection Steps

This chapter was divided into two steps. In the first step, the terms Open Innovation and Entrepreneurship were placed in the research field of the WoS database, limited to the period between 2011 and 2020. Then, the overall features of the publications were surveyed. The ten-year interval was chosen because it is a recent interval that can advance the understanding of open innovation and entrepreneurship in a digital economy, such as the current one.

In the second step, analysis of the bibliometric networks built with CiteSpace.

In the third step, the most cited publications were considered and compared with the authors who published the most in the same period. The actions of the research are shown in Figure 1.

Then, the general characteristics of the publications were inventoried in the WoS database, and the articles with the highest number of citations were investigated in detail to increase knowledge on the subject under consideration.

Figure 1. Stages of research
Source: Own elaboration.

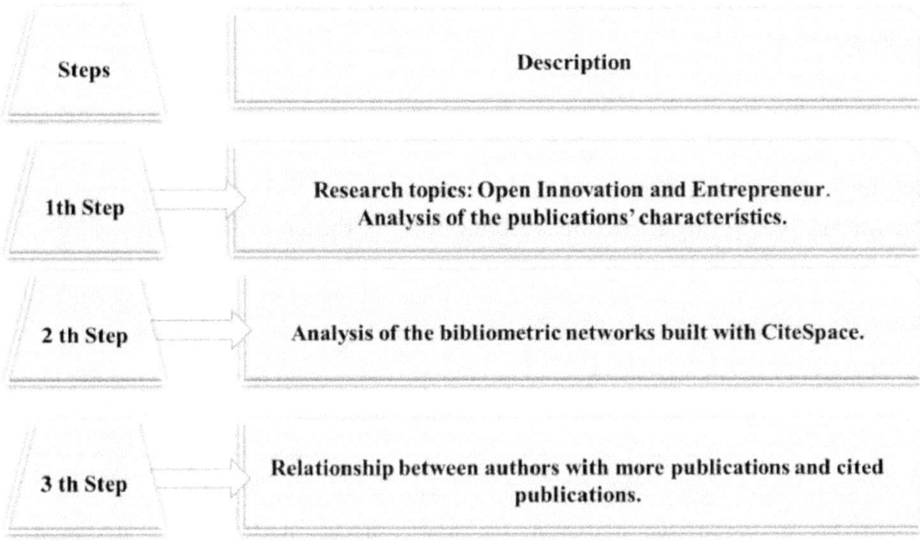

RESULTS

The research results showed the main features of scientific production related to the scope of the expression of the study.

Bibliometric analyses were performed using the Citespace program. The articles published between 2011 and 2020 were obtained from the Web of Science database (Web of Science Core Collection database maintained by Clarivate Analytics. Access date: March 2021) and submitted to analysis using bibliometric methods.

Bibliometric Analysis

Firstly, research was done on the topic "Open Innovation and Entrepreneurship", in the period defined for the study, in the Web of Science database. Four hundred twenty-nine publications were found. Thus, the following are the general characteristics of publications related to the theme according to the following categories: (1) Research areas, (2) Type of documents, (3) Annually published articles, (4) Prominent authors, (5) Source Title, (6) Main Institutions, (7) Main countries, (8) Main languages, (9) Keywords, and then the number of publications per author and the number of citations will be displayed.

Secondly, Network Analysis. CiteSpace was programmed with the following standards: timespan from 2011 to 2020; node type: subject category, countries, authors cited, journals, documents cited, keyword; criterion: 50 articles most cited articles per year.

Research Areas

Regarding the primary Research Areas in Open Innovation and Entrepreneurship publications, we highlight Business Economics as shown in Table 1.

Table 1. Distribution of articles by research areas

Research Areas	Total
Business Economics	293
Engineering	48
Public Administration	27
Science Technology Other Topics	27
Computer Science	26
Education Educational Research	26
Information Science Library Science	24
Environmental Sciences Ecology	23
Social Sciences Other Topics	21
Operations Research Management Science	17
Total	532

Source: Own elaboration.

The type of document published was analysed (Figure 5), standing out the articles' publication, representing 74,94% of the total records found in the Web of Science database. This means that the studies in this field of research are interdisciplinary. Different areas of research activities in a relational way in the construction of knowledge. In addition, the field is multidisciplinary, since multiple areas form it.

There is a Web of Science citation index where each author's cited documents and the documents quoted by them are mentioned (Figure 2).

Open innovation studies are mostly empirical articles (71%), published in peer-reviewed journals. 25% of the articles come from works approved in events and congresses, and the rest is composed of theoretical articles that seek to build theory in this field of study.

Figure 2. Distribution of articles by type of publication
Source: Own elaboration.

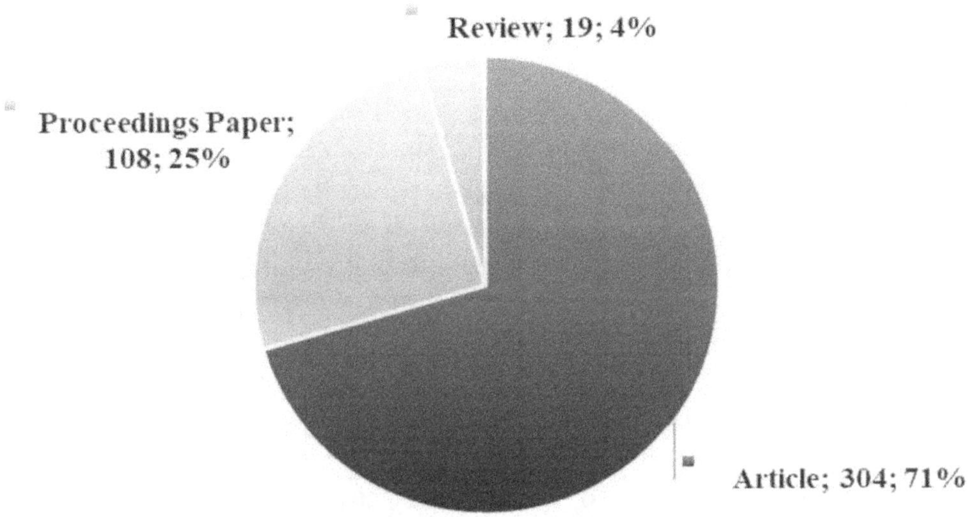

Annually Published Articles

According to Figure 3, it is possible to follow the growth of the publications. The years with the highest productivity were 2017 and 2020. Considering the number of publications, publications on open innovation and entrepreneurship appear increasingly, with significant growth since 2015, which shows the academic interest in the area and its progressive prominence in scientific studies.

Figure 3. Publications distributed per year
Source: Own elaboration.

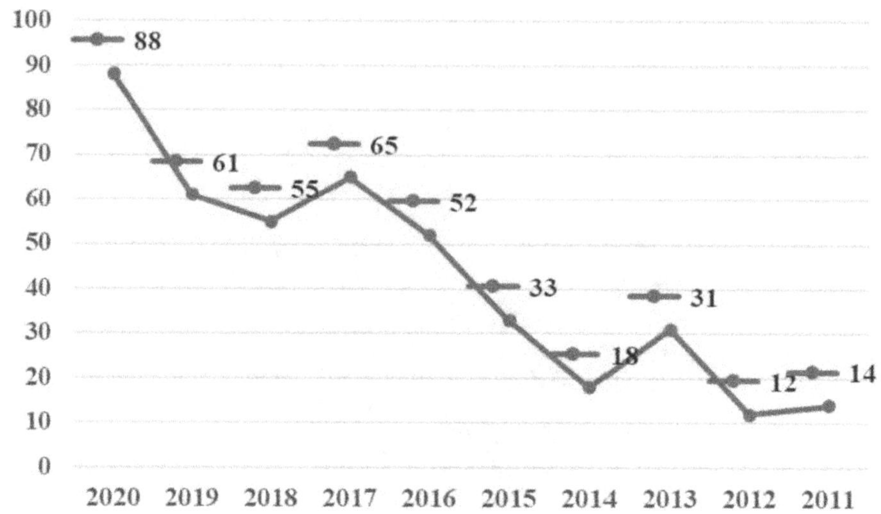

Main Authors

Table 2 presents the prominent authors who published articles related to Open Innovation and Entrepreneurship for the analyzed period. More relevant authors were not confirmed.

Table 2. Distribution of articles by authors

Author	Total
Yun, J.J.	10
Bogers, M.	8
Park, K.	7
Secundo, G.	5
Urbano, D.	5
Del Vecchio, P.	4
Miller, K.	4
Rangus, K.	4
Santoro, G.	4
Chaston, I.	3
Total	54

Source: Own elaboration.

The research showed that the author Yun, J.J. was the one who published the most research papers (10).

The author most dedicated to the subject is JinHyo Joseph Yun. The most cited work is the title "Entrepreneurial cyclical dynamics of open innovation", which addresses cases from Asia, such as South Korea and Japan, to discuss the entrepreneurial dynamics of open innovation. (Yun *et al.,* 2018). The author's most recent work addresses the culture of open innovation. Three types of culture for the dynamics of open innovation are discussed: leading culture of entrepreneurship, intrapreneurship and organizational entrepreneurship for open innovation dynamics (Yun *et al.,* 2020).

Type of Sources

Table 3 shows the prominent journals with the highest frequency of articles in the sample. In identifying the sources of publication, it was found that the journals with most scientific papers published, involving the theme, in Web of Science, stand out: Technological Forecasting and Social Change, International Entrepreneurship and Management Journal and Sustainability.

Table 3. Distribution of articles by source

Sources	Total
Technological Forecasting and Social Change	15
International Entrepreneurship and Management Journal	14
Sustainability	14
Service Industries Journal	9
Management Decision	8
R D Management	8
European Journal of Innovation Management	7
Industry and Innovation	7
International Journal of Innovation Management	7
Journal of Business Research	7
Total	96

Source: Own elaboration.

Table 3 shows the average number of citations calculated according to the proportion between the number of citations and publications. The most cited work of the "Technological Forecasting and Social Change" is by Popa *et al.* (2017), with

136 citations. Moderators, antecedents and results of the open innovation climate are discussed.

Main Organisations

The Organisations that most stood out and published works related to Open Innovation and Entrepreneurship are identified in Table 4.

Table 4. Distribution of articles by leading institutions

Organizations-Enhanced	Total	Organizations	Total
Daegu Gyeongbuk Institute of Science Technology DGIST	10	University of Salento	10
University of Salento	10	University of Copenhagen	9
University of California System	9	Daegu Gyeongbuk Institute of Science Technology DGIST	8
University of Copenhagen	9	University of California Berkeley	8
University of California Berkeley	8	Sangji University	6
Ramon Llull University	7	University of Cambridge8	6
University of Naples Federico II	7	Copenhagen Business School	5
University of Turin	7	Lappeenranta University of Technology	5
Autonomous University of Barcelona	6	Lulea University of Technology	5
ESADE Business School	6	Northumbria University	5
Total	79		67

Source: Own elaboration.

Active Organisation Table 4 show the ten mains' Organizations and Organizations-Enhanced that produced the most significant number of publications on the subject of study. Table 4 also shows a dominant organization in the group, the Daegu Gyeongbuk Institute of Science Technology DGIST and the University of Salento, with ten publications. The University of Salento, University of Turin, both in Italy, and the Autonomous University of Barcelona in Spain correspond to the authors with the highest productivity, are the origins institutions of Secundo, G., Santoro, G., and Urbano, D., respectively.

Main Countries

The number of articles distributed by significant countries is shown in Table 5 in the research area Open Innovation and Entrepreneurship.

Table 5. Distribution of articles by country

Country	Total
Italy	60
Spain	57
England	55
USA	52
Germany	34
China	26
Finland	22
Sweden	21
France	19
South Korea	18
Denmark	17
Switzerland	15
Australia	14
Portugal	14
Netherlands	12
Total	436

Source: Own elaboration.

Italy was the country that contributed most in the Research area of Open Innovation and Entrepreneurship with 60 publications, was followed by Spain, England, USA. Except for China, all the countries whose authors publish the most on the subject are part of the OECD, which shows that the debate on entrepreneurship and open innovation seems to interest economic and social development.

Main Languages

Most papers published in the study area are published in English, 420 in the Web of Science, as shown in Table 6, corresponding to 97,90% of the works.

Table 6. Distribution of articles by language

Language	Total
English	420
Spanish	4
Russian	2
Chinese	1
Lithuanian	1
Polish	1
Total	429

Source: Own elaboration.

English remains the priority language through which publications are carried out.

Relationship among the Most Cited Articles

Articles with a higher number of citations were identified and had a more significant influence in the area; these works are described in Table 7, ordered by the number of citations.

Table 7 shows the references of ten articles, most cited in the database, resulting from the research carried out for Open Innovation and Entrepreneurship.

Table 7. Articles in the number of citations (WoS)

TC	AY	Title	Author	Journal	Year
246	49,20	The open innovation research landscape: established perspectives and emerging themes across different levels of analysis	Bogers et. al.	Industry and Innovation 24(1), 8-40	2017
150	18,75	When Is Open Innovation Beneficial? The Role of Strategic Orientation	Cheng et. al.	Journal of Product Innovation Management 31(6), 1235-1253	2014
99	19,80	Antecedents, moderators, and outcomes of innovation climate and open innovation: An empirical study in SMEs	Popa et. al.	Technological Forecasting and Social Change 118, 134-142	2017
81	8,10	Entrepreneurship and open innovation in an emerging economy	Chaston, Ian; Scott, Gregory J.	Management Decision 50, 1161-1177	2012
80	8,00	Value creation by knowledge-based ecosystems: evidence from a field study	Van der Borgh et. al.	R & D Management 42(2), 150-169	2012

Continued on following page

Table 7 Continued

TC	AY	Title	Author	Journal	Year
80	7,27	Managing knowledge assets under conditions of radical change: The case of the pharmaceutical industry	Allarakhia, Minna; Steven, Walsh	Technovation 31, 105-117	2011
78	19,50	Coworking-spaces: how a phenomenon of the sharing economy builds a novel trend for the workplace and for entrepreneurship	Bouncken et. al.	Review of Managerial Science 12(1), 317-334	2018
76	19,00	Blockchain tokens and the potential democratisation of entrepreneurship and innovation	Chen, Yan	Business Horizons 61(4), 567-575	2018
74	12,33	Corporate accelerators: Building bridges between corporations and startups	Kohler, Thomas	Business Horizons 59(3), 347-357	2016
70	7,78	Socio-cultural factors and female entrepreneurship	Noguera et. al.	Int. Entrepreneurship and Management Journal 9(2), 183-197	2013

Notes: TC- Total citations; AY - Average per year
Source: Own elaboration.

In 2017 and 2014, two publications stand out, which obtained the highest number of citations, as shown in Table 14, showing that researchers in the area found them essential.

The survey in the database showed the article, The open innovation research landscape: established perspectives and emerging themes across different levels of analysis, published in the Industry and Innovation, written by Bogers, Marcel; Zobel, Ann-Kristin; Afuah, Allan; Almirall, Esteve; Brunswicker, Sabine; Dahlander, Linus; Frederiksen, Lars; Gawer, Annabelle; Gruber, Marc; Haefliger, Stefan; Hagedoorn, John; Hilgers, Dennis; Laursen, Keld; Magnusson, Mats G.; Majchrzak, Ann; McCarthy, Ian P.; Moeslein, Kathrin M. and Nambisan, Satish, in the year 2017, is ranked in the 1st position with 246 citations.

Network Analysis

Research Categories

The subject categories reveal the research areas with the most prominence in studies on open innovation. In this sense, according to Figure 4, the main research areas according to the number of citations are business & economics, management, business, engineering, and computer science. These areas have a purple ring around them, which shows the high centrality of intermediation; they are areas of knowledge that act as bridges of connection between other areas (Chen, 2006, 2016; Huang et al., 2020).

Figure 4. Research categories
Source: Own elaboration.

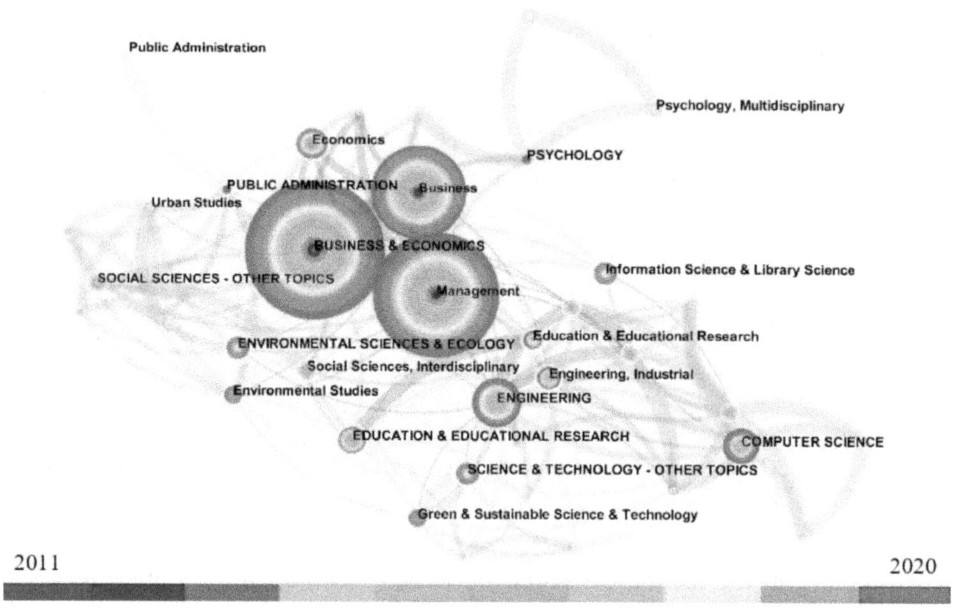

In addition, the colours of the edges represent the recentness of the relationships so that the "hotter" colours (yellow, orange, red) represent newer relationships. The relationships closest to the first years of the survey (2011), on the other hand, are more incredible colours, such as purple and blue. In this sense, the most recent relationships are established between psychology and public administration. The oldest relationships are established between education, economics, and engineering.

The areas in the red show an explosion of citations in the period; that is, they experience a sudden increase in the level of citations in a given period. They are green & sustainable Science and technology, Science & technology, education & educational research, environmental studies, environmental sciences & ecology, information science & library science, economics, and public administration.

The network has 49 nodes (subject categories) and 204 edges; each node relates approximately four times in terms of average. The network density is 0.1735 in a total of 1. Therefore, it can be considered low, implying the need to establish a higher level of interaction and relationships between the areas (Liu, 2011; Najberg et al., 2020).

Open innovation and entrepreneurship are multidisciplinary fields, as it has multiple research areas dedicated to the subject. In addition, it is a field marked by interdisciplinarity, in which the areas are interconnected with each other, whose researchers are in constant dialogue for the construction of scientific knowledge. The different subject categories represent specific approaches of each discipline for open innovation and entrepreneurship (Schoepflin & Glänzel, 2001).

Countries

The countries related to the studies' authors reflect possible places of dedication to open innovation and entrepreneurship. In this sense, Figure 5 shows the network of countries to which the authors are linked.

Figure 5 shows that the relationships between authors from different countries are primarily recent because the edges are mainly red. Older relationships are between countries like the United States and Canada; the United States and China; the United States and Portugal; Spain, Denmark, Colombia; England, Ireland, and Brazil.

The most significant nodes in the network represent the most prominent countries in terms of the number of citations: England, the United States, and Spain are predominant in terms of citations, present the most significant centrality of intermediation in the network, a fact demonstrated by the presence of the purple ring. As shown previously, the centrality of intermediation indicates that the authors of these countries are actors that connect other nodes in the network. Therefore, they establish publication networks between researchers from different countries in this case.

Countries with red nodes have an explosion of citations in some period, denoting the importance of their studies for the field.

The network is composed of 42 nodes (countries), 150 edges (relationships), and a density of 0.1742, which, like the network of subject categories, can also be considered low. In this sense, there is an opportunity to improve relationships between researchers of open innovation and entrepreneurship. An opportunity for improvement for studies in the area would be the increase in the density of the network of countries, which would reflect a more significant number of relationships between authors from different nations, which in turn would favour an increase in the flow of information (Najberg et al. al., 2020; Zhang & Fang, 2018). Thus, collective and collaborative research seems to be essential to make research in the context of open innovation and entrepreneurship increasingly robust (Huizingh, 2011).

Figure 5. Countries of the authors of the articles
Source: Own elaboration.

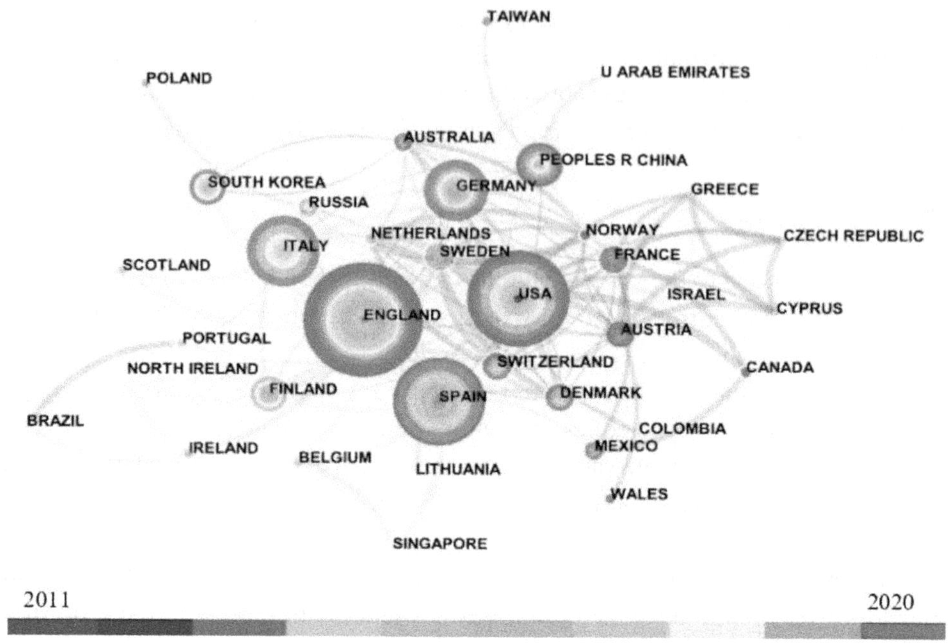

Authors of Articles

Figure 6 reveals the relationships established between the authors of the articles. The network of authors of the works is a network with many structural holes. Structural holes are interruptions in the flow of information between network nodes and given this relationship gap, each actor has access to different data flows within the network (Ahuja, 2000).

We understand that a network of authors with fewer structural holes is more beneficial for the field of open innovation and entrepreneurship studies (Ahuja, 2000; Burt, 2004). This is because denser and more connected research networks among authors could promote greater trust, productivity and resource sharing.

The network of authors is formed by 47 nodes and 36 edges, with a density of 0.0333. Among the networks presented in this work, this network has the lowest density, favouring the understanding that more partnerships can be established between researchers and different research groups.

The most prominent links within the network are established between the author's Paul Melo, Renata Martins Correa, Arnoldo José, and Bill O'Gorman. The oldest partnership between authors is based between David Urbano and Claudia Alvarez.

The most recent is the pairs Anna Claudia Pellicelli and Gabriele Santoro, as well as Pasquale-del-Vechio and Giustina Secundo.

It is essential to highlight that establishing a more significant number of links between authors can improve the field of studies in open innovation, which will favour the exchange of knowledge, and therefore, the advancement of the area.

Figure 6. Authors of articles
Source: Own elaboration.

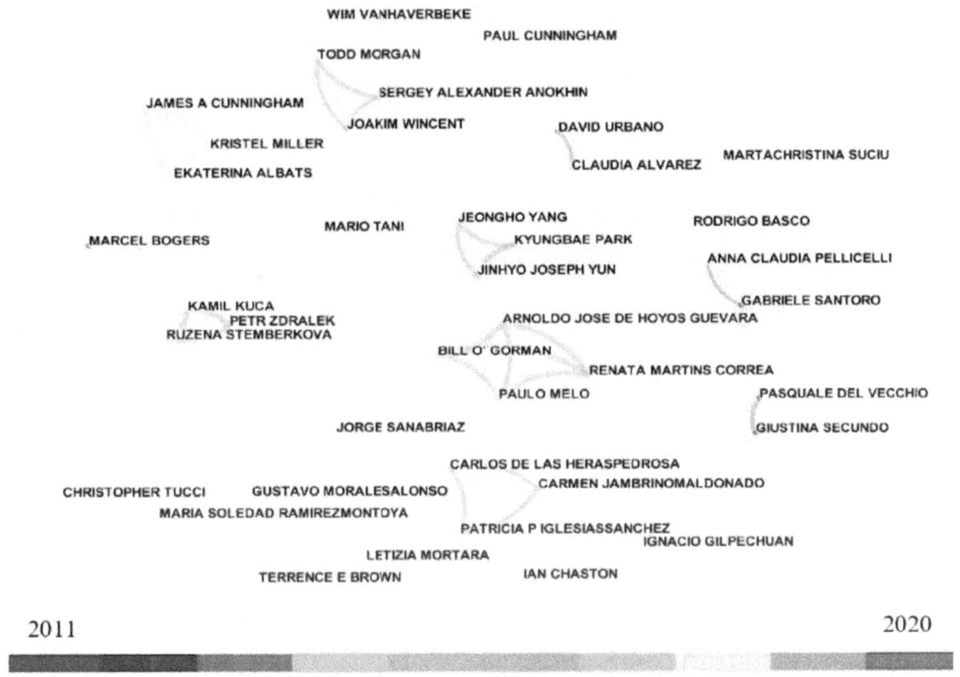

Journals

The network consists of 164 nodes, 352 edges, and a density of 0.0263. The low density can demonstrate that few journals concentrate the majority of the network's relationships. Visually, this can be identified through the dense and concentrated relationships established between the publications of the Small Business Economics, Entrepreneurship Theory and Practice, European Journal of Innovation Management, Journal of Business Research, Open Innovation: Research, Practices, and Policies, Harvard journals Business Review, among others.

The journals are generally related to innovation, management, technology, research and development, and entrepreneurship, and therefore retain their identity with the fields of open innovation and entrepreneurship.

The journals most cited in studies on open innovation and entrepreneurship are shown in Figure 7.

Figure 7. Main journals
Source: Own elaboration.

Works that Underpin the Studies

Considering that the documents raised represent a repository of knowledge, the analysis of the quotation of documents is a means by which it is possible to know the structure of a field of knowledge (Chen & Liu, 2020).

The network in Figure 8 shows the works most found in the references that made up our sample. The methodology used was the analysis of the document co-citation network to identify thematic groups in the research of open innovation and entrepreneurship and the relationships established between them.

Thus, the network contains the works most cited by researchers, making up the theoretical and empirical body on open innovation and entrepreneurship. In addition, the paper is divided into thematic clusters.

The network comprises 453 nodes, 1773 edges and has a density of 0.0173. The papers with the highest citation count and therefore have the most significant nodes are Dahlander and Gann (2010), Huizingh (2011), West and Bogers (2014), Parida et al. (2012), Chesbrough and Bogers (2014), Perkmann et al. (2013). It is possible to say that these are the works most mentioned by researchers in studies on open innovation and entrepreneurship. The works with greater intermediation centrality are Chaston and Scott (2012), Eftekhari and Bogers (2015), Parida et al. (2012), Perkmann et al. (2013), and West and Bogers (2014). For that reason, they represent bridges of connection between different works.

The most prominent thematic clusters in the studies labelled based on the keywords are innovation performance, science and technology, knowledge, business model, and ecosystem. Such themes are recurrent in the keywords of the works and may represent researchers' inclinations and interests in sub-themes within the field of open innovation and entrepreneurship. In addition, colours represent the years in which relationships were established so that clusters with warmer colours (red) are more recent clusters, and clusters with colder colours (blue) represent older relationships. Thereby. The essential authors about the number of citations (large nodes) emerged in clusters of more recent relationships (green, orange, red).

Figure 8. Works that underpin the studies
Source: Own elaboration.

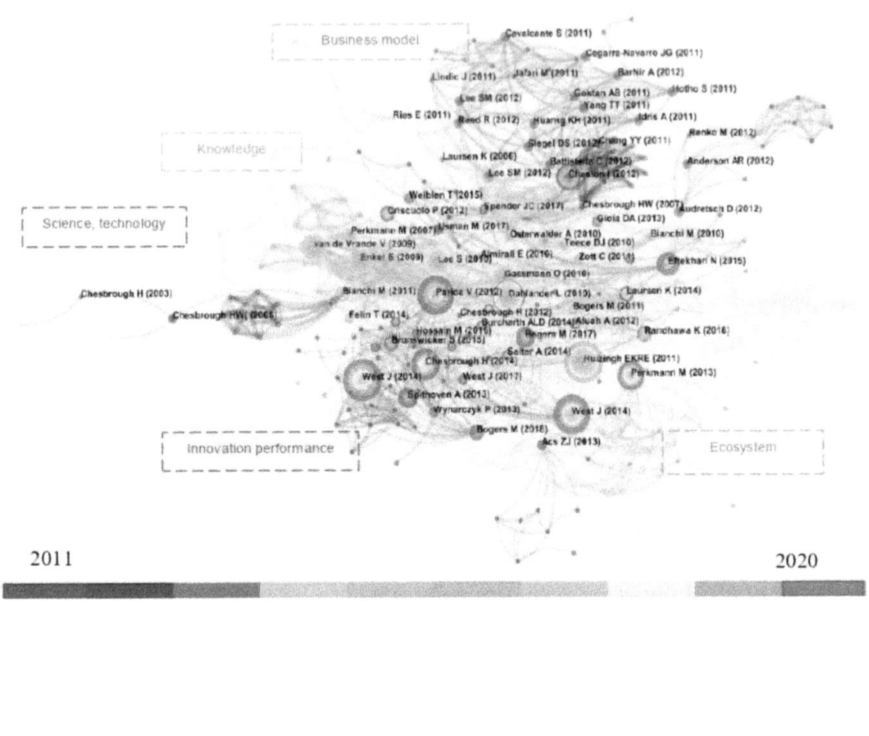

Main Keywords

According to Figure 9, the most frequent keywords in studies on open innovation and entrepreneurship are open innovation, entrepreneurship, technology, performance, research and development, SME - small-medium enterprise, capability, absorptive capacity, exploration, exploitation, collaboration, co-creation, competitive advantage, incubator, knowledge transfer, dynamic ability, high tech, among others. In general, we realize that the main keywords involve business strategy themes in dynamic environments.

The colours of the edges in red reveal that the most recent words encompass, for example, incubators, competitive advantage, startup, exploration and exploitation. This demonstrates the importance of open innovation and entrepreneurship for the development of the digital economy, especially concerning the promotion of startups and incubators. Startups are also important for sustainable development (Sunny & Shu, 2019), and for this reason, learning new skills (absorptive capacity) is fundamental for organizational survival, business performance, and society's improvement.

Figure 9. Main keywords
Source: Own elaboration.

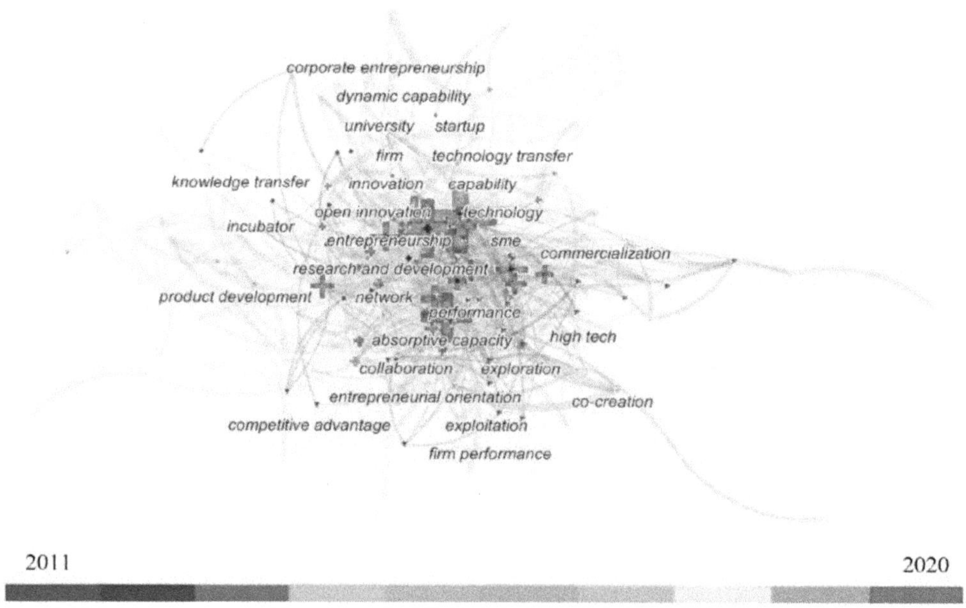

FINAL CONSIDERATIONS

The present paper aims to provide an overview of the publications landscape and knowledge structures for the research on Open Innovation and Entrepreneurship. The research results identified the main characteristics of scientific production in the period under the themes in study. After refining the search for the categories, it was decided to present only the articles that determine the year with the highest number of publications.

There is a multiplicity and diversity as to the authors who have published the most on the topic, a Yun, JJ research with ten articles stands out, and the Institute of Science and Technology DGIST and the University of Salento were found with ten publications. In addition, the country that published the most on the subject was Italy (60) papers.

Bibliometric analysis using CiteSpace reveals its potential to analyse the evolution of Open Innovation and Entrepreneurship in the last ten years. It was possible to identify that the areas that stood out were green and sustainable science, technology science, and technology. As far as the countries are concerned, the most significant nodes in terms of citation are England, the United States, and Spain.

Concerning the authors, the most prominent links in the network are between the author's Paul Melo, Renata Martins Correa, Arnoldo José, and Bill O'Gorman. Regarding the most published journals, it appears that few journals concentrate most of the network's relationships, such as Small Business Economics, Entrepreneurship Theory, and Practice, European Journal of Innovation Management.

The results cover previous bibliometric research studies of Open Innovation and Entrepreneurship combining co-citation analysis and keyword co-occurrence to understand the development of this field from different perspectives. The bibliometric visualization used in the second part of this article provides fundamental time data for country co-authorship, citation of articles, journals, and co-occurrence of keywords, adding a new dimension to the analysis and providing insights into the flow of the main trends and collaborations. Finally, co-occurrence analysis detected the most frequent keywords and identified emerging research trends and topics.

Thus, it is suggested for future research to select articles on national and international bases to compare results; use different search terms; perform the search for abstracts and keywords; carry out the bibliometric analysis of the references of the most cited articles, analyse other points different from those surveyed in the present study, such as: what are the emerging themes Open Innovation in entrepreneurship and corporate social responsibility and in which contexts, to analyse other contents different from those surveyed in this study.

Among other limitations of this study, we have: the information presented is limited to the articles selected only on an international basis, the search was carried out only by the title of the articles; bibliometric analysis is limited to authors, articles, years of publication, funding agencies, sources, institutions, countries, language and period.

It is an article with an excellent contribution to knowledge informing exciting facts on what CiteSpace can perform: Intellectual structure, emerging trends, and future research opportunities in Open Innovation and Entrepreneurship.

REFERENCES

Ahuja, G. (2000). Collaboration Networks, Structural Holes, and Innovation: A Longitudinal Study. *Administrative Science Quarterly*, *45*(3), 425–455. doi:10.2307/2667105

ANPEI. (2017). *Guia da Lei do Bem: o que é inovação para a Lei do Bem? Conheça o principal instrumento de fomento à inovação em empresas do Brasil*. Letras & Artes Comunicação.

Aquino, Y. (2018). *Governo regulamenta Marco Legal da Ciência*. Tecnologia e Inovação, Brasília, 8 fev. Agência Brasil.

Azevedo, C. E. F. (2017). *Incremento da cultura de inovação: passo essencial para o desenvolvimento da base industrial de defesa e ampliação do poder dissuasório*. Trabalho de Conclusão de Curso – Escola Superior de Guerra.

Azevedo, C.E.F. (2018). Os elementos de análise da cultura de inovação no setor de Defesa e seu modelo tridimensional. *Coleção Meira Mattos: revista das ciências militares*, *12*(45), 145-167.

Baggio, A. F., & Baggio, D. K. (2015). Empreendedorismo: Conceitos e definições. *Revista de empreendedorismo, inovação e tecnologia, 1*(1), 25-38.

Bogers, M., Chesbrough, H., & Moedas, C. (2018). Open Innovation: Research, Practices, and Policies. *California Management Review*, *60*(2), 5–16. doi:10.1177/0008125617745086

Bogers, M., Foss, N. J., & Lyngsie, J. (2018). The human side of open innovation: The role of employee diversity in firm-level openness. *Research Policy*, *47*(1), 218–223. doi:10.1016/j.respol.2017.10.012

Bogers, M., Zobel, A.-K., Afuah, A., Almirall, E., Brunswicker, S., Dahlander, L., Frederiksen, L., Gawer, A., Gruber, M., Haefliger, S., Hagedoorn, J., Hilgers, D., Laursen, K., Magnusson, M. G., Majchrzak, A., McCarthy, I. P., Moeslein, K. M., Nambisan, S., Piller, F. T., ... Ter Wal, A. L. J. (2017). The open innovation research landscape: Established perspectives and emerging themes across different levels of analysis. *Industry and Innovation*, *24*(1), 8–40. doi:10.1080/13662716.2016.1240068

Booksten, A. (1979). Explanations of the bibliometric distributions. *Collect Mange Summer-Fall*, *3*(2-3), 151–162. doi:10.1300/J105v03n02_04

Braga, M. N., Leite, M. M., & Felix, E. S. (2018). Empreendedorismo e gestão de mudanças como fator de desenvolvimento: Uma pesquisa de campo com os ambulantes do setor alimentício na cidade de Juazeiro do Norte–CE. *Revista Livre de Sustentabilidade e Empreendedorismo*, *3*(2), 48–76.

Burt, R. S. (2004). Structural holes and good ideas. *American Journal of Sociology*, *110*(2), 349–399. doi:10.1086/421787

Camps, D., Samar, M. E., Ávila, R. E., & Recuero, Y. (2006). Estudio bibliométrico de un volumen de la *revista Archivos de Medicina. Archives of Medicine*, *2*(3), 1–6.

Carlsson, B., Braunerhjelm, P., McKelvey, M., Olofsson, C., Persson, L., & Ylinenpää, H. (2013). The evolving domain of entrepreneurship research. *Small Business Economics*, *41*(4).

Castro, G. C., de Araujo, L. M., & Carvalho, P. K. F. (2021). Educação Empreendedora: Utilização das redes sociais como ferramentas potenciadoras do Marketing Digital em micro e pequenas empresas na cidade de Codó-MA. *Brazilian Journal of Development, Curitiba*, *7*(4), 41523–41534.

Chaston, I., & Scott, G. J. (2012). Entrepreneurship and open innovation in an emerging economy. *Management Decision*, *50*(7), 1161–1177. doi:10.1108/00251741211246941

Chen, C. (2006). CiteSpace II: Detecting and Visualising Emerging Trends and Transient Patterns in Scientific Literature. *Journal of the American Society for Information Science and Technology*, *57*(3), 359–377. doi:10.1002/asi.20317

Chen, C. (2016). CiteSpace: A practical guide for scientific mapping literature. *Novinka. Computer Science, Technology and Applications*.

Chen, C., & Song, M. (2019). Visualising a field of research: A methodology of systematic scientometric *reviews. PLoS One*, *14*(10), e0223994. doi:10.1371/journal.pone.0223994 PMID:31671124

Chen, C., Ibekwe-SanJuan, F., & Hou, J. (2010). The structure and dynamics of cocitation clusters: A multiple-perspective cocitation analysis. *Journal of the American Society for Information Science and Technology*, *61*(7), 1386–1409. doi:10.1002/asi.21309

Chen, X., & Liu, Y. (2020). Visualisation analysis of high-speed railway research based on CiteSpace. *Transport Policy*, *85*(3), 1–17. doi:10.1016/j.tranpol.2019.10.004

Chesbrough, H., & Brunswicker, S. (2015). A Fad or a Phenomenon? The Adoption of Open Innovation Practices in Large Firms. *Research Technology Management*, *57*(2), 16–25.

Chesbrough, H. (2006). *Open business models: How to thrive in the new innovation landscape*. Harvard Business School Press.

Chesbrough, H. (2006). Open innovation: A new paradigm for understanding industrial innovation. In Open innovation: Researching a new paradigm. Oxford University Press.

Chesbrough, H. (2012). *Inovação aberta: como criar e lucrar com a tecnologia*. Bookman.

Chesbrough, H. W. (2003). *Open Innovation: The New Imperative for Creating and Profiting from Technology*. Harvard Business School Press.

Chesbrough, H., & Bogers, M. (2014). Explicating Open Innovation Clarifying an Emerging Paradigm for Understanding Innovation. Oxford University Press.

Chesbrough, H., Vanhaverbeke, W., & West, J. (2006). *Open innovation: Researching a new paradigm*. Oxford University Press.

Chesbrough, H. W. (2017). The future of open innovation: The future of open innovation is more extensive, more collaborative, and more engaged with a wider variety of participants. *Research Technology Management*, *60*(1), 35–38. doi:10.1080/08956308.2017.1255054

Dahlander, L., & Gann, D. M. (2010). How open is innovation? *Research Policy*, *39*(6), 699–709. doi:10.1016/j.respol.2010.01.013

Davidsson, P. (2016). A "business researcher" view on opportunities for psychology in entrepreneurship research. *The Journal of Applied Psychology*, *65*(3), 628–636. doi:10.1111/apps.12071

Dodgson, M., Gann, D., & Salter, A. (2006). The role of technology in the shift towards open innovation: The case of Procter & Gamble. *R & D Management, 36*(3), 333–346. doi:10.1111/j.1467-9310.2006.00429.x

Dornelas, J. (2016). *Empreendedorismo: transformando ideias em negócios* (Vol. 6). Atlas.

Eckhardt, J. T., & Shane, S. A. (2003). Opportunities and entrepreneurship. *Journal of Management, 29*(3), 333–349. doi:10.1177/014920630302900304

Eftekhari, N., & Bogers, M. (2015). Open for Entrepreneurship: How Open Innovation Can Foster New Venture Creation. *Creativity and Innovation Management, 24*(4), 574–584. doi:10.1111/caim.12136

Fleming, L., & Waguespack, D. M. (2007). Brokerage, boundary spanning, and leadership in open innovation communities. *Organization Science, 18*(2), 165–180. doi:10.1287/orsc.1060.0242

Freel, M., & Robson, P. J. (2017). Appropriation strategies and open innovation in SMEs. *International Small Business Journal, 35*(5), 578–596. doi:10.1177/0266242616654957

Freitas, A. S., Filardi, F., Lott, A. C. O., & Braga, D. (2017). Inovação Aberta nas Empresas Brasileiras: Uma Análise da Produção Acadêmica no Período de 2003 a 2016. *Revista Ibero-Americana de Estratégia, 16*(3), 22–38. doi:10.5585/riae.v16i3.2497

Haubert, B., Schreiber, D., & Cristiano, M. P. (2019). Combinando o design thinking e a criatividade no processo de inovação aberta. *Gestão & Planejamento, 20*, 73–89. doi:10.21714/2178-8030gep.v.20.4823

Henttonen, K., & Lehtimäki, H. (2017). Open innovation in SMEs: Collaboration modes and strategies for commercialisation in technology-intensive companies in the forestry industry. *European Journal of Innovation Management, 20*(2), 329–347. doi:10.1108/EJIM-06-2015-0047

Hisrich, R. D., & Peter, M. P. (2004). *Empreendedorismo*. Bookman.

Huang, L., Zhou, M., Lv, J., & Chen, K. (2020). Trends in global research in forest carbon sequestration: A bibliometric analysis. *Journal of Cleaner Production, 252*, 1–17. doi:10.1016/j.jclepro.2019.119908

Huizingh, E. K. R. E. (2011). Open innovation: State of the art and future perspectives. *Technovation, 31*(1), 2–9. doi:10.1016/j.technovation.2010.10.002

Lauritzen, G. D., & Karafyllia, M. (2019). Perspective: Leveraging open innovation through paradox. *Journal of Product Innovation Management*, *36*(1), 107–121. doi:10.1111/jpim.12474

Lazzarotti, V., Bengtsson, L., Manzini, R., Pellegrini, L., & Rippa, P. (2017). Openness and innovation performance: An empirical analysis of openness determinants and performance mediators. *European Journal of Innovation Management*, *20*(3), 463–492. doi:10.1108/EJIM-06-2016-0061

Li, P.-Y., & Huang, K.-F. (2019). The antecedents of innovation performance: The moderating role of top management team diversity. *Baltic Journal of Management*, *14*(2), 291–311. doi:10.1108/BJM-07-2017-0202

Liang, T. P., & Liu, Y. H. (2018). Research Landscape of Business Intelligence and Big Data analytics: A Bibliometrics Study. *Expert Systems with Applications*, *111*, 2–10. doi:10.1016/j.eswa.2018.05.018

Lichtenthaler, U. (2011). Open innovation: Past research, current debates, and future directions. *The Academy of Management Perspectives*, *25*(1), 75–93.

Liu, C. H. (2011). The effects of innovation alliance on network structure and density of cluster. *Expert Systems with Applications*, *38*(1), 299–305. doi:10.1016/j.eswa.2010.06.064

Lopes, R., Almeida, M., & Lima, E. (2019). Desafios atuais e caminhos promissores para a pesquisa em empreendedorismo. *Revista de Administração de Empresas*, *59*(4), 284–292. doi:10.15900034-759020190406

Lu, Y. C., Matui, N., & Gracioso, L. (2019). Definição da inovação no âmbito da pesquisa brasileira: uma análise semântica. Revista Digital Biblioteconomia e Ciência da Informação, 17, 1-22.

Modak, N. M., Merigó, J. M., Weber, R., Manzor, F., & Ortúzar, J. D. D. (2019). Fifty years of Transportation Research journals: A bibliometric overview. *Transportation Research Part A, Policy and Practice*, *120*, 188–223. doi:10.1016/j.tra.2018.11.015

Najberg, E., Carvallho, J. B., Campos, W. Y. Y. Z., Rodriguez, M. V. R., & Bilhim, J. A. F. (2020). Higher education and professionalization of creative workers: State of the art. *Diálogo Com a Economia Criativa*, *5*(15), 33–57. doi:10.22398/2525-2828.51533-57

Pan Fagerlin, W., & Wang, Y. (2021). Top managers' communication efforts as a response to tensions in product innovation: An attention-based view. *Baltic Journal of Management*, *16*(1), 21–45. doi:10.1108/BJM-01-2020-0024

Parida, V., Westerberg, M., & Frishammar, J. (2012). Inbound Open Innovation Activities in High-Tech SMEs: The Impact on Innovation Performance. *Journal of Small Business Management*, *50*(2), 283–309. doi:10.1111/j.1540-627X.2012.00354.x

Park, E., & Kwon, S. J. (2018). Effects of innovation types on firm performance: An empirical approach in South Korean manufacturing industry. International. *Journal of Business Innovation and Research.*, *15*(2), 215–230. doi:10.1504/IJBIR.2018.089144

Perkmann, M., Tartari, V., McKelvey, M., Autio, E., Broström, A., D'Este, P., Fini, R., Geuna, A., Grimaldi, R., Hughes, A., Krabel, S., Kitson, M., Llerena, P., Lissoni, F., Salter, A., & Sobrero, M. (2013). Academic engagement and commercialisation: A review of the literature on university-industry relations. *Research Policy*, *42*(2), 423–442. doi:10.1016/j.respol.2012.09.007

Pinto, M. M. (2016). Tecnologia e inovação. b3. ed. rev. atual. – Florianópolis: Departamento de Ciências da Administração. UFSC.

Popa, S., Soto-Acosta, P., & Martinez-Conesa, I. (2017). Antecedents, moderators, and outcomes of innovation climate and open innovation: An empirical study in SMEs. *Technological Forecasting and Social Change*, *118*, 134–142. doi:10.1016/j.techfore.2017.02.014

Rauta, J. (2020). Ciência e movimento da inovação organizacional: um framework conceitual para diagnostico. *Revista de administração, sociedade e inovação*, *6*(2), 25-51.

Ribeiro, M. C., da Cruz, W. S., Procópio, J. G., & Soares, M. C. (2019). Características Empreendedoras dos Profissionais de Contabilidade de Um Município da Amazônia Paraense. *Revista Paraense de Contabilidade*, *4*(3), 64–77. doi:10.36562/rpc.v4i3.39

Rindova, V., Barry, D., & Ketchen, D. J. Jr. (2009). Entrepreneuring as emancipation. *Academy of Management Review*, *34*(3), 477–491. doi:10.5465/amr.2009.40632647

Rousseau, R. (2001). Indicadores bibliométricos y econométricos en la evaluación de instituciones científicas. *Acimed*, *9*(1), 50–60.

Santos, A. M., Acosta, A. C., Borghetti, L. B., & Balbinoti, S. G. (2016). Empreendedorismo: Inovação, criatividade e liderança. Revista Visão. *Gestão Organizacional*, *5*(1), 56–68.

Schoepflin, U., & Glänzel, W. (2001). Two decades of "Scientometrics", An interdisciplinary field represented by its leading journal. *Scientometrics*, *50*(2), 301–312. doi:10.1023/A:1010577824449

Schumpeter, J. (1982). Capitalismo, socialismo e democracia. Rio de Janeiro: Fundo de Cultura. (Original publication 1942)

Shane, S., & Venkataraman, S. (2000). The promise of entrepreneurship as a field of research. *Academy of Management Review*, *25*(1), 217–226. doi:10.5465/amr.2000.2791611

Sunny, S. A., & Shu, C. (2019). Investments, incentives, and innovation: Geographical clustering dynamics as drivers of sustainable entrepreneurship. *Small Business Economics*, *52*(4), 905–927. doi:10.100711187-017-9941-z

Thomas, E. (2018). From Closed to Open Innovation in Emerging Economies: Evidence from the Chemical Industry in Brazil. *Technology Innovation Management Review*, *8*(3), 26–37. doi:10.22215/timreview/1144

Turchi, L. M., & Morais, J. M. (2017). *Políticas de apoio à inovação tecnológica no Brasil: avanços recentes, limitações e propostas de ações*. Organizadores.

Van de Vrande, V., de Jong, J. P. J., Vanhaverbeke, W., & Rochemont, M. (2009). Open innovation in SMEs: Trends, motives and management challenges. *Technovation*, *29*(6-7), 423–437. doi:10.1016/j.technovation.2008.10.001

Vanhaverbeke, W. (2017). *Managing Open Innovation in SMEs*. Cambridge University Press. doi:10.1017/9781139680981

Wasserman, S., & Faust, K. (1994). *Social network analysis: Methods and applications*. Cambridge University Press. doi:10.1017/CBO9780511815478

West, J., & Bogers, M. (2014). Leveraging external sources of innovation: A review of research on open innovation. *Journal of Product Innovation Management*, *31*(4), 814–831. doi:10.1111/jpim.12125

West, J., Salter, A., Vanhaverbekec, W., & Chesbrough, H. (2014). Open innovation: The next decade. *Research Policy*, *43*(5), 805–811. doi:10.1016/j.respol.2014.03.001

Wiklund, J., Davidsson, P., Audretsch, D. B., & Karlsson, C. (2011). The future of entrepreneurship research. *Entrepreneurship Theory and Practice*, *35*(1), 1–9. doi:10.1111/j.1540-6520.2010.00420.x

Yun, J. H. J., Zhao, X., Jung, K. H., & Yigitcanlar, T. (2020). The culture for open innovation dynamics. *Sustainability*, *12*(12), 1–21. doi:10.3390u12125076

Yun, J. H. J., Won, D. K., & Park, K. B. (2018). Entrepreneurial cyclical dynamics of open innovation. *Journal of Evolutionary Economics*, *28*(5), 1151–1174. doi:10.100700191-018-0596-y

Yun, J. J., & Liu, Z. (2019). Micro-and macro-dynamics of open innovation with a quadruple-helix model. *Sustainability, 11*(12), 3301. doi:10.3390u11123301

Zhang, S., & Fang, Y. (2018). Research on Construction Project Organization Based on Social Network Analysis. *Wireless Personal Communications, 102*(2), 1867–1877. doi:10.100711277-018-5242-3

Zien, K., & Buckler, S. A. (1997). From Experience Dreams to Market: Crafting a Culture of Innovation. *Journal of Product Innovation Management, 14*(4), 274–287. doi:10.1111/1540-5885.1440274

Zupic, I., & Čater, T. (2015). Bibliometric Methods in Management and Organization. *Organizational Research Methods, 18*(3), 429–472. doi:10.1177/1094428114562629

ADDITIONAL READING

Chen, C. (2015). *How to use CiteSpace*. Leanpub.

Chen, C. (2017). Expert review. Science mapping: A systematic review of the literature. *Journal of Data and Information Science, 2*(2), 1–40. doi:10.1515/jdis-2017-0006

Chesbrough, H. W., & Crowther, A. K. (2006). Beyond high tech: Early adopters of open innovation in other industries. *R & D Management, 36*(3), 229–236. doi:10.1111/j.1467-9310.2006.00428.x

Chesbrough, H. W., & Euchner, J. (2011). The Evolution of Open Innovation: An interview with Henry Chesbrough. *Research Technology Management, 50*(1), 13–18. doi:10.5437/08956308X5405003

Chesbrough, H. W., & Rosenbloom, R. S. (2002). The Role of the Business Model in Capturing Value from Innovation: Evidence from Xerox Corporation's Technology Spin-Off Companies. *Industrial and Corporate Change, 11*(3), 529–555. doi:10.1093/icc/11.3.529

Rua, O. L., França, A., & Fernández, R. O. (2018). Key drivers of SMEs export performance: The mediating effect of competitive advantage. *Journal of Knowledge Management, 22*(2), 257–279. doi:10.1108/JKM-07-2017-0267

Van Lieshout, J. W. F. C., van der Velden, J. M., Blomme, R. J., & Peters, P. (2021). The interrelatedness of organizational ambidexterity, dynamic capabilities and open innovation: A conceptual model towards a competitive advantage. *European Journal of Management Studies, 26*(2/3), 39–62. doi:10.1108/EJMS-01-2021-0007

West, J., Salter, A., Vanhaverbeke, W., & Chesbrough, H. (2014). Open Innovation: The Next Decade. *Research Policy*, *43*(5), 805–811. doi:10.1016/j.respol.2014.03.001

Small, H. (1973). Co-citation in the scientific literature: A new measure of the relationship between two documents. *Journal of the American Society for Information Science*, *24*(4), 265–269. doi:10.1002/asi.4630240406

KEY TERMS AND DEFINITIONS

CiteSpace Analysis Software: Used for the bibliometric analysis of all papers, and the results of the analysis of literature clustering, scientific research collaboration, co-citations, and so on were visually displayed (Chen, 2006, 2015, 2017).

Cluster Analysis: Process of dividing a set of physical or abstract objects into multiple groups.

Entrepreneur: Search for opportunities beyond the resources you currently control (Stevenson, 2004; Carlsson, 2013).

Entrepreneurship: Cultural manifestation, which employs attitudes and behavioural forms that change from one region to another according to the way of life of each location (Braga et al., 2018).

Firm Performance: It is the ability to implement strategies effectively to achieve institutional goals.

Network Analysis: An analytical tool to explore a construction project as a temporary coalition network (the networks are made of co-cited references; links: are co-citation links; node type: is cited references) (Small, 1973).

Open Innovation: The open innovation concept is an emergent paradigm based on the assumption "that firms can and should use external ideas as well as internal ideas, and internal and external paths to market" (Chesbrough, 2003a, p. 59).

SME: Small and medium-sized enterprises.

Structural Holes: Interruptions in the flow of information between network nodes and given this relationship gap, each actor has access to different data flows within the network (Ahuja, 2000).

Chapter 6
Marketing and Open Innovation:
Toward Sustainable Innovation (SustaINovation)

Alpaslan Kelleci
https://orcid.org/0000-0003-1589-2905
Istanbul Gelisim University, Turkey

ABSTRACT

This chapter describes the interplay between marketing and innovation, between the "emergent marketing paradigm" and open innovation, and at a further level, between "sustainable marketing paradigm" and post open innovation, not to mention how these two disciplines provide ground for each other in increasing market share, boosting firm performance and producing value-added results for society. Over the last decade, both marketing and innovation have been navigating into a new phase. The third wave of open innovation, together with the "sustainable marketing paradigm," heralds a profound change concerning how sustainable value is created through open value networks (OVNs) in a post-innovation era.

INTRODUCTION

The marketing concept holds that the key to achieving organizational goals is to be more effective and efficient than competitors in determining and catering to the needs of target markets. In a similar manner, innovation enables the successful implementation and commercial utilization of new ideas to be more efficient and

DOI: 10.4018/978-1-7998-8665-5.ch006

effective to fulfill the needs and wants of target markets. That being the case, marketing and innovation are closely interconnected. As Drucker articulated long ago: "Because the purpose of business is to create a customer, the business enterprise has two—and only two—basic functions: marketing and innovation" (Drucker, n.d., p.20). By the same token, owing to its coordination between business functions, marketing acts as a source of innovation within firms. Consequently, it can be postulated that there exists an ipso facto convergence between marketing and innovation, subsequently, the new "emergent marketing paradigm" and open innovation, and at a further level, between "sustainable marketing paradigm" and post open innovation as shall be discussed in the subsequent sections.

Until the outset of the new millennium, both disciplines sought to create value within the closed doors of firms, regarding consumers as passive receivers, disregarding other prospective partners within the value chain. As substantial creators of value for consumers, clients, and society, over the last few decades, both marketing and innovation have been going through drastic changes concerning how they operate to achieve results through the utilization of co-creation, user-generated content, co-design, and co-innovation by means of crowdsourcing particularly via online digital platforms. Reinforcing this statement, Von Hippel (2005) stressed the importance of user-generated content in developing creative solutions and making innovations. Nishikawa et al. (2013) demonstrated that Japanese consumer goods brand Muji's user-generated furniture products outstrips designer-generated ones regarding unit sales, gross profit, and product novelty in the first year of introduction by harnessing the power of their users. Furthermore, aggregate sales data of user-generated products is further amplified over a longer period. Drawing on that empirical study, it could be inferred that user-driven innovative firms who mobilize external agents into their product development processes could reap substantial benefits in achieving superior market performance. However, this upstream approach to both marketing and innovation requires a deviation from conventional firm-centric business approaches.

Over the last few decades, there has been a paradigm shift in both marketing and innovation fields pertaining to how they create and deliver value. As an illustration, marketing's firm-centric value creation has transformed into participatory value co-creation, where customers, clients, and partners are perceived as co-producers and co-innovators. This view is supported by various researchers (Ramirez, 1999; Sheth et al., 2000; Prahalad & Ramaswamy, 2004) who argue that value is not created by the provider but instead in the customers' value-generating process. In conjunction with the transformation from exchange to value, the changing definition of marketing from 1985 to 2014 also reinforces the shift from the regnant exchange paradigm to the value paradigm, where the former dominated the discipline for almost two decades. To the same degree, with a paradigm change in marketing during the onset of the new millennium, innovation management had also been subjected to a profound change, from closed innovation paradigm to open innovation paradigm.

Taken together, the recent developments both in marketing and open innovation suggest that both disciplines have been gravitating from a linear to connected and networked, from hierarchical to democratized, from centralized to decentralized, and from firm-centric to society-centric. These shifts reveal a contradiction to the silo mentality of "marketing as usual" or "received marketing paradigm" and conventional corporate research labs.

This chapter explores several bodies of literature. First, the author begins with Hunt and Morgan's resource-advantage theory in explaining the significance of mobilizing external intangible resources, which is inherently ingrained in open innovation, to achieve a long-term competitive advantage based on marketing and innovation context. Secondly, the author describes the concurrent evolution of innovation and marketing and how a dyadic relationship exists between the "emergent marketing paradigm" and open innovation, and at a further level between the "sustainable marketing paradigm" and post open innovation. Then, the author attempts to clarify how the value creation concept is transformed in both disciplines, and how, in the present climate, sustainable value is co-created through open value networks in an age of cosmo-localism. Finally, the author touches on blockchain technologies, which facilitate sustainable innovation or post open innovation by means of including disintermediation or de-layerization in administrative processes and fractional or flexible ownership of content.

RESOURCE-ADVANTAGE THEORY IN CONNECTION WITH MARKETING AND OPEN INNOVATION

In the mid-1990s, Shelby Hunt and Robert Morgan developed the resource-advantage theory of competition (R-A theory) by synthesizing various research traditions (e.g., evolutionary economics and "Austrian" economics) as well as other theories, such as heterogenous demand theory, differential advantage theory, and the resource-based theory of the firm. In essence, R-A theory lays a theoretical foundation toward a general theory of marketing in addition to the process of competition. So far, the theory has been taken up by various academics and researchers, and it has been cited in several thousand articles and books (Hunt, 2015).

R-A theory rests on nine foundational premises; nevertheless, in the context of marketing and open innovation, two foundational premises (P6 and P8) are of substantial importance. The sixth premise (P6) defines *resources* as tangible and *intangible resources* as opposed to conventional resources, which are restricted to land, labor, and capital in neoclassical theory. In R-A theory, resources are expanded to include soft assets, such as informational (knowledge from external agents like customers and other stakeholders) and relational (relationship with suppliers and customers). These intangible resources are not easily replicated, unlike physical resources, since they are causally ambiguous, socially, or technologically complex and tacit. To put it another way, competitors will find it hard to reproduce soft assets since the process also calls for a different set of organizational competencies. Deploying soft assets demands thinking beyond "business as usual" practices where external ideas are smoothly diffused and mobilized by the organization. While R-A theory considers these soft assets as *organizational capital*, Falkenberg (1996) calls them *behavioral assets*, and Gummesson (1995) refers to them as *structural capital*.

Harnessing external resources requires a distinct organizational culture and climate, which favors to germinate and invigorate the knowledge and abilities of third parties within the organization (Vanhaverbeke & Cloodt, 2014). Deriving value from the creative contributions of others requires both attitude changes in management as well as changes in the operational settings. Companies with inflexible organizational cultures will form resistance to outside innovations as attested by "not invented here" (NIH) syndrome. Such organizations take pride in how they execute and accomplish, and they believe that their pre-existing solutions are better and superior. Thus, they tend to extract knowledge and value from firm appropriated resources. Research demonstrates that organizations tend to show strong biases against ideas from the outside (Piezunka & Dahlander, 2015).

Today, marketing and open innovation strive to create value by mobilizing intangible and external resources (e.g., co-creation, co-innovation, and crowdsourcing). At this point, it should also be noted that organizations do not even need to own these resources, unlike traditional companies of the industrial age. As an illustration, the relationships via crowdsourcing are never owned by firms, but it is the extraction of value from these relationships by means of building different platforms or by deploying different platformication strategies. In the present circumstances, organizational capital is considered by investors as the foremost ingredient of the wealth-creating capacity of a business enterprise or to determine the value of a firm.

R-A theory's eighth premise (P8), in alignment with marketing and open innovation, requires the management to recognize, understand, create, select, implement, and modify strategies. Hitherto the discipline of marketing over the last five decades emphasized firm-level actions and managerial perspectives from a micromarketing perspective. Additionally, the larger context of the market and the society was considered as static and given though broader social and institutional transformations have been materializing in today's fast-paced world. For example, we have been witnessing growing numbers of conscious consumers (particularly those of Gen Z and Gen Y), downshifters, voluntary simplifiers, and sustainable consumption patterns (Kelleci & Yıldız, 2021). In addition, the social unrest of masses, such as the Arab Spring, the Yellow Vest movement in France, and the Occupy movement in New York due to drastic income inequalities, and the erosion of citizens' systemic trust in institutions and their improvident CEOs give more strength to ever-increasing grassroots movements. All these developments give rise to digitally enabled social networks, which are associated with bottom-up, rather than top-down, self-organizational collaborative organizations (Grassroots, 2021). The recent social and institutional shifts indicate that both marketing and innovation management are compelled to modify their strategies in conformity with R-A theory, as shall be discussed below.

THE CONCURRENT EVOLUTION OF INNOVATION AND MARKETING: TOWARD OPEN INNOVATION

In the bygone days of the industrial period (1950–1990), brick-and-mortar innovations have taken quantum leaps in almost every area, particularly in space technologies, exploration of space and sea, and communication and information (Grinn, 2019). Companies were relatively smaller in size, and they were able to enjoy lucrative profit margins due to lesser competition. Furthermore, they were relying on their internal R&D to foster growth and profitability (Huston & Sakkab, 2006). In addition, during this period, the relationship between marketing and R&D was mainly unidirectional. To put it another way, these two functions run independently of one another. The communication between these two functions flowed from research to marketing; thus, new product developments came primarily from R&D (Horan, 1968). Consequently, marketing's function was predominantly to induce consumption or shape consumption patterns rather than complementing and leading R&D and innovation.

Since the early 1990s, the marketing function is more encompassing, and it takes multiple roles, such as identifying untapped market potential, reinforcing and leveraging R&D with latent needs and wants of markets, and establishing inter-functional coordination in organizations (Slater & Narver, 1994). Today, collaboration between marketing and innovation has grown tremendously as the world's innovation landscape had transformed into an open-innovation model. That being the case, both innovation and marketing disciplines have changed their approach to value-creation and value-delivery quite dissimilar to their traditional modus operandi. It does not mean that internal ideas and internal teams are not valued anymore. However, both disciplines' central approach to innovation and value creation shifted toward open-innovation and user-generated value creation, as in the case of Lego Ideas and Local Motors discussed below. Over the last few decades, both disciplines have been seeking to derive value from customers, clients, and value-chain partners. Even though the Swedish company Ikea is one of the earliest models of involving customers into the value chain by enabling them to install their own furniture through DIY practice, incorporating them directly into innovation processes have not been put into full effect until Procter & Gamble (P&G) put "connect & develop" at the onset of the new millennium.

P&G could be considered as the first company that put an open innovation model into practice even before Chesbrough introduced the term *open innovation* into the innovation literature. In 2001, P&G was suffering from declining growth. The company has realized that it would not meet its growth objectives by allocating more and more resources for internal R&D. The law of diminishing returns is appropriate to mention here as the law suggests that increasing a factor of production, in a similar manner in internal R&D, does not always lead to increased marginal productivity, and accordingly growth. P&G's CEO, A. G. Lafley, led the company to reinvent its innovation business model. Lafley canalized the company to procure 50% of its innovations from external sources, and it was against this milieu nouveau that the *connect and develop* (C+D) innovation model was developed. In 2005, C+D reached its original goal, with more than 50% of P&G innovation filled up by external networks. C+D's partnerships have yielded breakthrough innovations, such as the world's top-selling skin cream, Olay Regenerist, and Swiffer Duster, which is the market leader in 15 global markets. Today, the multinational has internalized its approach to open innovation, and it has more than 2000 successful agreements with partners all over the world (ideaCONNECTION, 2021).

Even though P&G is the first company to implement to derive value from external resources through the connect and develop innovation business model, the term *open innovation* was first coined by Chesbrough (2003, p. xxiv) who defined it as

a paradigm that assumes that firms can and should use external ideas as well as internal ideas, and internal and external paths to market, as the firms look to advance their technology. Open innovation combines internal and external ideas into architectures and systems whose requirements are defined by a business model.

The subsequent redefinition of open innovation by Chesbrough acknowledges that open innovation is not solely firm-centric: It also includes creative consumers (Berthon et al., 2007) and communities of user-innovators (West & Lakhani, 2008). Thus, innovation in this new period has changed since solely capitalizing on internal R&D through a centralized approach, and it has some constraints. First, it is not tenable to acquire every talent and retain them forever in an organization as it puts an enormous strain on an organization's finances. Secondly, attaining a variety of new perspectives through exogenous resources other than in-house resources is more effective, since there will always be someone smarter outside of the organization.

Proliferation of Open Innovation in the Age of Digital Economy

In parallel with the developments in World Wide Web technologies, such as Web 2.0 in 2004 and mobile technologies in 2007, the landscapes of both marketing and innovation have changed radically. What is different about the new world of marketing are the binary and interrelated concepts of conversations and engagement (Laudon & Laudon, 2020). Today, the key word in marketing is *interaction*. Marketing in this new period is based on creating online platforms and having customers, potential customers, and even critics engage in conversations.

The transformation in both marketing and innovation disciplines has been underpinned particularly by Web 2.0 technologies. It enabled a set of applications that allows user-generated content and crowdsourcing platforms over the internet. Web 2.0, unlike Web 1.0, which did not provide a means for interaction, allowed bidirectional as well as multidirectional interaction by employing social networks and digital platforms between firms and its users as well as among users themselves. The strength of such revolutionary technologies created new opportunities for both marketing and innovation disciplines to include users and other stakeholders in co-designing, co-innovation, and co-creation. Hafkesbrink and Schroll (2011) conceptualized the term *Innovation 3.0* to describe the next-generation innovation paradigm in the digital economy called *embedded innovation*.

Digital platforms enable business enterprises to develop crowdsourcing-based business models by harnessing the power of users, customers, and partners over the internet. As an illustration, in the first decade of the new millennium, the Lego Group, the Danish toy production company, was suffering from dwindling sales in the face of video and online games. Even though the group offered new products, such as computer games, and theme parks, they were still in the grip of declining market share in the industry. Pursuing a new growth strategy, the group launched an online crowdsourcing platform named Lego Ideas (formerly known as Lego Cuusoo) in 2008. The group's philosophy was based on the principle that people don't have to work for us to work with us (Robertson, 2014). Since the site's inception, customers have been sharing and voting for new Lego projects they wished to see as additions to the product line (The Leadership Network, 2021). The projects that are accepted into the 10K Club are reviewed by Lego experts (Lego Ideas, 2021). Lego Ideas is packed with hundreds of projects annually, and this enables the company to focus on the products that will sell the most. Furthermore, as users share their projects on social media sites to have voting support for their projects, Lego reaches new audiences and boosts its brand awareness.

In a similar fashion to the Lego Ideas platform, Local Motors is an American motor vehicle manufacturing company that has been thriving on open collaboration and co-creation since 2007. Local Motors believes that "the best and brightest ideas can—and should—come from anyone and anywhere, not just within the organization" (Local Motors, 2021). Local Motors employs a crowd-powered SaaS platform. The platform is called Launch Forth; it is a collaborative platform that empowers makers and solvers around the world used by the biggest and well-respected companies in the world, such as Airbus, HP, GE, Dominos, and Allianz (Crunchbase, 2021). Local Motors developed the world's first co-created, self-driving, electric, and 3D-printed shuttle named Olli. Local Motors could be considered as a sustainable-oriented company since Olli is built with 100% recyclable materials, and it has 90% fewer parts than a traditional vehicle, while the manufacturing process requires 40% less energy compared to traditional automobile manufacturing (Annunziata, 2021). Viewed in this way, Local Motors complies with the Sustainable Development Goals (SDG 12) of the United Nations (United Nations, 2021).

Besides this, Local Motors, thanks to 3D-printing technology, prevents the costly transport of bulky and heavy products, which helps to reduce carbon emissions (SDG 13), and emphasizes localization (SDG 10). Thanks to its digital manufacturing processes, the company is more resilient to fluctuations in production and stock levels (as the recent coronavirus outbreak has demonstrated), where products are bulky, heavy, and costly to ship in the industry. Thus, Local Motors has leveraged 3D printing to dramatically simplify and localize production. Digital manufacturing also enables mass customization and even personalization. Furthermore, it can allow companies to respond much more quickly to customers' changing needs. In essence, Local Motors employs an integrative approach to innovation by deriving benefits from sustainable open innovation, as shall be discussed below.

Today, even incumbent companies, such as South Korean multinational automotive manufacturer Hyundai seeks innovation through open innovation and collaborates with a large number of startups. For example, Hyundai CRADLE, which is Hyundai's corporate venturing and open innovation business, partners and invests extensively in primary global startups to speed up the development of advanced future automotive technologies for applications such as artificial intelligence (AI), mobility, autonomous driving, smart cities, or robotics. In addition, Hyundai plans to collaborate with competitive local partners and research facilities to test and validate innovative solutions for advanced mobility services (Hyundai Motor Group, 2021). Over and above that, in the framework of sustainable innovation (sustaINovation), Hyundai launched a next-generation NEXO vehicle, which is powered by a second-generation emission-free hydrogen fuel cell system. This technological innovation has been underpinned by various collaborators, such as local authorities and various governments.

Toward SustaINovation and Open Value Networks (OVNs)

So far, the current open innovation paradigm helped organizations to push up their creativity, subsequently leading to escalated sales, revenues, and increased customer engagement and brand awareness from a marketing perspective, as in the cases of Muji and Lego Ideas. However, such organizational accomplishments by means of earlier forms of open innovation still represent the carryovers of the short-term profit-oriented "received marketing paradigm" with the aim of maximizing shareholder value as advocated by Milton Friedman in the last quarter of the 20th century (Friedman, 1982). Put differently, even though the recent developments both in marketing and innovation have provided enormous benefits for business entities, these benefits were constrained in scope as they prioritized profit maximization over the society and the environment. Senior management has been primarily preoccupied with short-term, bottom-line performance, ignoring the long-term negative consequences of their actions.

Today, in parallel with the exacerbating environmental circumstances, such as climate change, deforestation, and carbon dioxide accumulation in the Anthropocene Epoch, both disciplines need to create inclusive value for all stakeholders as well as for the environment at a holistic level. It is evident that the current linear economic model does not seem tenable, given the carrying capacity of the planet. The regnant linear economic system appears to be in the grip of disintegration not due to the short-sightedness of organizations and governments but due to their underestimation of the future or the *ostrich effect*, which posits that people tend to bury their heads in the sand to avoid imminent danger. Given the severity of the situation and the environmental gridlock that humanity is facing today, the European Green Deal aims for a transformation from linear economic activities to circular economic activities and puts *SustaINovation* (sustainable innovation) at the heart of a new economic paradigm. Furthermore, the rising awareness of the society (particularly those of conscious consumers, Gen Y and Gen Z) at all levels reinforces the need for a transformation toward new sustainable practices. As Drucker articulated long ago, "Society has a right to expect the executives of its major organizations to anticipate major social problems and work at their solution" (Drucker, 1969, p. 192). Thus, as producers of results, both marketing and innovation executives must take the current open innovation paradigm to a further level in support of society and the environment. Both disciplines need to take environmental and social needs into consideration since "The needs of the society, if left unfilled, turn into social diseases. No institution, whether business or hospital, university or government agency, is likely to thrive in a diseased society" (P. F. Drucker, 1969, p. 192). The new fact in the present circumstances is that both marketing and innovation are liable for social as well as environmental quality and thus, both disciplines should transcend beyond positivist managerial epistemology. To Sheth and Sisodia (2006), "marketing as usual" is not working anymore, and marketing has been losing efficiency as well as effectiveness over time under the influence of the dominant social paradigm (DSP). In agreement with Sheth and Sisodia, both disciplines should repurpose how they create value by tapping into sustainability, SustaINovation, and sustainable marketing at the core level in the direction of shared value.

In consideration of the environmental and social deprivations, the Annual World Open Innovation Conference (WOIC), which was held in Rome in December 2019, sought to address both business and societal challenges in concert. Particularly after the spread of COVID-19 and the risk of more severe outbreaks in the future, scholars were inquisitive concerning "How might open innovation accelerate the coordination of business and other activities in the face of societal challenges?" (McGahan et al., 2021, p. 2). Societal challenges (e.g., rising inequities and polarities between the rich and the poor) require new structures and rearrangements. Speaking of the need for such a transformation, Peter Drucker put forward almost 30 years ago that

Every few hundred years in Western history there occurs a sharp transformation. Within a few short decades, society—its world view, its basic values, its social and political structures, its arts, its key institutions—rearranges itself. And the people born then cannot even imagine a world in which their grandparents lived and into which their own parents were born. (P. F. Drucker, 1994, p. 1)

Events, such as financial crisis of 2008–2009, the Occupy Movement, climate change, and institutional changes from retailing to e-tailing, the emergence of new revenue models, such as subscription-based and on-demand revenue models, together with changes in new business models from pay-to-have to pay-to-use also reinforce Drucker's aforementioned articulation. Last but not least, today, environmental concerns can no longer remain trivial matters for organizations, because of ecological challenges and risks, investor requirements, consumer expectations, employee priorities, and regulations and legislation (IBM Institute for Business Value, 2021).

At the onset of the new millennium, open innovation was still at its germinal stages, and it did not consider inclusive prosperity and shared value for the whole. That being the case, its scope has been constrained to boost organizational performance and maximize shareholder value to a great extent. However, considering today's environmental and social complexities, openness postulates to think beyond traditional boundaries, and it requires new ways of thinking to tackle growing global challenges at a multi-dimensional level. Hitherto, the management of open innovation has been grounded in the long-standing economic institutions of the industrial revolution, to be more specific, in traditional corporate organizations. Nevertheless, today, we have been witnessing transformational changes in the existing organizational structures in the form of open value networks (OVN) and more revolutionary, innovative outlets appearing as socially oriented innovation platforms, which incorporate the notions of shared value, shared prosperity, and inclusive growth. Institutions evolve through humanlike stages of birth, growth, maturity, and decline, as "the introduction of novel technologies, management practices, organizational structures and institutional solutions profoundly change the system in which they arise" (Galaz et al., 2012). In conjunction with these so-called transformations, the world has been witnessing a shift from profit-centric (for-profit) organizations to society-centric (for-benefit) organizations, as well as an upsurge in blockchain technologies that underpin these burgeoning institutions explosively, as shall be discussed in the following sections.

From Profit-Centric Organizations to Society-Centric Organizations and Changing Role of Marketing & Open Innovation

Starting from the 1960s until the new millennium, traditional profit-centric organizations under the influence of the dominant social paradigm (DSP) focused solely on creating economic value for their shareholders, taking societal and environmental issues at the periphery. In the narrow view of capitalism, a firm has been considered a self-contained entity, which has been "designed to increase its profits so long as it stays within the rules of the game" (Friedman, 1982). In line with the regnant economic system, CEOs have squeezed marketing executives to achieve shorter-term performance results. Thus, the scope of marketing has consequently been constrained to downstream marketing, which prioritized short-term-oriented metrics, such as customer profitability, customer lifetime value, and repeat purchases (Kelleci & Yıldız, 2021).

Corporate social responsibility (CSR) programs focused mostly on reputation building to attract more customers and to increase market share even though they had a limited connection to social and environmental issues. The role of marketing embraced a firm-centric approach to value creation. However, in the present circumstances, marketing should transcend beyond persuasion and demand creation to broader needs of the society, based on the principle of shared or inclusive value. The idea of shared value was initially tackled by Porter and Kramer in 2006 and was further explored in their 2011 *HBR* article (Porter & Kramer, 2011). Porter and Kramer provided exemplary organizations, such as Revolution Foods and Waste Concern, which tackled social and environmental problems and sought to create bilateral value. However, these organizations still carry the DNA of the industrial era's long-standing economic institutions that are built on the dominant ownership model, in which the design principles are built on shareholder finance and top-down management structures. Today, thanks to the rapid advancements in information technologies, we have been witnessing the rise of more revolutionary and groundbreaking organizations, such as open value networks (OVNs) and collaborative organizations, which strive to create far-reaching effects for all members of the society since the value concept is shifting from profit-oriented value maximization to well-being (WB) maximization (Kelleci & Yıldız, 2021).

These new types of organizations are also known as *social sector organizations* (SSO), which deal with social problems and introduce new social solutions. SSOs have been aiming to introduce innovative well-being solutions on the market, inclusive of people, society, and the environment (Morgan, 2015). OVNs appear to have high prospects to give rise to brand new socio-economic formations in the innovation landscape to transform the concept of "business as usual." These purpose-driven institutions seek to change innovation, production, and profit distribution processes dissimilar to those of traditional growth-oriented system, which has been under the influence of the DSP (Kilbournea et al., 2002).

The free software movement, which began in 1983 with the launching of the GNU project by Richard Stallman (Open-source-software movement, 2021), can be regarded as the origin of OVNs. The movement enabled the Wikipedia encyclopedia, the Linux operating system, and the Mozilla Firefox web browser. The free and open-source software movement has given rise to another wave in mass collaboration, called *commons-based peer production* (CBPP; Benkler, 2006). CBPP is a socially oriented mode of production that takes the free and open-source software movement to a further level by converging intangible resources (e.g., software, design) and local manufacturing technologies (Priavolou, 2018). It strives to pair easily accessible designs with distributed production capabilities, to facilitate local manufacturing via Internet-based technologies. The *design global, manufacture local* (DGML) approach is a form of CBPP that is based on the idea of cosmo-localism (Ramos, 2017). Cosmo-localism, to a large extent, rests on Bauwens' essay regarding misallocation as well as the mistreatment of material resources (e.g., minerals, soil, and water) and immaterial resources (e.g., knowledge and design). The current management practices under the DSP regard material resources as infinite and treat immaterial ones as if they are in short supply. Furthermore, traditional management practices do not consider spillover effects or negative external costs, such as climate change, changes in air, water, and soil quality, causing profound impacts on human health, the environment, and the ecosystem (Stern, 2006). Thus far, traditional pricing models have only included internal costs, which involved direct monetized costs of manufacturing a product and ignored the emissions, pollutants, and waste from production, in addition to the cost of disposing of the product at the end of its lifecycle. On the other hand, the external costs that engender depreciation in natural capital are passed on to the society in the form of taxes as well as medical and insurance payments.

Cosmo-localism aims to:

- Reduce or eliminate industrial waste through the development of localized circular economies (Ramos, 2017).
- Transform cities and regions into more resilient settlements in the face of financial and environmental shocks in addition to severe disease outbreaks, as in the case of the COVID-19 pandemic, through localized manufacturing of critical products (Ramos, 2017).
- Generate local jobs through localized manufacturing and the creation of new local investment avenues (Ramos, 2017).
- Minimize carbon and ecological footprints by reducing imported goods from distant countries since international trade contributes to carbon leakage (i.e., CO2 emission displacement; Feng et al., 2013), biodiversity loss (Lenzen et al., 2012), and deforestation (Liu, 2014), thus aggravating environmental and socio-economic inequality between developed and developing countries.

Collaborative organizations based on the CBPP movement, such as WikiHouse, Open-Source Ecology, Farm Hack, and Open Bionics, could be illustrated as representatives of post open innovation and the new socio-economic formations in the age of cosmo-localism (Manzini, 2015). More of these organizations seem to loom on the horizon since the advancement of information technology has added force to the diffusion of the CBPP movement (Benkler, 2006).

WikiHouse Foundation is a UK-registered nonprofit organization, which aims to foster open technologies and common infrastructures for housing and sustainable development by connecting companies, organizations, and governments. The foundation controls WikiHouse open-source digital construction platform, which enables common people to build a house without any special skills or training in house construction thanks to the contributions of a global community of professionals, such as architects, engineers, and builders. Participators can contribute to the development of tools and technologies by improving the existing designs and technologies and even developing new ones. Some participators, such as Architecture 00 and Momentum Engineering, support WikiHouse library with architectural design studios and structural engineering. WikiHouse library entails different house types and ready-to-use building layouts as well as technologies that include the sub-components of a house and its utilities. A stack of online tools allows the contributors of the community to share designs and experiences.

In essence, the foundation maintains the infrastructure and facilities as well as fostering cooperation in the ecosystem by coordinating interactions among the contributors and raising funds from donations. The foundation's mission is twofold: (1) to revolutionize the building industry by democratizing and simplifying the construction of sustainable, resource-light dwellings (WikiHouse, 2021); and (2) to expand the availability and relevance of architecture and its related services to the broader needs of the society other than exclusive needs of higher-end consumer segments in the construction market. Thus, WikiHouse manifests itself as a new type of hybrid organization that focuses on the social context by challenging and shaping "business as usual" artifacts in a new post innovation or sustaINovation era. In doing so, WikiHouse harnesses the power of CBPP, which allows dispersed individuals to self-organize and co-create non-rivalrous use-value in a globally networked information society.

In a similar fashion with WikiHouse, Open Source Ecology (OSE) is a nexus of farmers, engineers, architects, and supporters through the medium of the Global Village Construction Set (GVCS). GVCS is an open technological platform that entails "a set of the 50 most important machines that it takes for modern life to exist—everything from a tractor to an oven, to a circuit maker" (Open Source Ecology, 2021). In effect, through the GVCS platform, any machine could be built as in the case of the Lego Creator series, which allow users and fans to build multiple models based on the three-in-one concept (Lego, 2021), so users can develop vehicles or animals via subject-specific brick sets (Lego, 2021). OSE envisions a world of collaborative design for a transparent and inclusive economy of abundance, and it considers itself as a distributive enterprise that contradicts traditional organizational structures of the Industrial Age. Thus, it aims to shatter all forms of competitive waste by sharing all its intellectual assets through collaborative innovation to let others learn and truly accelerate innovation. To OSE, resources are wasted since mainstream companies allocate more funds for copyrights and patents than for research and development.

The Role of Blockchain Technologies that Underpin Sustainable Innovation

On the way toward sustainable innovation, blockchain appears as a prospective technology to find the roots of sustainable raw materials, sources of cleaner and renewable energy, distributed intellectual assets, and even equal employment policies and practices by integrating colossal activities of various value chain members over the decentralized platforms. Blockchain technologies have been gaining immense momentum after the pseudonymous Satoshi Nakamoto's white paper in 2008 concerning a peer-to-peer electronic cash system in the finance industry. Even though there are studies on blockchain technology, the majority of these studies are dedicated to the technical aspects, overlooking the role of blockchain in enabling decentralized platforms and governance in reducing inequalities, which is one of the sustainable development goals of the United Nations (SDG 10). Today, the blockchain has proved to be remarkably useful in areas such as predictive analytics, e-government,

IoT, and AI. These technologies are precursors of self-regulating systems in a new age of Cybernetics (i.e., the science of control). Self-regulating systems, thanks to the advancements particularly in AI, have already been manifesting themselves in the form of self-driving electric vehicles, life support systems (e.g., artificial hearth, medical ventilation apparatus), pilotless planes, and special algorithms which are employed to assess natural and environmental diseases, political upheavals as well as price volatilities in petroleum and other assets and consequently, make buy–sell decisions for stocks and other securities.

Blockchain appears to be substantial mediator as well as a facilitator of post open innovation or sustainable innovation since it provides trust among stakeholders. Research has demonstrated that open innovation is unpredictable and involves high risk (Yoon et al., 2016). Blockchain-based open innovation formulates the rules among multiple stakeholders in a trusted and immutable way that protects the rights of proprietors through its distributed features. Open innovation and particularly post open innovation through blockchain technologies also provides additional subsequent benefits (Fraga-Lamas & Fernández-Caramés, 2020):

- Stronger protection of intellectual property rights, such as processes of idea claiming, licensing, record keeping and non-disclosure agreements. Also, earnings from creative work, as in the case of Lego Ideas, and patent royalties are automatically claimed based on predetermined agreements.
- Fractional or flexible ownership of content among various stakeholders via smart contracts and divisible tokens in the third era of the internet, which is calle the "internet of value." There are already existing blockchain platforms that offer fractional ownership in arts, real estate, and agriculture (CoreLedger, 2021). In a similar fashion, joint ownership of intellectual property will be in the offing.
- Disintermediation or de-layerization in the administrative process will be more pronounced since blockchain enables open governance models. Also,

Blockchains are very useful in federal systems such as Germany or the European Union. Each member of the European Union acts as one or more members in a blockchain network and shares its data with the others over the joint blockchain. (European Data Portal, 2018)

- Access to open data with a high degree of privacy turned out to be realizable attainment. While data is open to all stakeholders over a decentralized system, members choose what data to share. Furthermore, blockchain and open data are closely interrelated regarding equality of information knowledge and access, as well as the reorganization of data exchange between multiple stakeholders.

CONCLUSION

This chapter sought to describe the interplay between marketing and innovation, between the "emergent marketing paradigm" and open innovation, and, at a further level, between "sustainable marketing paradigm" and post open innovation, not to mention how these two disciplines provide ground for each other in increasing market share, boosting firm performance and producing value-added results for the society.

Until the last decade of the 20th century, marketing and innovation have been considered as isolated disciplines, and the relationship between these two areas was by and large monodirectional. In-house R&D was the most important source of innovation, and all innovation activities were carried out behind the closed doors of companies. Marketing's function was constrained to utilize marketing mix and induce consumption rather than completing R&D and innovation. However, starting in the early 1990s, as competition has intensified and profits have dwindled, both marketing and innovation disciplines have started to search for alternative ways of creating new and modified logics to tap into the best and brightest ideas through external networks and resources and to reduce time to market (TTM) relative to direct competitors. Marketing played the role of orchestrator between R&D and customers, nurturing in-house R&D with external product ideas and thus acting as a facilitator of innovation via crowdsourcing platforms. However, the first wave of open innovation, which emerged in the early 2000s, was constrained in scope as it solely prioritized profit maximization, ignoring social and environmental considerations. The second wave of open innovation, together with the "emergent marketing paradigm," which started in the first decade of the 2000s, updated its approach to creating value by tackling social and environmental problems and endeavored to create bilateral value both for firms and society (Porter & Kramer, 2011).

Today, both marketing and innovation have been navigating into a new phase. The third wave of open innovation, together with the "sustainable marketing paradigm," heralds a profound change concerning how value is created and shared and how OVNs are gaining traction. With such massive transformations approaching, *raison d'être* of marketing needs to rethink its existing perspective and practices driven by markets and short-term financial outcomes (Sheth, 2011). The author presumes that OVNs will tremendously influence marketing and innovation management, and more importantly, hitherto organizational configurations and structures. Thus, in agreement with R-A theory, both marketing and innovation management should modify and transform their modus operandi to purpose-driven alternatives since inclusive growth for the whole society appears to gain substantial traction in the forthcoming period of post open innovation and cosmo-localism.

REFERENCES

Annunziata, M. (2021, March 17). *Reinventing mobility and manufacturing at once: Local Motors*. https://www.forbes.com/sites/marcoannunziata/2020/03/17/reinventing-mobility-and-manufacturing-at-once-local-motors/?sh=2df79db60d8b

Benkler, Y. (2006). *The wealth of networks: How social production transforms markets and freedom*. Yale University Press.

Berthon, P. R., Pitt, L. F., McCarthy, I., & Kates, S. M. (2007). When customers get clever: Managerial approaches. *Business Horizons*, *50*(1), 39–47. doi:10.1016/j.bushor.2006.05.005

Chesbrough, H. W. (2003). *Open innovation: The new imperative for creating and profiting from technology*. Harvard Business School Press.

CoreLedger. (2021, March 27). *How blockchain can divide indivisible goods for shared ownership*. Medium. https://medium.com/coreledger/how-blockchain-can-divide-indivisible-goods-for-shared-ownership-78c2aff048c

Crunchbase. (2021, June 2). *Launch Forth*. https://www.crunchbase.com/organization/launch-forth

Drucker, P. F. (1969). *The age of discontinuity: Guidelines to our changing society*. William Heinemann Ltd.

Drucker, P. F. (1994). *Post-capitalist society*. HarperCollins.

Drucker, P. F. (n.d.). *The Essential Drucker. HarperCollins*.

European Data Portal. (2018). *Open data and blockchain: A match made in heaven?* https://www.europeandataportal.eu/en/highlights/open-data-and-blockchain-match-made-heaven

Falkenberg, A. W. (1996). Marketing and the Wealth of Firms. *Journal of Macromarketing*, *16*(1), 4–24. doi:10.1177/027614679601600102

Feng, K., Davis, S. J., Sun, L., Li, X., Guan, D., Liu, W., Liu, Z., & Hubacek, K. (2013). Outsourcing CO2 within China. *Proceedings of the National Academy of Sciences of the United States of America*, *110*(28), 11654–11659. doi:10.1073/pnas.1219918110 PMID:23754377

Fraga-Lamas, P., & Fernández-Caramés, T. M. (2020). *Leveraging blockchain for sustainability and open innovation: A cyber-resilient approach toward EU Green Deal and UN Sustainable Development Goals*. IntechOpen.

Friedman, M. (1982). *Capitalism and freedom*. University of Chicago.

Galaz, V., Biermann, F., Crona, B., Loorbach, D., Folke, C., Olsson, P., Nilsson, M., Allouche, J., Persson, A., & Reischl, G. (2012). Planetary boundaries: Exploring the challenges for global environmental governance. *Current Opinion in Environmental Sustainability*, *4*(1), 80–87. doi:10.1016/j.cosust.2012.01.006

Grassroots. (2021, April 11). In *Wikipedia*. https://en.wikipedia.org/wiki/Grassroots#:~:text=A%20grassroots%20movement%20is%20one,%2C%20national%2C%20or%20international%20level

Grinn, L. E. (2019). *Kondratieff waves: The spectrum of opinions*. https://www.researchgate.net/publication/339484056_Kondratieff_Waves_The_Spectrum_of_Opinions

Gummesson, E. (1995). *Focus shifts in marketing: A new agenda for the third millenium* [Paper presentation]. Twentieth Anniversary Program of the Marketing Technology Center.

Hafkesbrink, J., & Schroll, M. (2011). Innovation 3.0: Embedding into community knowledge - collaborative organizational learning beyond open innovation. *Journal of Innovation Economics & Management*, *1*(7), 55–92. doi:10.3917/jie.007.0055

Horan, J. J. (1968). Working relationships between marketing and R&D: Early, relevant, two-way communications are key to success. *Research Management*, *11*(4), 217–223. doi:10.1080/00345334.1968.11755907

Hunt, S. D. (2015). *Marketing theory: Foundations, controversy, strategy, resource-advantage theory*. Routledge.

Huston, L., & Sakkab, N. (2006, March). Connect and develop: Inside Procter & Gamble's new model for innovation. *Harvard Business Review*, 1–17.

Hyundai Motor Group. (2021, April 23). *Reasons Hyundai seeks to boost innovation through*. https://tech.hyundaimotorgroup.com/article/reasons-hyundai-seeks-to-boost-innovation-through/

IBM Institute for Business Value. (2021, March 27). *The rise of the sustainable enterprise*. https://www.ibm.com/thought-leadership/institute-business-value/report/sustainable-enterprise

ideaCONNECTION. (2021, March 18). *An example of open innovation success with Procter & Gamble*. https://www.ideaconnection.com/open-innovation-success/An-Example-of-Open-Innovation-Success-with-Procter-Ga-00641.html

Kelleci, A., & Yıldız, O. (2021). A guiding framework for levels of sustainability in marketing. *Sustainability*, *13*(4), 1644. https://doi.org/10.3390/su13041644

Kilbournea, W. E., Beckmann, S. C., & Thelen, E. (2002). The role of the dominant social paradigm in environmental attitudes A multinational examination. *Journal of Business Research*, *55*(3), 193–204.

Laudon, K. C., & Laudon, J. P. (2020). *Management information systems: Managing the digital firm*. Pearson.

Lego. (2021, May 7). *Creator 3 in 1*. https://www.lego.com/tr-tr/themes/creator-3-in-1

Lego Ideas. (2021, March 20). *It's your time to shine*. https://ideas.lego.com/projects/create

Lenzen, M., Moran, D., Kanemoto, K., Foran, B., Lobefaro, L., & Geschke, A. (2012). International trade drives biodiversity threats in developing nations. *Nature*, *486*, 109–112.

Liu, J. (2014). Forest sustainability in China and implications for a telecoupled world. *Asia & the Pacific Policy Studies*, *1*(1), 230–250.

Local Motors. (2021, March 21). *We are unlike any manufacturer you have ever seen*. https://localmotors.com/company/

Manzini, E. (2015). *Design, when everybody designs: An introduction to design for social innovation*. MIT Press.

McGahan, A. M., Bogers, M. L., Chesbrough, H., & Holgersson, M. (2021). Tackling societal challenges with open innovation. *California Management Review*, *63*(2), 49–61.

Morgan, R. (2015). *Calculating social value: How can the social value of social purpose organisations be measured?* The Leverhulme Centre for the Study of Value School of Environment, Education and Development.

Nishikawa, H., Schreier, M., & Ogawa, S. (2013). User-generated versus designer-generated products: A performance assessment at Muji. Intern. *J. of Research in Marketing*, *30*, 160–167.

Open Source Ecology. (2021, May 2). *About*. https://www.opensourceecology.org/about-overview/

Open-source-software movement. (2021, April 15). In *Wikipedia*. https://en.wikipedia.org/wiki/Open-source-software_movement

Piezunka, H., & Dahlander, L. (2015). Distant search, narrow attention: How crowding alters organizations' filtering of suggestions in crowdsourcing. *Academy of Management Journal*, *58*(3), 856–880. https://doi.org/10.5465/amj.2012.0458

Porter, M. E., & Kramer, M. R. (2006). Strategy and society: The link between competitive advantage and corporate social responsibility. *Harvard Business Review*, *84*(12), 78–92.

Porter, M. E., & Kramer, M. R. (2011). Creating shared value: How to reinvent capitalism—and unleash a wave of innovation and growth. *Harvard Business Review*, (January–February), 62–77.

Prahalad, C., & Ramaswamy, V. (2004). *The future of competition: Co-creating unique value with customers*. Harvard Business Review Press.

Priavolou, C. (2018). The emergence of open construction systems: A sustainable paradigm in the construction sector? *Journal of Futures Studies*, *23*(2), 67–84.

Ramirez, R. (1999). Value co-production: Intellectual origins and implications for practice and research. *Strategic Management Journal*, *20*(1), 49–65.

Ramos, J. (2017). Cosmo-localization and leadership for the future. *Journal of Futures Studies*, *21*(4), 65–84.

Robertson, D. C. (2014). *Brick by brick: How LEGO rewrote the rules of innovation and conquered the global toy industry*. Random House.

Sheth, J. N. (2011, July). Impact of emerging markets on marketing: Rethinking existing perspectives and practices. *Journal of Marketing*, *75*, 166–182.

Sheth, J. N., & Sisodia, R. S. (2006). *Does marketing need reform? Fresh perspectives on the future*. M.E. Sharpe.

Sheth, J. N., Sisodia, R. S., & Sharma, A. (2000). The antecedents and consequences. *Journal of the Academy of Marketing Science*, *28*, 55–66.

Slater, S. F., & Narver, J. C. (1994). Market orientation, customer value, and superior performance. *Business Horizons*, *37*(2), 22–28. https://doi.org/10.1016/0007-6813(94)90029-9

The Leadership Network. (2021, March 20). *5 sustainable innovation practices that saved LEGO*. https://theleadershipnetwork.com/article/lego-sustainable-innovation

United Nations. (2021, March 21). *Ensure sustainable consumption and production patterns*. https://sdgs.un.org/goals/goal12

Vanhaverbeke, W., & Cloodt, M. (2014). Theories of the firm and open innovation. In H. Chesbrough, W. Vanhaverbeke, & J. West (Eds.), New Frontiers in Open Innovation (pp. 256–278). Oxford University Press.

Von Hippel, E. (2005). *Democratizing Innovation.* The MIT Press.

West, J., & Lakhani, K. R. (2008). Getting clear about communities in open innovation. *Industry and Innovation, 15*(2), 223–232. https://doi.org/10.1080/13662710802033734

WikiHouse. (2021, April 15). In *Wikipedia*. https://en.wikipedia.org/wiki/WikiHouse

Yoon, B., Shin, J., & Lee, S. (2016). Open innovation projects in SMEs as an engine for sustainable growth. *Sustainability*, *8*(2), 1–27.

ADDITIONAL READING

Allen, B. J., Chandrasekaran, D., & Basuroy, S. (2018). Design crowdsourcing: The impact on new product performance of sourcing design solutions from the "crowd.". *Journal of Marketing*, *82*(2), 106–123. doi:10.1509/jm.15.0481

Cui, A. S., & Wu, F. (2018). Customer involvement in innovation: A review of literature and future research direction. *Innovation & Strategy*, *15*, 63–98. doi:10.1108/S1548-643520180000015005

Dahl, D. W., Fuchs, C., & Schreier, M. (2015). Why and when consumers prefer products of user-driven firms: A social identification account. *Management Science*, *61*(8), 1978–1988. doi:10.1287/mnsc.2014.1999

Kelleci, A. (2022). Four-stage model of value creation for sustainability-oriented marketing: En route to participatory marketing. *Journal of Macromarketing*, *1*(42), 5–11. doi:10.1177/02761467211049668

Kostakis, V. (2018). In defense of digital commoning. *Organization*, *25*(6), 812–818. doi:10.1177/1350508417749887

Kostakis, V., Niaros, V., Dafermos, G., & Bauwens, M. (2015). Design global, manufacture local: Exploring the contours of an emerging productive model. *Futures*, *73*, 126–135. doi:10.1016/j.futures.2015.09.001

Kotler, P. (2020). Marketing and value creation. *Journal of Creating Value*, *6*(1), 10–11. doi:10.1177/2394964320903559

Nishikawa, H., Schreier, M., Fuchs, C., & Ogawa, S. (2017). The value of marketing crowdsourced new products as such: Evidence from two randomized filed experiments. *JMR, Journal of Marketing Research*, *30*(2), 525–539. doi:10.1509/jmr.15.0244

Schemmann, B., Herrmann, M. A., Chappin, M. M. H., & Heimeriks, G. (2016). Crowdsourcing ideas: Involving users in the ideation phase of new product development. *Research Policy*, *2*(45), 1145–1154. doi:10.1016/j.respol.2016.02.003

KEY TERMS AND DEFINITIONS

Co-Creation: Creating new product and services with external users.

Commons-Based Peer Production (CBPP): A new type of socio-economic production, in which numerous collaborators work on products and services over the Internet.

Cosmo-Localism: Localized and distributed production of digital commons under creative commons licenses.

Dominant Social Paradigm (DSP): Regnant political, social, and economic structures based on neo-classical school of thought.

Open Innovation: A new innovation paradigm, which is rested on developing goods and services with various stakeholders, such as suppliers, partners, and users.

Open Value Network: A new organizational formation based on digital infrastructures to support commons-based peer production.

User-Generated Content (UGC): All digital forms of content that have been curated or created by numerous users on various online platforms.

Chapter 7
Regional Cluster Evolution of Aerospace Industry in the Republic of Korea:
New Quadruple Helix and Open Innovation Perspective

Jun Gon Lee
Institute for Industrial Policy Studies, South Korea

Min Jae Park
Ajou University, South Korea

ABSTRACT

This study aims to present the evolution mechanism of the aerospace industry cluster in terms of new quadruple helix and open innovation. This study analyzed aerospace clusters located in Gyeongnam province in the Republic of Korea. It emphasizes the importance of active cooperation among industry, government, and university participating in innovation cluster. In addition, this study points out that the cooperation of clusters in other regions is also important. It also emphasizes that a common open innovation culture among participating actors strengthens these collaborative ecosystems. In the past, Korea has been dependent on imports for most of the civilian and military sectors from US as a latecomer in the aerospace industry. At present, however, it produces its own advanced trainer called the T-50. This has a unique development path as a latecomer, and the aerospace innovation cluster played a major role in this development.

DOI: 10.4018/978-1-7998-8665-5.ch007

INTRODUCTION

Balanced national development is one of the key industry policies in most countries. The balanced national development of the government of Republic of Korea (hereinafter, ROK) envisions providing regional specific and independent foundation of growth for ROK to become a regionally strong and balanced nation. The nine Key Issues of the 4th Balanced National Development Five Year Plan announced January of 2019 includes vitalizing the cluster for innovation city industries to facilitate local area growth by establishing and embarking on characteristic based development strategy (Presidential Committee for Balanced National Development Korea, 2019). It corresponds with public agencies relocated to local areas for respective innovation cities as well as promoting mutually beneficial development among innovation cities and neighboring areas.

Hence, the balanced development model to select and nurture various types of industrial clusters based on regional characteristics and supporting systems for the development of designated local areas is under development (Dubina et al., 2017). Proposals of numerous research and prospects regarding industrial clusters can be seen, and many of these research results provide grounds to adopt national industry policies (Asheim et al., 2016), but the research on the fast-changing industrial environment and industrial clusters for sustainable industry growth continues.

Porter (1998) describes industrial clusters as clusters with geographic concentrations of interconnected companies and institutions in a particular field. Clusters encompass an array of linked industries and other entities important to competition (Delgado et al., 2015). Commonly, aerospace industry leads technological innovation of other industries as it is an integrated system industry of advanced technology and manufacturing to converge machinery, electronic, parts, IT and etc. It features a unique characteristic as it has great ripple effect on relevant industries (Ortuzar, 2015), and functions as an index and scale to estimate the level of technological development per country. Most aerospace industry ecosystems are shaped with government-driven national strategies due to the long-term development cycle, large-scale investment, economies of scale, and technological/economical risks (Smith and Tranfield, 2005). Consequently, bipolarization of the market aggravates narrowing the path for market entry of latecomers due to some leading aerospace countries/companies with preeminent technology, economic and market.

However, latecomers continue to adopt nurturing policies for the growth of its aerospace industry because the aerospace industry is the key to every nation's defense (Niosi and Zhegu, 2010). Also, due to its application both in the defense and civil sector, it is not only the backbone to the defense industry, but a gateway to sustainable future-oriented and high-value added industry by enhancing international competitiveness and entering new markets with convergence of aerospace system and system integration technology of both defense and the civil sector (Hansik, 2008; Yuan et al., 2016). Such distinct characteristics of this industry compels latecomers to adopt the optimal solution and direction for nurturing and development at the national level since market entry and acquisition of technology in competition against leading countries or to achieve surpassing technological advancement in a short-time would be unrealistic (Lee and Yoon, 2015). Corresponding national policy to shape and nurture the national industrial cluster has led the development of the aerospace industry of Korea.

Many clusters include governmental and other institutions—such as universities, standards-setting agencies, think tanks, vocational training providers, and trade associations—that provide specialized training, education, information, research, and technical support (Etzkowitz and Zhou, 2017; Leydesdorff and Fritsch, 2006). It means to generate new knowledge and technology through mutually beneficial application of the government agency, private companies, universities, research labs and *etc.* within the designated area (Farinha et al., 2016). This can become a sustainable and mutually beneficial growth industrial model by maximizing the synergy effect via efficient connection with clusters from different industries. Various positive analyses prove the effects of external economies of scale which puts companies within the cluster to be advantageous in growth speed, innovation and etc. over stand-alone companies. Foremost, technological and economic uncertainty can gradually decrease since short distance makes smooth mutual interaction viable through mutual communication and cooperation as the cluster forms (Fitjar et al., 2016). At the end of this process, the cluster can contribute to promote innovation capacity, sustainable growth, new business development, job creation and industrial competitiveness. The notion and range of the simple industrial cluster is now being developed and defined to encompass generation and dissemination of knowledge from expanded innovation activities of governmental and other institutions-such as industrial partners, universities, research centers-as well as the establishment of mutual cooperative system as an innovation cluster (Farinha et al., 2016).

Korea constructed numerous industrial clusters around the country with the implementation of the Economic Development Five Year Plan since 1961. The former industrial cluster maintained minimum supporting facilities centered on the factory site, but the present concept of industrial cluster resembles estate that are designated and developed according to a comprehensive plan to add on education, research, business support, data processing facilities to the former functions of the simple industrial cluster. Also, collective installation of housing, cultural facilities, environmental facilities, parks, green areas, and medical welfare facilities took place for functional enhancement to the aforementioned facilities.

Table 1 shows a total of 1,207 industrial clusters in Korea and Gyeongsangnam-do (hereinafter, Gyeongnam) Province ranks the highest nationwide with 207.

Particularly, it has the highest number of national and general industrial clusters nationwide and is a prime example for numerous opportunities to generate mutually efficient synergy effect with various industrial clusters such as shipbuilding, aerospace, engine, and machinery. The ROK is in the process of implementing 2010 ~ 2019 plan for Korean Aerospace Industry' announced in 2010 to invigorate the aerospace industry. The Plan emphasizes the necessity to promote the aerospace industry as a new growth engine to compete against the group of 7 countries. Also, one of the major implementation items includes shaping the aerospace industrial cluster to promote the Gyeongnam Province as a strongpoint for aerospace industry.

Table 1. Overview of industrial cluster in Korea (As of Dec. 2018)

Type	Number of Cluster (%)	Number of Cluster in Gyeongnam
National	44 (3.7%)	8
General	664 (54.8%)	117
Urban High-Tech	27 (2.3%)	1
Agriculture	472 (39.3%)	81
Total	1,207 (100%)	207

Source: KILIS (2018)

Sacheon area of the Gyeongnam Province is designated as national aerospace industrial cluster to bring together relevant companies and institutions to center around the aerospace system integrator to shape the aerospace industrial cluster as well as to establish and implement long-term aerospace industry promotion plans driven by the local government. Hence, this research analyzes the success case of domestic aerospace industry by surveying the aerospace industrial cluster of the Gyeongnam Province and particularly, the Sacheon area. Also, with reference to cases overseas, this research will provide prospects to the development of Regional Innovation Systems by designating a development model of subjects-government, industry, academia/research-within a cluster linked with distinct clusters. This research analyzes the Korean aerospace cluster model for sustainable growth with relevance to systematic policy implementation of balanced national development and regional innovation systems. Particularly, this research aims to provide cluster development model and directions for aerospace latecomers and distinct industries planning to shape aerospace industrial clusters in the future. This is in the perspective of capacity enhancement of each subject and synergy maximization from mutual integration to strengthen independent functions of the government, industry, academia/research entities and effort to cooperate and link with clusters from other regions.

The sequence of study is as follows. Section 2 introduces existing studies of innovation cluster, regional innovation systems, and the introduction of South Korea's aerospace industry. Section 3 provides the analysis of Gyeongnam Province's aerospace business status and Framework Development: Porter's Diamond Model with New Quadruple Helix Perspective. And then, Section 4 offers practical and academic contributions of the research in conclusion. Finally, the conclusion is provided in Section 5.

LITERATURE REVIEW

Innovation Cluster and Regional Innovation System

Today, the world focuses its attention on technological innovation cluster as infrastructure to accelerate technological innovation in the hyper-competition environment. Technological innovation cluster is a network where major innovation subjects generate new innovation by organically combining within the cluster (Humphrey and Schmitz, 2000). In other words, technological innovation cluster is a concept that includes the addition of technological innovation related learning network of industrial partners, academia and research entities to the industrial cluster. Previous research called the network of industry-academia-research as the Triple helix (Etzkowitz and Leydesdorff, 2000; Etzkowitz and Zhou, 2017). It is a concept that embodies all entities involved in generating and disseminating knowledge such as universities, public research institutions, consulting firms, service providers in the knowledge based industry, and brokers (Etzkowitz and Zhou, 2017). Technological innovation cluster initially concentrated on the mutual interaction between internal innovative nodes, but networking with other strongpoints became important to accelerate innovation even more (Comunian and England, 2019; Lee and Park, 2019).

Cluster basically means the location of where relevant organizations organically bond and exist in various definitions and forms (Feser and Bergman, 2000). Clusters can be defined in various meanings according to its major function such as the production cluster, industrial cluster, cultural cluster, education cluster, and etc. Also, the categorization of a cluster depends on the major subject to determine whether it is civilian-led or government-led (Huang and Wang, 2018). OECD (1999) definition of a cluster encompasses independently strong companies, universities, research institutions, knowledge production agencies or knowledge based service providers such as knowledge providing firms, relevant organizations such as brokers or consultants, and customer network that are linked to the production chain that generate additional value.

Fundamentally, when integration provides competitive advantage, a cluster is inclined to form in a certain location and operates in a life-cycle of introduction-growth-maturity-decline stage (Trippl et al., 2015). Industrial cluster is used to describe a location of geographically amassed relevant organizations such as companies, specialized suppliers, service providers as well as firms and universities of associated industries, standard-setting bodies, and occupation groups. Cluster is a geographically concentrated body that refers to the vertical relationship between supplier and customer as well as the horizontal relationship among customer, technology, channel and etc. (Fornahl and Hassink, 2017; Trippl et al., 2015). Major feature of a cluster is that the internal components are interconnected and that official and unofficial mutual interaction among them is significant (OECD, 1999). The internal members seem as they are in a collectively competitive relationship with other clusters or competitors, but these internal members are in a cooperative relationship while they compete against each other.

Porter (1998)'s Diamond Model describes the industrial cluster. Namely, the Demand Conditions, Factor Conditions, Related and Supporting Industries and Firm Strategy, Structure and Rivalry are the 4 factors used to analyze not only the national competitiveness, but also the success and failure of a cluster. Porter suggests that the 2 driving powers to influence the development and direction of a cluster comes from the influence of the private sector and the strength of the government sector. Porter's Model can be summarized to give the following implications for business management: 1) Strategic importance of positioning, 2) Company follows the fate of the local area of its cluster, 3) Necessity to endeavor for the development of its cluster, 4) Necessity of common action by companies within the cluster (Delgado et al., 2015). Porter's theory mentions the following factors to have impact on the competitiveness of the cluster: 1) Enhancement of productivity, 2) Modification of direction and speed of innovation, 3) Promotion of new business formation. Moreover, it is said that the following factors dynamically shape, develop and evolve a cluster: 1) Historic factor matters, 2) The role of a handful of innovative companies is significant, 3) Innovation Cluster possesses a self-reinforcement cycle, 4) On the contrary to expansion and reproduction of these clusters, a cluster can decline due to internal factors.

Innovation cluster is a location that generates greater additional value to innovation competitiveness compared to other regions as innovation subjects are concentrated in a certain area to implement innovative activities (Engelberg et al., 2018; Frenken et al., 2015). In other words, Innovation cluster is an area that produces synergy from mutual interaction of established network-companies, universities, research centers, supporting facilities-with research, development and production activities. Innovation cluster is fundamentally different from the industrial cluster and others since technological innovation itself is a major function and goal at the same time (Feser and Bergman, 2000).

Prime examples of this cluster are science and techno parks that are built upon science technology and its major activities encompass the process of innovation for development of science technology and application to actual operation of business. Innovation cluster features general characteristics of a system and includes innovation subjects such as industry-academia-research, network relationships among innovation subjects, input of innovation resources, independent or collective culture of innovation subjects (Lorenzen, 2001; Tracy and Clark, 2003). Basically, the source of competitiveness can be found in the dissemination of knowledge required for technological innovation and the advantage to achieve technological innovation due to concentration. Also, agglomeration economy can be achieved because of the economies of scale and decrease in the distance cost (Clark et al., 2018; Cottineau et al., 2018). In the perspective of policy-making for science technology, the innovation cluster is not just a unit of competition that resembles national competitiveness, but also a convenient index to establish and implement policies.

Aerospace Industry of Korea

The development route for aerospace industry in each country can be categorized into the following 4 stages as in Figure 1 (KAIA, 2017). The stages are Maintenance/ Subcontract licensed assembly, License Production, Indigenous Development (medium-sized aircraft), and Advanced country. Korea is positioned in the third stage of Indigenous Development because certain level of design/development/ test & evaluation technology has been acquired, but advanced combat function or system integration technology in the large aircraft sector. It can be judged that Korea has entered the stage to independently develop mid-class aircraft. Implications for development plans will be provided to latecomers in the aerospace industry via case analysis of the Korea aerospace industry.

Figure 1. Level of Korea aerospace industry development
Source: *KAIA (2017)*

Korea aerospace industry began in 1951 with preventive maintenance and line maintenance conducted by the 80th Aircraft Depot and simple depot maintenance mainly on US aircraft to enhance maintenance capacity before 1970. Then aerospace industry went through a full-scale development stage in the late 1970s with the start of license-production to go beyond the simple depot maintenance level. First of all, Korean Air produced 500 MD helicopters under license from US Hughes (Currently known as Boeing) and put together the first Korean-made aircraft, the F-5E/F, on license-production which helped to start manufacturing aircraft parts. Meanwhile, the depot maintenance program on military jet engine was transferred to Samsung Precision (Currently known as Hanwha Aerospace) in the process. Then in 1982, F-5E/F military jet engine was produced under license from US GE and some parts were successfully produced domestically.

Since then, the aerospace industry took another step forward when the Korean Fighter Program (KFP) was approved in 1985. In this Program, technology related to the engine and parts of the airframe was transferred to Samsung Aerospace[1] as a result of producing F-16s under license from US General Dynamics (Currently known as Lockheed Martin). Domestic industrial partners produced parts and Samsung Aerospace ultimately assembled the aircraft, known as the KF-16, of the Korean Fighter Program which greatly contributed to lay the basic framework of domestic aerospace industry. It was also significant because the advanced trainer T-50 was developed as a result of transfer of technology. In the meanwhile, Agency of Defense Development (ADD) led KTX-1, military trainer program, in 1983. The first indigenous basic trainer, KT-1, was manufactured by the main contractor, Daewoo Heavy Industries[1], and industrial partners, Korean Air, Samsung Aerospace, LG Precision (Currently known as LIG Nex1) in 2000 after the prototype conducted its test flight in 1995. Since then, it went beyond the use of ROK Air Force for basic training and was exported to countries in South East Asia and Latin America where the discussions for exports continue till today, resulting in the reputation for its successful performance globally.

Feasibility study on the KTX-2 development program was initiated as part of the KFP offset, after successful completion of the KTX-1 Program in 1997. As a result, the decision was made to build a supersonic and lightweight aircraft that surpasses the role of a simple advanced trainer which led to the contractor-driven system development in 1997. Major stakeholders were Samsung Aerospace, Korean Air, Daewoo Heavy Industries, LG Precision, KIA Heavy Industries (Currently known as Hyundai WIA) and US Lockheed Martin provided and collaborated for technical support. Marking the 50th anniversary of ROK Air Force, the T-50 Golden Eagle produced from KTX-2 was delivered to the ROK Air Force as an advanced trainer after successful development. Also, it boasted of successful exports to Indonesia, Philippines, Iraq, Thailand, and etc. in the international markets. The Korean Fighter eXperiment (KF-X) to develop next generation fighters has been appropriated with the largest sum of budget since the establishment of the ROK. It is currently under co-development with Indonesia and led by KAI since 2014 with technical support from US Lockheed Martin.

Civilian aerospace parts industry is continuously expanding with KAI delivering A320 Wing Bottom Panel, A350 Wing Rib, A320 Wing Top Panel to Airbus as well as B787 wings and parts that connect the airframe to Boeing. Also, Korean Air manufactures B787 next generation aircraft airframe and wing structure for Boeing, airframe structure for Embraer, a specialized wingtip, Sharkelt, made of composite material on the A320 series, and provides cargo doors on the A350 for Airbus. While most deliveries are still dependent on the contracts signed by large companies like KAI, Korean Air, and Hanwha Aerospace, the number of exports are on the rise for small and medium sized aerospace part manufacturers.

Also, they have enhanced their sales, technical and quality assurance capacity to engage global aircraft OEMs with new business models of their own. In accordance to the increase of demand for civilian aircraft worldwide and shift in the defense business environment, business is becoming diversified in the civilian market for growth expansion. Particularly, the rapid market increase for low cost carriers in Korea has led to the establishment of civilian aircraft maintenance facilities and specialized aircraft maintenance companies to provide maintenance services for airframe, engine, and parts. Through these measures, the aircraft maintenance market is to grow gradually and production of low cost carriers is on its way (Park et al., 2012).

System integration technology and partial subsystem technology has been obtained through development experiences of government-driven supersonic aircraft, helicopters and etc. in the military aircraft manufacturing perspective (Moir and Seabridge, 2011), but experience and capacity in system integration and in the final assembly of civilian aircraft is insufficient. Particularly, as shown in Table 2, experiences in design capacity and production for airframe structure, parts, military engine has been acquired in the perspective of core technology for major aircraft components, but a large gap still exists with leaders in the aerospace industry pertaining to core items such as radar, avionics, flight control system, and S/W (Smith and Tranfield, 2005). Table 2 exhibits technology competitiveness of aerospace core system and Table 3 shows yearly manufacturing, status for domestic and export demand, and manufacturing by demand in the military and civil sectors of the aerospace industry.

Table 2. Technology competitiveness of aerospace core system

	Level of technology competitiveness compared to the world's highest level (= 100)			
	~ 60	60 ~ 70	70 ~ 80	80 ~
Fighter/Trainer	Radar	Avionics, Engine, Weapon, IRST Electronic Warfare	Not Applicable	Not Applicable
Helicopter	Weapon	Avionics, Engine, Flight Control	Not Applicable	Not Applicable
UAV	Propulsion IFF, GPS	Sensor, GPS, System Integration	Not Applicable	Data Link

Source: KIET (2017)

Table 3. Aviation and aerospace industry trend by year

	Manufacturing (US$M)	Domestic vs Export		Military vs Civil	
		Domestic (US$M)	Export (US$M)	Military (US$M)	Civil (US$M)
2011	2,358	5,930	1,019	1,344	1,014
2012	2,697	5,193	1,366	1,456	1,241
2013	3,606	5,766	1,652	2,019	1,587
2014	4,343	6,408	1,985	2,432	1,911
2015	4,886	7,215	2,563	2,878	2,008
2016	5,117	7,859	2,542	2,990	2,127
2017	3,969	5,436	2,086	1,757	2,212
2018	4,714	6,732	2,617	2,575	2,139
Average annual increase (%)	**11.7**	**3.5**	**15.9**	**13.6**	**11.8**

Source: KIET (2018)

The business environment for the field of aircraft manufacturing is still driven by the government with primary development in the defense sector which carries the growth of the entire aerospace industry, but continuous increase of nurturing civilian aircraft manufacturing business and the growth of global aircraft market heightens the growth rate in the civilian sector to close the gap with the defense sector (Lawrence and Braddon, 2017), Although the output of the civil sector in 2017 has reversed the output of the military sector for the first time since the statistics of the aerospace industry have been collected, it may lead to a significant drop in manufacturing due to domestic and export unstable situation. It is being diagnosed as a potential risk factor for the Korean aerospace industry.

The current position of manufacturers in the global aerospace industry according to the PwC's 2018 Aerospace Manufacturing Attractiveness Rankings (as shown in Table 4), Korea ranks 20th out of 209 countries worldwide and tops 4th and 5th in Industry and Economy respectively, but Geo-Political Risk is at 106th to resemble the tense environment in the Korean peninsula. Korea actively pursues enhancement of civilian sector development, invigoration of core parts and maintenance, investment for aerospace technology R&D, establishment of infrastructure and nurturing of aerospace industry cluster to achieve 7th place in the global aerospace industry as part of its aerospace industry advancement plan. Low attractiveness in the Geo-Political Risk will be resolved when inter-Korean exchange becomes vigorous, and North Korea opens its airspace for airliners to establish air routes making the Korean peninsula the most attractive hub in Asia.

Table 4. 2018 aerospace manufacturing attractiveness rankings

Country	Overall Rank	Cost	Labor	Infrastructure	Industry	Geo-political Risk	Economy
USA	1	7	1	5	1	4	10
Canada	2	9	3	9	3	3	23
Singapore	3	29	2	2	5	10	2
Switzerland	4	5	9	11	24	14	4
UK	5	15	14	4	12	8	20
Netherlands	6	19	7	3	37	9	7
Australia	7	2	10	20	17	6	22
Germany	8	28	6	10	8	2	11
Hong Kong	9	30	13	1	22	20	9
Japan	10	20	5	6	10	1	3
Ireland	11	6	15	24	27	35	16
Finland	12	14	4	15	39	17	44
Denmark	13	1	16	14	60	22	34
France	14	11	30	7	7	5	30
Sweden	15	21	21	12	26	11	27
Norway	16	4	12	19	53	21	25
Spain	17	10	27	8	14	17	43
New Zealand	18	38	11	22	42	25	37
Belgium	19	3	19	18	30	32	40
Korea	**20**	**34**	**26**	**16**	**4**	**106**	**5**

Source: PwC (2018)

CASE STUDY: AEROSPACE INDUSTRIAL CLUSTER IN SOUTH KOREA

Case Overview

Sacheon city's population is around 117 thousands according to the survey in February 2019, takes up 3.78% of the Gyeongnam province, ranks 16th out of 18 cities in terms of size in the Gyeongnam province, but Sacheon is the home to 72% of productions related to aerospace in Korea, 70% of jobs and 67% of companies (Gyeongnam Province, 2019). Sacheon has a long history with aircraft. Japan built air force bases in Sacheon to wage war against China during the Sino-Japanese War and US during the Pacific War. After the independence of Korea, military supervised the air strip of Sacheon for civilian aircraft operations which towed the development of the neighboring shipbuilding industry (Bitzinger, 1995; Kwon, 2018). Also, the location of air force training wing to nurture pilots and the test & evaluation group greatly contributed to the industries in the local areas. The turning point for Sacheon to become the aerospace industrial cluster it is today was when Samsung Aerospace constructed its production factory in the Sacheon area after being selected as the main contractor for production of KF-16s under license above mentioned.

As part of the government's policy to implement aerospace industry governance in 1997 after the IMF restructuring process, the three domestic aircraft manufacturers-Samsung Aerospace, Daewoo Heavy Industries and Hyundai Aerospace-were integrated to KAI in 1999. This promoted national competitiveness in the aerospace industry, invigorated local economy, and facilitated the formation of aerospace industrial cluster when its headquarters and partial establishments moved to Sacheon. Such measures to form a One-Single site acted as a facilitator to make Sacheon the national aerospace industrial cluster, increased efficiency of cooperating with industrial partners and clusters from other regions in the Gyeongnam province which continues to bring about remarkable development along with innovation activities (Lee and Yoon, 2015). As mentioned in the introduction, Gyeongnam province has 207 clusters, the highest number of industrial clusters in Korea, out of 1,207 clusters. Its survey of population in December of 2018 was at 3,447 thousands, number of companies at 274 thousands, jobs at 1,379 thousands making it the 4th most populated area in Korea after Seoul, Gyeonggi-do province, and Busan (Gyeongnam Province, 2019). It is a prime example for a local area to have numerous opportunities to generate mutually efficient synergy within the cluster with various industries such as shipbuilding, aerospace, engine, and machinery. There are total of 188 aerospace related companies in the Gyeongnam province and it is comprised of 2 aircraft system integrators, 1 engine manufacturer, leaving 185 companies that produce aircraft parts, engine parts, and auxiliary equipment (Gyeongnam Province,

2019). Direct involvement with the aerospace industry is limited to less than 3.0% of the entire number of companies in the Gyeongnam province and less than 4% of jobs, but it is the third most important industry after automobiles and shipbuilding with unique resemblance of the aerospace industry to both foreign and domestic.

Table 5 shows the area of distribution for companies in the Gyeongnam province with the highest number of 78(41.5%) in Jinju and Sacheon which are in the same zone. Out of the entire number of jobs related to the aerospace industry in the Gyeongnam province, 68.1% works in Jinju and Sacheon area, followed by 63(33.5%) companies in Changwon with 21.9% jobs. The formation of Korea's aerospace industrial cluster and its role centered in Sacheon, and the significance of mutual growth accompanied by industrial cooperation with industrial clusters in Changwon and Gimhae is noticeable.

Table 5. Status for aerospace business industry location in Gyeongnam Province (As of Dec. 2017)

	Number of Companies	**Number of Employee**
Gyeongnam Province	**188**	**11,735**
Sacheon	57	7,573
Changwon	63	2,572
Gimhae	22	389
Jinju	21	423

Source: Gyeongnam Province (2019)

In addition, as shown in Table 6 below, the regional manufacturing of Korea is led by the Gyeongnam Province where KAI, Hanwha Aerospace and related partners are concentrated, and Gimhae, where Korean Air is located, account for 91.7% of Korea's entire aerospace industry.

Table 6. Aviation and aerospace industry cluster trend by region (Unit: US$M)

	2016	2017	2018	2019	Share (%)
Gyeongnam	3,789	2,877	3,683	4,126	78.1
Gimhae	919	740	643	726	13.6
Gyeongbuk	192	128	138	191	2.9
Chungnam	119	98	84	90	1.8
Daejeon	44	54	64	68	1.4
Seoul	26	39	36	49	0.8
Gyeonggi	25	21	24	27	0.5
Incheon	3	2	25	37	0.5
Chungbuk	0	0	17	15	0.4
Total	5,117	3,969	4,714	5,329	100.0

Source: KAIA (2018)

Analytical Framework: Porter's Diamond Model with Quadruple Helix Perspective

Based on Porter's diamond model in Figure 2, we propose 4 endogenous variables such as Factor Conditions, Demand Conditions, Related and Supporting Industries and Firm Strategy, Structure and Rivalry and 2 exogenous variables like Chance and Government. The major purpose of this model is to judge the competitiveness of a certain company of a certain nationality in a certain industry that generates and maintains sustainable competitive advantage and to describe the reason for its success in global business management. To begin with, Factor Conditions, the first of the endogenous variables, resemble production elements and is categorized into human resources, material resources, physical resources, knowledge resources, capital resources and facility infrastructures. Second variable, Demand Conditions, resemble the demand composition of the subject nation or the characteristic of the consumers' needs, as well as the size and pattern of market demand of the subject nation. Third variable, Related and Supporting Industries, imply the existence of a supplier, industry or related industries that possess international competitiveness in country. Fourth variable, Firm Strategy, Structure and Rivalry, signifies the national environment and condition to create overall structure and strategy for establishment, organization, and operation of firms within the country as well as competitive relations in the domestic market. The first exogenous variable, Government, implicates the influence on the competitiveness of each country and industry levied by the macroeconomic and industry related policies on the 4 endogenous variables mentioned above. Secondly, Chance, resembles external factors that are beyond government control on variables such as production and consumption that are essential to achieve economic growth or industrial development domestically.

Figure 2. Michael Porter's diamond model
Source: *Porter (1990)*

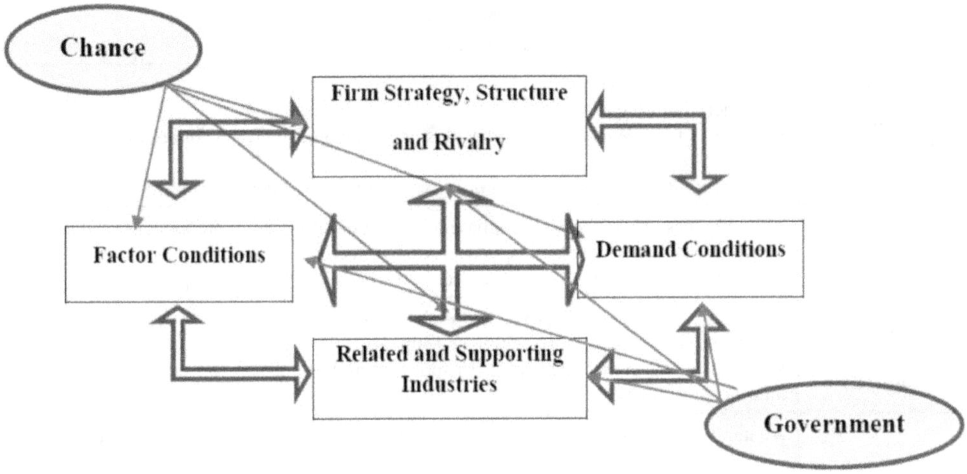

Korea's aerospace industry development follows the Innovation Cluster model based on the close cooperation between the aerospace cluster in Sacheon and neighboring industrial clusters. Table 7 and Figure 3 demonstrate the analysis results of aerospace development in the Sacheon area according to the Porter's Diamond Model.

As provided below in Figure 3, the main factor for Korea's development in the aerospace industry and the success of Sacheon aerospace cluster comes from the growth of government-driven programs and organic cooperation of industrial partners both foreign and domestic to assist the aircraft system integrating company. Particularly, industrial partners and related firms of KAI, Korea's only system integrator, are concentrated in Sacheon, Changwon, and Gimhae which puts all of them in a two-hour driving radius. Moreover, since most defense programs are driven by the government, government agencies (such as Defense Acquisition Program Administration, Defense Agency for Technology and Quality) to provide program management/supervision and quality/technical support have permanent presence within the industrial cluster which makes mutually close implementation of tasks and prompt decision making process possible (Dubina et al., 2017; Engelberg et al., 2018). Aerospace related universities, research centers and education/training institutions, aerospace related cultural exchanges have increase the maturity of the industrial cluster (Turkina et al., 2016).

Table 7. Porter's Diamond Model for Sacheon, Gyeongnam province Aerospace Cluster

Factor	Description
Firm Strategy, Structure and Rivalry	• Development of military aircraft centered on KAI, the Korea's only system integration company, and collaboration of small and medium sized industrial partners to manufacture civilian aircraft parts • Upgrade & modification, maintenance program centered on KAL and industrial partners to produce parts within the cluster • Continuous technical and quality enhancement for mutual growth
Factor Conditions	• Possess superior resources/infrastructure related to shipbuilding, automobiles, and machinery industry • Center of Ultra-Wideband industry cluster and integrated cluster for aircraft manufacturing/maintenance • Key point for transports like airports, express railways, freeways & ports
Demand Conditions	• Trainer (basic/advanced) and fighter/helicopter development requirement of the user • Increase of market size for low cost carriers in Korea • Continuous increase of civilian air transports both foreign and domestic
Related and Supporting Industries	• Centered on Sacheon aerospace industrial cluster, Changwon and Gimhae industrial cluster provides organic cooperation and support • Establishment of nurturing infrastructure such as research support, education and training, and aerospace cultural exchange
Government	• Established aerospace industry development plans and designated national industrial cluster • Relocation of government agencies and aerospace industry promotion policy of local governments • Government-driven support policy
Chance	• Increase of demand to develop Korean-made military aircraft for national security • Advancement of aerospace industry and accumulation of technology • Expansion of market and cooperation with technologically advanced countries through economic development

Previous industrial cluster development models analyzed the direction and performance of innovation from the Triple Helix perspective (Leydesdorff, 2012). However, this study suggests New Quadruple Helix Model to satisfy the need of a new approach regarding the environment of aerospace industry that involves various subjects. Key to the New Quadruple Helix Model is that the cooperation and competition model among the KAI centered Sacheon aerospace cluster and the manufacturer-based Changwon industrial cluster with companies to produce aircraft engine, parts, jig & fixture, and machine tools as well as the Korean Air-based Gimhae industrial cluster have brought growth beyond the domestic market to reach the global market. Eventually, the industrial characteristics of its location, linkage between related and supporting industries are highly important for each industrial cluster (Leydesdorff and Fritsch, 2006). Government, industries, universities, research centers and each industrial cluster should establish organic cooperative systems and shape the infrastructure not to simply amass factories for production, but to create an industrial ecosystem that leads local innovation growth (Etzkowitz and Zhou, 2017; Yoon and Nadvi, 2018).

Figure 3. New quadruple helix model

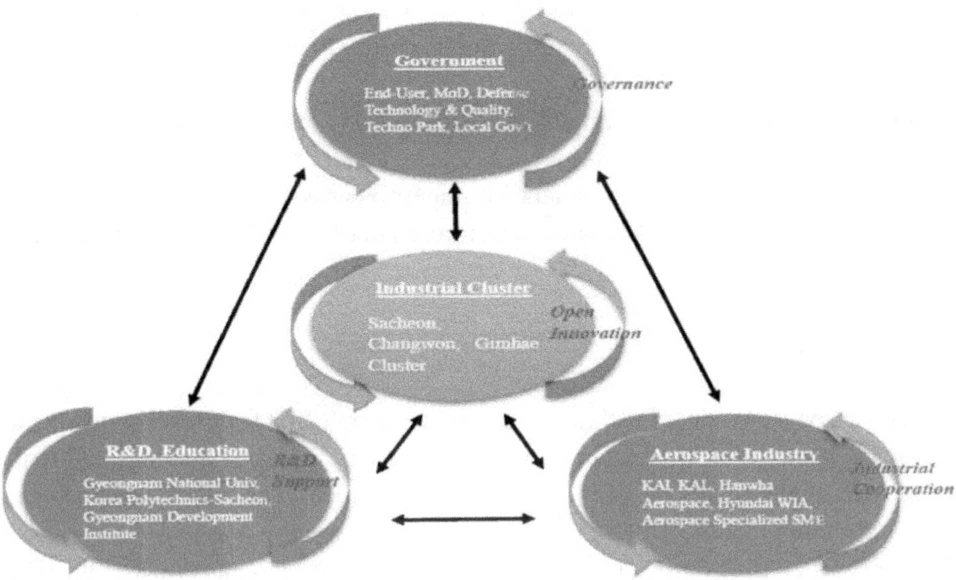

The unique characteristic of the aerospace industry makes latecomers enter the market or acquire technology that matches the level of leading countries or achieve greater technological performance in a short time realistically difficult (McGuire and Islam, 2015). Strategic promotion policy on a national level as well as convergence and mutual cooperation among firms within the cluster and respective local industrial clusters centered on the industrial cluster is required (Huang and Wang, 2018; Grillitsch et al., 2019). Convergence and technical cooperation of the government, industries, research centers and particularly, neighboring local industrial clusters is a must. The T-50 advanced trainer program is the best case to represent the successful convergence of the Sacheon aerospace industrial cluster with other local industrial clusters in Gyeongnam province as well as the cooperation of government, industries, and research centers through the New Quadruple Helix Model. KAI drove the successful development of the world's 12th supersonic aircraft, the T-50, and KT-1 basic trainer with the help of industrial partners in the aerospace industrial cluster. It achieved astonishing results by making deliveries to the ROK Air Force and exports to 7 countries.

Other successful examples of the aerospace industrial cluster include development of military-use unmanned aircraft, dual-use helicopter, satellites and maintenance, repair, and operation (MRO) services. Since then, Korea conducts independent R&D on upgraded aircraft weapon systems such as the next generation fighter development program (KF-X) and light armed helicopter (LAH) development program. Also, Korea is involved in international co-development program for large carrier A350 of Airbus as Tier 1 partner, as a co-developer in the B787 program of Boeing, and other programs such as the manufacturer of airframe structure to diversify the business portfolio. Also, MRO and space programs can draw various cooperation models such as continuous technical exchange, joint investment (Mathaisel, 2005), and co-development among national aerospace clusters beyond the cooperation of domestic aerospace clusters to enhance competitiveness for sustainable growth as in export diversification and expansion of foreign markets (Niosi and Zhegu, 2005).

DISCUSSION

Sacheon aerospace industrial cluster is a prime example that features expansion and growth of Open Innovation. Open Innovation is a paradigm that assumes that firms can and should use external ideas as well as internal ideas, and internal and external paths to market, as the firms look to advance their technology (Van de Vrande et al., 2009). Open Innovation combines internal and external ideas into architectures and systems whose requirements are defined by a business model (Chesbrough, 2006). Continuous influx of new knowledge and technology must take place in the local industrial clusters for establishment and growth of technology-based new industries where the government, companies, research institutions and universities as well as financial resources amass. Hence, it is necessary to continuously spread the R&D results and technology via open innovation inwardly and outwardly of local boundaries (De Wit et al., 2007). Particularly, the prime example of success in Open Innovation is the successful aerospace cluster built upon the business model and derivative technology developed from an aircraft portfolio that have utilized the same aircraft platform for multiple missions with the technical transition of the T-50 advanced trainer into various derivatives such as the FA-50 light attacker, TA-50 tactical basic trainer, and T-50B Black Eagle for aerobatics. KAI spearheaded the achievement of open innovation in cooperation with Sacheon aerospace cluster and neighboring industrial clusters. US Lockheed Martin was a critical partner on all forms of knowledge exchange and product commercialization internally, externally, and between two companies by coping with series of technology innovation processes such as joint research development, technology exchange, and co-marketing (Lee and Yoon, 2015).

This resulted in the successful development of the first Korean-made supersonic advanced trainer to nurture fighter pilots. It is under operation by the ROK Air Force and is globally exported to Southeast Asia and mid-eastern markets. Moreover, Sacheon aerospace industrial cluster endeavors to acquire and disseminate external technology and knowledge with technical collaboration, joint research and etc. with multiple subjects both in and out of the aerospace industrial cluster as their strategic and industrial partner to design and manufacture various civilian airframe structures and parts of global aircraft manufacturers such as Boeing and Airbus.

Thus, open innovation companies make influx of external advanced technologies into their systems and maximize their commercialization capacity of new technology through these activities for technological enhancement and continuous growth. Various methods of technology transfer and cooperation, mutually beneficial growth as well as maximization of capacity is sought after for Open Innovation in the aerospace industry to maintain long-term relationship between the main contractor and industrial partners on technology transfer, cooperation and trust-based partnership (Lorenzen, 2001). Unlike other industrial groups with shorter cycles, there is a great amount of time and investment spent from designing, developing, to testing and evaluating, not to mention the overall quality of the manufactured aircraft that could be affected from technology management, technology level and quality elements of the industrial partpner.

As for factor conditions, Sacheon plays a pivotal function such as production and technology development as it is located in the center of the extended aerospace industrial cluster that covers Changwon and Gimhae industrial clusters. Daejeon, a research cluster, is also in a radius of two hours' drive and government attempts to foster the aerospace industrial cluster as a key location. Moreover, Sacheon airport, neighboring Gimhae and Yeosu airport, KTX bullet train, freeway, Busan port and Gwangyang port comprise the international transportation infrastructure and extended transportation network in this area. The environment is perfect to nurture human talent at research and education institutions that provide aviation related and mechanical engineering studies such as the Mechanical and Aerospace Engineering of Gyeongsang National University, Mechatronics of Changwon National University, Korea Polytech, Aviation High School, Air Force Aviation Science High School. In the vicinity, there is the Korea Institute of Machinery & Materials of Changwon (KIMM), Research Center for Aircraft Parts Technology of Gyeongsang National University (ReCAPT), Korea Aerospace Research Institute (KARI), and etc. The infrastructure for the growth of the aerospace industry from development, production, research support, education & training to aviation cultural exchange is well established, but there is a need for continuous support and effort of the central and local government for increase of relevant business in the local areas to bring about economic growth, population influx, and community welfare enhancement.

As for demand conditions, KAI deemed as the key company of the aerospace industrial cluster, gathered its businesses that were spread around the country into the Sacheon area in 2006 to improve synergy effect of the aerospace industry. It embarked on building assembly factory for satellite programs and space center for test facilities in March of 2019. The stable demand of the ROK Air Force and the government driven military aircraft development programs brought growth in the Sacheon aerospace industrial cluster. It continues to develop with foreign exports and civilian aircraft parts businesses. However, there is a need for customer diversification under the current market environment of Korea that is concentrated on the military sector for the sake of economies of scale. Hence, enhancement of core technology and company competitiveness must take place for continuous exchange and business diversification with aviation markets that include foreign advanced aerospace industrial clusters of European and US companies (Lee and Yoon, 2015).

As for related and supporting industries, among 188 aerospace related companies in the Gyeongnam province, 78 (41.5%) are located in the driving range of Jinju and Sacheon to top the list and 68.1% of the entire jobs related to the aerospace industry within the Gyeongnam province is in the same regions as shown in Table 5. Sacheon and the Gyeongnam province is the home to majority of aerospace related domestic companies to form the country's largest aerospace industrial cluster. Associated firms are concentrated in Changwon and Gimhae areas to neighbor Sacheon, where the aircraft system integrator KAI is located. With the acknowledgement of the significance of domestic aerospace industry, the central and local government designated the aerospace industry as one of the knowledge-based machine industry and continues to implement strategic support to promote Sacheon as the hub of aerospace industry in Northeast Asia. There are ample amount of opportunities for the superior machine industry and R&D capacity of relevant industry groups based on the mutual exchange, cooperation and support among companies as well as the concentration of system integrator, engine manufacturer, parts, and other manufacturers within the aerospace industry cluster. However, it can be evaluated that the cluster that have grown on KAI-centric ecosystem for a long time, highly values qualitative elements such as cultural relationship and business relationship. Moreover, it is necessary to diversify growth through technology innovation and efficient management of business to reach global markets for each company.

As for Firm Strategy, Structure and Rivalry, it is necessary to take an innovative and strategic approach to acquire mutual cooperation of subjects and scale of economies-based advanced technology and flexible market for continuous and efficient development of the aerospace industry (Frenken et al., 2015). There are only 8 companies apart from KAI that have more than 200 employees including executives among the 57 aerospace related companies within the Sacheon aerospace industrial cluster. The reality is that the rest of the companies simply conduct subcontract productions and partially engineering development programs.

Many of these small size companies do not correspond to the standards, equipment, and certification required by the global markets. Majority of small and medium sized companies implement the strategy to acquire their orders from KAI, but the transition should be made to build a cooperative relationship structure of effectiveness and mutually beneficial exchanges of innovation resources. Independent innovation subjects, local government and KAI should lead this shift for the practical changes of technology and innovation growth of small and medium sized companies by establishing new strategic cooperation among companies, pioneering into new markets, and government providing financial support for R&D.

As for Government, the aerospace industry has been driven and managed by the government from the initial stages of the industry to present to achieve continuous and stable growth due to its unique industrial features and characteristics of the market size. Particularly, the central government drives long-term strategies on a large scheme with the basic philosophy to operate efficiently and systematically according to the 2010 ~ 2019 Plan for KAI. Policy regulations on military aircraft development programs, aircraft upgrade programs, MRO programs, offset programs and etc. generate stable demand and implements transfer of technology from foreign companies. Also, the government leads continuous industrial development linked with export promotion policies for domestic companies to tap global markets. The very existence of the industry is highly dependent on the role of the government considering the significance of the government compared to other industries. Sustainable growth of the aerospace industry can be made possible when the central government sets the goals, promotes policies, and the local government provides specific assistance within the industrial cluster. Particularly, the government's active sales diplomacy for global exports in the military sector could have significant ripple effect on the overall domestic aerospace industry. New market can be pioneered through healthy competition among companies, management and supervision for mutually beneficial growth, and new governance that fulfills the need for technological convergence with other industries and UAVs in the future under the regulations and procedures of the government.

As for Chance, challenges are anticipated due to the changes in the aerospace industry according to the aspect of technology trends. It is expected that mutually beneficial growth will take place as technology from other industries and the aerospace industry surpasses the existing technology such as the UAV and manned/unmanned interface as a result of convergence of technologies related to the 4th industrial revolution and automation, energy efficient technology based on innovation of fundamental technology, IT based integration and connection among industries, 3D printing technology, transition to software Value Chain. Opportunity should be expanded through strategic governance of selection and concentration under the uncertain transition of technology. Particularly, stable and continuous demand is expect in the military sector of the aerospace industry adopting the frame from national security of the world's only divided country. Demand in the aerospace industry will rise in an unpredictable growth opportunity when inter-Korean exchanges become popular and North Korea opens its airspace leading to new air routes. It is necessary to continuously evaluate and analyze opportunities in realistic and specific terms even though the leading aerospace countries will implement more measures to protect domestic technology and exercise greater influence corresponding to the market growth (Lee and Park, 2020).

CONCLUSION

Krause proposes the 11-step model demonstrated below in Table 8 as the catch-up model of latecomers' (Brauer, 2002). Initial steps, as the basic maintenance transition stage, include capability of performing simple maintenance to obtain fundamental understanding and capacity on defense technology. Assembly of imported components begins after step 3 and ultimately leads to completely independent R&D and production after perfecting the steps of production under license and co-production. It is the closest model to explain the direction of growth on weapon systems of Korea's aerospace defense industry and currently, Korea is between steps 9 and 10.

Table 8. Ladder of arms production

1	Capability of performing simple maintenance
2	Overhaul, refurbishment and rudimentary modification capabilities
3	Assembly of imported components, simple licensed production
4	Local production of components or raw materials
5	Final assembly of less sophisticated weapons; some local component production
6	Co-production or complete licensed production of less sophisticated weapons
7	Limited R&D improvements to local license-produced arms
8	Limited independent production of less sophisticated weapons; limited production of more advanced weapons
9	Independent R&D and production of less sophisticated weapons
10	Independent R&D and production of advanced arms with foreign components
11	Completely independent R&D and production

Source: Krause (1992)

Figure 4 below, also provides the framework of the complex products systems and military aerospace industry as well as the process of learning-by-doing implemented by Korea's aerospace industry as a latecomer (Lee and Yoon, 2015). In a nutshell, the development steps of Korea's defense industry are similar to the development process of general industries of latecomers according to the gradual transition from dependence on foreign technology to completely independent technology and R&D. Particularly, aerospace industry has achieved production, development and global exports through various methods such as license production, technology transfer, offset, and industrial partnership. The development and shaping of industrial clusters in Sacheon and Gyeongnam Province based on Open Innovation and the New Quadruple Helix Model plays a pivotal role to such enlargement and growth.

Figure 4. Process of Korea's learning-by-doing in military aircraft sector

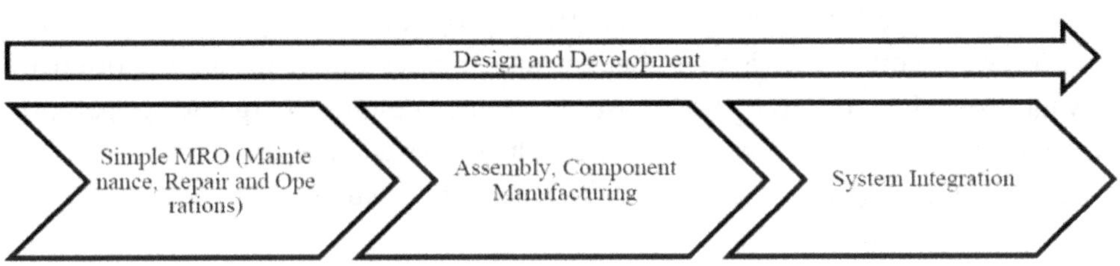

The breakdown of the development process of Sacheon aerospace industrial cluster can be seen in Figure 5. The growth in the initial stages, also known as the preliminary stage, of the aerospace industry was focused on F-16 license-production and production of simple parts to obtain manufacturing technologies of aviation parts and design capabilities. The intermediate stage to adopt a new growth engine established international industrial partnership and co-developed the T-50 advanced trainers to develop an indigenous aircraft and to obtain R&D technology for both military and civilian aviation parts. Currently, the advanced stage requires a jump into unmanned technology, mutual cooperation between civilian and military technology in terms of spin-on and spin-off, and expansion into technology for the space industry according to the changes in the global industrial environment.

Figure 5. Development stage of aerospace cluster

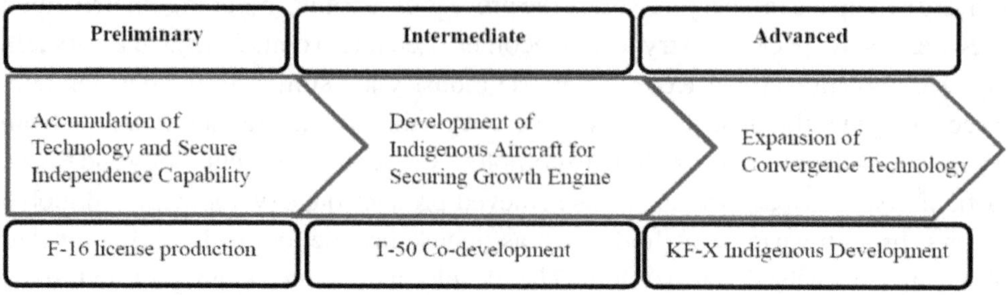

The unique characteristic of the aerospace industry makes it realistically impossible to achieve integration of indigenous aircraft systems and obtain system technology by overcoming the technological gap with the leading countries in short time. Particularly, military aircraft development programs follow government-driven procedures reflecting the defense budget and it is essential to be supported by relevant research institutions. It is most important to establish organic cooperation and close cooperation within the industrial cluster based on open innovation as the aircraft system integrator leads practical R&D of products, co-development and production with foreign partners.

Notably, the civilian aircraft structure programs are different from military aircraft programs since it is an intense and limitless competition market that requires growth by continuous co-development with advanced foreign aerospace companies and win supply contract based on the capacity of technology, quality assurance and business management of the aircraft system integrator, its industrial partners and the industrial cluster regardless of the supervision and the allocated budget of the government. The policy governance of the ROK government to restructure the aircraft manufacturing sector had contributed to the great success and direction of today's aerospace development in Sacheon and Gyeongnam Province.

Nevertheless, continuous promotion strategy of the central government on the aerospace industry and various supports on the aerospace cluster provided by the local government will sustain the industry and enable mutually beneficial growth of both large and small enterprises in this industry. Currently, the Korea's domestic aerospace industry is highly dependent on the military sector, which lowers the self-reliance of the industry, creating a fragile industrial structure in which the entire industry is overly dependent on certain industries. As shown in Table 3, in the case of 2017, the significant drop in manufacturing and discontinuance of delivery due to unstable domestic and export conditions are recognized as potential risk factors for the aerospace industry ecosystem. In order to overcome the current limitations and to achieve industrial self-sufficiency and sustainable growth, it is necessary to expand the market into the civilian sector and to reorganize industries such as entry into major countries through the Risk Sharing Program.

LIMITATIONS AND FURTHER STUDY

This research provides policy and industry-related implications to latecomers by analyzing Korea's aerospace industrial cluster, but acknowledges its limitations. First, the limitation is on generalizing the framework and implication of the research from a single case analysis. Hence, it is necessary to look into aerospace clusters in other countries to analyze common success factors and differences. Secondly, quantitative analysis via Social Network Analysis on connection patterns and strength based on transactions and exchange between subjects that actually comprise the cluster is required.

DISCLOSURE STATEMENT

No potential conflict of interest was reported by the authors.

REFERENCES

Asheim, B. T., Grillitsch, M., & Trippl, M. (2016). Regional innovation systems: Past–present–future. *Handbook on the Geographies of Innovation*, *36*, 45–62. doi:10.4337/9781784710774.00010

Bitzinger, R. A. (1995). South Korea's Defense Industry at the Crossroads. *Korean Journal of Defense Analysis*, *7*(1), 233–249. doi:10.1080/10163279509464539

Brauer, J. (2002). The arms industry in developing nations: history and post-cold war assessment. In *Arming the South* (pp. 101–127). Palgrave Macmillan. doi:10.1057/9780230501256_6

Chesbrough, H. W. (2003). The Era of Open Innovation. *MIT Sloan Management Review*, *44*(3), 35–41.

Clark, G. L., Feldman, M. P., Gertler, M. S., & Wójcik, D. (2018). *The New Oxford Handbook of Economic Geography*. Oxford University Press. doi:10.1093/oxfordhb/9780198755609.001.0001

Cottineau, C., Finance, O., Hatna, E., Arcaute, E., & Batty, M. (2018). Defining urban clusters to detect agglomeration economies. *Environment and Planning. B, Urban Analytics and City Science*. Advance online publication. doi:10.1177/2399808318755146

De Wit, J., Dankbaar, B., & Vissers, G. (2007). Open innovation: The new way of knowledge transfer? *Journal of Business Chemistry*, *4*(1), 11–19.

Delgado, M., Porter, M. E., & Stern, S. (2015). Defining clusters of related industries. *Journal of Economic Geography*, *16*(1), 1–38. doi:10.1093/jeg/lbv017

Dubina, I. N., Campbell, D. F., Carayannis, E. G., Chub, A. A., Grigoroudis, E., & Kozhevina, O. V. (2017). The balanced development of the spatial innovation and entrepreneurial ecosystem based on principles of the systems compromise: A conceptual framework. *Journal of the Knowledge Economy*, *8*(2), 438–455. doi:10.100713132-016-0426-0

Engelberg, J., Ozoguz, A., & Wang, S. (2018). Know thy neighbor: Industry clusters, information spillovers, and market efficiency. *Journal of Financial and Quantitative Analysis*, *53*(5), 1937–1961. doi:10.1017/S0022109018000261

Etzkowitz, H., & Leydesdorff, L. (2000). The dynamics of innovation: From National Systems and "Mode 2" to a Triple Helix of university–industry–government relations. *Research Policy*, *29*(2), 109–123. doi:10.1016/S0048-7333(99)00055-4

Etzkowitz, H., & Zhou, C. (2017). *The triple helix: University–industry–government innovation and entrepreneurship*. Routledge. doi:10.4324/9781315620183

Farinha, L., Ferreira, J., & Gouveia, B. (2016). Networks of innovation and competitiveness: A triple helix case study. *Journal of the Knowledge Economy*, *7*(1), 259–275. doi:10.100713132-014-0218-3

Feser, E. J., & Bergman, E. M. (2000). National industry cluster templates: A framework for applied regional cluster analysis. *Regional Studies*, *34*(1), 1–19. doi:10.1080/00343400050005844

Fitjar, R. D., Huber, F., & Rodríguez-Pose, A. (2016). 'Not too close, not too far: Testing the Goldilocks principle of 'optimal' distance in innovation networks'. *Industry and Innovation*, *23*(6), 465–487. doi:10.1080/13662716.2016.1184562

Fornahl, D., & Hassink, R. (2017). *The life cycle of clusters: A policy perspective*. Edward Elgar Publishing. doi:10.4337/9781784719289

Frenken, K., Cefis, E., & Stam, E. (2015). Industrial dynamics and clusters: A survey. *Regional Studies*, *49*(1), 10–27. doi:10.1080/00343404.2014.904505

Gyeongnam Province. (2019). *Statistics Database of Gyeongnam Province. Gyeongnam Province.* Research Report, Published by Gyeongnam Province, Rep. of Korea. https://www.gyeongnam.go.kr/data

Hasik, J. (2008). *Arms and Innovation: entrepreneurship and alliances in the twenty-first century defense industry.* University of Chicago Press. doi:10.7208/chicago/9780226318899.001.0001

Huang, C., & Wang, Y. (2018). Evolution of network relations, enterprise learning, and cluster innovation networks: The case of the Yuyao plastics industry cluster. *Technology Analysis and Strategic Management, 30*(2), 158–171. doi:10.1080/09537325.2017.1297786

Humphrey, J., & Schmitz, H. (2000). *Governance and upgrading: linking industrial cluster and global value chain research* (Vol. 120). Institute of Development Studies.

KAIA. (2017). *Level of Korea Aerospace Industry Development.* Korea Aerospace Industry Associations.

KAIA. (2018). *Trend of Export and Import of Aviation and Aerospace Industry in Korea.* Korea Aerospace Industry Associations.

KIET. (2017). *Report on Technology competitiveness of Aerospace core system in Korea.* Korea Institute for Industrial Economics and Trade.

KILIS. (2018). *Statistics on Industrial Cluster in Korea.* Korea Industrial Land Information System. https://www.industryland.or.kr/web/en/Center/Overview.jsp

Krause, K. (1992). *Arms and the State: Patterns of Military Expenditure and Trade. Cambridge.* Cambridge University Press. doi:10.1017/CBO9780511521744

Kwon, P. B. (2018). Mars and Manna: Defense Industry and the Economic Transformation of Korea under Park Chung Hee. *Korea Journal, 58*(3), 15–46. doi:10.25024/kj.2018.58.3.15

Lawrence, P., & Braddon, D. (2017). *Strategic issues in European aerospace.* Routledge. doi:10.4324/9781315242330

Lee, J. G., & Park, M. J. (2019). Rethinking the national defense R&D innovation system for latecomer: Defense R&D governance matrix. *Technological Forecasting and Social Change, 146*, 1–11. doi:10.1016/j.techfore.2019.05.012

Lee, J. G., & Park, M. J. (2020). Evaluation of technological competence and operations efficiency in the defense industry: The strategic planning of South Korea. *Evaluation and Program Planning, 79*, 1–11. doi:10.1016/j.evalprogplan.2019.101775 PMID:31865011

Lee, J. J., & Yoon, H. (2015). A comparative study of technological learning and organizational capability development in complex products systems: Distinctive paths of three latecomers in military aircraft industry. *Research Policy*, *44*(7), 1296–1313. doi:10.1016/j.respol.2015.03.007

Leydesdorff, L. (2012). The triple helix, quadruple helix and an N-tuple of helices: Explanatory models for analyzing the knowledge-based economy? *Journal of the Knowledge Economy*, *3*(1), 25–35. doi:10.100713132-011-0049-4

Leydesdorff, L., & Fritsch, M. (2006). Measuring the knowledge base of regional innovation systems in Germany in terms of a Triple Helix dynamics. *Research Policy*, *35*(10), 1538–1553. doi:10.1016/j.respol.2006.09.027

Lorenzen, M. (2001). Ties, trust, and trade: Elements of a theory of coordination in industrial clusters. *International Studies of Management & Organization*, *31*(4), 14–34. doi:10.1080/00208825.2001.11656825

Mathaisel, D. F. (2005). A lean architecture for transforming the aerospace maintenance, repair and overhaul (MRO) enterprise. *International Journal of Productivity and Performance Management*, *54*(8), 623–644. doi:10.1108/17410400510627499

McGuire, S., & Islam, N. (2015). Indigenous technological capabilities, emerging market firms and the aerospace industry. *Technology Analysis and Strategic Management*, *27*(7), 739–758. doi:10.1080/09537325.2014.959482

Moir, I., & Seabridge, A. (2011). *Aircraft Systems: Mechanical, electrical, and avionics subsystems integration* (Vol. 52). John Wiley & Sons.

Niosi, J., & Zhegu, M. (2005). Aerospace clusters: Local or global knowledge spillovers? *Industry and Innovation*, *12*(1), 5–29. doi:10.1080/1366271042000339049

Niosi, J., & Zhegu, M. (2010). Anchor tenants and regional innovation systems: The aircraft industry. *International Journal of Technology Management*, *50*(3/4), 263–284. doi:10.1504/IJTM.2010.032676

OECD. (1999). *Boosting innovation: The cluster approach*. OECD Publishing.

Ortuzar, G. (2015). Industry clusters and economic development. *Indiana Business Review*, *90*(1), 7–9.

Park, Y., Lee, S., & Lee, S. (2012). Patent analysis for promoting technology transfer in multi-technology industries: The Korean aerospace industry case. *The Journal of Technology Transfer*, *37*(3), 355–374. doi:10.100710961-010-9181-8

Porter, M. E. (1990). The Competitive Advantage of Nations. *Harvard Business Review*, *3-4*, 73–91.

Porter, M. E. (1998). Clusters and the new economics of competition. *Harvard Business Review*, *76*(6), 77–90. PMID:10187248

Presidential Committee for Balanced National Development Korea. (2019). *The 4th Balanced National Development Five Year Plan*. Rep. of Korea.

PwC. (2018). *Aerospace manufacturing attractiveness rankings*. pwc.com/us/en/industrial-products/publications/assets/pwc-aerospace-manufacturing-attractiveness-rankings-2018.pdf

Smith, D. J., & Tranfield, D. (2005). Talented suppliers? Strategic change and innovation in the UK aerospace industry. *R & D Management*, *35*(1), 37–49. doi:10.1111/j.1467-9310.2005.00370.x

Tracey, P., & Clark, G. L. (2003). Alliances, networks and competitive strategy: Rethinking clusters of innovation. *Growth and Change*, *34*(1), 1–16. doi:10.1111/1468-2257.00196

Trippl, M., Grillitsch, M., Isaksen, A., & Sinozic, T. (2015). Perspectives on cluster evolution: Critical review and future research issues. *European Planning Studies*, *23*(10), 2028–2044. doi:10.1080/09654313.2014.999450

Turkina, E., Van Assche, A., & Kali, R. (2016). Structure and evolution of global cluster networks: Evidence from the aerospace industry. *Journal of Economic Geography*, *16*(6), 1211–1234. doi:10.1093/jeg/lbw020

Van de Vrande, V., De Jong, J. P., Vanhaverbeke, W., & De Rochemont, M. (2009). Open innovation in SMEs: Trends, motives and management challenges. *Technovation*, *29*(6-7), 423–437. doi:10.1016/j.technovation.2008.10.001

Yuan, C., Liu, S., Yang, Y., & Shen, Y. (2016). On the contribution of defense innovation to China's economic growth. *Defence and Peace Economics*, *27*(6), 820–837. doi:10.1080/10242694.2014.901644

ENDNOTE

1 Currently, both Samsung Aerospace and Daewoo Heavy Industries were merged into Korea Aerospace Industries, KAI.

Chapter 8
Comparison of Innovation Policies Between the European Union and the United States of America

Carla Pires
https://orcid.org/0000-0003-4526-0271
CBIOS, Universidade Lusófona, Portugal

ABSTRACT

Innovation policies of the United States of America (USA) seem to be more effective and efficient than the innovation policies of the European Union (EU). In this work, a brief review about the innovation policies of the two regions is carried out, followed by their comparison and critical discussion. Unequivocally, the innovation policies of USA and EU support open innovation. In general, open innovation strategies lead to better economic performance, the growth of the number of jobs, and workers' better remunerations and quality of life than close innovation strategies. Both USA and EU recognize the importance of innovation to overcome the current pandemic crisis. In contrast with the innovation policies of EU, the innovation policies of USA support a higher investment in research and development (R&D), a more flexible regulation in some areas (e.g., copyright), and more coordinated agencies for the transposition of the laboratory inventions to the market ("Lab-to-Market"). This seems to contribute to a less fragmented market and a more effective promotion and marketing of new inventions in USA.

DOI: 10.4018/978-1-7998-8665-5.ch008

INTRODUCTION

Transformative innovation is crucial to stimulate technological and economic development, to promote business, or to ensure employment and financial return of investments (EPO & EUIPO, 2019). Innovation is a broad concept. For instance, new products or processes (more or less disruptive) or new forms of organization, management, or marketing in companies are considered innovative outcomes. Ideally, innovative outcomes should be more efficient than any previous solution in the market (Caraça et al., 2008). In this sense, entrepreneurial companies with new products and/or projects, such as startups (innovative emerging companies, such as some small and medium-sized enterprises) are potentially eligible to be supported by public and/or private policies (Torres et al., 2017).

Governance policies, including industrial policy, regulation, patent system, education, and funding, seem to play a crucial role in the promotion of innovation in diverse sectors (Andreoni & Chang, 2019; Congressional Budget Office, 2017). The exposure of companies to the global market, trade and flow of ideas can lead to more competitive and optimized business practices. These practices are likely to boost the productivity and efficiency of companies. In general, innovative business tend to be more competitive, specialized, and efficient than conventional business (Aspen Institute, 2019).

Between 2014 and 2016 in EU, 29.2% of jobs were ensured by companies/industries that owned and/or marketed trademarks and patents (about 2/3 of these industries marketed more than one Industrial Property Right - IPR). Overall, 63 million of people were employed in these industries, with 83.8 million of workers if taking indirect jobs into account. Industries intensively exploring IPRs provided better salaries, encompassed the majority of EU trade, and accounted for 45% of the EU's economic activity in terms of gross domestic product (GDP) (6.6 trillion euros). These companies achieved a trade surplus, which contributed to keep balanced the EU's foreign trade. Particularly, industries involved in the development of climate change mitigation technologies (CCMTs) or in the development of technologies related to the Fourth Industrial Revolution (4IR) have grown in the EU: CCMTs industries were related to 2.5% of employment and 4.7% of GDP, while 4IR industries were related to 1.9% of employment and 3.9% of GDP in 2014-2016 (EPO & EUIPO, 2019).

The Global Innovation Index (GII) was launched by the World Intellectual Property Organization (WIPO) in 2007. The calculation of GII is based on innovation metrics from more than 130 countries. This indicator goes beyond the traditional quantifications of the number of PhDs per country, the number of scientific papers or the investment in Research and Development (R&D) (WIPO, 2019). The GII is composed of diverse indicators, which are based on innovation inputs (e.g., resources in terms of institutions, human resources, infrastructure or sophistication of the market and business) and innovation outputs (e.g., creative, and scientific outputs: products, or processes) (WIPO, 2011). According to the Global Innovation Index (GII), the leading economies were located in North America, followed by Europe and Southwest Asia, East Asia, and Oceania (by geographic areas) in 2020. Regarding the 2020 GII ranking, innovation inputs and outputs were located in certain regions of the globe. These innovations were related to specific research areas. Thus, products or process should be diversified in both developed and developing countries (i.e., more and better innovation) (WIPO, 2019, 2020).

In this sense, the study aim was to carry out a brief review about the innovation policies in EU and USA, followed by their comparison and critical evaluation.

BACKGROUND

Innovation Policies: EU Policies

EU advocates a vision of open innovation. According to the concept of open innovation, both internal and external R&D ideas are determinant for the success of business. The philosophy of open innovation is based on the following premises: not only the best workers should be integrated in companies, i.e., it is necessary to look for highly qualified subjects in the external and internal environments; the development of better business models may be more relevant than getting to the market first; external R&D can create significant value (e.g., patent licenses); and benefits can be maintained through internal R&D (e.g., to exploit both generated and third-party IP).

In contrast, closed innovation is based on the development, production, and marketing of products, which were developed in-house R&D. In this paradigm, companies should preferably work with the best workers; products should be introduced in the market bythe initial developer; and companies that produce more and better products/inventions and first introduce these products in the market win. These companies should protect their inventions through IP rights to avoid that other businesses benefit from the developed ideas (European Commission, 2016).

Recognizing the importance of innovation for a more intelligible, inclusive, and sustainable economy, a significant amount of the EU GDP was invested in R&D (European Parliament, 2020; WIPO, 2019). In 2018, the five countries with the highest R&D investments (billion dollar) were, respectively: USA (511), China (452), Japan (166), Germany (119) and Republic of Correia (78) (WIPO, 2019). Switzerland, Sweden, Japan, and Germany, followed by US, OECD, China, Netherlands, Norway, EU, Australia, Portugal were the countries that registered the highest R&D investment by GDP, according to the latest data from the Organization for Economic Co-operation and Development (OECD) (2018) (OECD, 2020).

The market of EU is one of the largest in the world, although it remains fragmented. For instance, according to the European innovation scoreboard (2021), the innovation leaders were Belgium, Denmark, Finland, and Sweden and the emerging innovator were Romania, Bulgaria, Latvia, Poland, Slovakia, Hungary, and Croatia. These findings support that EU is a heterogeneous territory in terms of innovation (European Commission, 2021a). Moreover, there is a political recognition that innovation has not yet reached the most favorable environment in EU (European Parliament, 2020; WIPO, 2019). The objectives of EU innovation policies are, as follows:

1. To remove barriers, such as costly patents, market fragmentation or a limited *capacity* to produce new products; some of these barriers can cause product failure.
2. To optimize the functioning of public and private sectors. For instance, through the implementation of collaborative innovation partnerships between EU institutions, national and regional authorities, and businesses.
3. To increase the investment in innovation. An investment of 3% of EU GDP in R&D is expected until 2025, which can create 3.7 million of jobs and increase annual GDP by €795 billion (European Parliament, 2020).
4. To reinforce EU's position in the sector of science.
5. To support industrial innovation. For instance, through promoting technological investments (e.g., small, and medium-sized enterprises).
6. To move towards addressing social concerns, such as climate change, sustainable transport, or renewable energy.
7. To support the development of new technologies, for example through partnerships between industries and governments, products/inventions should be launched
8. To promote international cooperation, regarding research and innovation (European Union, 2019).

Diverse public agencies with the mission of managing research and innovation or other related activities are common in EU. For instance, Competitiveness and Innovation Agency (IAPMEI), the National Innovation Agency (ANI) and the Portuguese Industrial Association - Chamber of Commerce and Industry (AIPCCI) in Portugal. EU regularly publishes information on innovation through databases, statistics, journals, or other publications (European Commission, 2020b; European Union, 2019).

Among others, the main political achievements of EU on innovation are presented, as follows:

1. The development of metrics to quantify the diffusion of innovation through EU (e.g., Innovation Union Scoreboard and the Regional Innovation Scoreboard) and citizens' opinion (e.g., Innobarometer) in EU;
2. Horizon 2020, which is the financial instrument for the implementation of innovation in EU;
3. Other financial instruments: the European Commission in cooperation with the European Investment Bank Group created specific financial instruments to boost R&D, such as a facilitated access to loans (e.g.,'InnovFin - EU Finance for Innovators' or 'Investment Plan for Europe'). Additionally, companies including small and medium-sized enterprises were encouraged through the COSME (Competitiveness of Enterprises and SMEs) program,
4. Regulatory Instruments (e.g., Resolution of 6 July 2016 on synergies for innovation: the European Structural and Investment Funds, Horizon 2020 and other European innovation funds and EU programs);
5. The creation of an innovation council - the European Innovation Council (EIC) (European Parliament, 2020).
6. Political cohesion (e.g., the most developed regions allocate 80% of the European Regional Development Fund to innovation, aiming at prioritizing a low-carbon economy and ensuring the competitiveness of small and medium-sized enterprises);

In addition, several political measures were proposed, as follows: patent protection, standardization, public procurement, and smart regulation to attract innovative companies and businesses (European Parliament, 2020).

The EU's main science and technology program is Horizon 2020. This program support areas such as space exploration, nanotechnologies, micro and nano electronics, photonics, health and medicine, demographic change, computing, robotics, the internet, bio-saving, safe, clean, and efficient energies, climate change, waste and water management, safety of citizens, education sciences, gender equality, citizens' participation in science, ethics, open data, etc.

Particularly, the program of Horizon 2018-2020 was focused on a limited number of research topics, which directly assist the political priorities of Commission's. A budget of more than €7 billion financed 4 focus areas: (i) building a low-carbon, climate-resilient future; (ii) connection of economic and environmental gains, such as circular economy (e.g., recycling and reuse of products); (iii) digitizing and transforming European industry and services, with an emphasis on cybersecurity; (iv) increasing security in the EU (e.g., controlling cybercrime or other threats) (Horizon, 2020).

Among the recommendations of EU to foster innovation were (i) the increase of the number of researchers, with an estimated need for at least one million more researchers in the next decade, (ii) the achievement of the target of 3% of GDP in R&D or (iii) the removal of obstacles to the free movement of researchers. Consistent policies to promote research must be implemented across the EU. Finally, EU encourage curriculum adaptations to bridge the gaps of students' abilities and skills in various innovative areas (European Parliament, 2020).

Innovation Policies: USA

Open innovation strategies were also followed up by USA in public and private sector (Lee, Hwang, & Choi, 2012). In 2019, the USA science and technology plan (Trump administration) was focused on the following areas: rural connectivity and 5G; advanced production; artificial intelligence; transport systems; cybersecurity; digital economy; energy; health and medicine; innovative computing and electronics technologies; homeland and national security; transposition of products from the laboratory to the market (marketing); resilience in natural disasters; ocean science; response to the opioid epidemic; science related to Antarctic zone; privacy; quantum information science and space science or education and training of workers. The main governmental measures on R&D were, as follows:

1. To redefine the international system of weights and measures, with the aim of increasing the measurement accuracy.
2. To stimulate innovation through public participation (e.g., economic support programs and citizens' R&D projects).
3. To reduce the burden of research (e.g., reduction of regulatory and administrative problems).
4. To develop the Model of the Earth system (a model that uses artificial intelligence to identify extreme weather events).
5. To coordinate federal science and technology programs, for example to define priority intervention areas and strategic plans of the units.
6. To develop the science of lithium batteries, with the aim of ensuring the production of safer and longer-lasting batteries and,
7. To advance nanotechnology science (Executive Office of the President of united states, 2019).

In general, the 2019 and 2020 plans were similar concerning the medicine topics:

1. Development of new diagnosis methodologies, vaccines, and therapies (e.g., vaccine against COVID-2019 and other biological threats).
2. Modeling and forecasting of infectious diseases (e.g., models for the prediction and management of current and future pandemics).

3. Biomedicine and biotechnology (e.g., rapid containment and treatment of infectious diseases; with application of the principles of personalized medicine and artificial intelligence) and
4. Bio economics (e.g., the public benefit regarding human, plant, and animal spectrums should be stimulated, while enhancing economic growth).

R&D activities are also recognized by the USA government as a key factor to promote the competitiveness of business, the growth of economy or the increase of the number of jobs. USA government invest about $495 billion in R&D, which is the largest amount invested by a government in this type of activities (1/4 of the global R&D value). Particularly, the USA government favors the investment in areas where private industry shown a limited interest due to a likely scarce financial return, e.g., critical research areas to economy and/or national defense (United States Whitehouse, 2019).

The 2020 innovation plan of USA was designed to overcome the problems of the COVID-2019 crisis. There was a strong focus on data science and the facilitation of multisectoral partnerships and technology transfer, in order to facilitate the economic recovery of USA (e.g., investment in startups and creation of agencies/departments to manage funds, and the coordination between agencies to facilitate the transfer of products from the laboratory to the market). In addition, other measures were purposed in the 2020 innovation plan of USA, such as: the development of 5G technologies or the creation of specific departments in research agencies, aiming at coordinating the interactions between the public and private sectors. Among the missions of these new departments/agencies were (i) the development of advanced manufacturing (e.g., drug production, internet of things and robotics) or (ii) the promotion of safe and effective use of nuclear, renewable, and fossil energy, e.g., R&D about nuclear reactors (Executive Office of the President of United States, 2020).

The innovation policy goals of the recent elected President Joe Biden during campaign were (i) to be an active partner of industry, aiming at supporting R&D and domestic production, (ii) to be a stronger regulator, (iii) to increase investment in social goals (e.g., more opportunities for minorities), (iv) to support regional growth, (v) to create climate solutions, (vi) to increase significantly public investment in R&D, (vii) to increase substantially R&D funding in clean energy and advanced production, (viii) to increase public investment in education and the acquisition skills, (ix) to promote high- and low-skill immigration, (x) to enhance investment in rural broadband infrastructure, (xi) to reduce the digital divide, (xii) to apply higher taxes on business, (e,g, large corporations), (xiii) to develop stronger regulations (e.g.,. regulations on privacy and broadband providers, and more aggressive antitrust), (xiv) to limit Section 230 protections and (xv) to contain the investment in other areas, such as defense spending (Information Technology and Innovation Foundation, 2020).

MAIN FOCUS OF THE CHAPTER

The levels of innovation between different countries are clearly heterogenous, which may be related to their level of economic development. Innovation seems to be essential for developed and developing countries to stimulate the economy and competitiveness, to increase or maintain employment, to promote the well-being of society and to ensure a sustainable development (Gavriluţă, 2016; WIPO, 2019).

Overall, USA showed a better innovation performance than EU, although some EU countries presented a better GII rank than USA. According to the GII rank (2019): Switzerland (first place occupied by a Country of the Schengen area), Sweden (2nd place), followed by USA in 3rd (WIPO, 2019). This situation could be explained by diverse factors (i) a higher investment in R&D per GDP by USA than EU (USA = 2,820 vs. EU-28 = 2.025) (OECD, 2020), (ii) after the World War II" (1939 to 1945), the operational scientific and productive capacity was maintained in USA, with a reduction of these indicators in Europe, Pacific region, Japan and Asia, (iii) the brightest brains and skilled immigrants were welcomed by USA, after the World War II (iv) after returning to civilian life thousands of militaries quickly graduated, and (v) during the cold war, the environment of innovation was favored, because of an expressive investment in education and a significant competitiveness between countries (e.g., military, technological, or sports) (Aspen Institute, 2019). Finally, USA integrates a coordinated system of Institutes for Manufacturing Innovation (IMIs) that support the marketing of new inventions (Global Trade and Innovation Policy Alliance, 2019; Manufacturing USA, 2020). A structured and coordinated network of institutes to assist the launch of new products ("transfer of knowledge from the lab to the market") was not identified in EU, in opposition to USA (European Commission, 2020b; European Union, 2019).

Significant innovation asymmetries were identified between different regions in EU. According to the EU Innovation Scoreboard, the most innovative EU regions were Zurich in Switzerland, Helsinki, Finland, Stockholm or Sweden and Hovedstaden in Denmark. Czech Republic, Greece, and Italy were classified as moderately innovative countries, with some relevant innovation centers (e.g., Prague in the Czech Republic, Crete in Greece, and Friuli Venezia Giulia in Italy). Least innovative countries/regions may be helped through more coordinated policies according to the European Commission (European Commission, 2020a). In Portugal, ANI recommends (innovation measures): (i) the creation of added value from the knowledge generated by R&D, (ii) the collaboration between the industries and the generators of advanced knowledge, (iii) a straight supervision of the national innovation system, (iv) the development of public and private initiatives, (v) the identification of stakeholders' limitations or (vi) a better coordination between public and private entities (ANI, 2019).

European patent applications ensure protection of inventions (e.g. products or process) in up to 44 countries. Importantly, one in five European patent applications was from a small or medium-sized company in 2018 (a higher number than previous year). About two-thirds of these patents were commercially exploited (about 50% by the company and about 50% by the company in collaboration with a trading partner, usually from another European country). Small and medium-sized enterprises holding European patent applications were more likely to establish collaborations with companies from other geographical areas: North America (26%), Asia (21%) and the rest of the world (13%). Overall, the number of European patent applications commercially exploited (about two-thirds), and the percentage of international collaborations were limited (only, 13% to 26%). Thus, more collaborative strategies with extra-European partners are likely to be positive due to due to market expansion (e.g. growth of patent portfolios) (EPO, 2019). Unfortunately, the EU market is fragmented and present difficulties in producing and marketing the generated innovation. For instance, the establishment of partnerships between the public and private sector, the collaboration with non-European partners or the growth of investment in R&D (EU target for innovation: 3% of GDP) (European Parliament, 2020; WIPO, 2019).

As expected, there are common R&D areas between EU and USA (e.g., medicine and health, computing, cybersecurity, or nanotechnology). Additionally, specific R&D niches may be identified in both regions. For instance, EU was more focused on climate change or gender equality than USA, which abandoned the Paris agreement during the Trump administration (Executive Office of the President of United States, 2019; European Parliament, 2020; Horizon, 2020; USA Department of State, 2019).

Positively, coordinating structures to assist the productive activity of emergent innovations are frequent in USA (IMIs institutes) (Manufacturing USA, 2020). The mission of these institutes (lab-to-market initiatives) is to strength the entrepreneurial capacities of research organizations, to develop more effective forms of collaboration/ partnerships, to promote/optimize technology management, to transfer practices, to promote access for external innovators, to improve the participation of small business in R&D, to improve metrics and analyses and to advance innovation assessments (United States Studies Centre, 2019). Conversely, the most skeptical experts warn that the investment in R&D was reduced by the USA government in the last years e.g., fewer R&D stimulus in the private sector, such as less favorable credit. These limitations may negatively influence the future of R&D in USA (Global Trade and Innovation Policy Alliance, 2019).

Finally, governments, companies, and civil societies are obliged to face to meet the new economic, health and social challenges as a result of the current COVID-2019 pandemic crisis. Innovation is an irreplaceable tool to overcome the actual pandemic crisis, not only by offering new opportunities for the development of health technologies (e.g., therapies or vaccines against the COVID-19 virus), but also by generating new opportunities, products, processes and/or business models for companies (OECD, 2019; European Commission, 2020c).

Issues, Controversies, Problems

In this section, some of the strengths and weakness of EU and USA innovation policies are presented (e.g. patent waiver on COVID-2019 vaccines).

Strengths of EU Innovation Policies

Among the strengths of EU innovation policies are (i) the definition of financial instruments (e.g., Horizon 2020), (ii) the development of digital governments (e-Gov) (e.g., making public administrations more efficient, namely through a easiest access to public services by citizens) or (iii) the facilitation of the flow of non-personal data ("removal of unjustified restrictions on data location, regulatory competence and authority supervision, even when data is processed across borders") (European Commission, 2020ab; European Parliament, 2020).

EU support open innovation strategies to bridge their needs: "Fostering international cooperation in research and innovation is a strategic priority for the European Union so that we can access the latest knowledge and the best talent worldwide, tackle global societal challenges more effectively, create business opportunities in new and emerging markets, and use science di diplomacy as an influential instrument of external policy" (EC-OECD, 2018; Leijten, 2019). Open innovation advocates the dissemination of free trade, exchange of knowledge or marketing of innovative products and services, which favor the advancement of global innovation (Leijten, 2019). The firms benefiting from institutional and economic incentives and collaborating with other organizations (e.g., sharing scientific findings) seems to be more prepared to cooperate with partners, to access resources/inputs, to improve their technological and product projects (multilevel analyses of data from 601 European firms) (Oguguo et al., 2020).

In UE, public procurement of innovative strategies (PPP) is already producing positive outputs (European Commission, 2021b; Stojčić et al., 2020). PPPs occur "when the public sector uses its purchasing power to act as early adopter of innovative solutions which are not yet available on large scale commercial basis" (European Commission, 2021b). Positive innovation outputs were produced by PPPs in a study involving 41,623 firms. Innovation outputs may be improved if firms simultaneously receive financial support and innovation-oriented public procurement (Stojčić et al., 2020).

Weaknesses EU Innovation Policies

Among the weaknesses of EU innovation policies were (i) the absence of a digital single market (e.g., cybersecurity for business and citizens) (ii) a limited investment in R&D (e.g., despite the target of 3% of GDP, investment in R&D is stagnated), and (iii) constraints on applying copyright legislation in the digital age (e.g., the use of text and image from internet for commercial purposes) (Global Trade and Innovation Policy Alliance,2019). Concerning R&D collaborations, the cooperation between firms should be optimized in the future aiming at developing better products (Oguguo et al., 2020).

The innovation performance of EU Member States is annually presented in the EU Innovation Union Scoreboard, which may not be a precise and sensitive tool to design innovation policies. This indicator is associated with bias when compared to other metrics (e.g., "identification of and relation between input and output innovation indicators") (Edquist et al., 2018). EU regions are heterogeneous, regarding their industrial structure and regional innovation systems ("a process of economic diversification (structural change) in addition to mere economic growth (expansion)"). Overall, four types of innovators were identified in EU (innovation leaders, strong innovator, moderate innovators and modest innovators): Zürich, Stockholm and Copenhagen (innovation leaders, with a high score on both research and business innovation); growing industrial regions in Northern and Western Europe (strong innovators); most capital regions of Southern and Eastern Europe (with the exception of Prague) (moderate innovators; the industrial structure is characterized by service functions and public administration) and Southern and Eastern Europe, with focus on agriculture and small and medium enterprises in traditional sectors (modest innovators) (Asheim, 2019).

Regional innovation policies are based on relatively well-established networks, which may influence the type of interactions between different stakeholders. The redesign of networks of business and research may be needed due to changes in innovation policies (Rubach et al., 2017). Innovation policy analysis tends to overlook the deep asymmetries in production structures across EU member states, despite they are fundamental for the good functioning of European integration. Ideally, the economic structure of each EU member state should be individually analyzed, regarding the design of new politic recommendations and measures (Mamede, 2017).

Strengths of USA Innovation Policies

In USA, successful innovation contributes to raise per capita income and the standards of living and quality of life of citizens. Indirectly, innovative companies stimulate other firms to be innovative (Krumm, 2019). Among the strengths of the USA innovation policies are:

1. The commercialization of inventions is assisted by the participation of institutes, such as Institutes of Manufacturing Innovation (IMI), IMIs are based on a public-private partnership that brings together members of government, academia, and industry. There are 16 IMIs territorially dispersed: *Every day, Manufacturing USA leaves its mark on our industry and nation by bringing together manufacturing, academia and government to fuel a skilled U.S. workforce. The collaborations will galvanize domestic manufacturing supply chains; grow centers of technological excellence across the country; move products from lab to market in record time; revitalize the national economy; and affirm our global leadership* (https://www.manufacturingusa.com/institutes). Each IMI supports the production of different technologies, such as electronics, biotechnology, sensors, digital materials, artificial intelligence, etc. (Global Trade and Innovation Policy Alliance, 2019; Manufacturing USA, 2020). Advanced manufacturing institutes were launched to assist firms in finding competent partners (e.g., automobile production requires intricate chains of specialized subcontracting firms). These *institutes are strengthening regional economic clusters, creating, and reinforcing connections between firms that are geographically concentrated and reinforcing connections between firms that are geographically concentrated.* (Block et al., 2020).
2. The innovation system includes technological transfer measures, such as the *Bayh-Dole Act*. The *Bayh-Dole Act* is a bipartisan legislation of 1980, according to which universities, small businesses, and non-profit institutions may require IP rights, (e.g. reseach supported by the federal goverment). This regulation lead to a significant increase in the number of patent applications and granted patents for universities and
3. A strong protection of IP rights is ensured. For instance, patents may guarantee financial return in some cases. Positively, innovators´ trust and security to invest time and money in the development of new products or processes increase with the number of granted patents/IP rights (Global Trade and Innovation Policy Alliance, 2019; Manufacturing USA, 2020).
4. Government is committed to stimulate R&D, with significant federal resources being allocated to promote technological development (e.g., US$ 144 billion in 2017) (Gordon, 2019).

The protection of IP is predicted in the Us Constitution under Article 1, Section 8, giving Congress the power, "To promote the Progress of Science and useful Arts, by securing for limited to Authors and Inventors the exclusive Right to their respective

Writings and Discoveries", which reinforce the relevance of IP rights for the economy of USA (Global Trade and Innovation Policy Alliance, 2019; Manufacturing USA, 2020). Innovation policy measures, such as, granting of patents and funding of National Institutes of Health, supported the development of new pharmaceutical treatments, with clear social benefits (Kyle, 2020).

Weaknesses of USA Innovation Policies

In 2017, USA registered an alarming decrease in the ranking of innovation. USA dropped to 10th in the global ranking for net impact on global innovation and the share of global tech unicorn start-ups tumbled to 41% in 2017 (Krumm et al., 2019). Among the weaknesses of the USA innovation policies are:

1. Progressive decrease in R&D investment by the federal government, with only 0.62 of GDP in 2017 (the lowest value since 1955),
2. An inadequate investment in education (Galama, 2008; Global Trade and Innovation Policy Alliance, 2019),
3. Private sector reduction of investments in R&D (e.g., credits),
4. Lack of policies for stimulating innovation. According to the opinion of observers, "federal policies do little to support state and local initiatives; the federal government invests little and pays little attention to the service sector and the important role of companies and universities in the marketing process" (Global Trade and Innovation Policy Alliance, 2019),
5. The number of laws was reduced to improve the efficiency of markets during Trump administration, which may have negatively impacted innovation ("for every one new regulation issued, at least two prior regulations be identified for elimination"; "2-for-l" order) (Krumm, 2019).

University education should be encouraged to graduate highly qualified staff, who can operate in the innovation sector. Among the major research areas for innovative business are science technology, engineering, and mathematics (STEM). For instance, companies with active employee retention and promotion policies tend to maintain higher innovation standards and launch more products into the market (Aspen Institute, 2019).

Additionally, mobility of researchers was altered in some cases, as a consequence of the restrictive emigration policies of USA. This may have negatively impacted the performance some business, since highly skilled workers are required in innovative companies (Aspen Institute, 2019). Competitiveness, innovation, and prosperity of USA partially depends on the channeling of global talent (Dennis& Committee for Economic Development of The Conference Board, 2020). Thus, fewer restrictions on immigration (e.g., immigration of highly qualified staff), more international cooperation, higher investments, and implementation of spy networks to protect inventions were recommended in USA (Aspen Institute, 2019).

Despite the significant R&D investment in USA, some research areas were preferred. For instance, 56.0% (on average) of total federal public expenses in R&D for defense (1999 to 2017), with only 22.0% (on average) for health (Gordon, 2019).

In USA, the political corruption seems to limit corporate innovation at a local level, with less innovative firms in corrupt regions (e.g., predominance of firms with reduced patenting activities). This may be explained by a higher extortion risk and a decreased threat of competition in highly corrupt regions (Huang & Yuan, 2021).

Waiver on COVID-2019 Vaccines: EU vs. USA

The Biden Administration stated that the COVID-2019 vaccine waiver at the World Trade Organization (WTO) Agreement on Trade-Related Aspects of Intellectual Property Rights (TRIPS) Council, contrary to the opinion of EU (Global Trade and Innovation Policy Alliance, 2021). However, diverse disadvantages were highlighted, such as "removing the IP rights would make it more difficult for innovators to share the technology and know-how needed for manufacturers to produce genuine and effective vaccine"; "removing IP prevents the rights owners from controlling the efficacy and quality of vaccines that reach peoples' arms" or "removing IP undermines the innovation of the biotech sector and the quality of vaccines" (Global Trade and Innovation Policy Alliance, 2021; Property Rights Alliance, 2021).

SOLUTIONS AND RECOMMENDATIONS

Ideally, civil society should supervise innovation policies to control/limit the influence of political lobbies/doctrines in the dissemination of certain research areas (e.g., nuclear energy) or the disinvestment on potentially unprofitable innovations (e.g., medicines for the treatment of rare diseases, which cover a limited number of patients). A closer cooperation and dialogue between all stakeholders (e.g., academies, industry, and business) and policy makers is recommended to achieve efficient innovative policies. Historical paths, different needs, and national innovation systems should be considered in the design of innovation policies in EU or other countries (Makó et al., 2019). The regulatory agenda of USA includes the improvement of the national framework environment for innovation (Krumm, 2019).

Frequently, the investment of private sector on R&D is scarce aiming at minimizing the risk of potential losses, such as, when investments are too high (e.g., a high risk of investment loss). There is a significant positive effect of education and R&D on the outputs of innovation. Thus, collaborations between business, universities and R&D centers should be strengthened in EU (e.g., partnerships between the private sector and the elements of the innovation systems) (Pegkas et al., 2019). Ideally, innovation policies should be tailored by country, because of the heterogeneity of national innovation systems and the innovative capacity of each country (Tziogkidis et al., 2020). Besides assisting companies, innovation policies should encourage collaborations between firms/companies. Finally, entrepreneurship positively impact innovative business, which reinforce the importance of an open innovation framework (Pusthovrh & Jaklič, 2014).

Governments should support and promote innovation beyond the health sector, since some major international research projects were stopped during COVID-19 pandemic (WIPO, 2021). Academies, private and public groups, and civil society are encouraged to discuss the long-term implications of the pandemic crisis on economy, health, and innovation (George et al., 2020).

FUTURE RESEARCH DIRECTIONS

Studies about the impact of regulation and/or corruption on innovation are recommended. Further studies about the impact of grants or incentives (public or private) on innovation citizens' participation on decisions about innovative policies are suggested.

The impact of pandemic on innovation must be monitored, because of the lack of interest in some research areas at a global level. For instance, the impact of telehealth and tele-education on patients' health and students' learning outcomes, respectively. Positively, new disruptive technologies, such as vaccines against COVID-19 or other health technologies to mitigate the virus or to facilitate social interactions were developed during COVID-19 pandemic.

The emergence of these new technologies is monitored by international institutions, such as European Patent Office (EPO). Among these technologies are vaccines and therapeutics (e.g., candidate antiviral and symptomatic therapeutics or nucleic acids and antibodies to fight coronavirus), diagnostics and analytics (e.g., protein and nucleic acid assays and analytical protocols), informatics (e.g., bioinformatics or healthcare informatics) or the tracking of technologies for the new normal, such as (i) new devices, materials, and equipment (e.g., building materials, design of an aircraft's, automobile's, or other vehicle's interior, robots, masks, respirators, etc.), (ii) new procedures, actions, and activities (e.g., clean room technologies, air treatment, cleaning of air, ventilation to avoid recirculation of contaminated air, plastics with antiviral/antibacterial properties, spraying of disinfectants, UV disinfection using a photocatalyst, disinfection with ozone, thermal or ultrasound treatments, protections for patients or health professionals, negative pressure ventilators, such as mechanical ventilation without intubation, etc), (iii) new digital technologies (e.g., touchless, gesture-based interaction with public terminals in order to avoid the spread of germs or monitoring or tracking people with Covid-19 symptoms, wearing masks or washing hands, apps, using Artificial Intelligence and Machine Learning to help understand how the virus spreads, methods to detect virus infection in tissues etc.). This emergent research may be consulted at EPO website (under EPO's standard terms and conditions (https://www.epo.org/news-events/in-focus/fighting-coronavirus.html) (EPO, 2021).

CONCLUSION

Both EU and US innovation policies support that innovation led to better economic performance, an increase in employment and productivity, and a more sustainable economy. Additionally, these policies recommend an open innovation model, an easier mobility of researchers, national and international investment and cooperation between research centers and business, development of cybersecurity against spy networks, affordable education, and a more specialized and advanced qualification for workers (European Parliament, 2020; United States Whitehouse, 2019; Von der Leyen, 2019). Strong education strategies are required to prepare an appropriate workforce in innovative sectors in both regions. Education is especially relevant, since both regies are intended to become more competitive in the future (Aspen Institute, 2019; European Parliament, 2020).

Overall, USA performed better than EU in terms of innovation indicators (GII), although both regions were among the most innovative in the world (WIPO, 2019). R&D investment was higher in USA in comparison to EU. Additionally, some regulatory aspects seemed to be more flexible in USA than EU (e.g., fair use of copyright in USA), with USA integrating a coordinated system of institutes/agencies (IMIs) to support the marketing of new inventions. These differences may explain the better performance of USA over EU. Particularly, the coordinated system of institutes/agencies of USA seemed to facilitate the introduction of new inventions into the market and to avoid market fragmentation (Global Trade and Innovation Policy Alliance, 2019; Manufacturing USA, 2020; WIPO, 2019).

Some political measures are suggested to improve innovation in EU, such as more investment in R&D (e.g., 3% of GDP target is far from being achieved by most EU countries), creation of new agencies that support the introduction of new innovations into the market and allow an effective coordination between stakeholders (currently, coordination bodies are dispersed in EU and in general these entities do not work in an efficient networking), more investment for small and medium-sized enterprises, optimization of the communication between small and medium-sized enterprises and potential partners/markets outside the EU, less heterogeneous indices of innovation between different EU regions, and creation of more flexible innovation regulations in EU.

As expected, there are some common innovation areas between EU and USA, such as medicine, health, nanotechnology, or computing. Currently, the emerging problems of the pandemic crisis are a priority in both regions. During Trump administration, research on climate mitigation decreased in USA (Executive Office of the President of United States, 2019; European Parliament, 2020; Horizon, 2020; USA Department of State, 2019, 2020). However, the innovation policies of the recent elected President Joe Biden are more focused on climate change mitigation than the previous ones. Additionally, the innovation policies of the Biden administration support a higher focus on social inequalities and clean energies, and a lower investment on defense than the previous administration Trump (Information Technology and Innovation Foundation, 2020). Civil society should scrutiny innovation policies to limit the eventual influence of lobbies, corruption, and external interests.

The current pandemic crisis may positively and/or negatively influence innovation at a global level. For instance, collaborations on new innovations against COVID-19. COVID-19 should be maintained, but non-COVID-19 research should not be overlooked by policy makers, such as research on cancer, dementia, or social and economic sciences. The global lack of interest in some research areas, such as non-COVID-19 research must be supervised (WIPO, 2020).

DISCLOSURE

This chapter was based on a work developed during the frequency of the master's in public administration, ISCTE.IUL - *Instituto Universitário de Lisboa* (2019-2020).

ACKNOWLEDGMENT

ISCTE.IUL - *Instituto Universitário de Lisboa* and CBIOS - Research Center for Biosciences and Health Technologies, Universidade Lusófona de Humanidades e Tecnologias, Lisboa, Portugal.

REFERENCES

Andreoni, A., & Chang, H. J. (2019). The political economy of industrial policy: Structural interdependencies, policy alignment and conflict management. *Structural Change and Economic Dynamics*, *48*, 136–150. doi:10.1016/j.strueco.2018.10.007

Ani. (2019). *International Comparative Analysis of the National Innovation System.* Available: https://www.ani.pt/media/4880/relatorio_012_ani.pdf

Anišić, Z., Koldžin, D., & Freund, R. (2013). How to Support Open Innovations through Public Policies? *Annals of the Faculty of Engineering Hunedoara - International Journal of Engineering (Stevenage, England)*, *11*(2), 241–247.

Asheim, B. T. (2019). Smart specialisation, innovation policy and regional innovation systems: What about new path development in less innovative regions? *Innovation: The European Journal of Social Sciences*, *32*(1), 8–25.

Aspen Institute. (n.d.). *An innovation challenge for the United States.* Available: https://assets.aspeninstitute.org/content/uploads/2019/09/Aspen-Cyber-Group-An-Innovation-Challenge-for-the-United-States-10.2.19.pdf

Block, F., Keller, M. R., & Negoita, M. (2020). Network Failure and the Evolution of the US Innovation System. *Journal of Industry, Competition and Trade*, *20*(2), 235–247. doi:10.100710842-019-00324-1

Caraça, J., Lundvall, B. Å., & Mendonça, S. (2009). The changing role of science in the innovation process: From Queen to Cinderella? *Technological Forecasting and Social Change*, *76*(6), 861–867. doi:10.1016/j.techfore.2008.08.003

Congressional Budget Office. (n.d.). *How Might Changes in Federal Policies Boost Innovation and Productivity?* Available: https://www.cbo.gov/publication/52464

Dennis, A. (2020). *Boosting Immigration: Harnessing Global Talent to Increase US Competitiveness, Innovation, and Prosperity.* Committee for Economic Development of The Conference Board. Committee for Economic Development of The Conference Board.

EC-OECD. (2018). *STI policy taxonomy / ontology STIP monitoring and analysis (EC-OECD project).* Available: https://www. innovationpolicyplatform.org/stip-monitoring-and-analysis/sti-policytaxonomy-ontology

Edquist, C., Zabala-Iturriagagoitia, J. M., Barbero, J., & Zofío, J. L. (2018). On the meaning of innovation performance: Is the synthetic indicator of the Innovation Union Scoreboard flawed? *Research Evaluation*, *27*(3), 196–211. doi:10.1093/reseval/rvy011

EPO. (2019). *Market success for inventions: Patent commercialization scoreboard: European SMEs November 2019 | Key findings*. Available: http://documents.epo.org/projects/babylon/eponet.nsf/0/981A954C6D692D4DC125849A0054C147/$File/Patent_commercialisation_scoreboard_European_SMEs_key_findings_2019_en.pdf

EPO. (2021). *Fighting coronavirus*. Available: https://www.epo.org/news-events/in-focus/fighting-coronavirus.html

EPO & EUIPO. (2019). *IPR-intensive industries and economic performance in the European Union*. Available: https://www.boip.int/uploads/inline/WEB_IPR_intensive_Report_2019.pdf

European Commission. (2016). *Open Innovation Open Science to the World - a vision for Europe*. Available: http://publications.europa.eu/resource/cellar/3213b335-1cbc-11e6-ba9a-01aa75ed71a1.0001.02/DOC_2

European Commission. (2020a). *Regional Innovation Scoreboard*. Available: h Available: ttps://ec.europa.eu/growth/industry/policy/innovation/regional_en

European Commission. (2020b). *Enterprise Europe Network: Lisbon*. Available: https://een.ec.europa.eu/about/branches/pt/lisboa

European Commission. (2020c). *Economy: Coronavirus Crisis in EU*. Available: https://ec.europa.eu/info/live-work-travel-eu/health/coronavirus-response/economy_en

European Commission. (2021a). *European Innovation Scoreboard 2021*. Available: file:///C:/Users/cmbpi/Downloads/ET-AY-21-001-EN-N.pdf

European Commission. (2021b). *Public Procurement of Innovative Solutions*. Available: https://ec.europa.eu/digital-single-market/en/public-procurement-innovative-solutions

European Parliament. (2020). *Innovation policy*. Available: https://www.europarl.europa.eu/factsheets/en/sheet/67/innovation-policy

European Union. (2019). *Research and innovation*. Available: https://europa.eu/european-union/topics/research-innovation_pt

Executive Office of the President of United States. (2019). *Science & Technology Highlights*. Available: https://www.whitehouse.gov/wp-content/uploads/2019/02/Administration-2018-ST-Highlights.pdf

Executive Office of the President of United States. (2020). *Administration Research and Development Budget Priorities*. Available: https://www.whitehouse.gov/wp-content/uploads/2020/08/M-20-29.pdf

Galama, T., & Hosek, J. (2008). *U.S. Competitiveness in Science and Technology*. RAND Corporation.

Gavriluţă, A. F. (2016). Implications of Government on Sustainable Development. *Journal of Public Administration. Finance & Law*, *10*, 31–41.

George, G., Lakhani, K. R., & Puranam, P. (2020). What has changed? The Impact of Covid Pandemic on the Technology and Innovation Management Research Agenda. *Journal of Management Studies*, *57*(8), 1754-1758.

Global Trade and Innovation Policy Alliance. (2019). *National innovation policies: What Countries Do Best and How They Can Improve*. Available: https://www2.itif.org/2019-national-innovation-policies.pdf

Global Trade and Innovation Policy Alliance. (2021). *U.S. support of TRIPS waiver undermines efforts to fight COVID-19*. Available: https://gtipa.org/publications/2021/05/06/us-support-trips-trips-waiver-undermines-efforts-fight-covid-19

Gordon, J. L. (2019). The role of the State in fostering innovation activity: Case studies of the USA and Germany. *Brazilian Journal of Political Economy*, *39*(4), 571–590. doi:10.1590/0101-31572019-2899

Horizon. (2020). *Horizon 2020 sections and Focus areas*. Available: https://ec.europa.eu/programmes/horizon2020/en/h2020-sections

Huang, Q., & Yuan, T. (2021). Does Political Corruption Impede Firm Innovation? Evidence from the United States. *Journal of Financial and Quantitative Analysis*, *56*(1), 213–248. doi:10.1017/S0022109019000966

Information Technology and Innovation Foundation (ITIF). (2020). *President-Elect Biden's Agenda on Technology and Innovation Policy*. Available: https://itif.org/publications/2020/11/07/president-elect-bidens-agenda-technology-and-innovation-policy

Krumm, B. K. (2019). Regulatory Policy in the Trump Era and its Impact on Innovation. *Mercer Law Review*, *70*(3), 685–704. doi:10.2139srn.3404205

Kyle, M. K. (2020). The Alignment of Innovation Policy and Social Welfare: Evidence from Pharmaceuticals. *NBER Innovation Policy & the Economy*, *20*(1), 95–123. doi:10.1086/705640

Lee, S. M., Hwang, T., & Choi, D. (2012). Open innovation in the public sector of leading countries. *Management Decision, 50*(1), 147–162. doi:10.1108/00251741211194921

Leijten, J. (2019). Innovation policy and international relations: Directions for EU diplomacy. *European Journal of Futures Research, 7*(1), 1–21. doi:10.118640309-019-0156-1

Makó, C., Illéssy, M., & Heidrich, B. (2019). When Will Alpha and Omega Collide? In Search of the Theoretical Relevance of Eu Innovation Policies. *Vezetéstudomány / Budapest Management Review, 50*(11), 66–73.

Mamede, R. P. (2017). Structural asymmetries, innovation measurement and innovation policies in the EU. *Portuguese Journal of Social Science, 16*(3), 377–392. doi:10.1386/pjss.16.3.377_1

Manufacturing, U. S. A. (2020). *Institutes.* Available: https://www.manufacturingusa.com/institutes

OECD. (2019). *Embracing Innovation in Government: Global Trends in 2019.* Available: https://trends.oecd-opsi.org/embracing-innovation-in-government-global-trends-2019.pdf

OECD. (2020). *Gross domestic spending on R&D.* Available: https://data.oecd.org/rd/gross-domestic-spending-on-r-d.htm

Oguguo, P. C., Bodas Freitas, I. M., & Genet, C. (2020). Multilevel institutional analyses of firm benefits from R&D collaboration. *Technological Forecasting and Social Change, 151*, 119841. Advance online publication. doi:10.1016/j.techfore.2019.119841

Pegkas, P., Staikouras, C., & Tsamadias, C. (2019). Does research and development expenditure impact innovation? Evidence from the European Union countries. *Journal of Policy Modeling, 41*(5), 1005–1025. doi:10.1016/j.jpolmod.2019.07.001

Property Rights Alliance. (2021). *U.S. support of trips waiver undermines effort to fight COVID-19.* Available: https://www.propertyrightsalliance.org/news/u-s-support-of-trips-waiver-undermines-effort-to-fight-covid-19/

Rubach, S., Hoholm, T., & Håkansson, H. (2017). Innovation networks or innovation within networks. *IMP Journal, 11*(2), 178–206. doi:10.1108/IMP-09-2015-0057

Stojčić, N., Srhoj, S., & Coad, A. (2020). Innovation procurement as capability-building: Evaluating innovation policies in eight Central and Eastern European countries. *European Economic Review, 121*, 103330. Advance online publication. doi:10.1016/j.euroecorev.2019.103330

Torres Freire, C., Massami Maruyama, F., & Polli, M. (2017). Innovation and Entrepreneurship: Public Policies and Private Actions. *New Studies*, 50-76.

Tziogkidis, P., Philippas, D., Leontitsis, A., & Sickles, R. C. (2020). A data envelopment analysis and local partial least squares approach for identifying the optimal innovation policy direction. *European Journal of Operational Research*, *285*(3), 1011–1024. doi:10.1016/j.ejor.2020.02.023

United States Studies Centre. (n.d.). *Myths, crises and complacency: innovation policy in the United States and Australia.* Available: https://www.ussc.edu.au/analysis/innovation-policy-in-the-united-states-and-australia#unleashing-american-innovation

United States Whitehouse. (2019). *Research and development.* Available: https://www.whitehouse.gov/wp-content/uploads/2018/02/ap_18_research-fy2019.pdf

US Department of State. (n.d.). *On the US Withdrawal from the Paris Agreement.* Available: https://www.state.gov/on-the-u-s-withdrawal-from-the-paris-agreement/

Von der Leyen, U. (2019). *One the most ambitious Union: my program for Europe.* Available: https://ec.europa.eu/info/sites/info/files/political-guidelines-next-commission_pt.pdf

WIPO. (2011). *The Global Innovation Index: Insights and trends.* Available: https://www.wipo.int/wipo_magazine/en/2011/04/article_0005.html

WIPO. (2019). *The Global Innovation Index 2019.* Available: https://www.wipo.int/edocs/pubdocs/en/wipo_pub_gii_2019-chapter1.pdf and https://www.wipo.int/global_innovation_index/en/

WIPO. (2020). *The Global Innovation Index 2020* Available: https://www.globalinnovationindex.org/gii-2020-report

WIPO. (2021). *The GII calls on business and policy leaders around the world to sustain innovation.* Available: https://www.wipo.int/global_innovation_index/en/2020/#risks

ADDITIONAL READING

Aarden, E., Marelli, L., & Blasimme, A. (2021). The translational lag narrative in policy discourse in the United States and the European Union: A comparative study. *Humanities & Social Sciences Communications*, *8*(1), 1–9. doi:10.105741599-021-00777-y

Almeida, H., Hsu, P.-H., Li, D., & Tseng, K. (2021). More Cash, Less Innovation: The Effect of the American Jobs Creation Act on Patent Value. *Journal of Financial and Quantitative Analysis*, *56*(1), 1–28. doi:10.1017/S0022109019000954

Berné-Martínez, J. M., Arnal-Pastor, M., & Llopis-Amorós, M.-P. (2021). Reacting to the paradigm shift: QCA study of the factors shaping innovation in publishing, information services, advertising and market research activities in the European Union. *Technological Forecasting and Social Change*, *162*, 120340. Advance online publication. doi:10.1016/j.techfore.2020.120340

Buciuni, G., & Pisano, G. (2021). Variety of Innovation in Global Value Chains. *Journal of World Business*, *56*(2), 101167. Advance online publication. doi:10.1016/j.jwb.2020.101167

Hadjielias, E., Olufunmilola, L. D., Discua Cruz, A., Zekas, S., Christofi, M., & Sakka, G. (2021). How do digital innovation teams function? Understanding the team cognition-process nexus within the context of digital transformation. *Journal of Business Research*, *122*, 373–386. doi:10.1016/j.jbusres.2020.08.045

Hjelmar, U. (2021). The institutionalization of public sector innovation. *Public Management Review*, *23*(1), 53–69. doi:10.1080/14719037.2019.1665702

Huang, Q., & Yuan, T. (2021). Does Political Corruption Impede Firm Innovation? Evidence from the United States. *Journal of Financial and Quantitative Analysis*, *56*(1), 213–248. doi:10.1017/S0022109019000966

López-Rubio, P., Roig-Tierno, N., & Mas-Tur, A. (2021). Which regions produce the most innovation policy research? *Policy Studies*, 1–23. doi:10.1080/01442872.2021.1937595

Mortazavi, S., Eslami, M. H., Hajikhani, A., & Väätänen, J. (2021). Mapping inclusive innovation: A bibliometric study and literature review. *Journal of Business Research*, *122*, 736–750. doi:10.1016/j.jbusres.2020.07.030

Nylund, P. A., Brem, A., & Agarwal, N. (2021). Innovation ecosystems for meeting sustainable development goals: The evolving roles of multinational enterprises. *Journal of Cleaner Production*, *281*, 125329. Advance online publication. doi:10.1016/j.jclepro.2020.125329

Pustovrh, A., & Jaklič, M. (2014). National Innovation Policies in the Eu: A Fuzzy-Set Analysis. *Economic & Business Review*, *16*(1), 39–62. doi:10.15458/2335-4216.1179

Rush, H., Marshall, N., Bessant, J., & Ramalingam, B. (2021). Applying an ecosystems approach to humanitarian innovation. *Technological Forecasting and Social Change, 165*, 120529. doi:10.1016/j.techfore.2020.120529

Xie, X., & Wang, H. (2021). How to bridge the gap between innovation niches and exploratory and exploitative innovations in open innovation ecosystems. *Journal of Business Research, 124*, 299–311. doi:10.1016/j.jbusres.2020.11.058

KEY TERMS AND DEFINITIONS

Close Innovation: Internal innovative practices, with innovations occurring internally to organizations.

Indicators of Innovation: Any qualitative or quantitative metric to quantify innovation.

Innovation: Any process or product, management or marketing form, business or industrial activity, or other related activity that contribute to a significant improvement in the public or private sector.

Innovation Performance: Grade of achievements (low or high), as consequence of innovative practices.

Inventions: A technical solution to solve a specific technical problem.

Open Innovation: Collaborative innovative practices, with innovations occurring internally and externally to organizations.

Patents: A patent is an exclusive right over an invention, as a consequence of a contract between the state and the person making the application, which ensure the exclusive right to produce and commercialize a certain invention.

Research and Development: Scientific investigations in the public or private sector.

Chapter 9
Linking Open Innovation and Firm Performance

Francisco Musiello-Neto
University of Rovira i Virgili, Brazil

Orlando Manuel Martins Marques Lima Rua
Center for Organisational and Social Studies, Porto School of Accounting and Business, Polytechnic of Porto, Portugal & Research Center of Business Sciences, University of Beira Interior, Portugal

Mario Arias-Oliva
Complutense University of Madrid, Spain

ABSTRACT

This study aims to analyze the relationship between open innovation and firm performance. A quantitative methodology was adopted with a survey of 251 small and medium-sized enterprise (SME) top managers in the hospitality sector, particularly in hotels. The primary data collected were subjected to descriptive and inferential statistical analysis treatments, highlighting the application of the structural equations model. The findings show that open innovation enhances hotel performance. In practical terms, this study will guide, on the one hand, the firms' top managers of the hospitality sector in the definition of open innovation strategies to develop the relevant resources and capacities for achieving superior performance. On the other hand, it can contribute to the meaning of effective government programs to support firms in this sector.

DOI: 10.4018/978-1-7998-8665-5.ch009

INTRODUCTION

The open innovation management model has been one of management's most widely discussed topics (Huizingh, 2011). The concept of open innovation has quickly gained great prominence, both as an approach for contemporary top management concerning the business community and as a theoretical concept intensively studied by researchers (Podmetina et al., 2018).

Regarding the relationship between open innovation and organizational performance, the management competence of the firm depends on the ability of senior managers to mobilize and distribute the available resources, namely knowledge for the creation of organizational value (Alavi & Leidner, 2001). This issue positively reflects the results achieved by firms by leveraging their value chains, with strategic business objectives aligned through management innovation (West et al., 2014). The intentional use of knowledge input and output flow is intended to accelerate internal innovation and expand markets to retain external knowledge (Chesbrough & Crowther, 2006).

Open innovation is a strategy contemplated in the different management models, aiming at the superior performance of the organization (Finkelstein et al., 2009). This strategic component underlies the identification of key factors for recognizing opportunities and making decisions that affect organizational processes (Diaz-Fernandez et al., 2015). In this regard, top managers play a critical role, as their choices and actions create organizational contexts, responses to middle managers, and performances with ultimate impact on the organization (Smith, 2014). Managers (1) identify and develop new ideas to build, support, and stimulate employees involved in learning and processes, (2) contribute to the efficiency and coordination of existing capabilities that support new organizational capabilities, and (3) contribute leadership that enhances competitiveness (Lopez-Cabrales et al., 2015).

Companies that implemented open innovation, as a process of innovation in management, to direct the organization to the use of available resources, adapt to the new competitive environment before new strategic procedures, reduce organizational risk, expand competitive advantage and adaptability to the environment, to obtain superior performance (Lião et al., 2015). The shift in the management model from closed to open innovation emphasizes manager expertise, and it requires a more skilled workforce, especially concerning interpersonal skills (Reilly, 2018).

In this context, the justification of these assumptions (open innovation model and superior performance) is found in the narration of the facts that follow the vast literature on organizational theory, strategic management and management models, with particular emphasis on open innovation and the difficulties linked to management rooted in the concept of closed innovation (Aranha et al., 2017). Some authors (e.g., Almirall & Casadesus-Masanell, 2010; Leiponen & Helfat, 2010;

Huizingh, 2011) argue that few studies are published in the scientific literature on the benefits of the implementation of the *open* innovation model in open innovation organizations, especially in SMEs.

This research sought to evaluate the relationship between open innovation and firm performance. The following research question emerged: What is the relationship between open innovation and firm performance?

THEORETICAL BACKGROUND

Open Innovation

Chesbrough (2003a) perceived that the management innovation model was closed, about new ideas and discrimination in the marketplace. From this observation, this researcher identified two pressing questions for maintaining this management model for most of the 20th century: (1) do these companies have the best talent and, therefore, are their ideas the best? and (2) are we the creators, are we the best sellers of our ideas? For this author, the mobility of knowledge makes it impossible to keep the best R&D talents because they have a high cost for the organization. Regarding the gradual and progressive transformation of ideas, organizations need to look outward for alternative content (ideas and conceptions) to generate innovation to share costs and benefits. These transformations could quickly be exchanged in rapidly changing environments, which for the moment had been capitalized by companies.

In this new paradigm (open innovation), in which the external environment can and should be considered by the management innovation strategies, research departments are no longer the only source of innovation for organizations, which need to innovate with increasing speed. Thus, innovation becomes part of a continuous flow in a collaborative process, from the internal to the external environment and vice-versa (Chesbrough, 2003a). Given this context and the search for a management innovation concept and modelling that seeks robustness to the study, an extensive review of the literature on business models between 1997 to 2018 was sought in the academic literature that identified varied concepts provided by researchers (Vils et al., 2017).

From this perspective, studies of management innovation and business models began to attract attention at the beginning of this century, following the intensive growth in the business models literature. The main areas with conceptual highlights are e-business, information technology for organizations, strategy focused on value creation and competitive advantage, innovation and technology management, creation and acquisition of value by companies based on the organization of their internal processes and external relationships with customers and suppliers (Zott et al., 2011). Including, the openness of the organization has increasingly become a trend for management; it aims to analyze how a new management model can influence the superior performance of the company and innovation. In addition, the open innovation model identifies the main variables that can affect the relationship between innovation and performance (Lopes & De Carvalho, 2018).

The open innovation model highlights the need for firms to acquire valuable resources from third parties and share internal resources to develop new products and services (Teplov et al., 2019). However, this model does not clarify when and how a firm obtains external knowledge and shares internal knowledge (Kuo-Nan & Tidd, 2012).

Open innovation confronts managers with the company and market specifities, despite the individual character of each company and specific to the management model. According to Chesbrough (2003a), in general terms, open innovation is structured according to a tripod: strategy, structure/processes and culture. This author states that managers are already required to answer a series of questions considering many variables. With the open innovation model, the complexity of these analyses diminishes considerably.

According to Van de Vrande et al. (2009) and Huizingh (2011), some activities favor the firm to acquire new knowledge and technologies outside the boundaries of the organization, allowing intentional flow of knowledge input that will capture and benefit from external sources of knowledge to improve current development, such as:

1. analyze the modifications that customers have made to the products they have purchased, to learn what those customers' needs are, and how that product can be improved to meet those needs; and
2. (2) establish networks that allow companies to quickly fill specific knowledge needs without wasting time and resources to develop that knowledge internally.

These authors also state that partnerships can also evolve into formal alliances or the acquisition of technological capabilities, i.e.:

a. establish external stakes by investing in startups to maintain market opportunities; outsource R&D to acquire external, licensed or purchased knowledge; and
b. bring in key knowledge developed outside the boundaries of the organization.

These mechanisms highlight the creation of multiple organizational values beyond the product life cycle, which is evidence of management valuation because knowledge includes the ability to create, absorb and share information related to these projects, which is mainly peculiar to the culture of the organization (Teece, 2007). This change in management perspective makes open innovation relevant to a more significant number and variety of organizations. On the other hand, if successful, management innovation with the organisation's primary focus brings new growth for the companies generating open innovation. Both arguments illustrate the need to integrate open innovation into the initiative for company strategy (Teece, 2007).

Business innovation is based on technology as the potential to transform traditional industry practice structurally, but uncertainty remains about where and how these transformations can be realized. SMEs seek to adopt supportive tools to survive to maintain company competitiveness and agility in the competitive market (Tikakul & Thomson, 2018). Many large organisations have successfully implemented the open innovation model (e.g., IBM, Microsoft, Dell, Procter & Gamble, IBM, Espoo, Xerox, Lucent, General Electrics, and Nokia) (Chesbrough, 2006).

It thus becomes essential to create a new organizational maturity and management competencies for the modalities of interaction with the innovation fostering market, to identify the best opportunities to obtain, through alliances (partnerships), the relationships between strategic orientations (entrepreneurship and market) with product and process innovations (Yun et al., 2016). In addition, companies that employ external resources in their own business obtain advantages in terms of new product development the more accessible access to markets, knowledge and technology (Chesbrough, 2006).

West et al. (2006) maintain that external knowledge has the same importance as internal knowledge. In the concept of open innovation, other companies of any segment and size can absorb the technologies developed (internally and externally). And they foster a win-win relationship. Effective open innovation requires companies to share their basic knowledge while ensuring that they will not lose their essential knowledge and future competitive advantage (Hurmelinna-Laukkanen, 2011).

Huizingh (2011) reinforces that the characteristics of open innovation within organizations lose strength as the global organizational reality identifies a natural environment to the interaction and inter-relationship of knowledge transfer, both internally and externally, to the corporation. The flow of information and knowledge generated for the innovation process increasingly crosses corporate boundaries by disconnecting from the closed innovation management system, whether normative or best practices. Companies seek available resources to create value or use external resources in their business models (Chesbrough, 2003b). Lichtenthaler (2010) argues that there is no value creation effect of integrating a wide range of external parties such as suppliers, customers, competitors, consultants, research institutes and universities in the innovation process. Bahemia and Squire (2010) explain that the great benefit is the technological development or shortening of the product life cycle and understanding how this cycle (product) can stimulate innovation further down the production chain.

Chesbrough and Borgers (2014, 2019) define open innovation as using knowledge input and output flows to accelerate internal innovation and expand markets for external use of innovation, respectively. These authors further argue that the concept of open innovation proposes that the R&D model is transformed into knowledge inputs and outputs that they can manage purposefully, where firms can (1) develop input processes to seek and transfer external knowledge for their innovation activities, (2) create output channels to move new internal knowledge within the firm to other organizations in the surrounding environment, and (3) define specific mechanisms designed to direct these knowledge inputs and outputs.

The open innovation model defines requirements of the relationship between innovation and organizational processes, which generates new internal and external ideas and enables the formation of a new architecture, systems, and management platforms (Chesbrough, 2012). In addition to providing guidelines, management is responsible for delivering the active support needed to manage the change in business processes that new technologies impact, which facilitates the mitigation of stakeholder resistance and explicitly exhibits commitment through communication and actions to ensure succession (Kulkarni et al., 2017).

Firm Performance

For Filippetti and Guy (2020), firm performance depends not only on internal R&D resources and activities but also on the accumulation of knowledge and skill developed outside organizational boundaries, such as partnerships with other agents (e.g., suppliers, customers, research institutions, universities, etc.). The potential for business success depends on organizational performance, i.e., its ability to implement strategies effectively to achieve institutional goals (Randeree & Al Youha, 2009).

Tsinopoulos et al. (2018) extend this relationship (organizational structure vs environment) by adding open innovation practices such as cooperation with other organizations, using external R&D information, and introducing new work processes. In this way, the main goal of open innovation is to maximize firm performance (Ahn et al., 2015) and new product development choices and patents (Thakur-Wernz et al., 2019). On the other hand, Laursen and Salter (2006) state that open innovation is considered an antecedent of organizational performance because the firm obtains and uses external resources by establishing cooperative relationships with new partners (e.g., customers, suppliers, competitors, research institutions, governments). Moreover, the impact (direct or indirect) of open innovation activities on firm performance has been extensively investigated, including R&D cost-effectiveness (Caloghirou et al., 2004), patent production (Rothaermel & Alexandre, 2009), and the proportion of new products (Grimpe & Sofka, 2009; Laursen & Salter, 2006; Atuahene-Gima, 2005).

Miotti and Sachwald (2003) advocate that open innovation improves the firm's innovation performance, although some researchers have suggested that over-reliance on external knowledge may not benefit the firm's ability to innovate (Laursen & Salter, 2006). Indeed, the principle for improving open innovation performance lies in how the top manager leads his or her relationships with stakeholders and how one interacts with other stakeholders (Dahlander & Gann, 2010). The top manager can significantly leverage organisational performance to connect business processes and external knowledge. Therefore, organizational performance criteria are considered the foundation for designing and operating an internal performance measurement system (Dahlander & Gan, 2010).

For Wen et al. (2020), the relationship between customer experience and inbound open innovation positively influences firm performance. These researchers identify three elements in the process of this interaction: (1) resource acquisition, (2) resource integration, and (3) interaction mechanism. Resource acquisition and the interaction mechanism play a limited role in the mediation between customer knowledge and firm performance management. While resource integration has a more significant influence on the firm's results, i.e., its economic performance. Similarly, Wang (2019) postulates that in the case of research centres, the increase in open inbound innovation is essential for raising efficiency, tending to organizational performance.

In the coupled activities of open innovation, Wang et al. (2014) studied the relationship between firm performance and industry environment. The results showed that (a) decentralization generates a positive effect, increasing the influence of open innovation activities on the output, (b) formalization practices reduce this positive influence, (c) resource acquisition affects the firm's innovation positioning and (d) the importance of the top manager's knowledge about the organization, which can manage different levels of organization performance, as a precursor to possible alliances (partnerships) at the horizon and/or vertical level in knowledge acquisitions.

Sisodiya et al. (2013), regarding the key elements that allow open innovation to increase its effectiveness in a turbulent business context, state that open innovation depends on external connections and the ability to create and manage relationships with other firms. The relationships between open innovation and organizational performance should enhance the effects of open to entry innovation on organizational performance. The firm's ability to build relationships with other firms in an environment characterized by knowledge richness and flexibility in responsiveness and adaptability enhances the effects of open innovation on entry.

External innovation elements and channels can reduce the marginal returns of open innovation (Greco et al., 2016). When a firm combines internal patents and derived resources with inputs raised through external knowledge in the most profitable way, it achieves better efficiency and increased revenues (Dittrich & Duysters, 2007).

Open innovation also guides firms to broaden their mental models. In essence, it involves the creation of networks and relationships that tend to be greater than the aggregation of bilateral relationships (Eiteneyer et al., 2019). The open innovation framework implicitly postulates complementarity between knowledge inputs and outputs, positively impacting innovation performance (Cassiman & Valentini, 2016). Thus, the increased effectiveness of open innovation shows that firms possess strong relational capabilities, as those that have deployed open innovation have achieved higher financial performance (Ovuakporie et al., 2021).

Laursen and Salter (2006) propose that the relationship between open innovation activity and organizational performance is indispensable; however, they noted that innovation performance could vary along a continuum of novelty from radical to incremental.

Thus, it is intended to test the following hypothesis:

H1: Open innovation has a positive effect on firm performance.

RESEARCH METHODS

Sample Design and Data Collection

The sample was drawn from Portuguese hospitality sector firms. A questionnaire was used as the primary data source and was carried out from October 28th, 2018 to April 27th, 2019. The identification of firms was made through Portugal's Hotel, Restaurant and Similar Association (Associação da Hoteleira, Restauração e Similares de Portugal-AHRESP) database, which features 1727 hotels, of which 717 were disregarded for not having active e-mail. Thus, in this study, the authors have used non-probabilistic and convenient sampling.

Hotel executive directors were the elements of research, and the unit of analysis is individual. 348 responses were received, of which 97 were eliminated because (1) the survey was not fully covered, (2) the hotel had no employee designated for this purpose, and/or (3) the manager did not have time to respond to the survey. Thus, 251 complete and validated questionnaires were obtained, and the sample size was considered appropriate according to Krejcie et al. (1970). This score corresponds to a response rate of 24.85%, which is regarded as good as the average response rate of the top management survey is in the range of 15-20% (Menon et al., 1999). According to Hair et al. (2016), this sample size is considered suitable for data analysis using structural equation modelling of partial square composition (PLS-SEM). It allows analysis even with small sample sizes.

Measures

The researchers measured the constructs of this study with scales from previous research. The two dimensions of open innovation, inbound and outbound, were assessed using six items from Sisodiya et al. (2013) and five items from Cheng and Huizingh (2014). The two dimensions of organizational performance, market positioning and profit, were analyzed according to the ten items recommended by Spanos and Lioukas (2001).

RESULTS

Descriptive Analysis

Table 1 shows the descriptive statistics of the sample's demographics.

Table 1. Descriptive analysis

Item	%
Gender:	
Male	62.5
Female	37.5
Age (years old):	
1-25	19.3
26-35	26.9
36-45	42.6
46-55	8.4
> 55	2.8
Academic qualifications:	
Vocational qualification	55.6
Bachelor degree	28.9
Master degree	12.6
PhD	2.9
Professional experience (years):	
1	7.3
2-5	48.7
6-10	30.8
>10	13.2

Source: Own elaboration.

Partial Least Square Structural Equations Modeling (PLS-SEM)

Results of the Measurement Model

The reliability of the variables was studied by analyzing the internal stability and consistency of Cronbach's alpha, which must be greater than 0.7 (Chin, 2010). The Cronbach's alpha for both constructs is excellent (Table 2) (Pestana & Gageiro, 2010). Results show that the measurement model meets all general requirements. First, all reflective items have a load higher than 0.707, which means that the reliability of individual indicators (loading) is higher than 0.5. Second, all-composite reliability values and Cronbach's alpha values are higher than 0.70, suggesting acceptable model reliability. Third, the average variance extracted (AVE) values of all constructs are higher than 0.50, indicating an adequate convergent validity and implying that our set of indicators represents the same underlying construct (Hair et al., 2016).

Table 2. Standardized factor analysis loadings, CR, AVE, Mean and SD

First-order constructs	Item	Loadings	CR	AVE	Mean	SD
Open innovation			.962	.698		
(α = .957)	OI_9	.903			4.74	1.482
	OI_10	.897			4.71	1.523
	OI_3	.892			4.84	1.653
	OI_2	.888			4.67	1.666
	OI_5	.884			4.68	1.653
	OI_8	.862			4.84	1.497
	OI_4	.716			5.03	1.535
	OI_7	.698			4.53	1.622
	OI_6	.690			4.65	1.671
	OI_11	.686			4.53	1.621
	OI_1	.635			5.12	1.605
Firm performance			.949	.729		
(α = .940)	OP_1	.918			4.91	1.210
	OP_4	.913			4.77	1.261
	OP_2	.908			4.88	1.163
	OP_3	.902			4.83	1.283
	OP_7	.896			5.14	1.020
	OP_5	.880			5.13	1.037
	OP_6	.875			5.02	1.148

Source: Own elaboration.

The composite reliability coefficient was also used to test the convergent validity (Chin, 1998). As can be seen from Table 2, using the parameters of Gefen and Straub (2005) that advocate a minimum level of 0.6, the variables exponentially exceed the required value. In this study, the method proposed by Fornell and Larcker (1981) was used, which suggests using the AVE with a minimum value of 0.5 to prove convergent validity. All variables also did reach the required value.

Discriminant validity is determined by construct and is related to the level at which it differs and stands out from the other constructs of the model, thus making it necessary to have no correlations with other latent variables, and it can be gauged from the principle that all cross loads cannot be higher than the loading of each indicator (Hair et al., 2016). Henseler et al. (2015) propose Heterotrait-Monotrait Ratio (HTMT) to assess the discriminant validity, which is a new and advanced criterion and is one of the effective methods to evaluate it. Therefore, HTMT was used to assess the discriminant validity of the constructs, and its values are given in Table 3. All the values were less than 0.90; hence, discriminant validity was also established for all constructs.

Table 3. HTMT

HTMT	1.	2.
1. Open innovation		
2. Firm performance	.262	

Source: Own elaboration.

Results of the Structural Model

For this purpose, the significance of the model was assessed based on path coefficients, t-values, and standard errors. The hypotheses tested the direct and indirect effects through the bootstrapping procedure using Smart PLS 3 (Henseler et al., 2015). The PLS algorithm followed by bootstrapping techniques was used to calculate each exogenous construct's relative strength.

According to Chin (1998), the hypothesis is significant and advocates a minimum structural coefficient of 0.2. As displayed in Table 4, open innovation had a significant and positive relationship with competitive advantage ($\beta = 0.264$, $t = 4.755$; LL = 0.169, UL =0.383); thus, H1 is supported.

Table 4. Path analysis: direct effects

Hypothesis	Original Sample (O)	Sample Mean (M)	Standard Error (STERR)	T-Statistics (O / STERR)	L.L.	U.L.	Result
H1. OI -> CA	0.264	0.276	0.056	4.755*	0.169	0.383	Supported

Note: *p<0.001.
Source: Own elaboration.

DISCUSSION AND CONCLUSION

The results support the relationship between open innovation and firm performance. Some studies indicate that open innovation positively influences different measures of organizational performance (Carayannis & Grigoroudis, 2014; Popa et al., 2017). Therefore, SMEs can benefit from external knowledge, as they respond more effectively to the needs of markets, being more flexible than large organizations (Spithoven et al., 2013). On the other hand, they can increase their overall performance through open innovation (Popa et al., 2017).

Open innovation practices are strategic assets that generate sustainable competitive advantage and improve organizational performance of firms (Camisón & Villar-López, 2014). Previous studies suggest that open innovation helps firms gain competitive advantage (Goldman et al., 1994). This fact leads to higher organizational performance (OECD, 2005), as also the Resource-Based View considers organizational performance as a result of an organization's internal performance (Camisón & Villar-López, 2014). Moreover, in dynamic markets, the ability of organizations to leverage the benefits of open innovation makes their aptitude in solid connections with external organizations (Biscotti et al., 2018). Channels increase the effectiveness of inbound open innovation to enhance organizational performance.

For Chiang and Hung (2010), knowledge sharing is a vital aspect of innovation in which associative knowledge practices help to increase value for the innovator, increasing organizational open innovation. As a result of this interaction, SME involvement in external knowledge-seeking offers performance benefits, also improving innovation performance (Burnswicker & Vanhaverbeke, 2015). As an effect, several other studies suggest links between knowledge management, innovation, and performance (Santoro et al., 2018; López-Nicolás & Meroño-Cerdán, 2011), which, together with the open search of various external channels, influence firms' radical innovation performance (Chiang & Hung, 2010). The literature on open innovation integrates external knowledge transfer (Chesbrough, 2006). Simultaneously, Van de Vrande et al. (2009) emphasize how organizations deploying open innovation have improved their performance. Much of the work on open innovation focuses on the input rather than the output of innovation (Lichtenthaler, 2011; Chesbrough, 2003b), which requires firms to develop organizational policies and practices for the type of resources that best leverage the benefits of open innovation to increase organizational performance.

The theoretical contribution to substantiate the research hypothesis, based on the open innovation model, lies in organizational performance and its positive effect on leader's propensity for open innovation (Biscotti et al., 2018), external knowledge in *sourcing* strategies (Burnswicker & Vanhaverbeke, 2015), organizational innovation as a facilitator of technological innovation capabilities (Camisón & Villar-López, 2014), SMEs' flexibility to acquire external knowledge (Spithoven et al., 2013), and knowledge sharing (Chiang & Hung, 2010). On the other hand, the role of organizational culture (Tellis et al., 2009), customer acquisition (Arnold, Fang, & Palmatier, 2011), absorptive capabilities (Forés & Camisón, 2016), knowledge management (Santoro et al., 2018; López-Nicolás & Meroño-Cerdán, 2011), radical innovation (Chiang & Hung, 2010), and knowledge sharing (Vera & Crossan, 2004) provide theoretical contributions to highlight.

The practical contributions of this research proved to be essential for SMEs performance in the hospitality sector. Therefore, top managers should develop the firm's capabilities as they allow them to use organizational resources to obtain superior performance. This study contributes to developing new instruments and programs to support SMEs in the hospitality sector. By identifying the resources, technologies and dynamic capabilities that influence the firms' performance through the available and necessary resources, this study is beneficial for top managers because it stimulates entrepreneurial behaviors.

Some limitations stand out in the course of this study. The first one refers to the sending of the survey. The authors should also mention that given the number of firms studied (251), they chose to apply the survey to firms whose e-mail address was registered at AHRESP. Although the number of respondents is significant, a larger sample would allow a more refined analysis of the results. In addition, this is a non-probabilistic convenience sample. The second limitation concerns the metrics that assess innovation management and its superior performance. The researchers chose for respondents only top managers/leaders. However, because it is an electronic survey, this does not characterize whether the top manager responded to the survey. They also understand that evaluating the different constructs of this study based on a single person's opinion (top manager/leader) may not accurately reflect the reality of firms since decisions are made by a team that may have different views about the activity studied.

This research suggests some lines of future investigations, namely:

1. to analyze the mediating/moderating effect of environmental factors on the relationship between open innovation and competitive advantage in large firms and insufficiently structured sectors of the economy, to identify whether top managers have developed entrepreneurial skills when they perceive that in an external environment with a high level of hostility they can lead firms to achieve competitive advantage; and
2. replicate the research in other sectors of the economy, whether technology-intensive or not, or in quite structured sectors (automotive, pharmaceutical, agribusiness, etc.) to identify the existence of innovation ecosystems that support sectors where late technologies characterize innovations.

REFERENCES

Ahn, J. M. T., & Mortara, L. (2015). Open innovation: A new classification and its impact on firm performance in innovative SMEs. *Journal of Innovation Management*, *3*(2), 33–54. doi:10.24840/2183-0606_003.002_0006

Alavi, M., & Leidner, D. E. (2001). Review: Knowledge management and knowledge management systems: Conceptual foundations and research issues. *Management Information Systems Quarterly*, *25*(1), 107–133. doi:10.2307/3250961

Almirall, E., & Casadesus-Masanell, R. (2010). Open vs. Closed Innovation: A Model of Discovery and Divergence. *Academy of Management Review*, *35*(1), 27–47.

Aranha, E. A., Garcia, N. A. P., Silva, G. N. R., & Santos, P. (2017). Open Innovation and Business Model in Brazilian Small Business. *International Journal of Business Management and Economic Research*, *8*(5), 1008–1015.

Atuahene-Gima, K. (2005). Resolving the Capability–Rigidity Paradox in New Product Innovation. *Journal of Marketing*, *69*(4), 61–83. doi:10.1509/jmkg.2005.69.4.61

Bahemia, H., & Squire, B. (2010). A Contingent View of Open Innovation in new Prodtuct Development Projects. *International Journal of Innovation Management*, *14*(4), 603–627. doi:10.1142/S1363919610002799

Biscotti, A. M., Mafrolla, E., Giudice, M. D., & D'Amico, E. (2018). CEO turnover and the new leader propensity to open innovation: Agency-resource dependence view and social identity perspective. *Management Decision*, *56*(6), 1348–1364. doi:10.1108/MD-04-2017-0392

Burnswicker, S., & Vanhaverbeke, W. (2015). Open innovation in small and medium-sized enterprises (SMEs): External knowledge sourcing strategies and internal organizational facilitators. *Journal of Small Business Management*, *53*(4), 1241–1263. doi:10.1111/jsbm.12120

Caloghirou, Y., Kastelli, I., & Tsakanikas, A. (2004). Internal capabilities and external knowledge sources: Complementsor substitutes for innovative performance? *Technovation*, *24*(1), 29–39. doi:10.1016/S0166-4972(02)00051-2

Camisón, C., Forés, B., & Puig-Denia, A. (2016). Return on capital in Spanish tourism businesses: A comparative analysis of family vs non-family businesses.European. *Journal of Management and Business Economics*, *25*(3), 91–110. doi:10.1016/j.redeen.2016.04.002

Carayannis, E., & Grigoroudis, E. (2014). Linking innovation, productivity, and competitiveness: Implications for policy and practice. *The Journal of Technology Transfer*, *39*(2), 199–218. doi:10.100710961-012-9295-2

Cassiman, B., & Valentini, G. (2019). Open Innovation: Are inbound and outbound knowledge flows really complementary? *Strategic Management Journal*, *37*(6), 1034–1046. doi:10.1002mj.2375

Cheng, C. C. J., & Huizingh, E. K. R. E. (2014). When Is Open Innovation Beneficial? The Role of Strategic Orientation. *Journal of Product Innovation Management*, *31*(6), 1235–1253. doi:10.1111/jpim.12148

Chesbrough, H. W. (2003a). Xerox PARC-1. The Achievements and Limits of Closed Innovation. In H. W. Chesbrough (Ed.), *Open Innovation: the new imperative for creating and profiting from technology* (pp. 1–10). Harvard Business School Press.

Chesbrough, H. W. (2003b). The era of open innovation. *MIT Sloan Management Review*, *44*(3), 35–41.

Chesbrough, H. W. (2012). Open innovation: Where we've been and where we're going. *Research Technology Management*, *55*(4), 20–27. doi:10.5437/08956308X5504085

Chesbrough, H. W., & Bogers, M. (2014). Explaining open innovation: clarifying an emerging paradigm for understanding innovation. In H. W. Chesbrough, W. Vanhaverbeke & J. West (Eds.), New frontiers in open innovation (pp. 3-28). Oxford University Press.

Chesbrough, H. W., Bogers, M., Heaton, S., & Teece, D. J. (2019). Strategic Management of Open Innovation: A Dynamic Capabilities Perspective. *Berkeley Haas California Management Review*, *62*(1), 77–94. doi:10.1177/0008125619885150

Chesbrough, H. W., & Crowther, A. K. (2006). Beyond high tech: Early adopters of open innovation in other industries. *R & D Management*, *36*(3), 229–236. doi:10.1111/j.1467-9310.2006.00428.x

Chiang, Y.-H., & Hung, K.-P. (2010). Exploring open search estrategies and perceived innovation performance from the perspective of inter-organizational knowledge flows. *R & D Management*, *40*(3), 292–299. doi:10.1111/j.1467-9310.2010.00588.x

Chin, W. W. (1998). The Partial Least Squares approach to structural equation modelling. In G. A. Marcoulides (Ed.), *Modern methods for business research* (pp. 295–336). Lawrence Erlbaum Associates Publisher.

Chin, W. W. (2010). How to write up and report PLS analyses. In V. E. Vinzi, W. W. Chin, J. Henseler, & H. Wang (Eds.), *Handbook of Partial Least Squares: Concepts, Methods and Applications in Marketing and Related Fields* (pp. 655–690). Springer. doi:10.1007/978-3-540-32827-8_29

Dahlander, L., & Gann, D. M. (2010). How Open Is Innovation? *Research Policy*, *39*(6), 699–709. doi:10.1016/j.respol.2010.01.013

Dittrich, K., & Duysters, G. (2007). Networking as a Means to Strategy Change: The Case of Open Innovation in Mobile Telephony. *Journal Product Management*, *24*(6), 510–521. doi:10.1111/j.1540-5885.2007.00268.x

Eiteneyer, N., Bendig, D., & Brettel, M. (2019). Social capital and the digital crowd: Involving backers to promote new product innovativeness. *Research Policy*, *48*(8), 1–15. doi:10.1016/j.respol.2019.01.017

Filippetti, A., & Frederick, G. (2020). Labor market regulation, the diversity of knowledge and skill, and national innovation performance. *Research Policy*, *49*(1), 103867. doi:10.1016/j.respol.2019.103867

Finkelstein, S., Hambrick, D. C., & Cannella, A. A. (2009). *Strategic leadership: Theory and research on executives, top management teams, and boards*. Oxford University Press.

Fornell, C., & Larcker, D. (1981). Evaluating structural equation models with unobserved variables and measurement error. *JMR, Journal of Marketing Research*, *18*(1), 39–50. doi:10.1177/002224378101800104

Frank, T., & Rothaermel, M. T. A. (2009). Ambidexterity in Technology Sourcing: The Moderating Role of Absorptive Capacity. *Organization Science*, *20*(4), 759–780. doi:10.1287/orsc.1080.0404

Goldman, S. L., Nagel, R. N., & Preiss, K. (1995). *Agile Competitors and Virtual Organizations: Strategies for Enriching the Customer*. Van Nostrand Reinhold.

Greco, M., Grimaldi, M., & Criceli, L. (2016). An analysis of the open innovation effect on firm performance. *European Management Journal*, *34*(5), 501–516. doi:10.1016/j.emj.2016.02.008

Grimpe, C., & Sofka, W. (2009). Search patterns and absorptive capacity: Low- and high-technology sectorsin European countries. *Research Policy*, *38*(3), 495–506. doi:10.1016/j.respol.2008.10.006

Hair, J., Hult, G. T. M., Ringle, C., & Sarstedt, M. (2016). *A Primer on Partial Least Squares Structural Equation Modeling (PLS-SEM)*. Sage.

Henseler, J., Ringle, C. M., & Sarstedt, M. (2015). A new criterion for assessing discriminant validity in variance-based structural equation modeling. *Journal of the Academy of Marketing Science*, *43*(1), 115–135. doi:10.100711747-014-0403-8

Huizingh, E. K. (2011). Open innovation: State of the art and future perspectives. *Technovation*, *31*(1), 2–9. doi:10.1016/j.technovation.2010.10.002

Hurmelinna-Laukkanen, P. (2011). Enabling collaborative innovation–knowledge protection for knowledge sharing. *European Journal of Innovation Management*, *14*(3), 303–321. doi:10.1108/14601061111148816

Krejcie, R. V., & Morgan, D. W. (1970). Determining Sample Size for Research Activities. *Educational and Psychological Measurement*, *30*(3), 607–610. doi:10.1177/001316447003000308

Kulkarni, U., Robles-Flores, J. A., & Popovič, A. (2017). A business intelligence capability: The effect of top management and the mediating roles of user participation and analytical decision making orientation. *Journal of the Association for Information Systems*, *18*(7), 516–541. doi:10.17705/1jais.00462

Kuo-Nan, H., & Tidd, J. (2012). Open versus closed new service development: The influences of project novelty. *Technovation*, *32*(11), 600–608. doi:10.1016/j.technovation.2012.07.002

Laursen, K., & Salter, A. (2006). Open for innovation: The role of openness in explaining innovation performance among U.K. manufacturing firms. *Strategic Management Journal*, *27*(2), 131–150. doi:10.1002mj.507

Leiponen, A., & Helfat, C. E. (2010). Innovation objectives, knowledge sources, and the benefits of breadth. *Strategic Management Journal*, *31*(2), 224–236. doi:10.1002mj.807

Lião, Y.-W., Wang, Y.-M., & Tu, Y.-M. (2015). Understanding the dynamics between organizational IT investment strategy and market performance: A system dynamics approach. *Computers in Industry*, *71*, 46–57. doi:10.1016/j.compind.2015.02.006

Lichtenthaler, U. (2010). Intellectual property and open innovation: An emperical analysi. *International Journal of Technology Management*, *52*(3/4), 372–391. doi:10.1504/IJTM.2010.035981

Lichtenthaler, U. (2011). Open innovation: Past research, current debates, and future directions. *The Academy of Management Perspectives*, *25*(1), 75–93.

Lopes, A. V. B. V., & De Carvalho, M. M. (2018). Evolution of the open innovation paradigm: Towards a contingent conceptual model. *Technological Forecasting and Social Change*, *132*, 284–298. doi:10.1016/j.techfore.2018.02.014

Lopez-Cabrales, A., Bornay-Barrachina, M., & Diaz-Fernandez, M. (2017). Leadership and dynamic capabilities: The role of HR systems. *Personnel Review*, *46*(2), 255–276. doi:10.1108/PR-05-2015-0146

López-Nicolás, C., & Merono-Cerdán, A. L. (2011). Strategic knowledge management, innovation and performance. *International Journal of Information Management*, *31*(6), 502–509. doi:10.1016/j.ijinfomgt.2011.02.003

Menon, A., Bharadwaj, S. G., Adidam, P. T., & Edison, S. W. (1999). Antecedents and consequences of marketing strategy making: A model and a test. *Journal of Marketing*, *63*(2), 18–40. doi:10.1177/002224299906300202

Miotti, L., & Sachwald, F. (2003). Co-operative R&D: Why and with whom? *Research Policy*, *32*(8), 1481–1499. doi:10.1016/S0048-7333(02)00159-2

Organisation for Economic Co-Operation And Development. (2005). *Guidelines for Collecting and Interpreting Innovation* (3rd ed.). OECD Statistical Office of the European Communities. Retrieved from: www.oecd.org/edu/teacherpolicy

Ovuakporie, O. D., Pillai, K. G., Wang, C., & Wei, Y. (2019). Differential moderating effects of strategic and operational reconfiguration on the relationship between open innovation practices and innovation performance. *Research Policy*, *50*(1), 104–146.

Pestana, M. H., & Gageiro, J. N. (2010). *Análise de Dados para Ciências Socais: The Complementarity of SPSS* (5th ed.). Edições Sílabo.

Podmetina, D., Soderquist, K. E., Petraite, M., & Teplov, R. (2018). Developing a competency model for open innovation from the individual to the organisational level. *Management Decision*, *56*(6), 1306–1335. doi:10.1108/MD-04-2017-0445

Popa, S., Soto-Acosta, P., & Martinez-Conesa, L. (2017). Antecedents, moderators, and outcomes of innovation climate and open innovation: An empirical study in sme's. *Technological Forecasting and Social Change*, *118*, 134–142. doi:10.1016/j.techfore.2017.02.014

Randeree, K., & Al Youha, H. (2009). Strategic management of performance: An examination of public sector organizations in the United Arab Emirates. *The International Journal of Knowledge. Culture and Change Management*, *9*(4), 123–134.

Reilly, P. (2018). Building customer centricity in the hospitality sector: The role of talent management. *Worldwide Hospitality and Tourism Themes*, *10*(1), 42–56. doi:10.1108/WHATT-10-2017-0068

Santoro, G., Ferraris, A., Giacosa, E., & Giovando, G. (2018). How sme's engage in open innovation: A survey. *Journal of the Knowledge Economy*, *9*(2), 651–574. doi:10.100713132-015-0350-8

Sisodiya, S. R., Johnson, J. L., & Grégoire, Y. (2013). Inbound open innovation for enhanced performance: Enablers and opportunities. *Industrial Marketing Management*, *42*(5), 836–849. doi:10.1016/j.indmarman.2013.02.018

Smith, W. (2014). Dynamic decision making: A model of senior leaders managing strategic paradoxes. *Academy of Management Journal*, *37*(6), 1592–1623. doi:10.5465/amj.2011.0932

Spanos, Y., & Lioukas, S. (2001). An Examination into the Causal Logic of Rent Generation: Contrasting porter's competitive strategy framework and the resource-based perspective. *Strategic Management Journal*, *22*(10), 907–934. doi:10.1002mj.174

Spithoven, A., Vanhaverbeke, W., & Roijakkers, N. (2013). Open innovation practices in SMEs and large enterprises. *Small Business Economics*, *41*(3), 537–562. doi:10.100711187-012-9453-9

Teece, D. J. (2007). Explicating dynamic capabilities: The nature and microfoundations of (sustainable) enterprise performance. *Strategic Management Journal*, *28*(13), 1319–1350. doi:10.1002mj.640

Teplov, R., Albats, E., & Podmetina, D. (2019). What Does Open Innovation Mean? Business Versus Academic Perceptions. *International Journal of Innovation Management*, *23*(1), 805–811. doi:10.1142/S1363919619500026

Thakur-Wernz, P., Cantwell, J., & Samant, S. (2019). Impact of international entry choices on the nature and type of innovation: Evidence from emerging economy firms from the Indian bio-pharmaceutical industry. *International Business Review, 28*(6), 101601. Advance online publication. doi:10.1016/j.ibusrev.2019.101601

Tikakul, C., & Thomson, A. (2018). International Lessons in Knowledge Management: A Study of Western & Eastern Manufacturing SMEs. *Electronic Journal of Knowledge Management, 16*(2), 113–130.

Tsinopoulos, C., Sousa, C. M. P., & Yan, J. (2018). Process Innovation: Open Innovation and the Moderating Role of the Motivation to Achieve Legitimacy. *Journal of Product Innovation Management, 35*(1), 27–48. doi:10.1111/jpim.12374

Van De Vrande, V., De Jong, J. P. J., Vanhaverbeke, W., & De Rochemont, M. (2009). Open innovation in sme's: Trends, motivations and management challenges. *Technovation, 29*(6-7), 423–437. doi:10.1016/j.technovation.2008.10.001

Vera, D., & Crossan, M. (2005). Strategic Leadership and Organizational Learning. *Academy of Management Review, 29*(2), 222–240. doi:10.2307/20159030

Vils, L., Mazzieri, M., Rodrigues, G., Da Silva, A., & Queiroz, M. J. (2017). Business model innovation: A bibliometric review. *International Journal of Innovation, 5*(3), 311–324. doi:10.5585/iji.v5i3.243

Wang, D. (2019). Association between technological innovation and firm performance in small and medium-sized enterprises. *International Journal of Innovation Science, 11*(2), 227–240. doi:10.1108/IJIS-04-2018-0049

Wang, F. K., & Wu, H. (2014). Service strategies of small cloud service providers: A case study of a small cloud service provider and its clients in Taiwan. *International Journal of Information Management, 34*(3), 406–415. doi:10.1016/j.ijinfomgt.2014.01.007

Wen, J., Kozak, M., Yang, S., & Liu, F. (2020). COVID-19: Potential effects on Chinese citizens' lifestyle and travel. *Tourism Review*. Advance online publication. doi:10.1108/TR-03-2020-0110

West, J., Salter, A., Vanheverbeke, W., & Chesbrough, H. (2014). Open innovation: The next decade. *Research Policy, 43*(5), 805–811. doi:10.1016/j.respol.2014.03.001

West, J., Vanhaverbeke, W., & Chesbrough, C. (2006). Open innovation: A research agenda. In H. Chesbrough, W. Vanhaverbeke, & J. West (Eds.), Open innovation: Researching a new paradigm (pp. 285–307). Oxford University Press.

Yun, J. J., Won, D. K., & Park, K. (2016). Dynamics from open innovation to evolutionary change. *Journal of Open Innovation*, *2*(7), 1–22. doi:10.118640852-016-0033-0

Zott, C., Amit, R., & Massa, L. (2011). The business model: Recent development and future research. *Journal of Management*, *37*(4), 1019–1042. doi:10.1177/0149206311406265

ADDITIONAL READING

Chesbrough, H. W., & Crowther, A. K. (2006). Beyond high tech: Early adopters of open innovation in other industries. *R & D Management*, *36*(3), 229–236. doi:10.1111/j.1467-9310.2006.00428.x

Chesbrough, H. W., & Euchner, J. (2011). The Evolution of Open Innovation: An interview with Henry Chesbrough. *Research Technology Management*, *50*(1), 13–18. doi:10.5437/08956308X5405003

Chesbrough, H. W., & Rosenbloom, R. S. (2002). The Role of the Business Model in Capturing Value from Innovation: Evidence from Xerox Corporation's Technology Spin-Off Companies. *Industrial and Corporate Change*, *11*(3), 529–555. doi:10.1093/icc/11.3.529

Chesbrough, H. W., Salter, A. J., Vanhaverbeke, W., & West, J. (2014). Open Innovation: The Next Decade. *Research Policy*, *43*(5), 805–811. doi:10.1016/j.respol.2014.03.001

Lisi, I. E. (2018). Determinants and Performance Effects of Social Performance Measurement Systems. *Journal of Business Ethics*, *152*(1), 225–251. doi:10.100710551-016-3287-3

Rua, O. L., França, A., & Fernández, R. O. (2018). Key drivers of SMEs export performance: The mediating effect of competitive advantage. *Journal of Knowledge Management*, *22*(2), 257–279. doi:10.1108/JKM-07-2017-0267

Van Lieshout, J. W. F. C., van der Velden, J. M., Blomme, R. J., & Peters, P. (2021). *The interrelatedness of organizational ambidexterity, dynamic capabilities and open innovation: a conceptual model towards a competitive advantage. European Journal of Management Studies.* doi:10.1108/EJMS-01-2021-0007

KEY TERMS AND DEFINITIONS

Firm Performance: It is the ability to implement strategies effectively to achieve institutional goals.

Hospitality Sector: Sector of the tourism industry that comprises a growing competitive activity that sustains a representative position in the tourism production chain and requires the ability to constantly adapt to the changes, needs and desires of the customer, as the satisfaction, safety and pleasure of the tourist have a vital role in generating wealth and employment in any country, with implications for the economy, the environment and the population.

Open Innovation: The open innovation concept is an emergent paradigm based on the assumption "that firms can and should use external ideas as well as internal ideas, and internal and external paths to market" (Chesbrough, 2003a, p. 59).

SME: Small and medium-sized enterprises.

Chapter 10
Critical Barriers to Overcome When Corporates Engage With Startups:
The Open Innovation Perspective

Alessia Pisoni
University of Insubria, Italy

Sveva Giovannoni
University of Insubria, Italy

Alberto Onetti
University of Insubria, Italy

ABSTRACT

The chapter aims at investigating the different implementation modes of open innovation (OI) adopted by companies when engaging with startups. In the last years, a significant body of literature has been published on OI-related issues. Research on OI is multidisciplinary and scattered among different fields of research. Based on this, the authors perform a comprehensive and systemized literature review to identify and describe the most critical issues to be considered when companies engage with startups. Specifically, they aim to identify the main barriers to corporate-startup collaboration and, in doing so, to provide a comprehensive framework able to shed new light on the proposed issue and to provide guidance to future research directions.

DOI: 10.4018/978-1-7998-8665-5.ch010

INTRODUCTION

Today's world is characterized by globalization, keen competition, and shortening of product life cycles. The survival/growth aspect constitutes a critical issue for incumbents and, at the same time, it represents a significant opportunity for new entrants that can disrupt the market and rewrite the rules of the game. What represents a problem for established firms can be another's opportunity. Innovation is strictly linked to entrepreneurship, and being an entrepreneur means having a clear strategy in mind. Innovation is becoming more democratic and many of the new ideas no longer originate internally; instead, they can come from anywhere and anyone (King & Lakhani, 2013).

According to Chesbrough (2006) some erosion factors mined the old paradigm of Closed Innovation and shifted the attention to the new one of Open Innovation. Chesbrough not only stated that firms should use both internal and external ideas in their innovation process, but they can also profit from explore internal ideas outside the firm both in the research stage or in the development stage. This logic behind Open Innovation seems to be built on a landscape of abundant knowledge (Chesbrough, 2003, 2006, 2012a; Chesbrough & Euchner, 2011; Chesbrough et al., 2014a,b). Today's modern technologies are mainly linked to ICT and ICT-related sectors, and the logic behind the innovation process is fully reversed. The old idea of a central R&D lab is based on a deep vertical integration and this approach does not make sense in today's world characterized by abundance of knowledge, where the value of knowledge is in the outside. Today firms are likely to collaborate for many reasons: to reduce costs, to reduce risks, to achieve economies of scale, to reduce time to market, and to promote shared learning (Lichtenthaler & Lichtenthaler, 2009).

The rapidity of technological change and the complex nature of technologies drive the fact that only few organizations can nowadays afford to maintain in-house knowledge and expertise in every potentially relevant area (Chesbrough & Crowther, 2006; Chesbrough et al., 2014a; Van Lieshout et al., 2021). Companies are increasing the use of Open Innovation strategies adoption in order to face this new era of distributed knowledge, but many of them are having difficulties in implementing and managing OI activities – many entrepreneurs are also misperceiving risks and opportunities that Open Innovation presents (King & Lakhani, 2013).

New ventures and established firms are intrinsically different one from the other – large firms have resources, economies of scale, power and a proven business model, on the other hand, startups lack corporates' characteristics but have fresh and promising ideas, more agility in terms of organization, a risk taker attitude, and ambitions to grow rapidly – these differences rise real challenges to engage one with the other (Weiblen & Chesbrough, 2015; Chesbrough & Rosenbloom, 2012). Different modes of engaging with startups have been highlighted during the last few years. Weiblen and Chesbrough (2015) described Corporate Venture Capital (CVC), Corporate Incubation, outside-in startup programs, and inside-out platform startup programs. Similarly, Mind the Bridge/Nesta (2017) provide six categories of Open Innovation implementation: exposure, trend spotting, accelerators, procurement, investments, and acquisitions (Onetti, 2019).

The Chapter aims at investigating the different implementation modes of Open Innovation adopted by companies when engaging with startups. The authors aim to identify the main barriers to corporate-startup collaboration and, in doing so, to provide a comprehensive framework able to shed new light on the proposed issue and to provide guidance to future research directions. Questions such as: "How can corporates and startups collaborate successfully?"; more specifically, "Which are the different 'forms/modes' of Open Innovation activities/implementations that they adopt?", "Which difficulties do corporates and startups encounter when engaging in asymmetric partnerships?", "Which factors lead to a successful implementation of Open Innovation activities?", define the chapter research goal.

The remainder of the chapter is structured as follows. First, the authors introduce the topic investigated, i.e. corporate-startup collaboration and the different form according to which such collaborations take place. Then, the authors present the systematic literature review approach adopted and discuss results on the main factors that enable and/or inhibit successful implementation of corporate-startup collaboration within the Open Innovation perspective. Lastly, concluding remarks and suggestions for future research directions complete the chapter.

CORPORATE-STARTUP COLLABORATION: THE OPEN INNOVATION PERSPECTIVE

According to Chesbrough (2003, 2012a,b, 2006, 2014a,b), Open Innovation describes "an emergent model of innovation in which firms draw on research and development that may lie outside their own boundaries", "it [OI] is a distributed innovation process based on purposively managed knowledge flows across organizational boundaries". This means that value is created by utilizing both internal and external ideas. Moreover, this implies also that internal ideas can be marketed in order to create additional value. So, ideas can come both from inside and outside the organization's boundaries and the internal ideas can step outside the firm both in the research stage or in the development stage. The logic behind OI appears to be built on a "landscape of abundant knowledge" (Chesbrough, 2006), this means that the knowledge created internally must be used readily or taken to the external market, and that a firm's internal pathways to market are not bounded to the use of internal knowledge only.

However, companies are not always ready to understand that they can take advantage of this wealth of information by using other's ideas to exploit their business to commercialize their own ideas that don't add value to their business otherwise (Chesbrough, 2006). Nowadays, firms are likely to collaborate for many different reasons: to reduce costs, to reduce risks, to achieve scale economies, to reduce time to market, and to promote shared learning.

In this respect, network is a crucial aspect of analysis in OI processes and implies the interaction among different typologies of actors (Chesbrough, 2003; Fichter, 2009; Padilla-Melendez et al., 2013). A wide range of areas and domains have been analyzed so far (Chesbrough et al., 2014a,b) and different units of analysis have been taken into consideration by scholars, such as large corporations, small and medium-sized companies (SMEs), and also high-tech startups (Weiblen & Chesbrough, 2015).

New ventures and established firms are intrinsically different one from the other: large firms have resources, economies of scale, power and a proven business model, on the other hand, startups lack corporates' characteristics but have fresh promising ideas, more agility in terms of organization, a risk taker attitude, and ambitions to grow rapidly. These different approaches rise real challenges to engage one with the other (Weiblen & Chesbrough, 2015). These scholars consider that in recent times the efforts to collaborate seems to be increasing, this is particularly happening in the tech industry, which needs speed and innovation.

As anticipated different modes of engaging with startups have been highlighted during the last few years. Weiblen and Chesbrough (2015) described Corporate Venture Capital (CVC), Corporate Incubation, outside-in startup programs, and inside-out platform startup programs. Recently, Kohler (2016) investigates how corporates internalise Open Innovation and identifies the following ways to promote corporate-startup engagement: (1) corporates supporting pilot projects: the corporation funds the development of innovative solution made by startups, rather than do it internally, to explore innovation and market opportunities; (2) corporates becoming startup customers: often a corporation that interacts with multiple startups, learns about different solutions and choses the one offering the best product for its needs; (3) corporates becoming startup distribution partners: based on an established partnership, startups can rely on the company's distribution networks; (4) corporates investing in startups: corporate often backs and supports startups in exchange of new market access and capabilities; (5) corporates acquiring startups: startups acquisition is an impactful way to solve specific business problems and to enter new market. Similarly, Mind the Bridge/Nesta (2017) provide six categories of Open Innovation implementation: exposure, trend spotting (through innovation outposts), accelerators, procurement, investments, and acquisitions (Onetti, 2019). More specifically, exposure is realized with one-off events and resource sharing and represent a first step for corporates to begin their engagement with startups (Onetti, 2019). Corporates gain exposure to innovative products and services and get awareness about innovative technologies, in doing so corporates can showcase their commitment to entrepreneurship and innovation and obtain a positive return in terms of communications and/or corporate social responsibility strategies. Moreover, companies that want to stay update about the latest technological trends, and engage with the most innovative startups, may also get exposure to the well-known innovation hubs of Silicon Valley and Israel (Mind the Bridge, 2017, 2018, 2019, 2020). In doing so, they establish a presence, either with a team or an office, to get exposure to those hubs via so-called "Corporate Innovation Outposts" (Mind the Bridge, 2017, 2018, 2019, 2020). Corporate accelerators can expose large firms to emerging trends and technologies, and allow employees to get exposure to an entrepreneurial mindset thus positively influencing corporate culture (Onetti, 2019). While accelerators typically focus on early-stage startups, more mature startups, the so-called "scaleups" (Onetti, 2019; Mind the Bridge, 2017), could also commercially engage with corporates. Finally, investments and acquisitions represent more structured form of corporate-startups engagement. By investing in a startup, a corporate monitors and supports its development path from a privileged position (i.e. as an insider), while by acquiring a startup, a corporate may internalize innovation as well as talents (acqui-hire) (Onetti, 2019; Pisoni & Onetti, 2018).

Concluding, scholars do not identify a "single best model for engagement", the model to be adopted depends on the goals that companies want to achieve through the engagement (Weiblen & Chesbrough, 2015; Onetti, 2019).

CRITICAL FACTORS TO BE CONSIDERED WHEN CORPORATES ENGAGE WITH STARTUPS: A SYSTEMATIC LITERATURE REVIEW APPROACH

As previously pointed out, the authors' aim is to devote a deeper assessment in understanding the specific factors that enable and/or inhibit the successful implementation of corporate-startup collaborations. Accordingly, a wide literature review, adopting a multistep systematic approach (Tranfield et al., 2003), has been performed to provide a comprehensive framework able to shed new light on the proposed issue and to provide guidance for future research directions. Thus, the purpose was threefold: (1) to investigate the state of the art (and the progress) of a specific stream of research by analyzing scholars' contributions to a specific topic; (2) to identify factors that enable and/or hinder corporate-startup collaboration and to develop a framework as well; (3) and, to provide future research directions.

In order to perform the review process, the authors, on the basis of prior experience and preliminary assessment of the existing literature, identified a broad

range of keywords such as: "Open Innovation", "collaboration", and "asymmetric partnership" combined with "startup" and "new ventures". The authors searched for these concepts on title, abstract and/or keywords in Scopus (Elsevier), which is the most comprehensive database of peer-reviewed journals in the fields of management, organization, and social science. Moreover, Web of Science and Google Scholar were used too, to identify additional contributions.
The following set of inclusion and exclusion criteria have been considered:

- document type: both articles and conference papers;
- only contributions written in English, to facilitate comparison of different works;
- only contributions published in the last twenty years, as the research focuses on the latest studies on the topic.

Figure 1. Systematic literature review process
Source: Own elaboration.

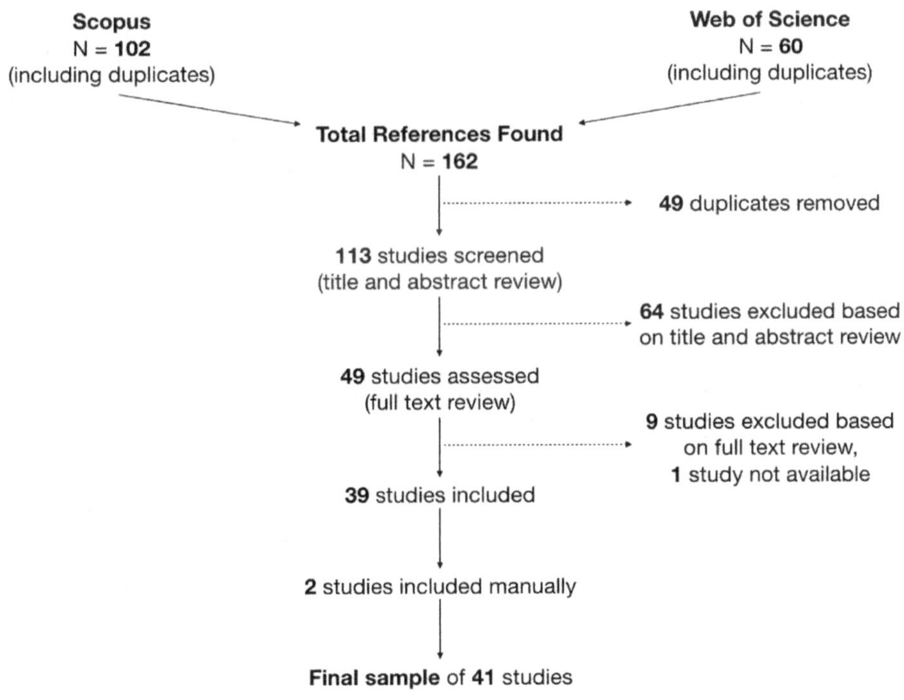

The results were then combined with those emerging both from a further snowballing search and from cross-references. All materials were labelled and stored, and duplications (i.e., journal articles that may appear more than once when searching different keywords) were deleted. Overall, 113 abstracts have been considered and those papers not considered relevant to the research have been discarded (the ones with a too broad perspective on OI and not focused on factors that enable and/or inhibit the successful implementation of corporate-startup collaboration). In doing so, the relevant literature screening process ended up with 41 papers considered relevant to enhance the understanding on corporate-startup collaborations (Figure 1).

The next step involved the in-depth analysis of each article. Each one of the 41 selected contributions was in depth analyzed and coded according to the following categories: article type (empirical/conceptual/review), methodology (qualitative/quantitative), type of data collected/analyzed (survey/interview/secondary data/sample size/geographic scope) and exploratory factors studied. Furthermore, data regarding the objective of the analysis and key findings were collected and treated as qualitative information to describe the key aspects under investigation and to provide future research directions in this stream of research.

The vast majority of the 41 contributions considered are manly based only on qualitative analysis performed adopting a case study approach. Different industries and geographies have been investigated by scholars in their studies. More specifically, the vast majority of studies focus on the automotive industry, on ICT and software development, and on pharmaceutical and biotech sector. Other studies also consider: aeronautical, beverage, chemical, electronics, fashion, financial, furniture, graphics, household manufacturing, infrastructure, insurance, materials, marketing, mining, nanotechnology, oil, semiconductors, textile, tourism, transportation, and water treatment. As regards the countries investigated, USA and Germany are considered in the vast majority of studies.

CRITICAL BARRIERS TO OVERCOME WHEN CORPORATES ENGAGE WITH STARTUPS

As anticipated, qualitative analysis, performed adopting a case study approach, allows to in depth analyze the difficulties that both large established firms and startups face when engaging in Open Innovation activities, and to identify which are the best practices that serve as facilitators to overcome these obstacles. More specifically, the barriers identified in the considered contributions are: culture, complexity and communication among the most frequent ones; the transfer of accumulated experience; the availability of qualified human resources; intellectual leadership; the concepts of autonomy, authority and risk; the difficulties in finding partners; managing the power unbalance; a differentiated value proposition; the "Not-Invented-Elsewhere Syndrome"; and the need for on-going iteration (Table 1).

The first contribution citing difficulties encountered during the implementation of Open Innovation activities is the one of Minshall et al. (2010). They found out that understanding how to transfer accumulated experience is a key problem in order to improve firms' performances, both startups and large firms desire a network in which is possible to share experiences and issues. They also highlight the fact that any kind of OI approach would never reach a point of completion. According to Oughton et al. (2013), who analyzed the cases of asymmetric partnerships of SMEs and multinational corporations, the main difficulties that arise are related to culture, complexity and communication. While Tamburis and Bonacci (2014) investigated the role of innovation networks in the pharmaceutical sector as a mean of knowledge transfer and found out that the main sources of problems are funding, sustainability, the availability of qualified human resources, the availability of data and tools (which is an aspect related to communication), and intellectual leadership.

In this respect, De Fabricio et al. (2015) conducted a study that focuses on strengthening the OI model of a Chinese multinational corporation subsidized in Brazil by using startups and technology parks. They suggest that breaking the cultural barriers between the two countries was the most difficult aspect. Moreover, Kohler (2016) carried out a case study on corporate accelerators and pointed out that corporate complexity is what creates problems to startups. Accordingly, he suggests that corporate accelerators should be designed to act like shields able to protect startups from it.

Jackson and Richter (2017) identified inhibitors to the collaboration between large firms and new ventures in accelerator programs. The main ones are related to culture (conflicts in basic beliefs or propositions), autonomy, authority, and risk. Mercandetti et al. (2017), by analyzing collaboration between SMEs and startups, found out that in these asymmetric partnerships the most difficult aspect is the one related to find possible partners to engage with. Additionally, Spender et al. (2017) – thanks to the literature review that they have conducted – pointed out that it is still not clear how the power unbalance with VCs and established firms can be managed by startups in an efficient way.

In addition, Mahmoud-Jouini et al. (2018) shed new light on the key factors in building a corporate accelerator capability, they highlighted the problem of designing a differentiated value proposition for startups based on corporate's assets capitalization. Moreover, Wikhamn and Styhre (2018) investigated a large biopharmaceutical enterprise's outbound Open Innovation activities and highlighted problems related to communication about building attractive assets proposals, and to the so called Not-Invented- Elsewhere Syndrome (NIE), which is a syndrome related to those assets that were previously selected as potential spinouts and that therefore gained a growing interest within the organization. These assets were formerly view as off-strategy and then they could get revalued. Wouters et al. (2018), then, attempted to provide a tool to better understand which is the value of a startup's offering to an established business, and which are the resources needed to help a startup to obtain its offering. They found out that startups are not that good in communication.

Table 1. Barriers to overcome when corporates engage with startups: summary

Barriers	References
Culture	Oughton et al. (2013); De Fabricio et al. (2015); Jackson and Richter (2017)
Complexity	Oughton et al. (2013); Kohler (2016)
Communication	Oughton et al. (2013); Tamburis and Bonacci (2014); Wikhamn and Styhre (2018); Wouters et al. (2018)
Transfer of Accumulated Experience	Minshall et al. (2010)
Availability of Qualified HR	Tamburis and Bonacci (2014)
Intellectual Leadership	Tamburis and Bonacci (2014)
Authority, Autonomy and Risk	Jackson and Richter (2017)
Finding Partners	Mercandetti et al. (2017)
Managing the Power Unbalance	Spender et al. (2017)
Differentiated Value Proposition	Mahmoud-Jouini et al. (2018)
Not-Invented-Elsewhere Syndrome (NIE)	Wikhamn and Styhre (2018)
Need for On-Going Iteration	Minshall et al. (2010)

Source: Authors' elaboration.

FACILITATORS FOR A SUCCESSFUL IMPLEMENTATION OF OPEN INNOVATION ACTIVITIES

Scholars also pointed out some "facilitators" as being effective when corporates engage with startups. Among these, the following are the most cited: having specialist teams with appropriate skills; running transparent processes; a continuous and effective communication; having shared roadmaps; a strong commitment from executives; a good problem definition; building special and flexible contracts; identifying a corporate champion accountable for the relationship; creating a collaborative work environment; recognize startups' work; do not limit startups' freedom; proactively manage relationships; partners' commitment; employees' engagement; provide mentorships; offering startups funds; having an independent team of startups advocates; being part of a large and committed external network; having long-term objectives; constructing non-traditional KPIs; treating startups as partners; assignment of dedicated business developers; and creating synergy effects.

More specifically, Minshall et al. (2010) pointed out that, in order to successfully transfer accumulated experience, an on-going iteration of both content and activities is needed. Oughton et al.'s study (2013) suggests that to overcome culture, complexity and communication problems, companies need to implement a good combination of facilitators based on hiring a team of specialists that have the appropriate skills, building and running transparent processes, having a continuous and effective communication, and sharing the roadmaps of the program. In this respect, the case study of Tamburis and Bonacci (2014) does not provide best practices to overcome communication, availability of qualified human resources and intellectual leadership issues, but it highlights which are the benefits that can be achieved if the problems are solved: agility, creativity, focus, speed, and cost advantages.

The facilitators that De Fabricio et al. (2015) pointed out to overcome cultural barriers issues refer to the flow of knowledge that must be guaranteed in all directions, a good interaction between teams which is necessary, and explicit and tacit knowledge that are both essentials. These aspects can be reconducted to a continuous and effective communication and a collaborative work environment. Moreover, Kohler (2016) suggests that corporate accelerators should be designed to act like shields able to protect startups from complexity. Kohler continues proposing that corporate must not limit startups' freedom and that is essential to customize the program on the basis of startups' needs in order to achieve successful results. Jackson and Richter (2017) pointed out that actions like regular interactions and active governance can result useful to reduce the impact of inhibitors linked to culture, authority and risk. These two facilitators can be exemplified by a continuous and effective communication, and by proactively managed relationships. Mahmoud-Jouini et al. (2018) then shed light on the key factors in building a corporate accelerator capability. In doing so, they pointed out that developing a specific program to proactively manage relationships and the assignment of dedicated business developers can increase the probability of the accelerator's success. Wouters et al. (2018) then attempted to provide a tool to better understand which is the value of a startup's offering to an established business, and which are the resources needed to help a startup to obtain its offering. They pointed out that startups are not that good in communication and that by offering mentorship to startups and producing the "Innovative Offering Value Proposition" and the "Leveraging Assistance Value Proposition" can lead to successful asymmetric partnerships.

Reichmann and Simpson (2016) studied roadmaps and roadblocks in early drug discovery and found out that, to pass over the roadblocks, there's the need of innovative management models that ensure relationships that are managed in a proactive way. Moreover, a transparent framework for widely acceptable Intellectual Property agreements and a strong commitment of all the parties involved are necessary. According to Kupp et al.'s contribution (2017), which analyzed the "hub:raum" case study, it is possible to highlight five major success factors for corporate accelerators: transparent and aligned goals (shared roadmaps), an independent team of startup advocates, a large and committed external network, top-management support, and long-term objectives. Moreover, it is crucial to develop and use significant performance indicators (that can be different from traditional KPIs).

Chesbrough (2012b), in his paper that assess General Electric's ecomagination challenge, was able to highlight as crucial factor for a successful Open Innovation initiative the strong commitment from the top-management. While Rainone et al. (2014) conducted a case study on a New Product Development (NPD) company with twenty-five years of experience and pointed out that facilitators when engaging with small companies include: over-communication, provide a clear problem definition, building special and flexible contracts and payment terms, identify a "corporate champion" (defined as someone from the established enterprise who is held accountable for the partnership with the new venture), develop and maintain a collaborative work environment, recognize startups' work and importance as a partner by providing them referrals or testimonials. In addition, Allen et al. (2016) examined the power of reciprocal knowledge sharing in a context of geographic proximity and found out that in their case study, it is not the location that influences the innovation success, what instead appears to have a positive impact on it is the communication intensity. More specifically, a variable like the location of OI activities can positively influence the success of partnerships. In this respect, De Fabricio et al. (2015) pointed out that technological parks allow and foster interactions with startups and universities. As said, Allen et al. (2016) proposed that location for sure influences the number of occurring communications between partners – but it doesn't necessarily guarantee their innovation success. Also the literature review conducted by Vrontis and Christofi (2019) on R&D internationalization and innovation shed light on some interesting issues: the first one is that "there's a direct positive impact of cross-regional knowledge integration on innovation quality, as well as a positive interaction effect of cross-regional knowledge integration and distributed R&D for innovation quality" (Vrontis & Christofi, 2019, p.7). Then they pointed out that a "modularization of work across locations is not effective when the underlying tasks are less familiar, routinized and analyzable – performance through modularization is enhanced only when the level of analyzability and routines is high [...] coordination across locations based on information sharing positively influences innovation performance when R&D captive centers perform tasks of low familiarity" (Vrontis & Christofi, 2019, p. 9). Moreover, the creation of innovation networks and ecosystems seems to allow to foster partnership's engagement. Tamburis and Bonacci (2014) in their paper investigated the importance of innovation networks in the healthcare industry as a mean of knowledge transfer. De Fabricio et al. (2015) suggested that developing a strong innovation ecosystem is essential to develop disruptive innovations. While, Shao and Shi (2018) suggested that the spillover effects and technology transfer of a well embedded cross-border innovation center within its local ecosystem are possible in the long run.

In addition, Wikhamn and Styhre (2016) provided an in-depth case study of how a large pharmaceutical company implemented a successful Open Innovation activity. What they found out is that employees' engagement resulted in a more open and dynamic environment, as well as an improved entrepreneurial image of the corporation. In addition, Hogenhuis et al. (2017) – with their contribution – wanted to prove the thesis that solutions implemented in the early stages of the interactions between established firms and young ventures, have a positive impact on the outcome of the asymmetric partnership. The barriers of asymmetric partnerships resulted addressed by offering mentorships and offering startup funds. Moreover, these "exemplary" large firms taken into consideration in their study differed from the others in terms of effective communication. In this respect, Livieratos and Lepeniotis (2017) assessed the state of European CVC programs in the electric utilities industry, and found out that the companies included in their case study – that represent best practices – were characterized by a strong commitment from the executives and by the alignment of partners' time schedules. Moreover, Richter et al. (2017) conducted and abductive study of OI using corporate accelerators and pointed out that senior management commitment is what drives a successful cooperation. They believe that KPIs are useless and it is better to develop customized measures that match specific purposes. Moreover, they have shown that it is essential to treat startups as real partners, not as subcontractors. Additionally, Selig et al. (2018) contributed at better understanding corporate accelerators, and in their case study they highlighted the importance of top-management support – that they define as "mandatory" –, and of synergy effects with other Open Innovation activities. In doing so, they also pointed out that control must go beyond traditional KPIs.

Allmendinger and Berger (2019), aiming to understand when startups are willing to engage in asymmetric partnership, found out that overly bureaucratic contracts scare the entrepreneurs and that – on the other hand – open and frequent communication, combined with customized and flexible contracts can attract them. While De Groote and Backmann (2019) while investigating how incumbents select startups as partners in Open Innovation activities - by implementing a multiple case study approach – pointed out that proactively managed relationships and activities, and partners' commitment are the factors that lead to a successful partnership. Gutmann (2019), who performed an integrative review on Corporate Venturing modes, found out that creating a collaborative work environment where people, processes, and technologies are organized with the aim to foster individual and team creativity is important to create environments where innovation flourishes.

Table 2. Facilitators for a successful implementation of open innovation activities by corporate and startup: a summary from the literature review

Facilitators	References
Specialist Teams (with appropriate skills)	Oughton et al. (2013)
Transparent Processes	Oughton et al. (2013); Reichmann and Simpson (2016); Kupp et al. (2017)
Continuous and Effective Communication	Oughton et al. (2013); Rainone et al. (2014); De Fabricio et al. (2015); Allen et al. (2016); Hogenhuis et al. (2017); Jackson and Richter (2017); Allmendinger and Berger (2019)
Shared Roadmaps	Oughton et al. (2013); Kupp et al. (2017); Livieratos and Lepeniotis (2017)
Strong Commitment from Executives	Chesbrough (2012b); Kupp et al. (2017); Livieratos and Lepeniotis (2017); Richter et al. (2017); Selig et al. (2018)
Problem Definition	Rainone et al. (2014)
Special/Flexible Contracts (Customization)	Rainone et al. (2014); Kohler (2016); Allmendinger and Berger (2019)
Identify a Corporate Champion	Rainone et al. (2014)
Collaborative Work Environment	Rainone et al. (2014); De Fabricio et al. (2015); Gutmann (2019)
Recognize Startups' Work	Rainone et al. (2014)
Not Limit Startups' Freedom	Kohler (2016)
Proactively Managed Relationships	Reichmann and Simpson (2016); Jackson and Richter (2017); Mahmoud-Jouini et al. (2018); De Groote and Backmann (2019)
Partners' Commitment	Reichmann and Simpson (2016); De Groote and Backmann (2019)
Employees' Engagement	Wikhamn and Styhre (2016)
Mentorships	Hogenhuis et al. (2017); Wouters et al. (2018)
Offering Startup Funds	Hogenhuis et al. (2017)
Independent Team of Startup Advocates	Kupp et al. (2017)
Large and Committed External Network	Kupp et al. (2017)
Long-term Objectives	Kupp et al. (2017)
Non-traditional KPIs	Kupp et al. (2017); Richter et al. (2017); Selig et al. (2018)
Startups Treated as Partners	Richter et al. (2017)
Assignment of Dedicated Business Developers	Mahmoud-Jouini et al. (2018)
Synergy Effects	Selig et al. (2018)

Source: Authors' elaboration.

CONCLUSION AND FUTURE RESEARCH DIRECTIONS

Open Innovation is of crucial importance in today's world characterized by globalization, keen competition, and shortening of product life cycles. Chesbrough (2006) not only stated that firms should use both internal and external ideas in their innovation process, but they can also profit from step internal ideas outside the firm both in the research stage or in the development stage. Therefore, companies are increasing the use of Open Innovation strategies in order to face this new era of distributed knowledge, but many of them are having difficulties in implementing and managing OI activities. More specifically, network is considered as being a crucial aspect of analysis in OI processes and implies the interaction among different typologies of actors (Chesbrough, 2003; Fichter, 2009; Padilla-Melendez et al., 2013). A wide range of areas and domains have been analyzed so far (Chesbrough et al., 2014; Gassmann et al., 2010) and different units of analysis have been taken into consideration by scholars, such as large corporations, small and medium-sized companies (SMEs), and also high-tech startups (Weiblen & Chesbrough, 2015; Rua et al., 2018).

The Chapter focuses on the latter aspect, i.e. corporate-startup collaboration. To identify the main barriers to corporate-startup collaboration and, in doing so, to provide a comprehensive framework able to shed new light on the proposed issue and to provide guidance to future research directions, a comprehensive and systematized literature review was performed. Contributions reviewed in the analysis pointed out that the main problematic issues to be faced for a successful collaboration are mainly linked to cultural barriers and communication (Oughton et al., 2013; Tamburis & Bonacci, 2014; De Fabricio et al., 2015; Jackson & Richter, 2017; Wikhamn and Styhre, 2018; Wouters et al., 2018). In addition, the most effective facilitators emerging from the "best practices" considered in the studies analyzed include continuous and effective communication, a strong commitment by top-management and building and maintaining proactively managed relationships (Chesbrough, 2012b; Oughton et al., 2013; Rainone et al., 2014; De Fabricio et al., 2015; Allen et al., 2016; Reichmann & Simpson, 2016; Hogenhuis et al., 2017; Jackson & Richter, 2017; Kupp et al., 2017; Livieratos & Lepeniotis, 2017; Richter et al., 2017; Mahmoud-Jouini et al., 2018; Selig et al., 2018; Allmendinger & Berger, 2019; De Groote & Backmann, 2019). Other scholars also argued that in many circumstances, finding the right partner to engage with is not that easy both for startups and for corporates (Holzmann et al., 2014). In addition, from the SLR emerged that in many cases also variables like trust and location of OI activities can positively affect the success of partnerships (De Fabricio et al., 2015; Allen et al., 2016; Vrontis & Christofi, 2019). Moreover, the creation and the development of innovation networks and ecosystems can foster partnership's engagement (Tamburis & Bonacci, 2014; De Fabricio et al., 2015; Shao & Shi, 2018).

Accordingly, future research directions should try to provide more evidence of how corporate-startup collaboration happens. The systematic literature review presented in this chapter calls for more empirical studies, both qualitative and quantitative, to provide a more comprehensive framework of the issue under investigation and to provide practical insights to entrepreneurs, managers and practitioners.

REFERENCES

Allen, T. J., Gloor, P. A., Fronzetti Colladon, A., Woemer, S. L., & Raz, O. (2016). The power of reciprocal knowledge sharing relationships for startup success. *Journal of Small Business and Enterprise Development*, *23*(3), 636–651. doi:10.1108/JSBED-08-2015-0110

Allmendinger, M. P., & Berger, E. S. C. (2019). Selecting corporate firms for collaborative innovation: Entrepreneurial decision making in asymmetric partnerships. *International Journal of Innovation Management.*

Blank, S. (2010). *What's A Startup? First Principles.* Steveblank.com

Chesbrough, H., Vanhaverbeke, W., & West, J. (Eds.). (2014b). *New frontiers in open innovation.* Oxford University Press. doi:10.1093/acprof:oso/9780199682461.001.0001

Chesbrough, H. W. (2003). *Open innovation: The new imperative for creating and profiting from technology*. Harvard Business School Press.

Chesbrough, H. W. (2006). *Open innovation: the new imperative for creating and profiting from technology*. Harvard Business Review Press.

Chesbrough, H. W. (2012a). Open innovation: Where we've been and where we're going. *Research Technology Management*, *55*(4), 20–27. doi:10.5437/08956308X5504085

Chesbrough, H. W. (2012b). GE's ecomagination Challenge: An experiment in Open Innovation. *California Management Review*, *54*(3), 140–154. doi:10.1525/cmr.2012.54.3.140

Chesbrough, H. W., & Crowther, A. K. (2006). Beyond high tech: Early adopters of open innovation in other industries. *R & D Management*, *36*(3), 229–236. doi:10.1111/j.1467-9310.2006.00428.x

Chesbrough, H. W., & Euchner, J. (2011). The Evolution of Open Innovation: An interview with Henry Chesbrough. *Research Technology Management*, *50*(1), 13–18. doi:10.5437/08956308X5405003

Chesbrough, H. W., & Rosenbloom, R. S. (2002). The Role of the Business Model in Capturing Value from Innovation: Evidence from Xerox Corporation's Technology Spin-Off Companies. *Industrial and Corporate Change*, *11*(3), 529–555. doi:10.1093/icc/11.3.529

Chesbrough, H. W., Salter, A. J., Vanhaverbeke, W., & West, J. (2014a). Open Innovation: The Next Decade. *Research Policy*, *43*(5), 805–811. doi:10.1016/j.respol.2014.03.001

De Fabricio, R. S., Da Silva, F. R., Simões, E., Galegale, N. V., & Akabane, G. K. (2015). Strengthening of Open Innovation model: Using startups and technology parks. *IFAC-PapersOnLine*, *48*(3), 14–20. doi:10.1016/j.ifacol.2015.06.051

De Groote, J., & Backmann, J. (2019). Initiating open innovation collaborations between incumbents and startups: How can David and Goliath get along? *International Journal of Innovation Management*, *2050011*, 1–33.

Fichter. (2009) Innovation communities: the role of networks of promotors in Open Innovation. *R&D Management, 39*(4), 357-371.

Gassmann, O., Enkel, E., & Chesbrough, H. W. (2010). The future of open innovation. *R & D Management*, *40*(3), 213–221. doi:10.1111/j.1467-9310.2010.00605.x

Gutmann, T. (2019). Harmonizing corporate venturing modes: An integrative review and research agenda. *Management Review Quarterly*, *69*(2), 121–157. doi:10.100711301-018-0148-4

Hogenhuis, B. N., Van Den Hende, E. A., & Hultink, E. J. (2017). Unlocking the innovation potential in large firms through timely and meaningful interactions with young ventures. *International Journal of Innovation Management*, *21*(1), 1–29. doi:10.1142/S1363919617500098

Jackson, P., & Richter, N. (2017). Situational logic: An analysis of open innovation using corporate accelerators. *International Journal of Innovation Management*, *21*(7), 1–21. doi:10.1142/S1363919617500621

King, A., & Lakhani, K. R. (2013). Using Open Innovation to identify the best ideas. *MIT Sloan Management Review*, *55*(1), 41–48.

Kohler, T. (2016). Corporate accelerators: Building bridges between corporations and startups. *Business Horizons*, *59*(3), 347–357. doi:10.1016/j.bushor.2016.01.008

Kupp, M., Marval, M., & Borchers, P. (2017). Corporate accelerators: Fostering innovation while bringing together startups and large firms. *The Journal of Business Strategy*, *38*(6), 47–53. doi:10.1108/JBS-12-2016-0145

Lichtenthaler, U., & Lichtenthaler, E. (2009). A Capability-Based framework for Open Innovation: Complementing absorptive capacity. *Journal of Management Studies*, *46*(8), 1315–1338. doi:10.1111/j.1467-6486.2009.00854.x

Lisi, I. E. (2018). Determinants and Performance Effects of Social Performance Measurement Systems. *Journal of Business Ethics*, *152*(1), 225–251. doi:10.100710551-016-3287-3

Livieratos, A. D., & Lepeniotis, P. (2017). Corporate venture capital programs of European electric utilities: Motives, trends, strategies and challenges. *The Electricity Journal*, *30*(2), 30–40. doi:10.1016/j.tej.2017.01.006

Mahmoud-Jouini, S. B., Duvert, C., & Esquirol, M. (2018). Key factors in building a Corporate Accelerators Capability. *Research Technology Management*, *61*(4), 26–34. doi:10.1080/08956308.2018.1471274

Mercandetti, F., Larbig, C., Tuozzo, V., & Steiner, T. (2017). Innovation by Collaboration between Startups and SMEs in Switzerland. *Technology Innovation Management Review*, *7*(12), 23–31. doi:10.22215/timreview/1125

Mind the Bridge. (2017b). *European Corporate Innovation Outposts in Silicon Valley. The Who's Who*. Available at: https://mindthebridge.com/research/

Mind the Bridge. (2018). *European Innovation Economy in Silicon Valley*. Available at: https://mindthebridge.com/research/

Mind the Bridge. (2019). *Corporate Innovation in Silicon Valley: Outposts and Investment Flow*. Available at: https://mindthebridge.com/research/

Mind the Bridge. (2020). *Corporate Innovation in Silicon Valley*. Available at: https://mindthebridge.com/research/

Mind the Bridge – NESTA. (2017a), *Open Innovation in Europe. A Snapshot of the SEP Europe's Corporate Startup Stars 2017*. Retrieved from: https://www.nesta.org.uk/blog/open-innovation-in-europe-a-snapshot-of-the-sep-europes-corporate-startup-stars-2017/

Minshall, T., Mortara, L., Valli, R., & Probert, D. (2010, June). Making 'asymmetric' partnerships work: Partnering between small start-ups and larger firms presents challenges – but some have found ways to overcome them. *Research Technology Management*, *53*(May), 53–63. doi:10.1080/08956308.2010.11657631

Onetti, A. (2019). Turning Open Innovation into Practice: Trends in European Corporates. *Journal of Business Strategy, 42*(1), 51-58.

Oughton, D., Mortara, L., & Minshall, T. (2013). Managing asymmetric relationships in open innovation: lessons from multinational companies and SMEs. In *Open Innovation in the Food and Beverage Industry* (pp. 276–293). Woodhead Publishing Series in Food Science, Technology and Nutrition. doi:10.1533/9780857097248.3.276

Padilla-Meléndez, A., Del Aguila-Obra, A. R., & Lockett, N. (2013). Shifting sands: Regional perspectives on the role of social capital in supporting open innovation through knowledge transfer and exchange with small and medium-sized enterprises. *International Small Business Journal, 31*(3), 296–318. doi:10.1177/0266242612467659

Pisoni, A., & Onetti, A. (2018). When startups exit: Comparing strategies in Europe and the USA. *The Journal of Business Strategy, 39*(3), 26–33. doi:10.1108/JBS-02-2017-0022

Rainone, D., Rainone, M., & Musial, L. (2014). How to work with small companies to expand your open innovation capabilities. *Open Innovation: New Product Development Essentials From the PDMA.*

Reichmann, M., & Simpson, P. B. (2016). Open innovation in early drug discovery: Roadmaps and roadblocks. *Drug Discovery Today, 21*(5), 779–788. doi:10.1016/j.drudis.2015.12.008 PMID:26743597

Richter, N., Jackson, P., & Schildhauer, T. (2017). Outsourcing creativity: An abductive study of open innovation using corporate accelerators. *Creativity and Innovation Management, 27*(1), 69–78. doi:10.1111/caim.12252

Rua, O. L., França, A., & Fernández, R. O. (2018). Key drivers of SMEs export performance: The mediating effect of competitive advantage. *Journal of Knowledge Management, 22*(2), 257–279. doi:10.1108/JKM-07-2017-0267

Selig, C. J., Gasser, T., & Baltes, G. H. (2018). How corporate accelerators foster organizational transformation: An internal perspective. *2018 IEEE International Conference on Engineering, Technology and Innovation.* 10.1109/ICE.2018.8436287

Shao, Y., & Shi, L. (2018). Cross-border open innovation of early stage tech incubation: A case study of forge, the first UK-China accelerator program. *Journal of Open Innovation, 4*(3), 37. doi:10.3390/joitmc4030037

Spender, J. C., Corvello, V., Grimaldi, M., & Rippa, P. (2017). Startups and open innovation: A review of the literature. *European Journal of Innovation Management, 20*(1), 4–30. doi:10.1108/EJIM-12-2015-0131

Tamburis, O., & Bonacci, I. (2014). Innovation networks in healthcare as mean of knowledge transfer. *IFKAD 2014: 9th International Forum on Knowledge Asset Dynamics: Knowledge and Management Models for Sustainable Growth.*

Tranfield, D., Denyer, D., & Smart, P. (2003). Towards a methodology for developing evidence-informed management knowledge by means of systematic review. *British Journal of Management, 14*(3), 207–222. doi:10.1111/1467-8551.00375

Van Lieshout, J.W.F.C., van der Velden, J.M., Blomme, R.J., & Peters, P. (2021). The interrelatedness of organizational ambidexterity, dynamic capabilities and open innovation: a conceptual model towards a competitive advantage. *European Journal of Management Studies.*

Vrontis, D., & Christofi, M. (2019). R&D internationalization and innovation: A systematic review, integrative framework and future research directions. *Journal of Business Research, 128*(2).

Weiblen, T., & Chesbrough, H. W. (2015). Engaging with startups to enhance corporate innovation. *California Management Review, 57*(2), 66–90. doi:10.1525/cmr.2015.57.2.66

Wikhamn, B. R., & Styhre, A. (2016). Open innovation as a facilitator for corporate exploration. *International Journal of Innovation Management, 21*(6), 1–20.

Wikhamn, B. R., & Styhre, A. (2018). Managerial challenges of outbound open innovation: A study of a spinout initiative in AstraZeneca. *R & D Management, 49*(4), 652–667.

Wouters, M., Anderson, J. C., & Kirchberger, M. (2018). New-technology startups seeking pilot customers: Crafting a pair of value propositions. *California Management Review, 60*(4), 101–124. doi:10.1177/0008125618778855

KEY TERMS AND DEFINITIONS

Asymmetric Partnership: Corporate and startups/scaleups are intrinsically different one from the other: large firms have resources, economies of scale, power and a proven business model, on the other hand startups lack corporates' characteristics but have fresh promising ideas, more agility in terms of organization, a risk taker attitude, and ambitions to grow rapidly. Accordingly, managing the power unbalance is a critical issue when corporates engage with startups.

Barriers: Problematic issues to be faced for implementing a successful corporate-startup collaboration. Among these, cultural barriers, complexity, and communication-related issues emerge as being the most frequently mentioned by scholars.

Corporate-Startup Collaboration: When corporates engage with startups to develop innovation. Collaborations happen in different forms: Corporate Venture Capital (CVC), Corporate Incubation, outside-in startup programs, and inside-out platform startup programs. More recently, additional categories have also been identified: exposure, trend spotting, accelerators, procurement, investments, and acquisitions.

Facilitators: "Best practices" to be considered as ways to facilitate asymmetric partnerships between corporates and startups. Among these, the most important emerging from the SLR are a continuous and effective communication among the parties, the strong commitment by the top-management in building and maintaining proactively managed relationships, the creation and the development of innovation networks and ecosystems to foster partnership's engagement.

Open Innovation: The open innovation paradigm describes a "distributed innovation process," i.e., how companies' innovation processes profit by mixing internal and external ideas.

Scaleup: A scaleup is the next development stage of a startup. It could be defined in different ways. In this chapter, it is intended as a company that raised at least $1M in funding (including both capital raised through VC and the stock market) since foundation, with at least one recent funding event.

Startup: Startups are new business projects (also described as "experiment") with a strong commitment to innovation and marked ambitions of growth, the so-called "scalability."

Compilation of References

Abulrub, A.-H., & Lee, J. (2012). Open innovation management: Challenges and prospects. *Procedia: Social and Behavioral Sciences*, *41*, 130–138. doi:10.1016/j.sbspro.2012.04.017

Ahn, J. M. T., & Mortara, L. (2015). Open innovation: A new classification and its impact on firm performance in innovative SMEs. *Journal of Innovation Management*, *3*(2), 33–54. doi:10.24840/2183-0606_003.002_0006

Ahn, J. M., Minshall, T., & Mortara, L. (2017). Understanding the human side of openness: The fit between open innovation modes and CEO characteristics. *R & D Management*, *47*(5), 727–740. doi:10.1111/radm.12264

Ahuja, G. (2000). Collaboration Networks, Structural Holes, and Innovation: A Longitudinal Study. *Administrative Science Quarterly*, *45*(3), 425–455. doi:10.2307/2667105

Akbar, Y. A., & Tracogna, A. (2018). The Sharing Economy and the Future of the Hotel Industry: Transaction cost theory and platform economics. *International Journal of Hospitality Management*, *71*, 91–101. doi:10.1016/j.ijhm.2017.12.004

Alavi, M., & Leidner, D. E. (2001). Review: Knowledge management and knowledge management systems: Conceptual foundations and research issues. *Management Information Systems Quarterly*, *25*(1), 107–133. doi:10.2307/3250961

Alexander, A. T., Miller, K., & Fielding, S. (2015). Open for business: Universities, entrepreneurial academics and open innovation. *International Journal of Innovation Management*, *19*(06), 1540013. doi:10.1142/S1363919615400137

Alexy, O., Bascavusoglu-Moreau, E., & Salter, A. J. (2016). Toward an Aspiration-Level Theory of Open Innovation. *Industrial and Corporate Change*, *25*(2), 289–306. doi:10.1093/icc/dtw003

Allen, T. J., Gloor, P. A., Fronzetti Colladon, A., Woerner, S. L., & Raz, O. (2016). The power of reciprocal knowledge sharing relationships for startup success. *Journal of Small Business and Enterprise Development*, *23*(3), 636–651. doi:10.1108/JSBED-08-2015-0110

Allmendinger, M. P., & Berger, E. S. C. (2019). Selecting corporate firms for collaborative innovation: Entrepreneurial decision making in asymmetric partnerships. *International Journal of Innovation Management*.

Almirall, E., & Casadesus-Masanell, R. (2010). Open vs. Closed Innovation: A Model of Discovery and Divergence. *Academy of Management Review*, *35*(1), 27–47.

Alshenqeeti, H. (2014). Interviewing as a data collection method: A critical review. *Sciedu Press*, *3*(1), 39–45. doi:10.5430/elr.v3n1p39

Andreoni, A., & Chang, H. J. (2019). The political economy of industrial policy: Structural interdependencies, policy alignment and conflict management. *Structural Change and Economic Dynamics*, *48*, 136–150. doi:10.1016/j.strueco.2018.10.007

Ani. (2019). *International Comparative Analysis of the National Innovation System*. Available: https://www.ani.pt/media/4880/relatorio_012_ani.pdf

Anišić, Z., Koldžin, D., & Freund, R. (2013). How to Support Open Innovations through Public Policies? *Annals of the Faculty of Engineering Hunedoara - International Journal of Engineering (Stevenage, England)*, *11*(2), 241–247.

Anning-Dorson, T. (2018). Innovation and competitive advantage creation. *International Marketing Review*, *35*(4), 580–600. doi:10.1108/IMR-11-2015-0262

Annunziata, M. (2021, March 17). *Reinventing mobility and manufacturing at once: Local Motors*. https://www.forbes.com/sites/marcoannunziata/2020/03/17/reinventing-mobility-and-manufacturing-at-once-local-motors/?sh=2df79db60d8b

ANPEI. (2017). *Guia da Lei do Bem: o que é inovação para a Lei do Bem? Conheça o principal instrumento de fomento à inovação em empresas do Brasil*. Letras & Artes Comunicação.

Antonioli, D., Marzucchi, A., & Montresor, S. (2012). Regional Innovation Policy and Innovative Behaviour: Looking for Additional Effects. *European Planning Studies*, *22*(1), 64–83. doi:10.1080/09654313.2012.722977

Anwar, M. (2018). Business Model Innovation and SME performance - Does Competitive Advantage mediate? *International Journal of Innovation Management*, *22*(7), 1–31. doi:10.1142/S1363919618500573

Aquino, Y. (2018). *Governo regulamenta Marco Legal da Ciência*. Tecnologia e Inovação, Brasília, 8 fev. Agência Brasil.

Aranha, E. A., Garcia, N. A. P., Silva, G. N. R., & Santos, P. (2017). Open Innovation and Business Model in Brazilian Small Business. *International Journal of Business Management and Economic Research*, *8*(5), 1008–1015.

Arnold, E. (2004). Evaluating research and innovation policy: A systems world needs systems evaluation. *Research Evaluation*, *13*(1), 3–17. doi:10.3152/147154404781776509

Asheim, B. T. (2019). Smart specialisation, innovation policy and regional innovation systems: What about new path development in less innovative regions? *Innovation: The European Journal of Social Sciences*, *32*(1), 8–25.

Asheim, B. T., Grillitsch, M., & Trippl, M. (2016). Regional innovation systems: Past–present–future. *Handbook on the Geographies of Innovation, 36*, 45–62. doi:10.4337/9781784710774.00010

Aspen Institute. (n.d.). *An innovation challenge for the United States*. Available: https://assets.aspeninstitute.org/content/uploads/2019/09/Aspen-Cyber-Group-An-Innovation-Challenge-for-the-United-States-10.2.19.pdf

Astuti, E., Suhadak, Rahayu, S. M., & Wilopo. (2018). The influence of information technology strategy and management support to the internal business process, competitive advantage, financial and non-financial performance of the company. *International Journal of Web Information Systems, 14*(3), 317–333. doi:10.1108/IJWIS-11-2017-0079

Atuahene-Gima, K. (2005). Resolving the Capability–Rigidity Paradox in New Product Innovation. *Journal of Marketing, 69*(4), 61–83. doi:10.1509/jmkg.2005.69.4.61

Auh, S., & Menguc, B. (2005). Balancing exploration and exploitation: The moderating role of competitive intensity. *Journal of Business Research, 58*(12), 1652–1661. doi:10.1016/j.jbusres.2004.11.007

Avalos-Quispe, G. A., & Hernández-Simón, L. M. (2019). Open Innovation in SMEs: Potential and Realized Absorptive Capacity for Interorganizational Learning in Dyad Collaborations with Academia. *Journal of Open Innovation: Technology, Market, and Complexity, 5*(3), 1–14.

Avalos-Quispe, G., & Hernandez-Simon, L. (2019). Open Innovation in SMEs: Potential and Realized Absorptive Capacity for Interorganizational Learning in Dyad Collaborations with Academia. *Journal of Open Innovation, 5*(3), 72. doi:10.3390/joitmc5030072

Azevedo, C.E.F. (2018). Os elementos de análise da cultura de inovação no setor de Defesa e seu modelo tridimensional. *Coleção Meira Mattos: revista das ciências militares, 12*(45), 145-167.

Azevedo, C. E. F. (2017). *Incremento da cultura de inovação: passo essencial para o desenvolvimento da base industrial de defesa e ampliação do poder dissuasório*. Trabalho de Conclusão de Curso – Escola Superior de Guerra.

Baggio, A. F., & Baggio, D. K. (2015). Empreendedorismo: Conceitos e definições. *Revista de empreendedorismo, inovação e tecnologia, 1*(1), 25-38.

Bahemia, H., & Squire, B. (2010). A Contingent View of Open Innovation in new Prodtuct Development Projects. *International Journal of Innovation Management, 14*(4), 603–627. doi:10.1142/S1363919610002799

Barge-Gil, A. (2013). Open Strategies and Innovation Performance. *Industry and Innovation, 20*(7), 585–610. doi:10.1080/13662716.2013.849455

Barney, J. (1991). Firm Resources and Sustained Competitive Advantage. *Journal of Management, 17*(1), 99–120. doi:10.1177/014920639101700108

Barney, J. B. (2001). Resource-based theories of competitive advantage: A ten-year retrospective on the resource-based view. *Journal of Management*, *27*(6), 643–650. doi:10.1177/014920630102700602

Benkler, Y. (2006). *The wealth of networks: How social production transforms markets and freedom*. Yale University Press.

Beraha, I. (2019). Ocena inovativnih performansi Republike Srbije. *Ekonomski vidici, 25*(3-4), 137-151.

Berchicci, L. (2013). Towards an open R&D system: Internal R&D investment, external knowledge acquisition and innovative performance. *Research Policy*, *42*(1), 11–127. doi:10.1016/j.respol.2012.04.017

Bernal-Torres, C. A., & Frost-González, S. (2015). Innovación abierta en empresas colombianas: Reto a superar. *Revista Venezolana de Gerencia*, *20*(70), 262–267. doi:10.31876/revista.v20i70.19996

Berthon, P. R., Pitt, L. F., McCarthy, I., & Kates, S. M. (2007). When customers get clever: Managerial approaches. *Business Horizons*, *50*(1), 39–47. doi:10.1016/j.bushor.2006.05.005

Bianchi, M., Campodall'Orto, S., Frattini, F., & Vercesi, P. (2010). Enabling open innovation in small- and medium-sized enterprises: How to find alternative applications for your technologies. *R & D Management*, *40*(4), 414–430. doi:10.1111/j.1467-9310.2010.00613.x

Bilińska-Reformat, K., Kucharska, B., Twardzik, M., & Dolega, L. (2019). Sustainable development concept and creation of innovative business models by retail chains. *International Journal of Retail & Distribution Management, 47*(1), 2-18.

Birkinshaw, J., & Mol, M. J. (2009). The sources of management innovation: When firms introduce new management practices. *Journal of Business Research*, *62*(12), 1269–1280. doi:10.1016/j.jbusres.2009.01.001

Biscotti, A. M., Mafrolla, E., Giudice, M. D., & D'Amico, E. (2018). CEO turnover and the new leader propensity to open innovation: Agency-resource dependence view and social identity perspective. *Management Decision*, *56*(6), 1348–1364. doi:10.1108/MD-04-2017-0392

Bitzinger, R. A. (1995). South Korea's Defense Industry at the Crossroads. *Korean Journal of Defense Analysis*, *7*(1), 233–249. doi:10.1080/10163279509464539

Björkdahl, J., Fallahi, S., & Holmén, M. (2018). Organizing for parallel business models in established firms. In Academy of Management Proceedings (Vol. 2018, No. 1, p. 14950). Academy of Management. doi:10.5465/AMBPP.2018.14950abstract

Blank, S. (2010). *What's A Startup? First Principles*. Steveblank.com

Block, F., Keller, M. R., & Negoita, M. (2020). Network Failure and the Evolution of the US Innovation System. *Journal of Industry, Competition and Trade*, *20*(2), 235–247. doi:10.100710842-019-00324-1

Bogers, M., Chesbrough, H., & Moedas, C. (2018). Open innovation: Research, practices, and policies. *California Management Review*, *60*(2), 5–16. doi:10.1177/0008125617745086

Bogers, M., Foss, N. J., & Lyngsie, J. (2018). The human side of open innovation: The role of employee diversity in firm-level openness. *Research Policy*, *47*(1), 218–223. doi:10.1016/j.respol.2017.10.012

Bogers, M., Zobel, A.-K., Afuah, A., Almirall, E., Brunswicker, S., Dahlander, L., Frederiksen, L., Gawer, A., Gruber, M., Haefliger, S., Hagedoorn, J., Hilgers, D., Laursen, K., Magnusson, M. G., Majchrzak, A., McCarthy, I. P., Moeslein, K. M., Nambisan, S., Piller, F. T., ... Ter Wal, A. L. J. (2017). The open innovation research landscape: Established perspectives and emerging themes across different levels of analysis. *Industry and Innovation*, *24*(1), 8–40. doi:10.1080/13662716.2016.1240068

Booksten, A. (1979). Explanations of the bibliometric distributions. *Collect Mange Summer-Fall*, *3*(2-3), 151–162. doi:10.1300/J105v03n02_04

Braga, M. N., Leite, M. M., & Felix, E. S. (2018). Empreendedorismo e gestão de mudanças como fator de desenvolvimento: Uma pesquisa de campo com os ambulantes do setor alimentício na cidade de Juazeiro do Norte–CE. *Revista Livre de Sustentabilidade e Empreendedorismo*, *3*(2), 48–76.

Brauer, J. (2002). The arms industry in developing nations: history and post-cold war assessment. In *Arming the South* (pp. 101–127). Palgrave Macmillan. doi:10.1057/9780230501256_6

Burnswicker, S., & Vanhaverbeke, W. (2015). Open innovation in small and medium-sized enterprises (SMEs): External knowledge sourcing strategies and internal organizational facilitators. *Journal of Small Business Management*, *53*(4), 1241–1263. doi:10.1111/jsbm.12120

Burt, R. S. (2004). Structural holes and good ideas. *American Journal of Sociology*, *110*(2), 349–399. doi:10.1086/421787

Caloghirou, Y., Kastelli, I., & Tsakanikas, A. (2004). Internal capabilities and external knowledge sources: Complementsor substitutes for innovative performance? *Technovation*, *24*(1), 29–39. doi:10.1016/S0166-4972(02)00051-2

Camisón, C., Forés, B., & Puig-Denia, A. (2016). Return on capital in Spanish tourism businesses: A comparative analysis of family vs non-family businesses.European. *Journal of Management and Business Economics*, *25*(3), 91–110. doi:10.1016/j.redeen.2016.04.002

Camps, D., Samar, M. E., Ávila, R. E., & Recuero, Y. (2006). Estudio bibliométrico de un volumen de la *revista Archivos de Medicina. Archives of Medicine*, *2*(3), 1–6.

Candi, M., Roberts, D. L., Marion, T., & Barczak, G. (2018). Social strategy to gain knowledge for innovation. *British Journal of Management*, *29*(4), 731–749. doi:10.1111/1467-8551.12280

Caraça, J., Lundvall, B. Å., & Mendonça, S. (2009). The changing role of science in the innovation process: From Queen to Cinderella? *Technological Forecasting and Social Change*, *76*(6), 861–867. doi:10.1016/j.techfore.2008.08.003

Carayannis, E., & Grigoroudis, E. (2014). Linking innovation, productivity, and competitiveness: Implications for policy and practice. *The Journal of Technology Transfer*, *39*(2), 199–218. doi:10.100710961-012-9295-2

Carlsson, B., Braunerhjelm, P., McKelvey, M., Olofsson, C., Persson, L., & Ylinenpää, H. (2013). The evolving domain of entrepreneurship research. *Small Business Economics*, *41*(4).

Carrasco-Carvajal, O., & García-Pérez-De-Lema, D. (2021). Innovation Capability and Open Innovation and its Impact on Performance in SMEs: An Empirical Study in Chile. *International Journal of Innovation Management*, *25*(04), 2150039. doi:10.1142/S1363919621500390

Carvalheira, A. M., & Moreira, A. (2015). Searching for opportunities and trust in international markets. In L. C. Carvalho (Ed.), *Handbook of Research on Entrepreneurial Success and Its Impact on Regional Development* (pp. 675–701). IGI Global. doi:10.4018/978-1-4666-9567-2.ch028

Carvalho, A. S., & Moreira, A. C. (2015). Open innovation profile in small and medium-sized firms. The perspective of technology centres and business associations. *International Journal of Innovation and Learning*, *18*(1), 4–22. doi:10.1504/IJIL.2015.070242

Cassiman, B., & Valentini, G. (2019). Open Innovation: Are inbound and outbound knowledge flows really complementary? *Strategic Management Journal*, *37*(6), 1034–1046. doi:10.1002mj.2375

Castro, G. C., de Araujo, L. M., & Carvalho, P. K. F. (2021). Educação Empreendedora: Utilização das redes sociais como ferramentas potenciadoras do Marketing Digital em micro e pequenas empresas na cidade de Codó-MA. *Brazilian Journal of Development, Curitiba*, *7*(4), 41523–41534.

Chaston, I., & Scott, G. J. (2012). Entrepreneurship and open innovation in an emerging economy. *Management Decision*, *50*(7), 1161–1177. doi:10.1108/00251741211246941

Chen, C. (2006). CiteSpace II: Detecting and Visualising Emerging Trends and Transient Patterns in Scientific Literature. *Journal of the American Society for Information Science and Technology*, *57*(3), 359–377. doi:10.1002/asi.20317

Chen, C. (2016). CiteSpace: A practical guide for scientific mapping literature. *Novinka. Computer Science, Technology and Applications.*

Chen, C., Ibekwe-SanJuan, F., & Hou, J. (2010). The structure and dynamics of cocitation clusters: A multiple-perspective cocitation analysis. *Journal of the American Society for Information Science and Technology*, *61*(7), 1386–1409. doi:10.1002/asi.21309

Chen, C., & Song, M. (2019). Visualising a field of research: A methodology of systematic scientometric *reviews. PLoS One*, *14*(10), e0223994. doi:10.1371/journal.pone.0223994 PMID:31671124

Chen, C.-Y., Lin, Y.-L., & Chu, P.-Y. (2013). Facilitators of national innovation policy in a SME-dominated country: A case study of Taiwan. *Innovation*, *15*(4), 405–415. doi:10.5172/impp.2013.15.4.405

Cheng, C. C. J., & Huizingh, E. K. R. E. (2014). When Is Open Innovation Beneficial? The Role of Strategic Orientation. *Journal of Product Innovation Management*, *31*(6), 1235–1253. doi:10.1111/jpim.12148

Chen, X., & Liu, Y. (2020). Visualisation analysis of high-speed railway research based on CiteSpace. *Transport Policy*, *85*(3), 1–17. doi:10.1016/j.tranpol.2019.10.004

Chesbrough, H. (2006). Open innovation: A new paradigm for understanding industrial innovation. In H. Chesbrough, W. Vanhaverbeke, & J. West (Eds.), Open innovation: Researching a new paradigm (pp. 1–12). Oxford University Press.

Chesbrough, H. (2006). Open innovation: A new paradigm for understanding industrial innovation. In Open innovation: Researching a new paradigm. Oxford University Press.

Chesbrough, H. W., & Bogers, M. (2014). Explaining open innovation: clarifying an emerging paradigm for understanding innovation. In H. W. Chesbrough, W. Vanhaverbeke & J. West (Eds.), New frontiers in open innovation (pp. 3-28). Oxford University Press.

Chesbrough, H. W., & Bogers, M. (2014). Explicating open innovation: clarifying an emerging paradigm for understanding innovation. In H. W. Chesbrough, W. Vanhaverbeke & J. West (Eds.), New frontiers in open innovation (pp. 3-28). Oxford University Press.

Chesbrough, H., & Bogers, M. (2014). Explicating Open Innovation Clarifying an Emerging Paradigm for Understanding Innovation. Oxford University Press.

Chesbrough, H. (2003). *Open innovation: The new imperative for creating and profiting from technology*. Harvard Business School Press.

Chesbrough, H. (2004). Managing Open Innovation. *Research Technology Management*, *47*(1), 23–26. doi:10.1080/08956308.2004.11671604

Chesbrough, H. (2006). *Open business models: How to thrive in the new innovation landscape*. Harvard Business School Press.

Chesbrough, H. (2012). *Inovação aberta: como criar e lucrar com a tecnologia*. Bookman.

Chesbrough, H. W. (2003). *Open Innovation* (1st ed.). Harvard Business School Publishing.

Chesbrough, H. W. (2003). The Era of Open Innovation. *MIT Sloan Management Review*, *44*(3), 35–41.

Chesbrough, H. W. (2003a). The era of open innovation. *MIT Sloan Management Review*, *44*(3), 35–41.

Chesbrough, H. W. (2003b). *Open Innovation: The New Imperative for Creating and Profiting from Technology*. Harvard Business School Press.

Chesbrough, H. W. (2003b). Xerox PARC-1. The Achievements and Limits of Closed Innovation. In H. W. Chesbrough (Ed.), *Open Innovation: the new imperative for creating and profiting from technology* (pp. 1–10). Harvard Business School Press.

Chesbrough, H. W. (2006). *Open innovation: the new imperative for creating and profiting from technology*. Harvard Business Review Press.

Chesbrough, H. W. (2012). Open innovation: Where we've been and where we're going. *Research Technology Management*, *55*(4), 20–27. doi:10.5437/08956308X5504085

Chesbrough, H. W. (2012b). GE's ecomagination Challenge: An experiment in Open Innovation. *California Management Review*, *54*(3), 140–154. doi:10.1525/cmr.2012.54.3.140

Chesbrough, H. W. (2017). The future of open innovation: The future of open innovation is more extensive, more collaborative, and more engaged with a wider variety of participants. *Research Technology Management*, *60*(1), 35–38. doi:10.1080/08956308.2017.1255054

Chesbrough, H. W., & Appleyard, M. M. (2007). Open Innovation and Strategy. *California Management Review*, *50*(1), 57–76. doi:10.2307/41166416

Chesbrough, H. W., Bogers, M., Heaton, S., & Teece, D. J. (2019). Strategic Management of Open Innovation: A Dynamic Capabilities Perspective. *Berkeley Haas California Management Review*, *62*(1), 77–94. doi:10.1177/0008125619885150

Chesbrough, H. W., & Crowther, A. K. (2006). Beyond high tech: Early adopters of open innovation in other industries. *R & D Management*, *36*(3), 229–236. doi:10.1111/j.1467-9310.2006.00428.x

Chesbrough, H. W., & Euchner, J. (2011). The Evolution of Open Innovation: An interview with Henry Chesbrough. *Research Technology Management*, *50*(1), 13–18. doi:10.5437/08956308X5405003

Chesbrough, H. W., & Rosenbloom, R. S. (2002). The Role of the Business Model in Capturing Value from Innovation: Evidence from Xerox Corporation's Technology Spin-Off Companies. *Industrial and Corporate Change*, *11*(3), 529–555. doi:10.1093/icc/11.3.529

Chesbrough, H., & Brunswicker, S. (2015). A Fad or a Phenomenon? The Adoption of Open Innovation Practices in Large Firms. *Research Technology Management*, *57*(2), 16–25.

Chesbrough, H., Vanhaverbeke, W., & West, J. (2006). *Open innovation: Researching a new paradigm*. Oxford University Press.

Chesbrough, H., Vanhaverbeke, W., & West, J. (Eds.). (2014b). *New frontiers in open innovation*. Oxford University Press. doi:10.1093/acprof:oso/9780199682461.001.0001

Chiang, Y.-H., & Hung, K.-P. (2010). Exploring open search estrategies and perceived innovation performance from the perspective of inter-organizational knowledge flows. *R & D Management*, *40*(3), 292–299. doi:10.1111/j.1467-9310.2010.00588.x

Chiaroni, D., Chiesa, V., & Frattini, F. (2011). The open innovation journey: How firms dynamically implement the emerging innovation management paradigm. *Technovation*, *31*(1), 34–43. doi:10.1016/j.technovation.2009.08.007

Chin, W. W. (1998). The Partial Least Squares approach to structural equation modelling. In G. A. Marcoulides (Ed.), *Modern methods for business research* (pp. 295–336). Lawrence Erlbaum Associates Publisher.

Chin, W. W. (2010). How to write up and report PLS analyses. In V. E. Vinzi, W. W. Chin, J. Henseler, & H. Wang (Eds.), *Handbook of Partial Least Squares: Concepts, Methods and Applications in Marketing and Related Fields* (pp. 655–690). Springer. doi:10.1007/978-3-540-32827-8_29

Chung, K. L., & D'Annunzio, N. (2018). Talent Management Practices of Small Mediumsized in the hospitality sector: na entrepreneurial owner-manager perspective. *WorldWide Hospitaity and Tourisn Themes, 10*(1), 101-116.

Clark, G. L., Feldman, M. P., Gertler, M. S., & Wójcik, D. (2018). *The New Oxford Handbook of Economic Geography*. Oxford University Press. doi:10.1093/oxfordhb/9780198755609.001.0001

Coelho, D. A., & Matias, J. C. (2010). Innovation in the organisation of management systems in Portuguese SMEs. *International Journal of Entrepreneurship and Innovation Management, 11*(3), 324–329. doi:10.1504/IJEIM.2010.031905

Congressional Budget Office. (n.d.). *How Might Changes in Federal Policies Boost Innovation and Productivity?* Available: https://www.cbo.gov/publication/52464

CoreLedger. (2021, March 27). *How blockchain can divide indivisible goods for shared ownership.* Medium. https://medium.com/coreledger/how-blockchain-can-divide-indivisible-goods-for-shared-ownership-78c2aff048c

Cornell University. INSEAD, & The World Intellectual Property Organization. (2020). *Global Innovation Index 2020: Who Will Finance Innovation?* Available at: https://www.wipo.int/edocs/pubdocs/en/wipo_pub_gii_2020.pdf

Cottineau, C., Finance, O., Hatna, E., Arcaute, E., & Batty, M. (2018). Defining urban clusters to detect agglomeration economies. *Environment and Planning. B, Urban Analytics and City Science*. Advance online publication. doi:10.1177/2399808318755146

Crescenzi, R., Nathan, M., & Rodríguez-Pose, A. (2016). Do inventors talk to strangers? On proximity and collaborative knowledge creation. *Research Policy, 45*(1), 177–194. doi:10.1016/j.respol.2015.07.003

Crunchbase. (2021, June 2). *Launch Forth*. https://www.crunchbase.com/organization/launch-forth

Czarnitzki, D., & Licht, G. (2006). Additionality of public R&D grants in a transition economy. The case of Eastern Germany. *Economics of Transition, 14*(1), 101–131. doi:10.1111/j.1468-0351.2006.00236.x

Dahlander, L., & Gann, D. M. (2010). How Open Is Innovation? *Research Policy, 39*(6), 699–709. doi:10.1016/j.respol.2010.01.013

Dantas, J. G., & Moreira, A. C. (2011). *O Processo de Inovação*. LIDEL.

Davidsson, P. (2016). A "business researcher" view on opportunities for psychology in entrepreneurship research. *The Journal of Applied Psychology*, *65*(3), 628–636. doi:10.1111/apps.12071

De Fabricio, R. S., Da Silva, F. R., Simões, E., Galegale, N. V., & Akabane, G. K. (2015). Strengthening of Open Innovation model: Using startups and technology parks. *IFAC-PapersOnLine*, *48*(3), 14–20. doi:10.1016/j.ifacol.2015.06.051

De Groote, J., & Backmann, J. (2019). Initiating open innovation collaborations between incumbents and startups: How can David and Goliath get along? *International Journal of Innovation Management*, *2050011*, 1–33.

De Wit, J., Dankbaar, B., & Vissers, G. (2007). Open innovation: The new way of knowledge transfer? *Journal of Business Chemistry*, *4*(1), 11–19.

Delgado, M., Porter, M. E., & Stern, S. (2015). Defining clusters of related industries. *Journal of Economic Geography*, *16*(1), 1–38. doi:10.1093/jeg/lbv017

Dennis, A. (2020). *Boosting Immigration: Harnessing Global Talent to Increase US Competitiveness, Innovation, and Prosperity.* Committee for Economic Development of The Conference Board. Committee for Economic Development of The Conference Board.

Díaz-Puente, J. M., Cazorla, A., & Ríos, I. (2009). Policy Support for the Diffusion of Innovation among SMEs: An Evaluation Study in the Spanish Region of Madrid. *European Planning Studies*, *17*(3), 365–387. doi:10.1080/09654310802618028

Distamont, A., Khongmalai, O., Rassameethes, R., & Distanont, S. (2018). Collaborative triangle for effective community water resource management in Thailand. *Kasetsart Journal of Social Sciences*, *39*(3), 374–380. doi:10.1016/j.kjss.2017.07.015

Distanont, A., & Khongmalai, O. (2018). The Role of Innovation in Creating Competitive Advantage. *Kasetsart Journal of Social Sciences*, *41*(1), 15–21. doi:10.1016/j.kjss.2018.07.009

Dittrich, K., & Duysters, G. (2007). Networking as a means to strategy change: The case of open innovation in mobile telephony. *Journal of Product Innovation Management*, *24*(6), 510–521. doi:10.1111/j.1540-5885.2007.00268.x

Divisekera, S., & Nguyen, V. K. (2018). Determinants of innovation in tourism evidence from Australia. *Tourism Management*, *67*, 157–167. doi:10.1016/j.tourman.2018.01.010

Dodgson, M., Gann, D., & Salter, A. (2006). The role of technology in the shift towards open innovation: The case of Procter & Gamble. *R & D Management*, *36*(3), 333–346. doi:10.1111/j.1467-9310.2006.00429.x

Dornelas, J. (2016). *Empreendedorismo: transformando ideias em negócios* (Vol. 6). Atlas.

Drechsler, A., & Weißschädel, S. (2018). An IT strategy development framework for small and medium enterprises. *Information Systems and e-Business Management*, *16*(1), 93–124. doi:10.100710257-017-0342-2

Drucker, P. F. (1969). *The age of discontinuity: Guidelines to our changing society*. William Heinemann Ltd.

Drucker, P. F. (1994). *Post-capitalist society*. HarperCollins.

Drucker, P. F. (n.d.). *The Essential Drucker. HarperCollins.*

Dubina, I. N., Campbell, D. F., Carayannis, E. G., Chub, A. A., Grigoroudis, E., & Kozhevina, O. V. (2017). The balanced development of the spatial innovation and entrepreneurial ecosystem based on principles of the systems compromise: A conceptual framework. *Journal of the Knowledge Economy*, *8*(2), 438–455. doi:10.100713132-016-0426-0

Đuričin, S., & Beraha, I. (2016). SME clustering in Serbia: finding the right business partners and improving the business environment for SMEs. In S. M. E. Clustering (Ed.), *Finding the right business partners and improving the business environment for SMEs* (pp. 213–236). Konrad Adenauer Stiftung.

Đuričin, S., & Beraha, I. (2021). Assessment of the Innovation Capacity of Business Entities in the Republic of Serbia. In *Finance, Innovation and Technology: new models and structures* (pp. 179–198). Institute of Economics - Ss. Cyril & Methodius University.

Đuričin, S., & Beraha, I. (2021). Identifying medium-sized agricultural enterprises with the greatest potential for innovation development. *Ekonomika Poljoprivrede*, *68*(1), 213–227. doi:10.5937/ekoPolj2101213D

Eckhardt, J. T., & Shane, S. A. (2003). Opportunities and entrepreneurship. *Journal of Management*, *29*(3), 333–349. doi:10.1177/014920630302900304

EC-OECD. (2018). *STI policy taxonomy / ontology STIP monitoring and analysis (EC-OECD project).* Available: https://www. innovationpolicyplatform.org/stip-monitoring-and-analysis/sti-policytaxonomy-ontology

Edler, J., Berger, M., Dinges, M., & Gok, A. (2012). The practice of evaluation in innovation policy in Europe. *Research Evaluation*, *21*(3), 167–182. doi:10.1093/reseval/rvs014

Edler, J., Cunningham, P., Gök, A., & Shapira, P. (2016). *Handbook of Innovation Policy Impact*. Edward Elgar Publishing. doi:10.4337/9781784711856

Edler, J., & Fagerberg, J. (2017). Innovation policy: What, why, and how. *Oxford Review of Economic Policy*, *33*(1), 2–23. doi:10.1093/oxrep/grx001

Edquist, C., Zabala-Iturriagagoitia, J. M., Barbero, J., & Zofío, J. L. (2018). On the meaning of innovation performance: Is the synthetic indicator of the Innovation Union Scoreboard flawed? *Research Evaluation*, *27*(3), 196–211. doi:10.1093/reseval/rvy011

Eftekhari, N., & Bogers, M. (2015). Open for Entrepreneurship: How Open Innovation Can Foster New Venture Creation. *Creativity and Innovation Management*, *24*(4), 574–584. doi:10.1111/caim.12136

Eiteneyer, N., Bendig, D., & Brettel, M. (2019). Social capital and the digital crowd: Involving backers to promote new product innovativeness. *Research Policy*, *48*(8), 1–15. doi:10.1016/j.respol.2019.01.017

Elmquist, M., Fredberg, T., & Ollila, S. (2009). Exploring the field of open innovation. *European Journal of Innovation Management*, *12*(3), 326–345. doi:10.1108/14601060910974219

Engelberg, J., Ozoguz, A., & Wang, S. (2018). Know thy neighbor: Industry clusters, information spillovers, and market efficiency. *Journal of Financial and Quantitative Analysis*, *53*(5), 1937–1961. doi:10.1017/S0022109018000261

Enkel, E., Gassmann, O., & Chesbrough, H. (2009). Open R&D and open innovation: Exploring the phenomenon. *Journal compilation. R & D Management*, *39*(4), 311–316. doi:10.1111/j.1467-9310.2009.00570.x

EPO & EUIPO. (2019). *IPR-intensive industries and economic performance in the European Union*. Available: https://www.boip.int/uploads/inline/WEB_IPR_intensive_Report_2019.pdf

EPO. (2019). *Market success for inventions: Patent commercialization scoreboard: European SMEs November 2019 | Key findings*. Available: http://documents.epo.org/projects/babylon/eponet.nsf/0/981A954C6D692D4DC125849A0054C147/$File/Patent_commercialisation_scoreboard_European_SMEs_key_findings_2019_en.pdf

EPO. (2021). *Fighting coronavirus*. Available: https://www.epo.org/news-events/in-focus/fighting-coronavirus.html

Etzkowitz, H., & Leydesdorff, L. (2000). The dynamics of innovation: From National Systems and "Mode 2" to a Triple Helix of university–industry–government relations. *Research Policy*, *29*(2), 109–123. doi:10.1016/S0048-7333(99)00055-4

Etzkowitz, H., & Zhou, C. (2017). *The triple helix: University–industry–government innovation and entrepreneurship*. Routledge. doi:10.4324/9781315620183

European Commission (2020). *European Innovation Score board 2020*. Luxembourg: Publications Office of the European Union. Available at: file:///C:/Users/Isidora/Downloads/ET-AY-20-002-EN-N%20Online%20(1).pdf

European Commission. (2016). *Open Innovation Open Science to the World - a vision for Europe*. Available: http://publications.europa.eu/resource/cellar/3213b335-1cbc-11e6-ba9a-01aa75ed71a1.0001.02/DOC_2

European Commission. (2020). *User guide to the SME Definition*. European Commission.

European Commission. (2020a). *Regional Innovation Scoreboard*. Available: h Available: ttps://ec.europa.eu/growth/industry/policy/innovation/regional_en

European Commission. (2020b). *Enterprise Europe Network: Lisbon*. Available: https://een.ec.europa.eu/about/branches/pt/lisboa

European Commission. (2020c). *Economy: Coronavirus Crisis in EU*. Available: https://ec.europa.eu/info/live-work-travel-eu/health/coronavirus-response/economy_en

European Commission. (2021a). *European Innovation Scoreboard 2021*. Available: file:///C:/Users/cmbpi/Downloads/ET-AY-21-001-EN-N.pdf

European Commission. (2021b). *Public Procurement of Innovative Solutions*. Available: https://ec.europa.eu/digital-single-market/en/public-procurement-innovative-solutions

European Data Portal. (2018). *Open data and blockchain: A match made in heaven?* https://www.europeandataportal.eu/en/highlights/open-data-and-blockchain-match-made-heaven

European Parliament. (2020). *Innovation policy*. Available: https://www.europarl.europa.eu/factsheets/en/sheet/67/innovation-policy

European Union. (2019). *Research and innovation*. Available: https://europa.eu/european-union/topics/research-innovation_pt

Executive Office of the President of United States. (2019). *Science & Technology Highlights*. Available: https://www.whitehouse.gov/wp-content/uploads/2019/02/Administration-2018-ST-Highlights.pdf

Executive Office of the President of United States. (2020). *Administration Research and Development Budget Priorities*. Available: https://www.whitehouse.gov/wp-content/uploads/2020/08/M-20-29.pdf

Falkenberg, A. W. (1996). Marketing and the Wealth of Firms. *Journal of Macromarketing*, *16*(1), 4–24. doi:10.1177/027614679601600102

Farinha, L., Ferreira, J., & Gouveia, B. (2016). Networks of innovation and competitiveness: A triple helix case study. *Journal of the Knowledge Economy*, *7*(1), 259–275. doi:10.100713132-014-0218-3

Fayoumi, A., & Loucopoulos, P. (2016). Conceptual modeling for the design of intelligent and emergent information systems. *Expert Systems with Applications*, *59*(15), 174–194. doi:10.1016/j.eswa.2016.04.019

Felício, J. A., Caldeirinha, V., & Dutra, A. (2019). Ambidextrous capacity in small and medium-sized enterprises. *Journal of Business Research*, *101*, 607–614. doi:10.1016/j.jbusres.2019.02.061

Feng, K., Davis, S. J., Sun, L., Li, X., Guan, D., Liu, W., Liu, Z., & Hubacek, K. (2013). Outsourcing CO2 within China. *Proceedings of the National Academy of Sciences of the United States of America*, *110*(28), 11654–11659. doi:10.1073/pnas.1219918110 PMID:23754377

Ferreira, J. L. M., & Teixeira, A. A. C. (2018). Open innovation and knowledge for fostering business ecosystems. *Journal of Innovation & Knowledge*, *4*(4), 253–255. doi:10.1016/j.jik.2018.10.002

Feser, E. J., & Bergman, E. M. (2000). National industry cluster templates: A framework for applied regional cluster analysis. *Regional Studies*, *34*(1), 1–19. doi:10.1080/00343400050005844

Fichter. (2009) Innovation communities: the role of networks of promotors in Open Innovation. *R&D Management, 39*(4), 357-371.

Filippetti, A., & Frederick, G. (2020). Labor market regulation, the diversity of knowledge and skill, and national innovation performance. *Research Policy*, *49*(1), 103867. doi:10.1016/j.respol.2019.103867

Finkelstein, S., Hambrick, D. C., & Cannella, A. A. (2009). *Strategic leadership: Theory and research on executives, top management teams, and boards*. Oxford University Press.

Fisher, M. (2007). Strengthening the empirical base of operations management. *Manufacturing & Service Operations Management*, *9*(4), 368–382. doi:10.1287/msom.1070.0168

Fitjar, R. D., Huber, F., & Rodríguez-Pose, A. (2016). 'Not too close, not too far: Testing the Goldilocks principle of 'optimal' distance in innovation networks'. *Industry and Innovation*, *23*(6), 465–487. doi:10.1080/13662716.2016.1184562

Fleming, L., & Waguespack, D. M. (2007). Brokerage, boundary spanning, and leadership in open innovation communities. *Organization Science*, *18*(2), 165–180. doi:10.1287/orsc.1060.0242

Foreman-Peck, J. (2013). Effectiveness and efficiency of SME innovation policy. *Small Business Economics*, *41*(1), 55–70. doi:10.100711187-012-9426-z

Fornahl, D., & Hassink, R. (2017). *The life cycle of clusters: A policy perspective*. Edward Elgar Publishing. doi:10.4337/9781784719289

Fornell, C., & Larcker, D. (1981). Evaluating structural equation models with unobserved variables and measurement error. *JMR, Journal of Marketing Research*, *18*(1), 39–50. doi:10.1177/002224378101800104

Fraga-Lamas, P., & Fernández-Caramés, T. M. (2020). *Leveraging blockchain for sustainability and open innovation: A cyber-resilient approach toward EU Green Deal and UN Sustainable Development Goals*. IntechOpen.

Franco, M., & Haase, H. (2016). Internationalisation of born globals: The role of strategic alliances. *European Journal of International Management*, *10*(2), 181–201. doi:10.1504/EJIM.2016.074471

Franco, M., Haase, H., & Pereira, A. (2016). Empirical study about the role of social networks in SME performance. *Journal of Systems and Information Technology*, *18*(4), 383–403. doi:10.1108/JSIT-06-2016-0036

Frank, T., & Rothaermel, M. T. A. (2009). Ambidexterity in Technology Sourcing: The Moderating Role of Absorptive Capacity. *Organization Science*, *20*(4), 759–780. doi:10.1287/orsc.1080.0404

Freel, M., & Robson, P. J. (2017). Appropriation strategies and open innovation in SMEs. *International Small Business Journal*, *35*(5), 578–596. doi:10.1177/0266242616654957

Freitas, A. S., Filardi, F., Lott, A. C. O., & Braga, D. (2017). Inovação Aberta nas Empresas Brasileiras: Uma Análise da Produção Acadêmica no Período de 2003 a 2016. *Revista Ibero-Americana de Estratégia*, *16*(3), 22–38. doi:10.5585/riae.v16i3.2497

Frenken, K., Cefis, E., & Stam, E. (2015). Industrial dynamics and clusters: A survey. *Regional Studies*, *49*(1), 10–27. doi:10.1080/00343404.2014.904505

Friedman, M. (1982). *Capitalism and freedom*. University of Chicago.

Fusch, P., Fusch, G. E., & Ness, L. R. (2018). Denzin's paradigm shift: Revisiting triangulation in qualitative research. *Journal of Social Change*, *10*(1), 19–32. doi:10.5590/JOSC.2018.10.1.02

Galama, T., & Hosek, J. (2008). *U.S. Competitiveness in Science and Technology*. RAND Corporation.

Galaz, V., Biermann, F., Crona, B., Loorbach, D., Folke, C., Olsson, P., Nilsson, M., Allouche, J., Persson, A., & Reischl, G. (2012). Planetary boundaries: Exploring the challenges for global environmental governance. *Current Opinion in Environmental Sustainability*, *4*(1), 80–87. doi:10.1016/j.cosust.2012.01.006

Garcia, R., Araújo, V., Mascarini, S., Santos, E. G., & Costa, A. R. (2019). How long-term university-industry collaboration shapes the academic productivity of research groups. *Innovation*, 1–15.

Gassmann, O., & Enkel, E. (2004). Towards a Theory of Open Innovation: Three Core Process Archetypes. *R&D Management Conference*, 1-18.

Gassmann, O., Enkel, E., & Chesbrough, H. (2010). The future of open innovation. *R & D Management*, *40*(3), 213–221. doi:10.1111/j.1467-9310.2010.00605.x

Gavriluţă, A. F. (2016). Implications of Government on Sustainable Development. *Journal of Public Administration. Finance & Law*, *10*, 31–41.

Gefen, D., & Straub, D. (2005). A practical guide to factorial validity using PLS-graph: Tutorial and annotated example. *Communications of the Association for Information Systems*, *16*(1), 91–109. doi:10.17705/1CAIS.01605

George, G., Lakhani, K. R., & Puranam, P. (2020). What has changed? The Impact of Covid Pandemic on the Technology and Innovation Management Research Agenda. *Journal of Management Studies*, *57*(8), 1754-1758.

Global Trade and Innovation Policy Alliance. (2019). *National innovation policies: What Countries Do Best and How They Can Improve.* Available: https://www2.itif.org/2019-national-innovation-policies.pdf

Global Trade and Innovation Policy Alliance. (2021). *U.S. support of TRIPS waiver undermines efforts to fight COVID-19*. Available: https://gtipa.org/publications/2021/05/06/us-support-trips-trips-waiver-undermines-efforts-fight-covid-19

Goksoy, A., Vayvay, O., & Ergeneli, N. (2013). Gaining competitive advantage through innovation strategies: An application in warehouse management processes. *American Journal of Business and Management*, *2*(4), 304–321.

Goldman, S. L., Nagel, R. N., & Preiss, K. (1995). *Agile Competitors and Virtual Organizations: Strategies for Enriching the Customer*. Van Nostrand Reinhold.

Gordon, J. L. (2019). The role of the State in fostering innovation activity: Case studies of the USA and Germany. *Brazilian Journal of Political Economy*, *39*(4), 571–590. doi:10.1590/0101-31572019-2899

Grassroots. (2021, April 11). In *Wikipedia*. https://en.wikipedia.org/wiki/Grassroots#:~:text=A%20grassroots%20movement%20is%20one,%2C%20national%2C%20or%20international%20level

Greco, M., Grimaldi, M., & Criceli, L. (2016). An analysis of the open innovation effect on firm performance. *European Management Journal*, *34*(5), 501–516. doi:10.1016/j.emj.2016.02.008

Grimpe, C., & Sofka, W. (2009). Search patterns and absorptive capacity: Low- and high-technology sectorsin European countries. *Research Policy*, *38*(3), 495–506. doi:10.1016/j.respol.2008.10.006

Grinn, L. E. (2019). *Kondratieff waves: The spectrum of opinions*. https://www.researchgate.net/publication/339484056_Kondratieff_Waves_The_Spectrum_of_Opinions

Gronum, S., Verreynne, M. L., & Kastelle, T. (2012). The Role of Networks in Small and Medium-Sized Enterprise Innovation and Firm Performance. *Journal of Small Business Management*, *50*(2), 257–282. doi:10.1111/j.1540-627X.2012.00353.x

Gummesson, E. (1995). *Focus shifts in marketing: A new agenda for the third millenium* [Paper presentation]. Twentieth Anniversary Program of the Marketing Technology Center.

Gutmann, T. (2019). Harmonizing corporate venturing modes: An integrative review and research agenda. *Management Review Quarterly*, *69*(2), 121–157. doi:10.100711301-018-0148-4

Gyeongnam Province. (2019). *Statistics Database of Gyeongnam Province. Gyeongnam Province.* Research Report, Published by Gyeongnam Province, Rep. of Korea. https://www.gyeongnam.go.kr/data

Hafkesbrink, J., & Schroll, M. (2011). Innovation 3.0: Embedding into community knowledge - collaborative organizational learning beyond open innovation. *Journal of Innovation Economics & Management*, *1*(7), 55–92. doi:10.3917/jie.007.0055

Hair, J., Hult, G. T. M., Ringle, C., & Sarstedt, M. (2016). *A Primer on Partial Least Squares Structural Equation Modeling (PLS-SEM)*. Sage.

Hasik, J. (2008). *Arms and Innovation: entrepreneurship and alliances in the twenty-first century defense industry*. University of Chicago Press. doi:10.7208/chicago/9780226318899.001.0001

Haubert, B., Schreiber, D., & Cristiano, M. P. (2019). Combinando o design thinking e a criatividade no processo de inovação aberta. *Gestão & Planejamento, 20*, 73–89. doi:10.21714/2178-8030gep.v.20.4823

Henseler, J., Ringle, C. M., & Sarstedt, M. (2015). A new criterion for assessing discriminant validity in variance-based structural equation modeling. *Journal of the Academy of Marketing Science, 43*(1), 115–135. doi:10.100711747-014-0403-8

Henttonen, K., & Lehtimäki, H. (2017). Open innovation in SMEs: Collaboration modes and strategies for commercialisation in technology-intensive companies in the forestry industry. *European Journal of Innovation Management, 20*(2), 329–347. doi:10.1108/EJIM-06-2015-0047

Herrera, L., & Sánchez-González, G. (2013). Firm size and innovation policy. *International Small Business Journal, 31*(2), 137–155. doi:10.1177/0266242611405553

Hisrich, R. D., & Peter, M. P. (2004). *Empreendedorismo*. Bookman.

Hogenhuis, B. N., Van Den Hende, E. A., & Hultink, E. J. (2017). Unlocking the innovation potential in large firms through timely and meaningful interactions with young ventures. *International Journal of Innovation Management, 21*(1), 1–29. doi:10.1142/S1363919617500098

Hong, J. F. L., Zhao, X., & Stanley, S. R. (2019). Collaborative-based HRM practices and open innovation: A conceptual review. *International Journal of Human Resource Management, 30*(1), 31–62. doi:10.1080/09585192.2018.1511616

Horan, J. J. (1968). Working relationships between marketing and R&D: Early, relevant, two-way communications are key to success. *Research Management, 11*(4), 217–223. doi:10.1080/00345334.1968.11755907

Horizon. (2020). *Horizon 2020 sections and Focus areas.* Available: https://ec.europa.eu/programmes/horizon2020/en/h2020-sections

Huang, C., & Wang, Y. (2018). Evolution of network relations, enterprise learning, and cluster innovation networks: The case of the Yuyao plastics industry cluster. *Technology Analysis and Strategic Management, 30*(2), 158–171. doi:10.1080/09537325.2017.1297786

Huang, L., Zhou, M., Lv, J., & Chen, K. (2020). Trends in global research in forest carbon sequestration: A bibliometric analysis. *Journal of Cleaner Production, 252*, 1–17. doi:10.1016/j.jclepro.2019.119908

Huang, Q., & Yuan, T. (2021). Does Political Corruption Impede Firm Innovation? Evidence from the United States. *Journal of Financial and Quantitative Analysis, 56*(1), 213–248. doi:10.1017/S0022109019000966

Hughes, M., & Morgan, R. E. (2007). Deconstructing the relationship between entrepreneurial orientation and business performance at the embr.,ic stage of firm growth. *Industrial Marketing Management, 36*(5), 651–661. doi:10.1016/j.indmarman.2006.04.003

Huizingh, E. K. (2011). Open innovation: State of the art and future perspectives. *Technovation, 31*(1), 2–9. doi:10.1016/j.technovation.2010.10.002

Humphrey, J., & Schmitz, H. (2000). *Governance and upgrading: linking industrial cluster and global value chain research* (Vol. 120). Institute of Development Studies.

Hungund, S., & Mani, V. (2019). Benchmarking of factors influencing adoption of innovation in software product SMEs: An empirical evidence from India. *Benchmarking*, *26*(5), 1451–1468. doi:10.1108/BIJ-05-2018-0127

Hunt, S. D. (2015). *Marketing theory: Foundations, controversy, strategy, resource-advantage theory*. Routledge.

Hurmelinna-Laukkanen, P. (2011). Enabling collaborative innovation–knowledge protection for knowledge sharing. *European Journal of Innovation Management*, *14*(3), 303–321. doi:10.1108/14601061111148816

Huston, L., & Sakkab, N. (2006, March). Connect and develop: Inside Procter & Gamble's new model for innovation. *Harvard Business Review*, 1–17.

Hyundai Motor Group. (2021, April 23). *Reasons Hyundai seeks to boost innovation through.* https://tech.hyundaimotorgroup.com/article/reasons-hyundai-seeks-to-boost-innovation-through/

IBM Institute for Business Value. (2021, March 27). *The rise of the sustainable enterprise.* https://www.ibm.com/thought-leadership/institute-business-value/report/sustainable-enterprise

ideaCONNECTION. (2021, March 18). *An example of open innovation success with Procter & Gamble.* https://www.ideaconnection.com/open-innovation-success/An-Example-of-Open-Innovation-Success-with-Procter-Ga-00641.html

Ilmudeen, A., Bao, Y., Alharbi, I. M., & Zubair, N. (2021). Revisiting dynamic capability for organizations' innovation types: Does it matter for organizational performance in China? *European Journal of Innovation Management*, *24*(2), 507–532. doi:10.1108/EJIM-06-2019-0144

Inês, A. I., Pires, P. M., Leite, M. P., & Moreira, A. C. (2021). As pequenas e médias empresas e o desafio da inovação aberta. *Gestao e Desenvolvimento*, *29*, 199–221. doi:0.34632/gestaoedesenvolvimento.2021.10030

Information Technology and Innovation Foundation (ITIF). (2020). *President-Elect Biden's Agenda on Technology and Innovation Policy*. Available: https://itif.org/publications/2020/11/07/president-elect-bidens-agenda-technology-and-innovation-policy

Ioncica, M., Madalina, T., Catalina, B., & Incica, D. (2008). The factors of competitiveness in the hospitality industry and the competitive strategy of firms. *Academia de Studii Economice, Buscuresti. Piata Romana*, *17*(2), 213–218.

Isento, G. (2015). *S.T.E.P. eleva-te para trabalhares em altura*. https://www.publico.pt/2015/11/12/p3/noticia/step-elevate-para-trabalhares-em-altura-1824869

Jackson, P., & Richter, N. (2017). Situational logic: An analysis of open innovation using corporate accelerators. *International Journal of Innovation Management*, *21*(7), 1–21. doi:10.1142/S1363919617500621

KAIA. (2017). *Level of Korea Aerospace Industry Development*. Korea Aerospace Industry Associations.

KAIA. (2018). *Trend of Export and Import of Aviation and Aerospace Industry in Korea*. Korea Aerospace Industry Associations.

Kaleka, A. (2002). Resources and capabilities driving competitive advantage in export markets: Guidelines for industrial exports. *Industrial Marketing Management*, *31*(3), 273–283. doi:10.1016/S0019-8501(00)00148-6

Keizer, J. A., Dijkstra, L., & Halman, J. I. M. (2001). Explaining Innovative Efforts of SMEs: An exploratory Survey among SMEs in the Mechanical and Electrical Engineering Sector in The Netherlands. *Technovation*, *22*(1), 1–13. doi:10.1016/S0166-4972(00)00091-2

Kelleci, A., & Yıldız, O. (2021). A guiding framework for levels of sustainability in marketing. *Sustainability*, *13*(4), 1644. https://doi.org/10.3390/su13041644

KIET. (2017). *Report on Technology competitiveness of Aerospace core system in Korea*. Korea Institute for Industrial Economics and Trade.

Kilbournea, W. E., Beckmann, S. C., & Thelen, E. (2002). The role of the dominant social paradigm in environmental attitudes A multinational examination. *Journal of Business Research*, *55*(3), 193–204.

KILIS. (2018). *Statistics on Industrial Cluster in Korea*. Korea Industrial Land Information System. https://www.industryland.or.kr/web/en/Center/Overview.jsp

King, A., & Lakhani, K. R. (2013). Using Open Innovation to identify the best ideas. *MIT Sloan Management Review*, *55*(1), 41–48.

Knabke, T., & Olbrich, S. (2018). Building novel capabilities to enable business intelligence agility: Results from a quantitative study. *Information Systems and e-Business Management*, *16*(3), 493–546. doi:10.100710257-017-0361-z

Kohler, T. (2016). Corporate accelerators: Building bridges between corporations and startups. *Business Horizons*, *59*(3), 347–357. doi:10.1016/j.bushor.2016.01.008

Koplin, J., Seuring, S., & Mesterharm, M. (2007). Incorporating sustainability into supply management in the automotive industry – the case of the Volkswagen AG. *Journal of Cleaner Production*, *15*(11-12), 1053–1062. doi:10.1016/j.jclepro.2006.05.024

Krause, K. (1992). *Arms and the State: Patterns of Military Expenditure and Trade. Cambridge*. Cambridge University Press. doi:10.1017/CBO9780511521744

Krejcie, R. V., & Morgan, D. W. (1970). Determining Sample Size for Research Activities. *Educational and Psychological Measurement*, *30*(3), 607–610. doi:10.1177/001316447003000308

Krumm, B. K. (2019). Regulatory Policy in the Trump Era and its Impact on Innovation. *Mercer Law Review*, *70*(3), 685–704. doi:10.2139srn.3404205

Kulkarni, U., Robles-Flores, J. A., & Popovič, A. (2017). A business intelligence capability: The effect of top management and the mediating roles of user participation and analytical decision making orientation. *Journal of the Association for Information Systems*, *18*(7), 516–541. doi:10.17705/1jais.00462

Kuo-Nan, H., & Tidd, J. (2012). Open versus closed new service development: The influences of project novelty. *Technovation*, *32*(11), 600–608. doi:10.1016/j.technovation.2012.07.002

Kupp, M., Marval, M., & Borchers, P. (2017). Corporate accelerators: Fostering innovation while bringing together startups and large firms. *The Journal of Business Strategy*, *38*(6), 47–53. doi:10.1108/JBS-12-2016-0145

Kwon, P. B. (2018). Mars and Manna: Defense Industry and the Economic Transformation of Korea under Park Chung Hee. *Korea Journal*, *58*(3), 15–46. doi:10.25024/kj.2018.58.3.15

Kyle, M. K. (2020). The Alignment of Innovation Policy and Social Welfare: Evidence from Pharmaceuticals. *NBER Innovation Policy & the Economy*, *20*(1), 95–123. doi:10.1086/705640

Lasagni, A. (2012). How Can External Relationships Enhance Innovation in SMEs? New Evidence for Europe. *Journal of Small Business Management*, *50*(2), 310–339. doi:10.1111/j.1540-627X.2012.00355.x

Laudon, K. C., & Laudon, J. P. (2020). *Management information systems: Managing the digital firm*. Pearson.

Lauritzen, G. D., & Karafyllia, M. (2019). Perspective: Leveraging open innovation through paradox. *Journal of Product Innovation Management*, *36*(1), 107–121. doi:10.1111/jpim.12474

Laursen, K., & Salter, A. (2006). Open for innovation: The role of openness in explaining innovation performance among U.K. manufacturing firms. *Strategic Management Journal*, *27*(2), 131–150. doi:10.1002mj.507

Lawrence, P., & Braddon, D. (2017). *Strategic issues in European aerospace*. Routledge. doi:10.4324/9781315242330

Lazzarotti, V., Bengtsson, L., Manzini, R., Pellegrini, L., & Rippa, P. (2017). Openness and innovation performance: An empirical analysis of openness determinants and performance mediators. *European Journal of Innovation Management*, *20*(3), 463–492. doi:10.1108/EJIM-06-2016-0061

Lee, J. G., & Park, M. J. (2019). Rethinking the national defense R&D innovation system for latecomer: Defense R&D governance matrix. *Technological Forecasting and Social Change*, *146*, 1–11. doi:10.1016/j.techfore.2019.05.012

Lee, J. G., & Park, M. J. (2020). Evaluation of technological competence and operations efficiency in the defense industry: The strategic planning of South Korea. *Evaluation and Program Planning*, *79*, 1–11. doi:10.1016/j.evalprogplan.2019.101775 PMID:31865011

Lee, J. J., & Yoon, H. (2015). A comparative study of technological learning and organizational capability development in complex products systems: Distinctive paths of three latecomers in military aircraft industry. *Research Policy*, *44*(7), 1296–1313. doi:10.1016/j.respol.2015.03.007

Lee, S. M., Hwang, T., & Choi, D. (2012). Open innovation in the public sector of leading countries. *Management Decision*, *50*(1), 147–162. doi:10.1108/00251741211194921

Lee, S., Miyoung, J., & Haemoon, O. (2018). Enhancing customers' positive responses: Applying sensory marketing to the hotel website. *Journal of Global Scholars of Marketing Science*, *28*(1), 68–85. doi:10.1080/21639159.2017.1410772

Lego Ideas. (2021, March 20). *It's your time to shine*. https://ideas.lego.com/projects/create

Lego. (2021, May 7). *Creator 3 in 1*. https://www.lego.com/tr-tr/themes/creator-3-in-1

Leijten, J. (2019). Innovation policy and international relations: Directions for EU diplomacy. *European Journal of Futures Research*, *7*(1), 1–21. doi:10.118640309-019-0156-1

Leiponen, A., & Helfat, C. E. (2010). Innovation objectives, knowledge sources, and the benefits of breadth. *Strategic Management Journal*, *31*(2), 224–236. doi:10.1002mj.807

Lenzen, M., Moran, D., Kanemoto, K., Foran, B., Lobefaro, L., & Geschke, A. (2012). International trade drives biodiversity threats in developing nations. *Nature*, *486*, 109–112.

Leydesdorff, L. (2012). The triple helix, quadruple helix and an N-tuple of helices: Explanatory models for analyzing the knowledge-based economy? *Journal of the Knowledge Economy*, *3*(1), 25–35. doi:10.100713132-011-0049-4

Leydesdorff, L., & Fritsch, M. (2006). Measuring the knowledge base of regional innovation systems in Germany in terms of a Triple Helix dynamics. *Research Policy*, *35*(10), 1538–1553. doi:10.1016/j.respol.2006.09.027

Liang, T. P., & Liu, Y. H. (2018). Research Landscape of Business Intelligence and Big Data analytics: A Bibliometrics Study. *Expert Systems with Applications*, *111*, 2–10. doi:10.1016/j.eswa.2018.05.018

Lião, Y.-W., Wang, Y.-M., & Tu, Y.-M. (2015). Understanding the dynamics between organizational IT investment strategy and market performance: A system dynamics approach. *Computers in Industry*, *71*, 46–57. doi:10.1016/j.compind.2015.02.006

Lichtenthaler, U. (2010). Intellectual property and open innovation: An emperical analysi. *International Journal of Technology Management*, *52*(3/4), 372–391. doi:10.1504/IJTM.2010.035981

Lichtenthaler, U. (2011). Open innovation: Past research, current debates, and future directions. *The Academy of Management Perspectives*, *25*(1), 75–93.

Lichtenthaler, U., & Lichtenthaler, E. (2009). A capability-based framework for open innovation: Complementing absorptive capacity. *Journal of Management Studies*, *46*(8), 1315–1338. doi:10.1111/j.1467-6486.2009.00854.x

Li, P.-Y., & Huang, K.-F. (2019). The antecedents of innovation performance: The moderating role of top management team diversity. *Baltic Journal of Management*, *14*(2), 291–311. doi:10.1108/BJM-07-2017-0202

Lisi, I. E. (2018). Determinants and Performance Effects of Social Performance Measurement Systems. *Journal of Business Ethics*, *152*(1), 225–251. doi:10.100710551-016-3287-3

Liu, C. H. (2011). The effects of innovation alliance on network structure and density of cluster. *Expert Systems with Applications*, *38*(1), 299–305. doi:10.1016/j.eswa.2010.06.064

Liu, J. (2014). Forest sustainability in China and implications for a telecoupled world. *Asia & the Pacific Policy Studies*, *1*(1), 230–250.

Livieratos, A. D., & Lepeniotis, P. (2017). Corporate venture capital programs of European electric utilities: Motives, trends, strategies and challenges. *The Electricity Journal*, *30*(2), 30–40. doi:10.1016/j.tej.2017.01.006

Local Motors. (2021, March 21). *We are unlike any manufacturer you have ever seen.* https://localmotors.com/company/

Lööf, H., & Heshmati, A. (2006). On the relationship between innovation and performance: A sensitivity analysis. *Economics of Innovation and New Technology*, *15*(4-5), 317–344. doi:10.1080/10438590500512810

Lopes, A. V. B. V., & De Carvalho, M. M. (2018). Evolution of the open innovation paradigm: Towards a contingent conceptual model. *Technological Forecasting and Social Change*, *132*, 284–298. doi:10.1016/j.techfore.2018.02.014

Lopes, R., Almeida, M., & Lima, E. (2019). Desafios atuais e caminhos promissores para a pesquisa em empreendedorismo. *Revista de Administração de Empresas*, *59*(4), 284–292. doi:10.15900034-759020190406

Lopez-Cabrales, A., Bornay-Barrachina, M., & Diaz-Fernandez, M. (2017). Leadership and dynamic capabilities: The role of HR systems. *Personnel Review*, *46*(2), 255–276. doi:10.1108/PR-05-2015-0146

López-Nicolás, C., & Merono-Cerdán, A. L. (2011). Strategic knowledge management, innovation and performance. *International Journal of Information Management*, *31*(6), 502–509. doi:10.1016/j.ijinfomgt.2011.02.003

Lorenzen, M. (2001). Ties, trust, and trade: Elements of a theory of coordination in industrial clusters. *International Studies of Management & Organization*, *31*(4), 14–34. doi:10.1080/00208825.2001.11656825

Love, J. H., & Roper, S. (2015). SME innovation, exporting and growth: A review of existing evidence. *International Small Business Journal*, *33*(1), 28–48. doi:10.1177/0266242614550190

Lu, Y. C., Matui, N., & Gracioso, L. (2019). Definição da inovação no âmbito da pesquisa brasileira: uma análise semântica. Revista Digital Biblioteconomia e Ciência da Informação, 17, 1-22.

Mahmoud-Jouini, S. B., Duvert, C., & Esquirol, M. (2018). Key factors in building a Corporate Accelerators Capability. *Research Technology Management*, *61*(4), 26–34. doi:10.1080/08956308.2018.1471274

Makó, C., Illéssy, M., & Heidrich, B. (2019). When Will Alpha and Omega Collide? In Search of the Theoretical Relevance of Eu Innovation Policies. *Vezetéstudomány / Budapest Management Review*, *50*(11), 66–73.

Malik, K., Glynn, S., Butler, J., & Miles, I. (2003). Developing innovation policies for the knowledge economy in Europe. *Innovation*, *5*(2-3), 225–233. doi:10.5172/impp.2003.5.2-3.225

Mamede, R. P. (2017). Structural asymmetries, innovation measurement and innovation policies in the EU. *Portuguese Journal of Social Science*, *16*(3), 377–392. doi:10.1386/pjss.16.3.377_1

Manufacturing, U. S. A. (2020). *Institutes*. Available: https://www.manufacturingusa.com/institutes

Manzini, E. (2015). *Design, when everybody designs: An introduction to design for social innovation*. MIT Press.

Maradana, R. P., Pradhan, R. P., Dash, S., Gaurav, K., Jayakumar, M., & Chatterjee, D. (2017). Does innovation promote economic growth? Evidence from European countries. *Journal of Innovation and Entrepreneurship*, *6*(1), 1. doi:10.118613731-016-0061-9

Marcolin, F., Vezzetti, E., & Montagna, F. (2017). How to practice open innovation today: What, where, how and why. *Creative Industries Journal*, *10*(3), 258–291. doi:10.1080/17510694.2017.1393178

Martie-Louise, V., Williams, A. M., Ritchie, B. W., Gronum, S., & Betts, K. S. (2019). Innovation Diversity and Uncertainty in Small and Medium Sized Tourism Firms. *Tourism Management*, *72*, 257–269. doi:10.1016/j.tourman.2018.11.019

Martínez-Martínez, A., Cegarra, J. G. C. N., García-Pérez, A., & Moreno-Ponce, A. (2019). Environmental knowledge strategy: Driving success of the hospitality industry. *Management Research Review*, *42*(6), 662–680. doi:10.1108/MRR-02-2018-0091

Martins, S. O., & Lino, J. A. (2014). Influência das Práticas de Inovação Aberta na Prospecção de Conhecimentos para a Criação de Valor em Ambientes de Alta Complexidade sob Condições de Incerteza e Imprevisibilidade. *Revista de Administração e Inovação*, *11*(1), 295–318. doi:10.5773/rai.v11i1.1320

Mathaisel, D. F. (2005). A lean architecture for transforming the aerospace maintenance, repair and overhaul (MRO) enterprise. *International Journal of Productivity and Performance Management*, *54*(8), 623–644. doi:10.1108/17410400510627499

McGahan, A. M., Bogers, M. L., Chesbrough, H., & Holgersson, M. (2021). Tackling societal challenges with open innovation. *California Management Review*, *63*(2), 49–61.

McGuire, S., & Islam, N. (2015). Indigenous technological capabilities, emerging market firms and the aerospace industry. *Technology Analysis and Strategic Management*, *27*(7), 739–758. doi:10.1080/09537325.2014.959482

Menon, A., Bharadwaj, S. G., Adidam, P. T., & Edison, S. W. (1999). Antecedents and consequences of marketing strategy making: A model and a test. *Journal of Marketing*, *63*(2), 18–40. doi:10.1177/002224299906300202

Mercandetti, F., Larbig, C., Tuozzo, V., & Steiner, T. (2017). Innovation by Collaboration between Startups and SMEs in Switzerland. *Technology Innovation Management Review*, *7*(12), 23–31. doi:10.22215/timreview/1125

Milici, A., Ferreira, F., Pereira, L., Carayannis, E., & Ferreira, J. J. (2021). Dynamics of open innovation in small- and medium-sized enterprises: A metacognitive approach. *IEEE Transactions on Engineering Management*, 1–14. Advance online publication. doi:10.1109/TEM.2020.3042458

Mind the Bridge – NESTA. (2017a), *Open Innovation in Europe. A Snapshot of the SEP Europe's Corporate Startup Stars 2017*. Retrieved from: https://www.nesta.org.uk/blog/open-innovation-in-europe-a-snapshot-of-the-sep-europes-corporate-startup-stars-2017/

Mind the Bridge. (2017b). *European Corporate Innovation Outposts in Silicon Valley. The Who's Who*. Available at: https://mindthebridge.com/research/

Mind the Bridge. (2018). *European Innovation Economy in Silicon Valley*. Available at: https://mindthebridge.com/research/

Mind the Bridge. (2019). *Corporate Innovation in Silicon Valley: Outposts and Investment Flow*. Available at: https://mindthebridge.com/research/

Mind the Bridge. (2020). *Corporate Innovation in Silicon Valley*. Available at: https://mindthebridge.com/research/

Minshall, T., Mortara, L., Valli, R., & Probert, D. (2010, June). Making 'asymmetric' partnerships work: Partnering between small start-ups and larger firms presents challenges – but some have found ways to overcome them. *Research Technology Management*, *53*(May), 53–63. doi:10.1080/08956308.2010.11657631

Miotti, L., & Sachwald, F. (2003). Co-operative R&D: Why and with whom? *Research Policy*, *32*(8), 1481–1499. doi:10.1016/S0048-7333(02)00159-2

Modak, N. M., Merigó, J. M., Weber, R., Manzor, F., & Ortúzar, J. D. D. (2019). Fifty years of Transportation Research journals: A bibliometric overview. *Transportation Research Part A, Policy and Practice, 120*, 188–223. doi:10.1016/j.tra.2018.11.015

Moir, I., & Seabridge, A. (2011). *Aircraft Systems: Mechanical, electrical, and avionics subsystems integration* (Vol. 52). John Wiley & Sons.

Moreira, A. C. (2009). Desafios das PME num contexto de globalização. *Revista Percursos & Ideias, 1*, 43–58.

Morgan, R. (2015). *Calculating social value: How can the social value of social purpose organisations be measured?* The Leverhulme Centre for the Study of Value School of Environment, Education and Development.

Motohashi, K. (2001). *RIETI Discussion Paper Series 01-E-006 Use of plant level micro-data for SME innovation policy evaluation in Japan*. Academic Press.

Najberg, E., Carvallho, J. B., Campos, W. Y. Y. Z., Rodriguez, M. V. R., & Bilhim, J. A. F. (2020). Higher education and professionalization of creative workers: State of the art. *Diálogo Com a Economia Criativa, 5*(15), 33–57. doi:10.22398/2525-2828.51533-57

Niosi, J., & Zhegu, M. (2005). Aerospace clusters: Local or global knowledge spillovers? *Industry and Innovation, 12*(1), 5–29. doi:10.1080/1366271042000339049

Niosi, J., & Zhegu, M. (2010). Anchor tenants and regional innovation systems: The aircraft industry. *International Journal of Technology Management, 50*(3/4), 263–284. doi:10.1504/IJTM.2010.032676

Nishikawa, H., Schreier, M., & Ogawa, S. (2013). User-generated versus designer-generated products: A performance assessment at Muji. Intern. *J. of Research in Marketing, 30*, 160–167.

Nuryakin, M. (2018). Competitive advantage. and product innovation key sucesso of batik sme's marketing performance in Indonesia. *Academy of Strategic Management, 17*(2), 1–17.

Nyheim, McFadden, & Connolly. (2005). Technology strategies for the hospitality industry. Upper Saddle River, NJ: Pearson Prentice Hall.

Odriozola-Fernández, I., Berbegal-Mirabent, J., & Merigó-Lindahl, J. M. (2019). Open innovation in small and medium enterprises: A bibliometric analysis. *Journal of Organizational Change Management, 32*(5), 533–557. doi:10.1108/JOCM-12-2017-0491

OECD. (1999). *Boosting innovation: The cluster approach*. OECD Publishing.

OECD. (2019). *Embracing Innovation in Government: Global Trends in 2019*. Available: https://trends.oecd-opsi.org/embracing-innovation-in-government-global-trends-2019.pdf

OECD. (2020). *Gross domestic spending on R&D*. Available: https://data.oecd.org/rd/gross-domestic-spending-on-r-d.htm

Oguguo, P. C., Bodas Freitas, I. M., & Genet, C. (2020). Multilevel institutional analyses of firm benefits from R&D collaboration. *Technological Forecasting and Social Change*, *151*, 119841. Advance online publication. doi:10.1016/j.techfore.2019.119841

Onetti, A. (2019). Turning Open Innovation into Practice: Trends in European Corporates. *Journal of Business Strategy, 42*(1), 51-58.

Open Source Ecology. (2021, May 2). *About.* https://www.opensourceecology.org/about-overview/

Open-source-software movement. (2021, April 15). In *Wikipedia*. https://en.wikipedia.org/wiki/Open-source-software_movement

Organisation for Economic Co-Operation and Development (OECD). (2007, Setembro 28). *Teachers Matter. Attracting, Developing and Retaining Effective Teachers. Country Note Korea*. Retieved from www.oecd.org/edu/teacherpolicy

Organisation for Economic Co-Operation And Development. (2005). *Guidelines for Collecting and Interpreting Innovation* (3rd ed.). OECD Statistical Office of the European Communities. Retrieved from: www.oecd.org/edu/teacherpolicy

Ortega-Argilés, R., Vivarelli, M., & Voigt, P. (2009). R&D in SMEs: A paradox? *Small Business Economics*, *33*(1), 3–11. doi:10.100711187-009-9187-5

Ortuzar, G. (2015). Industry clusters and economic development. *Indiana Business Review*, *90*(1), 7–9.

Oughton, D., Mortara, L., & Minshall, T. (2013). Managing asymmetric relationships in open innovation: lessons from multinational companies and SMEs. In *Open Innovation in the Food and Beverage Industry* (pp. 276–293). Woodhead Publishing Series in Food Science, Technology and Nutrition. doi:10.1533/9780857097248.3.276

Ovuakporie, O. D., Pillai, K. G., Wang, C., & Wei, Y. (2019). Differential moderating effects of strategic and operational reconfiguration on the relationship between open innovation practices and innovation performance. *Research Policy*, *50*(1), 104–146.

Padilla-Meléndez, A., Del Aguila-Obra, A. R., & Lockett, N. (2013). Shifting sands: Regional perspectives on the role of social capital in supporting open innovation through knowledge transfer and exchange with small and medium-sized enterprises. *International Small Business Journal*, *31*(3), 296–318. doi:10.1177/0266242612467659

Pan Fagerlin, W., & Wang, Y. (2021). Top managers' communication efforts as a response to tensions in product innovation: An attention-based view. *Baltic Journal of Management*, *16*(1), 21–45. doi:10.1108/BJM-01-2020-0024

Parida, V., Westerberg, M., & Frishammar, J. (2012). Inbound open innovation activities in high-tech SMEs: The impact on innovation performance. *Journal of Small Business Management*, *50*(2), 283–309. doi:10.1111/j.1540-627X.2012.00354.x

Park, E., & Kwon, S. J. (2018). Effects of innovation types on firm performance: An empirical approach in South Korean manufacturing industry. International. *Journal of Business Innovation and Research.*, *15*(2), 215–230. doi:10.1504/IJBIR.2018.089144

Park, J., Song, H., & Qiu, R. T. R. A. (2019). Review of research on turism demand forecasting: Lauching the annals of tourism research curated collection on tourism demand forecasting. *Annals of Tourism Research*, *75*, 338–362. doi:10.1016/j.annals.2018.12.001

Park, Y., Lee, S., & Lee, S. (2012). Patent analysis for promoting technology transfer in multi-technology industries: The Korean aerospace industry case. *The Journal of Technology Transfer*, *37*(3), 355–374. doi:10.100710961-010-9181-8

Pece, A. M., Simona, O. E. O., & Salisteanu, F. (2015). Innovation and Economic Growth: An Empirical Analysis for CEE Countries. *Procedia Economics and Finance*, *26*, 461–467. doi:10.1016/S2212-5671(15)00874-6

Pegkas, P., Staikouras, C., & Tsamadias, C. (2019). Does research and development expenditure impact innovation? Evidence from the European Union countries. *Journal of Policy Modeling*, *41*(5), 1005–1025. doi:10.1016/j.jpolmod.2019.07.001

Perkmann, M., Tartari, V., McKelvey, M., Autio, E., Broström, A., D'Este, P., Fini, R., Geuna, A., Grimaldi, R., Hughes, A., Krabel, S., Kitson, M., Llerena, P., Lissoni, F., Salter, A., & Sobrero, M. (2013). Academic engagement and commercialisation: A review of the literature on university-industry relations. *Research Policy*, *42*(2), 423–442. doi:10.1016/j.respol.2012.09.007

Pestana, M. H., & Gageiro, J. N. (2010). Análise de Dados para Ciências Socais: A Complementaridade do SPSS (5th ed.). Edições Sílabo.

Pestana, M. H., & Gageiro, J. N. (2010). *Análise de Dados para Ciências Socais: The Complementarity of SPSS* (5th ed.). Edições Sílabo.

Philipson, S. (2019). Sources of innovation: Consequences for knowledge production and transfer. *Journal of Innovation & Knowledge.*

Pierre, A., & Fernandez, A. S. (2018). Going deeper into SMEs' innovation capacity: An empirical exploration of innovation capacity factors. *Journal of Innovation Economics & Management*, *25*(1), 139–181. doi:10.3917/jie.pr1.0019

Piezunka, H., & Dahlander, L. (2015). Distant search, narrow attention: How crowding alters organizations' filtering of suggestions in crowdsourcing. *Academy of Management Journal*, *58*(3), 856–880. https://doi.org/10.5465/amj.2012.0458

Pihlajamaa, M., Kaipia, R., Säilä, J., & Tanskanen, K. (2017). Can supplier innovations substitute for internal R&D? A multiple case study from an absorptive capacity perspective. *Journal of Purchasing and Supply Management*, *23*(4), 242–255. doi:10.1016/j.pursup.2017.08.002

Pinto, M. M. (2016). Tecnologia e inovação. b3. ed. rev. atual. – Florianópolis: Departamento de Ciências da Administração. UFSC.

Pisoni, A., & Onetti, A. (2018). When startups exit: Comparing strategies in Europe and the USA. *The Journal of Business Strategy*, *39*(3), 26–33. doi:10.1108/JBS-02-2017-0022

Podmetina, D., Soderquist, K. E., Petraite, M., & Teplov, R. (2018). Developing a competency model for open innovation from the individual to the organisational level. *Management Decision*, *56*(6), 1306–1335. doi:10.1108/MD-04-2017-0445

Popa, S., Soto-Acosta, P., & Martinez-Conesa, I. (2017). Antecedents, moderators, and outcomes of innovation climate and open innovation: An empirical study in SMEs. *Technological Forecasting and Social Change*, *118*, 134–142. doi:10.1016/j.techfore.2017.02.014

PORDATA. (2017). *Pequenas e Médias Empresas (PME).* Obtido de Empresas e Pessoal: https://www.pordata.pt/Subtema/Portugal/Pequenas+e+M%C3%A9dias+Empresas+(PME)-378

Porter, M. E. (1985). *Competitive Advantage*. Free Press.

Porter, M. E. (1990). *Competitive Advantage of Nations*. Free Press. doi:10.1007/978-1-349-11336-1

Porter, M. E. (1990). The Competitive Advantage of Nations. *Harvard Business Review*, *3-4*, 73–91.

Porter, M. E. (1998). Clusters and the new economics of competition. *Harvard Business Review*, *76*(6), 77–90. PMID:10187248

Porter, M. E., & Kramer, M. R. (2006). Strategy and society: The link between competitive advantage and corporate social responsibility. *Harvard Business Review*, *84*(12), 78–92.

Porter, M. E., & Kramer, M. R. (2011). Creating shared value: How to reinvent capitalism—and unleash a wave of innovation and growth. *Harvard Business Review*, (January–February), 62–77.

Prahalad, C., & Hamel, G. (1995). *Competindo pelo Futuro*. Campus.

Prahalad, C., & Ramaswamy, V. (2004). *The future of competition: Co-creating unique value with customers*. Harvard Business Review Press.

Presidential Committee for Balanced National Development Korea. (2019). *The 4th Balanced National Development Five Year Plan*. Rep. of Korea.

Priavolou, C. (2018). The emergence of open construction systems: A sustainable paradigm in the construction sector? *Journal of Futures Studies*, *23*(2), 67–84.

Property Rights Alliance. (2021). *U.S. support of trips waiver undermines effort to fight COVID-19*. Available: https://www.propertyrightsalliance.org/news/u-s-support-of-trips-waiver-undermines-effort-to-fight-covid-19/

PwC. (2018). *Aerospace manufacturing attractiveness rankings*. pwc.com/us/en/industrial-products/publications/assets/pwc-aerospace-manufacturing-attractiveness-rankings-2018.pdf

Radicic, D., Pugh, G. T., Hollanders, H., & Wintjes, R. (2014). *The Impact of Innovation Support Programmes on SME Innovation in Traditional Manufacturing Industries: An Evaluation for Seven EU Regions*. UNU-MERIT Working Paper No. 2014-033.

Radziwon, A., & Bogers, M. (2019). Open innovation in SMEs: Exploring inter-organizational relationships in an ecosystem. *Technological Forecasting and Social Change*, *146*, 573–587. doi:10.1016/j.techfore.2018.04.021

Rainone, D., Rainone, M., & Musial, L. (2014). How to work with small companies to expand your open innovation capabilities. *Open Innovation: New Product Development Essentials From the PDMA*.

Rajalo, S., & Vadi, M. (2021). Collaboration potential between low-capacity SMEs and academic researchers determined by symmetry of motivation. *Technovation*, *107*(C), 102304. doi:10.1016/j.technovation.2021.102304

Ramirez, R. (1999). Value co-production: Intellectual origins and implications for practice and research. *Strategic Management Journal*, *20*(1), 49–65.

Ramos, J. (2017). Cosmo-localization and leadership for the future. *Journal of Futures Studies*, *21*(4), 65–84.

Randeree, K., & Al Youha, H. (2009). Strategic management of performance: An examination of public sector organizations in the United Arab Emirates. *The International Journal of Knowledge. Culture and Change Management*, *9*(4), 123–134.

Ranga, M., & Etzkowitz, H. (2013). Triple Helix Systems: An Analytical Framework for Innovation Policy and Practice in the Knowledge Society. *Industry and Higher Education*, *27*(4), 237–262. doi:10.5367/ihe.2013.0165

Raposo, M. L., Ferreira, J. J., & Fernandes, C. I. (2014). Local and cross-border SME cooperation: Effects on innovation and performance. *Revista Europea de Dirección y Economía de la Empresa*, *23*(4), 157–165. doi:10.1016/j.redee.2014.08.001

Rauta, J. (2020). Ciência e movimento da inovação organizacional: um framework conceitual para diagnostico. *Revista de administração, sociedade e inovação*, *6*(2), 25-51.

Razumova, M., Ibáñez, J. L., & Rey-Maquieira, J. P. (2015). Drivers of environmental innovation in majorcan hotels. *Journal of Sustainable Tourism*, *23*(10), 1529–1549. doi:10.1080/09669582.2015.1062016

Reichmann, M., & Simpson, P. B. (2016). Open innovation in early drug discovery: Roadmaps and roadblocks. *Drug Discovery Today*, *21*(5), 779–788. doi:10.1016/j.drudis.2015.12.008 PMID:26743597

Reilly, P. (2018). Building customer centricity in the hospitality sector: The role of talent management. *Worldwide Hospitality and Tourism Themes*, *10*(1), 42–56. doi:10.1108/WHATT-10-2017-0068

Ribau, C. P., Moreira, A. C., & Raposo, M. (2017). SMEs innovation capabilities and export performance: An entrepreneurial orientation view. *Journal of Business Economics and Management*, *18*(5), 920–934. doi:10.3846/16111699.2017.1352534

Ribau, C. P., Moreira, A. C., & Raposo, M. (2019). The role of exploitative and exploratory innovation in export performance: An analysis of plastics industry SMEs. *European Journal of International Management*, *13*(2), 224–246. doi:10.1504/EJIM.2019.098149

Ribeiro, M. C., da Cruz, W. S., Procópio, J. G., & Soares, M. C. (2019). Características Empreendedoras dos Profissionais de Contabilidade de Um Município da Amazônia Paraense. *Revista Paraense de Contabilidade*, *4*(3), 64–77. doi:10.36562/rpc.v4i3.39

Richter, N., Jackson, P., & Schildhauer, T. (2017). Outsourcing creativity: An abductive study of open innovation using corporate accelerators. *Creativity and Innovation Management*, *27*(1), 69–78. doi:10.1111/caim.12252

Rigby, D., & Zook, C. (2002). Open market innovation. *Harvard Business Review*, *80*(10), 80–89. PMID:12389463

Rindova, V., Barry, D., & Ketchen, D. J. Jr. (2009). Entrepreneuring as emancipation. *Academy of Management Review*, *34*(3), 477–491. doi:10.5465/amr.2009.40632647

Robertson, D. C. (2014). *Brick by brick: How LEGO rewrote the rules of innovation and conquered the global toy industry*. Random House.

Rohrbeck, R., Hölzle, K., & Gemunenden, H. (2009). Gemünden opening up for competitive advantage How Deutsche Telekom creates an open innovation ecosystem. *R & D Management*, *39*(4), 420–430. doi:10.1111/j.1467-9310.2009.00568.x

Rousseau, R. (2001). Indicadores bibliométricos y econométricos en la evaluación de instituciones científicas. *Acimed*, *9*(1), 50–60.

Rowley, J. (2002). Using case studies in research. *Management Research Review*, *25*(1), 16–27.

Rua, O. L., França, A., & Fernández, R. O. (2018). Key drivers of SMEs export performance: The mediating effect of competitive advantage. *Journal of Knowledge Management*, *22*(2), 257–279. doi:10.1108/JKM-07-2017-0267

Rubach, S., Hoholm, T., & Håkansson, H. (2017). Innovation networks or innovation within networks. *IMP Journal*, *11*(2), 178–206. doi:10.1108/IMP-09-2015-0057

Santoro, G., Ferraris, A., Giacosa, E., & Giovando, G. (2018). How SMEs Engage in Open Innovation: A Survey. *Journal of the Knowledge Economy*, *9*(2), 561–574. doi:10.100713132-015-0350-8

Santoro, G., Ferraris, A., & Winteler, D. J. (2019). Open innovation practices and related internal dynamics: Case studies of Italian ICT SMEs. *EuroMed Journal of Business*, *14*(1), 47–61. doi:10.1108/EMJB-05-2018-0031

Santoro, G., Mazzoleni, A., Quaglia, R., & Solima, L. (2021). Does age matter? The impact of SMEs age on the relationship between knowledge sourcing strategy and internationalization. *Journal of Business Research*, *128*(C), 779–787. doi:10.1016/j.jbusres.2019.05.021

Santos, A. M., Acosta, A. C., Borghetti, L. B., & Balbinoti, S. G. (2016). Empreendedorismo: Inovação, criatividade e liderança. Revista Visão. *Gestão Organizacional*, *5*(1), 56–68.

Schmiemann, M. (2009). *SMEs were the main drivers of economic growth between 2004 and 2006.* Obtido de https://ec.europa.eu/eurostat/documents/3433488/5284033/KS-SF-09-071-EN.PDF/7e1c1766-90e8-453d-aa57-352a1842dc2b

Schoepflin, U., & Glänzel, W. (2001). Two decades of "Scientometrics", An interdisciplinary field represented by its leading journal. *Scientometrics*, *50*(2), 301–312. doi:10.1023/A:1010577824449

Schumpeter, J. (1982). Capitalismo, socialismo e democracia. Rio de Janeiro: Fundo de Cultura. (Original publication 1942)

Selig, C. J., Gasser, T., & Baltes, G. H. (2018). How corporate accelerators foster organizational transformation: An internal perspective. *2018 IEEE International Conference on Engineering, Technology and Innovation.* 10.1109/ICE.2018.8436287

Shane, S., & Venkataraman, S. (2000). The promise of entrepreneurship as a field of research. *Academy of Management Review*, *25*(1), 217–226. doi:10.5465/amr.2000.2791611

Shao, Y., & Shi, L. (2018). Cross-border open innovation of early stage tech incubation: A case study of forge, the first UK-China accelerator program. *Journal of Open Innovation*, *4*(3), 37. doi:10.3390/joitmc4030037

Shearmur, R., & Doloreux, D. (2016). How open innovation processes vary between urban and remote environments: Slow innovators, market-sourced information and frequency of interaction. *Entrepreneurship and Regional Development*, *28*(5/6), 337–357. doi:10.1080/08985626.2016.1154984

Sheth, J. N. (2011, July). Impact of emerging markets on marketing: Rethinking existing perspectives and practices. *Journal of Marketing*, *75*, 166–182.

Sheth, J. N., & Sisodia, R. S. (2006). *Does marketing need reform? Fresh perspectives on the future*. M.E. Sharpe.

Sheth, J. N., Sisodia, R. S., & Sharma, A. (2000). The antecedents and consequences. *Journal of the Academy of Marketing Science*, *28*, 55–66.

Silva, A. D., Ferreira, F. A., Carayannis, E. G., & Ferreira, J. J. (2021). Measuring SMEs' propensity for open innovation using cognitive mapping and MCDA. *IEEE Transactions on Engineering Management*, *68*(2), 396–407. doi:10.1109/TEM.2019.2895276

Silva, L. F., & Moreira, A. C. (2021). Alignment in collaborative new product development. Comparing small and large firms. *International Journal of Business Innovation and Research*, *24*(2), 167–196. doi:10.1504/IJBIR.2021.112813

Simão, L., & Franco, M. (2018). External knowledge sources as antecedents of organizational innovation in firm workplaces: A knowledge-based perspective. *Journal of Knowledge Management*, *22*(2), 237–256. doi:10.1108/JKM-01-2017-0002

Simões, P. C., Moreira, A. C., & Mendes Dias, C. (2020). Portugal's changing defense industry: Is the triple helix model of knowledge society replacing state leadership model? *Journal of Open Innovation*, *6*(4), 183. doi:10.3390/joitmc6040183

Singh, S. K., Gupta, S., Busso, D., & Kamboj, S. (2021). Top management knowledge value, knowledge sharing practices, open innovation and organizational performance. *Journal of Business Research*, *128*(C), 788–798. doi:10.1016/j.jbusres.2019.04.040

Sisodiya, S. R., Johnson, J. L., & Grégoire, Y. (2013). Inbound open innovation for enhanced performance: Enablers and opportunities. *Industrial Marketing Management*, *42*(5), 836–849. doi:10.1016/j.indmarman.2013.02.018

Slater, S. F., & Narver, J. C. (1994). Market orientation, customer value, and superior performance. *Business Horizons*, *37*(2), 22–28. https://doi.org/10.1016/0007-6813(94)90029-9

Smith, D. J., & Tranfield, D. (2005). Talented suppliers? Strategic change and innovation in the UK aerospace industry. *R & D Management*, *35*(1), 37–49. doi:10.1111/j.1467-9310.2005.00370.x

Smith, W. (2014). Dynamic decision making: A model of senior leaders managing strategic paradoxes. *Academy of Management Journal*, *37*(6), 1592–1623. doi:10.5465/amj.2011.0932

Spanos, Y., & Lioukas, S. (2001). An Examination into the Causal Logic of Rent Generation: Contrasting porter's competitive strategy framework and the resource-based perspective. *Strategic Management Journal*, *22*(10), 907–934. doi:10.1002mj.174

Spender, J. C., Corvello, V., Grimaldi, M., & Rippa, P. (2017). Startups and open innovation: A review of the literature. *European Journal of Innovation Management*, *20*(1), 4–30. doi:10.1108/EJIM-12-2015-0131

Spithoven, A., Vanhaverbeke, W., & Roijakkers, N. (2012). Open innovation practices in SMEs and large enterprises. *Small Business Economics*, *41*(3), 537–562. doi:10.100711187-012-9453-9

Stojčić, N., Srhoj, S., & Coad, A. (2020). Innovation procurement as capability-building: Evaluating innovation policies in eight Central and Eastern European countries. *European Economic Review*, *121*, 103330. Advance online publication. doi:10.1016/j.euroecorev.2019.103330

Suh, Y., & Kim, M. S. (2012). Effects of SME collaboration on R&D in the service sector in open innovation. *Innovation (North Sydney, N.S.W.)*, *14*(3), 349–362. doi:10.5172/impp.2012.14.3.349

Sunny, S. A., & Shu, C. (2019). Investments, incentives, and innovation: Geographical clustering dynamics as drivers of sustainable entrepreneurship. *Small Business Economics*, *52*(4), 905–927. doi:10.100711187-017-9941-z

Tamburis, O., & Bonacci, I. (2014). Innovation networks in healthcare as mean of knowledge transfer. *IFKAD 2014: 9th International Forum on Knowledge Asset Dynamics: Knowledge and Management Models for Sustainable Growth.*

Teece, D. J. (2007). Explicating dynamic capabilities: The nature and microfoundations of (sustainable) enterprise performance. *Strategic Management Journal, 28*(13), 1319–1350. doi:10.1002mj.640

Teixeira, A. C., & Lopes, M. (2012). Open innovation in Portugal. *Acta Oeconomica, 62*(4), 435–458. doi:10.1556/aoecon.62.2012.4.2

Teplov, R., Albats, E., & Podmetina, D. (2019). What Does Open Innovation Mean? Business Versus Academic Perceptions. *International Journal of Innovation Management, 23*(1), 805–811. doi:10.1142/S1363919619500026

Thakur-Wernz, P., Cantwell, J., & Samant, S. (2019). Impact of international entry choices on the nature and type of innovation: Evidence from emerging economy firms from the Indian bio-pharmaceutical industry. *International Business Review, 28*(6), 101601. Advance online publication. doi:10.1016/j.ibusrev.2019.101601

The Leadership Network. (2021, March 20). *5 sustainable innovation practices that saved LEGO.* https://theleadershipnetwork.com/article/lego-sustainable-innovation

The Next Big Idea. (n.d.). *Startups - Vertequip.* Obtido em maio de 2019, de The Next Big Idea: https://thenextbigidea.pt/startups/vertiquip

Thomas, E. (2018). From Closed to Open Innovation in Emerging Economies: Evidence from the Chemical Industry in Brazil. *Technology Innovation Management Review, 8*(3), 26–37. doi:10.22215/timreview/1144

Tikakul, C., & Thomson, A. (2018). International Lessons in Knowledge Management: A Study of Western & Eastern Manufacturing SMEs. *Electronic Journal of Knowledge Management, 16*(2), 113–130.

Torkkeli, M., Kotonen, T., & Ahonen, P. (2007). Regional open innovation system as a platform for SMEs: A survey. *International Journal of Foresight and Innovation Policy, 3*(5), 336–350. doi:10.1504/IJFIP.2007.016456

Torres Freire, C., Massami Maruyama, F., & Polli, M. (2017). Innovation and Entrepreneurship: Public Policies and Private Actions. *New Studies*, 50-76.

Torres, L., Ibarra, E., & Arenas, A. (2015). Open innovation practices: A literature review of case studies. *Journal of Advanced Management Science, 3*(4), 362–367. doi:10.12720/joams.3.4.362-367

Tracey, P., & Clark, G. L. (2003). Alliances, networks and competitive strategy: Rethinking clusters of innovation. *Growth and Change, 34*(1), 1–16. doi:10.1111/1468-2257.00196

Tranfield, D., Denyer, D., & Smart, P. (2003). Towards a methodology for developing evidence-informed management knowledge by means of systematic review. *British Journal of Management, 14*(3), 207–222. doi:10.1111/1467-8551.00375

Trippl, M., Grillitsch, M., Isaksen, A., & Sinozic, T. (2015). Perspectives on cluster evolution: Critical review and future research issues. *European Planning Studies*, *23*(10), 2028–2044. doi:10.1080/09654313.2014.999450

Tsai, K.-H., & Yang, S.-Y. (2013). Firm innovativeness and business performance: The joint moderating effects of market turbulence and competition. *Industrial Marketing Management*, *43*(8), 1279–1294. doi:10.1016/j.indmarman.2013.06.001

Tsinopoulos, C., Sousa, C. M. P., & Yan, J. (2018). Process Innovation: Open Innovation and the Moderating Role of the Motivation to Achieve Legitimacy. *Journal of Product Innovation Management*, *35*(1), 27–48. doi:10.1111/jpim.12374

Turchi, L. M., & Morais, J. M. (2017). *Políticas de apoio à inovação tecnológica no Brasil: avanços recentes, limitações e propostas de ações*. Organizadores.

Turkina, E., Van Assche, A., & Kali, R. (2016). Structure and evolution of global cluster networks: Evidence from the aerospace industry. *Journal of Economic Geography*, *16*(6), 1211–1234. doi:10.1093/jeg/lbw020

Tziogkidis, P., Philippas, D., Leontitsis, A., & Sickles, R. C. (2020). A data envelopment analysis and local partial least squares approach for identifying the optimal innovation policy direction. *European Journal of Operational Research*, *285*(3), 1011–1024. doi:10.1016/j.ejor.2020.02.023

Ulku, H. (2004). *R&D, Innovation, and Economic Growth: An Empirical Analysis*. IMF Working Paper No. 04/185.

United Nations. (2021, March 21). *Ensure sustainable consumption and production patterns*. https://sdgs.un.org/goals/goal12

United States Studies Centre. (n.d.). *Myths, crises and complacency: innovation policy in the United States and Australia*. Available: https://www.ussc.edu.au/analysis/innovation-policy-in-the-united-states-and-australia#unleashing-american-innovation

United States Whitehouse. (2019). *Research and development*. Available: https://www.whitehouse.gov/wp-content/uploads/2018/02/ap_18_research-fy2019.pdf

US Department of State. (n.d.). *On the US Withdrawal from the Paris Agreement*. Available: https://www.state.gov/on-the-u-s-withdrawal-from-the-paris-agreement/

Vaivode, I. (2015). Triple Helix Model of University–Industry–Government Cooperation in the Context of Uncertainties. *Procedia: Social and Behavioral Sciences*, *213*, 1063–1067. doi:10.1016/j.sbspro.2015.11.526

Van De Vrande, V., De Jong, J. P. J., Vanhaverbeke, W., & De Rochemont, M. (2009). Open innovation in sme's: Trends, motives and management challenges. *Technovation*, *29*(6-7), 423–437. doi:10.1016/j.technovation.2008.10.001

Van Lieshout, J.W.F.C., van der Velden, J.M., Blomme, R.J., & Peters, P. (2021). The interrelatedness of organizational ambidexterity, dynamic capabilities and open innovation: a conceptual model towards a competitive advantage. *European Journal of Management Studies.*

Vanhaverbeke, W., & Cloodt, M. (2014). Theories of the firm and open innovation. In H. Chesbrough, W. Vanhaverbeke, & J. West (Eds.), New Frontiers in Open Innovation (pp. 256–278). Oxford University Press.

Vanhaverbeke, W. (2017). *Managing Open Innovation in SMEs*. Cambridge University Press. doi:10.1017/9781139680981

Vera, D., & Crossan, M. (2005). Strategic Leadership and Organizational Learning. *Academy of Management Review*, *29*(2), 222–240. doi:10.2307/20159030

Veugelers, R. (2008). The Role of SMEs in Innovation in the EU. A Case for Policy Intervention? *Review of Business and Economic Literature*, *0*(3), 239–262.

Vils, L., Mazzieri, M., Rodrigues, G., Da Silva, A., & Queiroz, M. J. (2017). Business model innovation: A bibliometric Review. *International Journal of Innovation*, *5*(3), 311–324. doi:10.5585/iji.v5i3.243

Von der Leyen, U. (2019). *One the most ambitious Union: my program for Europe*. Available: https://ec.europa.eu/info/sites/info/files/political-guidelines-next-commission_pt.pdf

Von Hippel, E. (2005). *Democratizing Innovation.* The MIT Press.

Vrgovic, P., Vidicki, P., Glassman, B., & Walton, A. (2012). Open innovation for sme's in developing countries-an intermediated communication network model for collaboration beyond obstacles. *Innovation (North Sydney, N.S.W.)*, *14*(3), 290–302. doi:10.5172/impp.2012.14.3.290

Vrontis, D., & Christofi, M. (2019). R&D internationalization and innovation: A systematic review, integrative framework and future research directions. *Journal of Business Research*, *128*(2).

Wahyuni, D. (2012). The research design maze: Understanding paradigms, cases, methods and methodologies. *Journal of Applied Management Accounting Research*, *10*(1), 69–80.

Wang, D. (2019). Association between technological innovation and firm performance in small and medium-sized enterprises. *International Journal of Innovation Science*, *11*(2), 227–240. doi:10.1108/IJIS-04-2018-0049

Wang, F. K., & Wu, H. (2014). Service strategies of small cloud service providers: A case study of a small cloud service provider and its clients in Taiwan. *International Journal of Information Management*, *34*(3), 406–415. doi:10.1016/j.ijinfomgt.2014.01.007

Wasserman, S., & Faust, K. (1994). *Social network analysis: Methods and applications*. Cambridge University Press. doi:10.1017/CBO9780511815478

Weiblen, T. (2014). The open business model: Understanding an emergent concept. *Journal of Multi Business Model Innovation and Technology*, *2*(1), 35–66. doi:10.13052/jmbmit2245-456X.212

Weiblen, T., & Chesbrough, H. W. (2015). Engaging with startups to enhance corporate innovation. *California Management Review*, *57*(2), 66–90. doi:10.1525/cmr.2015.57.2.66

Wendra, W., Sule, E. T., Joeliaty, J., & Azis, Y. (2019). Exploring dynamic capabilities, intellectual capital and innovation performance relationship: Evidence from the garment manufacturing. *Business: Theory and Practice*, *20*, 123–136. doi:10.3846/btp.2019.12

Wen, J., Kozak, M., Yang, S., & Liu, F. (2020). COVID-19: Potential effects on Chinese citizens' lifestyle and travel. *Tourism Review*. Advance online publication. doi:10.1108/TR-03-2020-0110

West, J., Vanhaverbeke, W., & Chesbrough, C. (2006). Open innovation: A research agenda. In H. Chesbrough, W. Vanhaverbeke, & J. West (Eds.), Open innovation: Researching a new paradigm (pp. 285–307). Oxford University Press.

West, J., & Bogers, M. (2013). Leveraging External Sources of Innovation: A Review of Research on Open Innovation. *Journal of Product Innovation Management*, *31*(4), 814–831. doi:10.1111/jpim.12125

West, J., & Lakhani, K. R. (2008). Getting clear about communities in open innovation. *Industry and Innovation*, *15*(2), 223–232. https://doi.org/10.1080/13662710802033734

West, J., Salter, A., Vanheverbeke, W., & Chesbrough, H. (2014). Open innovation: The next decade. *Research Policy*, *43*(5), 805–811. doi:10.1016/j.respol.2014.03.001

Wikhamn, B. R., & Styhre, A. (2016). Open innovation as a facilitator for corporate exploration. *International Journal of Innovation Management*, *21*(6), 1–20.

Wikhamn, B. R., & Styhre, A. (2018). Managerial challenges of outbound open innovation: A study of a spinout initiative in AstraZeneca. *R & D Management*, *49*(4), 652–667.

WikiHouse. (2021, April 15). In *Wikipedia*. https://en.wikipedia.org/wiki/WikiHouse

Wiklund, J., Davidsson, P., Audretsch, D. B., & Karlsson, C. (2011). The future of entrepreneurship research. *Entrepreneurship Theory and Practice*, *35*(1), 1–9. doi:10.1111/j.1540-6520.2010.00420.x

WIPO. (2011). *The Global Innovation Index: Insights and trends*. Available: https://www.wipo.int/wipo_magazine/en/2011/04/article_0005.html

WIPO. (2019). *The Global Innovation Index 2019*. Available: https://www.wipo.int/edocs/pubdocs/en/wipo_pub_gii_2019-chapter1.pdf and https://www.wipo.int/global_innovation_index/en/

WIPO. (2020). *The Global Innovation Index 2020* Available: https://www.globalinnovationindex.org/gii-2020-report

WIPO. (2021). *The GII calls on business and policy leaders around the world to sustain innovation.* Available: https://www.wipo.int/global_innovation_index/en/2020/#risks

Wosche, T., Haase, H., & Kratzer, J. (2017). Resource scarcity in sme's: Effects on incremental and radical innovations. *Management Research Review*, *40*(2), 195–217. doi:10.1108/MRR-10-2015-0239

Wouters, M., Anderson, J. C., & Kirchberger, M. (2018). New-technology startups seeking pilot customers: Crafting a pair of value propositions. *California Management Review*, *60*(4), 101–124. doi:10.1177/0008125618778855

Xiaobao, P., Wei, S., & Yuzhen, D. (2013). Framework of open innovation in SMEs in an emerging economy: Firm characteristics, network openness, and network information. *International Journal of Technology Management*, *62*(2/3/4), 223–250. doi:10.1504/IJTM.2013.055142

Yoon, B., Shin, J., & Lee, S. (2016). Open innovation projects in SMEs as an engine for sustainable growth. *Sustainability*, *8*(2), 1–27.

Yuan, C., Liu, S., Yang, Y., & Shen, Y. (2016). On the contribution of defense innovation to China's economic growth. *Defence and Peace Economics*, *27*(6), 820–837. doi:10.1080/10242694.2014.901644

Yuan, X., & Li, X. (2019). The combination of different open innovations: A longitudinal case study. *Chinese Management Studies*, *13*(2), 342–362. doi:10.1108/CMS-02-2018-0410

Yun, J. H. J., Won, D. K., & Park, K. B. (2018). Entrepreneurial cyclical dynamics of open innovation. *Journal of Evolutionary Economics*, *28*(5), 1151–1174. doi:10.100700191-018-0596-y

Yun, J. H. J., Zhao, X., Jung, K. H., & Yigitcanlar, T. (2020). The culture for open innovation dynamics. *Sustainability*, *12*(12), 1–21. doi:10.3390u12125076

Yun, J. J., & Liu, Z. (2019). Micro-and macro-dynamics of open innovation with a quadruple-helix model. *Sustainability*, *11*(12), 3301. doi:10.3390u11123301

Yun, J. J., Won, D. K., & Park, K. (2016). Dynamics from open innovation to evolutionary change. *Journal of Open Innovation*, *2*(7), 1–22. doi:10.118640852-016-0033-0

Zhang, D., Linderman, K., & Schroeder, R. G. (2012). The moderating role of contextual factors on quality management practices. *Journal of Operations Management*, *30*(1-2), 12–23. doi:10.1016/j.jom.2011.05.001

Zhang, S., & Fang, Y. (2018). Research on Construction Project Organization Based on Social Network Analysis. *Wireless Personal Communications*, *102*(2), 1867–1877. doi:10.100711277-018-5242-3

Zien, K., & Buckler, S. A. (1997). From Experience Dreams to Market: Crafting a Culture of Innovation. *Journal of Product Innovation Management*, *14*(4), 274–287. doi:10.1111/1540-5885.1440274

Zimmermann, R., Ferreira, L., & Moreira, A. C. (2020). How supply chain strategies moderate the relationship between innovation capabilities and business performance. *Journal of Purchasing and Supply Management*, *26*(5), 100658. doi:10.1016/j.pursup.2020.100658

Zott, C., Amit, R., & Massa, L. (2011). The business model: Recent development and future research. *Journal of Management*, *37*(4), 1019–1042. doi:10.1177/0149206311406265

Zupic, I., & Čater, T. (2015). Bibliometric Methods in Management and Organization. *Organizational Research Methods*, *18*(3), 429–472. doi:10.1177/1094428114562629

About the Contributors

Orlando Lima Rua holds a Habilitation and a PhD in Management. He is a Management Professor at the Porto School of Accounting and Business (ISCAP) of the Polytechnic of Porto (P. PORTO) and a researcher at the Center for Organisational and Social Studies (CEOS.PP) and the Research Center of Business Sciences (NECE).

* * *

Mamun Ala has a PhD in applied economics (international trade regulation) from the Centre for Regulation and Market Analysis, University of South Australia. His other postgraduate qualifications include MPhil in Management, MEco, MBA and Med. Mamun brings a wealth of academic experience working with the Australian Institute of Business, University of South Australia and Flinders University. As an experienced and well-published researcher, he is currently involved with several projects including the notion of system of innovation for low-tech industry, the impact of universal patent regime on developing countries, and the ethical aspects of product design and manufacturing.

Mario Arias-Oliva is PhD in Management by Rovira i Virgili University and PhD in Information Science by Complutense University of Madrid. He is part of the International Advisory Board of the Centre for Business Information Ethics (Meiji University, Tokyo, Japan). His research filed is technology acceptance, publishing in international top journals papers about cryptocurrency acceptance, cyborg technologies and robotics. He has present papers in more than a hundred International Conferences, and he has been President of the Scientific Commeette in three International Conferences. Currently he is Profesor of Marketing in Complutense University of Madrid.

Larissa Barbieri has a Degree in Pedagogy (2016) and Letters (2018) from Faculdade de Educação São Luís (FESL). Graduated in Institutional Psychopedagogy from the Faculty of Education São Luís (2018) and in Neuropsychology (2020) from the Faculty of Education São Luís (FESL). It works in the areas of Education, Environmental Education, Tourism, Management, Sustainability.

Luciana Barbieri da Rosa graduated in Business Administration - Bachelor's Degree from Faculdade de Educação São Luis - FESL (2007) and Full Degree from the Special Teacher Education Graduation Program for Professional Education - PEG (UFSM - 2015). Specialist in Environmental Education from the Federal University of Santa Maria / RS (UFSM-2009) and Specialist in Public Management from the Federal University of Santa Maria (UAB / UFSM - 2015). Master in Business Administration from the Postgraduate Program in Business Administration PPGA (UFSM - 2013). PhD in Business Administration from the Postgraduate Program in Business Administration PPGA (UFSM - 2019). He is currently a teacher trainer at the Federal Institute of Rondônia (UAB / IFRO), a member of the research groups: Ecoinovar (UFSM), Innovation and Technology Management (GEITEC / UNIR) and Innovation and Organizational Sustainability (UFSM). It operates in the areas of: Innovation, Sustainability, Education, Strategy, Marketing and Production.

Isidora Beraha is a Research Associate at the Institute of Economic Sciences in Belgrade. The fields of her scientific interest include business economics, value chain analysis, research and innovation systems, local economic development, entrepreneurship and small and SMEs. She has published a significant number of scientific papers in the mentioned fields. Since 2019, she has been president of the Scientific Council and Head of the Center for Basic Research of the Institute of Economic Sciences. She is a member of the Serbian Scientific Society of Economists, Society of Economists of Belgrade and Entrepreneurship Research and Education Network of Central European Universities (ERENET).

Sonja Đuričin is a Senior Research Associate at the Institute of Economic Sciences in Belgrade. The fields of her scientific interest include business economics and agricultural economics, innovation, financial management, strategic management, entrepreneurship and SMEs, local economic development. She is an author or co-author of many scientific and professional papers published in domestic and international publications. Since 2016, she has been an assistant professor at Belgrade Banking Academy teaching Management Accounting and Cost Accounting. She is a member of the Scientific Council of the Institute of Economic Sciences. Since 2018, she has been member of the Board of Directors of the Institute of Economic Sciences, and since 2019 the Head of the Center for cooperation with business sector. She is one of the editors of the Economic Analysis Journal and the editor-in chief of the annual publication "National Network of Medium Enterprises in RS", published by IES. She is a member of the Scientific Society of Economists of Serbia and ERENET (Entrepreneurship Research and Education Network of Central European Universities).

Sveva Giovannoni is research fellow at the Research Centre for Innovation and Life Sciences Management (CrESIT). She is passionate about Open Innovation and startups and she holds a MSc in Global Entrepreneurship Economics and Management. During her MSc she engaged with startups focused on cryptocurrencies, blockchain technology and sustainability. Nowadays, she works in the ICT field, helping corporates to achieve their business goals by improving their IT infrastructure – guiding them through their journey to the cloud.

Maria Hespanha obtained a Bachelor's degree from the University of Coimbra, Portugal and a Master's degree in Management from the University of Aveiro, Portugal. Additionally, she has a Postgraduate degree in Information Management and Healthcare Business Intelligence, from the NOVA University of Lisbon, Portugal.

Ana Inês holds a Bachelor's degree in Applied Foreign Languages, with a specialization in Business Relations, from the Catholic University of Portugal. She has a Master's Degree in Management from the University of Aveiro, Portugal.

Kuldeep Kaur is a Lecturer at the Australian Institute of Business. She has a strong career history with industry and academia. Kuldeep also worked with the University of South Australia and Flinders University and has taught various subjects at undergraduate and postgraduate levels. She has over a seven-year of experience working in the industry, including companies like Nestle and Cadbury. Kuldeep holds a PhD in organisational behaviour, and the central focus of her research is on organisational climate and its impacts on attitudes and behaviour. She is a competent researcher and loves to extract new relationships in different variables with advanced knowledge of statistical techniques.

Alpaslan Kelleci has considerable industry experience in B2B marketing, business development and sourcing. Throughout his professional business career, he made substantial contributions in developing new product ranges, lifting up sales revenues as well as firm recognition. Additionally, he managed diverse innovation activities ranging from incremental to disruptive; marketing to process. Dr. Kelleci is an Assistant Professor and has been teaching E-commerce, Introduction to Sustainability, and Sustainability Management in Aviation. His research areas are open innovation, sustainability management, sustainable innovation, sustainable open innovation, sustainability marketing, and sustainable production & consumption.

Maria Carolina Martins-Rodrigues is an International PhD in Management, University of Extremadura, Spain Post-graduate in Knowledge management, University of Belgrano, Buenos Aires, Argentina, and a research fellow of CIEO (Algarve University). Her research interests currently are Sustainability, innovation, Knowledge Management, Entrepreneurship, Social Responsibility and Business Management. Has co-authored over 20 articles and book chapters and published in several scientific journals. She has also organized Iberian Conference on Entrepreneurship and international Conferences of Sustainability and Innovation. Founder member and vice-president of the direction of Empreend - Portuguese Association for Entrepreneurship. Was Professor in University Aberta (UAb) and University Moderna. In TAX Administration was Tax Administration Technician Advisor acting as coordinator in the International Relations Services Directorate (DSRI). and was Head of the Tax Service.

António C. Moreira obtained a Bachelor's degree in Electrical Engineering and a Master's degree in Management, both from the University of Porto, Portugal. He received his Ph.D. in Management from the University of Manchester, England. He has a solid international background in industry leveraged working for a multinational company in Germany as well as in Portugal. He has also been involved in consultancy projects and research activities. He is an Associate Professor at the Department of Economics, Management, Industrial Engineering, and Tourism, University of Aveiro, Portugal, where he headed the Bachelor and Master Degrees in Management for five years. He is member of GOVCOPP research unit.

Francisco Musiello-Neto has a Master's Degree in Administration with an emphasis on Human Resources & Organizations from the Federal University of Paraíba (2003). Doctoral candidate at Universitat Rovira i Virgili (Thesis). University professor since 1995. Specialist in Management, and currently in the Open Innovation Management Model. Over the past 20 years, he has intensified academic production on the themes of organizational culture and organizational structure. And more recently on corporate risk, organizational strategy, competitive advantage, corporate risk and organizational performance in the Hospitality Sector.

Alberto Onetti is Full Professor of Entrepreneurship and Management at the University of Insubria, where he is also responsible for the Master Degree in Global Entrepreneurship, Economics and Management (GEEM). Since 2006 he has been Visiting Professor at College of Business of San Francisco State University. In 2009 he has been appointed as Chairman of the Californian Mind the Bridge Foundation. He has committed himself along the years to research in the entrepreneurship and corporate strategy. He has authored and co-authored insofar over 100 publications.

Carla Pires is PhD in Social Pharmacy and invited Professor at Universidade Lusófona's Research Center for Biosciences and Health Technologies, Portugal. She has more than 40 indexed publications. Her research interests include health communication, social pharmacy, pharmacy practice, and other. https://orcid.org/0000-0003-4526-0271.

Patrícia Pires has a Bachelor's degree in Languages and Business Relations and a Master's Degree in Management, both from the University of Aveiro, Portugal. She also has a Postgraduate degree in Retail Management, from Águeda School of Technology and Management, Portugal.

Alessia Pisoni is Associate Professor at the Department of Economics - University of Insubria, where she teaches Innovation Management. She holds a Ph.D. in Economics of Production and Development, and coordinates the research unit of the Research Centre for Innovation and Life Sciences Management (CRESIT). Since 2010, she has also been collaborating with Mind the Bridge Foundation's research activities on European ICT startup ecosystems. Nowadays, her research interests are in the area of innovation, internationalization and entrepreneurship. She is author of an extensive list of articles and books in the fields of innovation, entrepreneurship, corporate governance, and international business.

Dilraj Wadhwa is a Lecturer in Human Resource Management at Australian Institute of Business. She has a PhD in Human Resource Management. She has a successful career in higher education. Dilraj also taught at Flinders University and University of South Australia. She has over a decade of experience in supervision and leadership with demonstrated ability to work both independently and as an integral part of a team.

Index

A

B

C

D

E

F

G

H

I

L

N

O

P

Q

R

S

T

U

V

W

www.ingramcontent.com/pod-product-compliance
Lightning Source LLC
LaVergne TN
LVHW081335300926
849161LV00008B/1981